A

STATEMENT OF REASONS

FOR NOT BELIEVING

THE DOCTRINES OF TRINITARIANS,

CONCERNING

THE NATURE OF GOD AND THE PERSON OF CHRIST.

By ANDREWS NORTON.

THIRD EDITION,

WITH ADDITIONS, AND A BIOGRAPHICAL NOTICE
OF THE AUTHOR.

BOSTON:
WALKER, WISE, AND COMPANY,
PUBLISHERS FOR THE
AMERICAN UNITARIAN ASSOCIATION,
21 BROMFIELD ST.
1859.

University Press, Cambridge:
Printed by Welch, Bigelow, and Company.

EDITORIAL NOTE.

The present edition of the "Statement of Reasons" contains some additions and corrections made by the author in an interleaved copy of the work; and a few sentences have been omitted. The principal additions will be found on pp. 97, 98, 103, 104, and 238, 239, of this volume, corresponding with pp. 54, 59, and 172 of the edition of 1833.

The translation of passages quoted from the Gospels has, for the most part, been conformed to that contained in the author's "Translation of the Gospels, with Notes," recently published. The changes thus made, however, seldom affect the sense.

The Biographical Notice of Mr. Norton, by the Rev. Dr. Newell, was first published in the Christian Examiner for November, 1853.

The editor has taken the liberty to add a few notes and references in different parts of the volume. These, with the exception of one note of considerable length which concludes the Appendix, are carefully distinguished by being enclosed in brackets. Whatever is so enclosed is editorial, except where brackets occur in the course of quotations made by the author.

An Index to passages of Scripture quoted or referred to, and a General Index, have also been added to the work.

E. A.

CAMBRIDGE, April, 1856.

CONTENTS.

STATEMENT OF REASONS.

SECTION III.

SECTION IV.

SECTION V.

SECTION VI.

SECTION VII.

SECTION VIII.

SECTION IX.

SECTION X.

SECTION XI.

APPENDIX.

NOTE A.

NOTE B.

NOTE C.

BY THE EDITOR.

BIOGRAPHICAL NOTICE

OF

MR. NORTON,

BY THE

REV. WILLIAM NEWELL, D.D.,

PASTOR OF THE FIRST CHURCH IN CAMBRIDGE, MASS.

THE name of Andrews Norton has long been widely known as that of one of the ablest theologians and most accomplished critics of our time; standing, in his department of service, at the head of the Unitarian movement in this country. His memory will be ever admiringly cherished by those who sympathized with him in his religious views, and who knew him in the fulness of his fine powers, as it will be honored by all who are ready to do homage to a true man, wherever he may be found; by all who in a generous spirit can reverence sincere piety and virtue, rich genius and learning, patient industry and independent thought, consecrated to the highest aims, in whatever quarter of the Christian camp their light may shine.

When such a man passes away, we cannot but pause at his tomb, and hearken to the voices that come up to us from the receding past, louder and louder, as we listen, speaking of his labors and virtues. Both for the instruction of the living, and in justice and gratitude to the dead, we must glance, if we can do no more, over the scenes through which he has moved and the work which he has done. We propose to give a brief, though necessarily an imperfect, sketch of the life, character, and services of this faithful and gifted servant of Christ and of God, with a full appreciation, we trust, of his high merits, but in that spirit of simple truth which he loved so well, and which was one of the marked characteristics of the whole man.

Mr. Norton was a native of Hingham, Massachusetts. He was a direct descendant of Rev. John Norton of that town, who was a nephew of the celebrated John Norton, minister of Ipswich, and afterwards of Boston. His father, Samuel Norton, was a well-known and much respected citizen of Hingham, often employed in its public trusts, whose agreeable conversation and manners are spoken of by those who remember him. He was educated in the tenets of Calvinism, but, as he grew older, the views which it presents of the character and government of God were so revolting to him, that for a time he was almost driven into utter unbelief, until, under the light of truer and brighter views, he found faith and peace. He was a man of great devoutness of mind, delighting to see and to speak of the Creator's wisdom and love in all his works. He died in 1832, at the advanced age of eighty-eight. He married Miss Jane Andrews, of Hingham, a sister of Rev. Dr. Andrews, for so many years the minister of Newburyport. Another of her brothers died from a wound received at the battle of Brandywine. She lived to the age of eighty-five, and died in 1840.

Andrews Norton, the youngest child of his parents, was born December 31, 1786. From childhood he was remarkable for his love of books and his proficiency in his studies. Having completed his preparatory course at the Derby Academy, in Hingham, in 1801 he entered the Sophomore class in Harvard College, and was distinguished throughout his academical career for his high scholarship and correct deportment. He graduated in 1804, the youngest of his class, at the age of eighteen. The natural seriousness and religious tone of his mind determined him at once in the choice of his profession, and led him, on leaving college, to commence his preparation for the ministry. He became a Resident Graduate at Cambridge, but not being in haste to preach, he quietly pursued a course of literary and theological study, and laid the foundation of that high mental culture and large erudition which afterwards distinguished him. In this scholastic, but not idle nor fruitless retirement, he continued for a few years, residing partly at Cambridge, partly at his father's house in Hingham, until, in October, 1809, after preaching for a few weeks in Augusta, Maine, he accepted the office of Tutor in Bowdoin College.

Here he remained a year, and some of the friendships which he then formed lasted through life. After this he returned to Cambridge, which henceforward became his fixed and chosen residence. In 1811, he was elected Tutor in Mathematics in Harvard College, but resigned his office at the close of the year. Mr. Norton had now reached that point in his career at which the rich fruits of genius and scholarship, that had been so long ripening in the shade, were to be brought before the public eye, and to receive their due appreciation. It will be remembered that his entrance on his theological studies was nearly coincident with the breaking out of the controversy between the *orthodox* and *liberal* parties in theology, occasioned by the election, in 1805, of Rev. Dr. Ware, then minister of Hingham, to the Hollis Professorship. Without going into the history of that controversy, it is sufficient to say, that it was amidst the strong and constantly increasing excitement which it produced, that Mr. Norton's early manhood was passed. The atmosphere of the times and the character of his associates contributed, no doubt, to strengthen the decided bent of his mind towards the theological and metaphysical questions which formed the subjects of discussion of the day. In the society of such men as Buckminster, Thacher, Channing, Eliot, Frisbie, Farrar, Kirkland, and others of kindred opinions and spirit, his attachment to the principles of the liberal school must have received added impulse and strength. In 1812, he undertook the publication of " The General Repository and Review," a work "in which," to use his own words, "the tone of opposition to the prevailing doctrines of Orthodoxy was more explicit, decided, and fundamental than had been common among us." Its straightforward boldness in the expression of opinions which then seemed new and heretical, while it was admired and approved by some, startled others, even of the liberal party, who thought that the time for it was not yet ripe. It was conducted with signal ability, but after the second year was discontinued for want of support. It was too bold, and probably somewhat too learned, to win general favor. But it did its work and left its mark. In 1813 he was appointed Librarian of the College. He discharged the duties of his new office with his accustomed fidelity and judgment, and under his direction much was done during his eight years' service towards improving the condition of the library, then in many points, as in some now, lamentably deficient. He relinquished the charge of it in 1821; but he always retained a warm interest in its welfare, and was a generous contributor to it through life. In 1813, the same year in which he became Librarian, he was also chosen Lecturer on Biblical Criticism and Interpretation, under the bequest of Hon. Samuel Dexter. The revered names of Buckminster and Channing stand associated with his, as his predecessors elect in this office. Eminent as they were, it is not too much to say, that their successor did not fall below even their mark; that in a peculiar fitness for the place, he was in some respects before them; and that he carried out what they had only begun, or hoped to begin. Mr. Norton preached occasionally in the pulpits of Boston and the neighborhood, and, though he lacked the popular gifts of a public speaker, his services were held in acceptance by those who were best able to appreciate his true merits. At one time during the vacancy at the New South, previous to the election of Mr. Thacher, many of the members of that Society, as we have been informed, would have been glad to invite Mr. Norton to become their pastor. His lectures in Cambridge on subjects of Biblical Criticism were greatly admired; and there were persons who went out from Boston to hear them, whenever they were delivered.

In 1819, upon the organization of the Divinity School and the establishment of the Dexter Professorship of Sacred Literature, Mr. Norton was chosen by the Corporation to fill that office. He was inaugurated on the 10th of August, 1819; and the discourse which he delivered on that occasion, republished by him in his recent volume of "Tracts on Christianity," ought to be in the hands of every student of theology. He held his office till his resignation in 1830; "bringing to it," — to use the words of one of his associates in the Divinity School, still living and honored among us,* — "his large and ever-increasing stores of knowledge; imparting it in the clearest manner; never

* Professor Willard.

dogmatizing, in an ill sense of the word; but, on the contrary, fortifying his doctrines, solemnly and deliberately established in his own mind, with all the arguments and proofs that his critical studies and logical power could furnish." In 1821, he was married to Miss Catharine Eliot, daughter of Samuel Eliot, Esq., a wealthy and highly respected merchant of Boston, and a munificent benefactor of the College, whose son, Charles Eliot,* a young man of rare promise, early cut off, had been Mr. Norton's intimate coadjutor and friend. It is sufficient to say, that in this union he found all the happiness which earth has to give, and all that the truest sympathy and love can bestow. In 1822, he was bereaved of another of the dear friends whose society had been among the choicest blessings of his life, — the highly gifted and pure-minded Frisbie. He delivered an address before the University at his interment, and the following year published a collection of his literary remains, with a short memoir. In the discussions which took place in 1824-25, respecting the condition and wants of the College, and the relation between the Corporation and the Immediate Government, he took a prominent part both with voice and pen. In 1824, he published his "Remarks on a Report of a Committee of the Board of Overseers" proposing certain changes in the instruction and discipline of the College. In February, 1825, he appeared before the Board of

* The Miscellaneous Writings of Charles Eliot, with a biographical memoir by Mr. Norton, were printed in 1814.

Overseers in behalf of the memorial of the Resident Instructors, relative to "the mode in which, according to the charter of the institution, the Corporation of the same ought of right to be constituted." Edward Everett, then Professor of Greek Literature in the University, spoke in the morning, and Mr. Norton in the afternoon and evening, in support of the memorial. Mr. Norton's speech was afterwards published. His admiration of the poetry of Mrs. Hemans induced him, in 1826, to undertake the collection and republication of her works in this country, in a style suited to his estimation of their merits; and in an article in the Examiner during that year, followed by other articles on the same subject at different times, he labored to impress on the public mind his own sense of their richness and beauty. In the spring of 1828, partly for the benefit of his health, partly for the enjoyment of the tour, he went to England. He enjoyed so much during this visit, and formed so many pleasant acquaintances, especially with those whom he had long admired in their writings (Mrs. Hemans among others), that, in a career so quiet and uneventful as his for the most part was, it took its place among the most interesting recollections of his life. After the resignation of his Professorship, in 1830, he continued to devote himself to literary and theological pursuits. At the earnest solicitation of a friend (Rev. William Ware, we believe), urging the republication of his article on "Stuart's Letters to Channing," he undertook to revise and enlarge it; and the result of his labors — a new work in fact, the most able, thorough, and learned refutation of the Trinitarian doctrine that has yet appeared — was given to the press in 1833, under the title of "A Statement of Reasons for not believing the Doctrines of Trinitarians concerning the Nature of God and the Person of Christ." In 1833-34, he edited, in connection with his friend, Charles Folsom, Esq., "The Select Journal of Foreign Periodical Literature," a quarterly publication, the plan and object of which are to some extent indicated by the title. It contained also remarks and criticisms by the editors, and some longer articles by Mr. Norton. In 1837, he published the first volume of his elaborate work on the "Genuineness of the Gospels." In 1839, at the invitation of the Alumni of the Divinity School, he delivered the annual discourse before them, afterwards published, "On the Latest Form of Infidelity." Those who remember him as he appeared on that occasion, speaking to many of them for the last time, will not soon forget the impressions of that day, deepened by the evident feebleness of his health, by his slow, impressive utterance, and the "sweetly solemn" tones of that well-known voice, speaking out with slightly tremulous earnestness the deep convictions of a truth-loving, Christ-loving man, as with eagle eye he saw danger in the distance, where others saw only an angel of light, and with a prophet's earnestness sounded the alarm. The publication of Mr. Norton's discourse led to a controversy, in which he further illustrated and de-

2*

fended the views which he had expressed respecting the "Modern German School of Infidelity."

In 1844 appeared the second and third volumes of his work on the "Genuineness of the Gospels," completing the important and laborious investigation, which had occupied him for so many years, of the historical evidence on this subject. With the exception of his volume of "Tracts on Christianity," printed in 1852, composed chiefly of the larger essays and discourses which had before appeared in a separate form, this was his last published book.

Mr. Norton's life, certainly the most prominent portion of it, moved through sunshine. Clouded as it was by occasional bereavement, the common lot, and by the infirm health of his latter days, it was yet, in other respects, a singularly happy one. He was surrounded with every earthly blessing. He had within his reach all that can feed the intellect, or gratify the taste. He had leisure and opportunity for his chosen work. And all around him was an atmosphere of purity and peace. His strong and tender affections bloomed fresh and green to the last, in the sunny light of a Christian home. He loved and was loved, where to love and to be loved is a man's joy and crown. He had both the means and the heart to do good. And so, in tranquil labor, in calm reflection, in grave discussion of high themes, or in the play of cheerful conversation, amid the books and the friends he loved, "faded his late declining years away." His strength had been for a long time very gradually failing, as by the decay of a premature old age. In the autumn of 1849, it was suddenly prostrated by severe illness, from the effects of which he never entirely recovered. By the advice of his physician, he passed the following summer at Newport, with such great and decided benefit to his health from the change of air, that it was resolved to make it in future his summer residence. But in the spring of 1853, it was evident that his strength was declining, and that the bracing sea-breeze had lost its power to restore it. He became more and more feeble, till, at the close of the summer, he was unable to leave his room; but his mind remained strong and unclouded almost to the last. He was fully aware that the end drew nigh. And he met death, as we should expect that he above most men would meet it, with all a Christian's firmness, tranquilly, trustingly, with a hope full of immortality, reposing on the bosom of the Father. His patience, serenity, gentleness, his calm faith in God, the heavenliness of his spirit, the sweetness of his smile, illumined and sanctified the house of death. He gradually sunk away, till on Sunday evening, September 18, the quivering flame of life went out, and the shining light within ascended to the Father of lights.

The life of Mr. Norton was that of a diligent student and thinker, doing his work in the still air of the library, and withdrawn from the stir and rush of the great world, yet not indifferent to its movements, nor unconcerned in its welfare. He mingled little in political affairs, though in them, as in everything else, he had his own distinct judgment and decided action, when the time called. He took no prominent part in the moral reforms of the day. A lover of his country, a lover of his kind, he expressed his patriotism and his philanthropy in quiet, individual ways. Whatever he did for others, there was no sounding of a trumpet before him. He went little into general society. He had enough, as we have seen, to occupy his time and his thoughts, without going out of his little world into the larger. The delicacy of his health and the languidness of his animal spirits, added to the studiousness of his habits and his natural reserve, made him somewhat of a recluse. But his house, with its kind and sincere hospitality, was always open, nor was his heart cold, or his hand shut.

He was never idle; but he chose to labor in his own way, apart from the crowd. He knew that he should labor more happily and more usefully so. He kept aloof from public excitements. He had no taste for public meetings. He had not the showy, popular gifts, which fit a man for the speeches of the platform; nor the impulsive social temperament, which throws itself into the boiling current of the times. He was, both by nature and on principle, disinclined to enter into the associated movements of denominational warfare. He objected to the Unitarian name. He did not favor the formation of the Unitarian Association. On this point he differed decidedly, but quietly and amicably, from the majority of his brethren. No man prized the truths of Liberal Christianity more highly than he, or held them with a firmer grasp; but he believed that they would make their way more surely, and in the end more rapidly, with less irritating friction against the popular modes of faith, and with less peril, both from without and from within, if left to the quiet channels of individual speech and individual effort. He therefore studiously kept aloof from any distinct, formal organization, even for the maintenance and diffusion of doctrines dearer to him than life.

And yet this reserved, independent, solitary thinker, moving in his own orbit, towards his chosen goal, carried with him by a mastery which he did not seek, and by a gravitation which was but the natural result of his intellectual greatness, a host of other minds that rejoiced in his kingly light. By the massive power of his mind and the weight of his learning, by the force of his character and the impressive authority of his word, spoken and written, he wielded for many years an influence in the body to which he belonged, such as few other men among us have ever possessed. This influence, as quiet as it was powerful, was exerted partly through his stated teachings in the Divinity School at Cambridge, partly through his private conversational intercourse, partly through the occasional articles and the more elaborate works which came forth, "few and far between," from his scrupulous pen. What he was and did in his several fields of theological service is well understood by many of our readers; but those who knew little of him will be glad to know more, and those who knew him best will love to read over again the recollections of the past, and to dwell on the memory of what they owe him.

Mr. Norton brought to the Professorship of Sacred Literature a combination of rich qualifications, natural and acquired, for his high office, such as is rarely found, such as we can hardly hope to see again, approximating the ideal of the consummate theologian described by him in his Inaugural Discourse; — an acute and vigorous intellect, disciplined in all its faculties by laborious study, trained to habits of clear and exact reasoning, and remarkable alike for its powers of analysis and discrimination, for the logical ability with which it grappled with the questions before it, for the intense and sustained concentration of its strength on its chosen subjects, and for the native sagacity and good sense with which it saw its way to the hidden truth; varied and extensive learning, as finished and accurate as it was full; a most pure and nicely critical taste; a fine imagination, that stood back in waiting as the handmaid to his robust understanding; a complete command of his accumulated resources; an inwardly enthusiastic devotion to the studies which he had embraced, and the highest appreciation of their nobleness and importance; a masterly familiarity with the science of Scriptural interpretation, and with the whole circle of theological science; a love of original and independent investigation, going back to the fountain-head, and never satisfying itself with guesses or traditions; an indefatigable assiduity and patience of examination and of pursuit in the researches which formed the business of his life; the most scrupulous carefulness in the statement of facts; a simple lucidness of expression and daylight distinctness of thought, even in the abstrusest themes, as of one who believed that intelligible ideas can be conveyed in intelligible words, and that no others are worth having; a conscientious slowness in forming his conclusions, combined with great strength, earnestness, and decision in maintaining the opinions at which he at length arrived; a confidence that justified itself to those who knew him in the results of his so cautiously conducted inquiries, and a conscious authority which impressed his convictions on others; and with and above all other gifts, surrounding them with a sacred halo, the profound religiousness of his nature, seen, not shown, the depth and calm intensity of his faith in Christianity and in Christ, the elevated seriousness of his views of life and duty, and the purity, delicacy, uprightness, of his whole character.

The influence of such a man, both in his instructions and his example, on the minds which were brought into contact with him at the Divinity School in Cambridge, can hardly be overrated. They regarded him with peculiar reverence and admiration. They listened with eagerness and profound interest to his decided and luminous words, so aptly expressive of his decided and luminous thoughts. Even if they were not prepared to accept his conclusions, they did not the less admire the strength and fulness with which they were set forth. His admirable elucidations of Scripture, his searching criticisms on the various readings or various theories of interpretation, his convincing expositions of Christian doctrine, his solemn and impressive representations of the character and teachings of Christ, his interesting unwritten (yet, it seemed to us, as complete and exact, both in thought and language, as if they had been written) dissertations on some point of theological or metaphysical inquiry, his wise hints and counsels to the young preacher, uttered in that peculiar manner of his which gave them a double force, will never be forgotten by those who heard them. Even those who on some points are not in sympathy with him, love to bear testimony to his high merits. The voluntary tribute which Dr. Furness rendered to him some years since in his work on "Jesus and his Biographers," is as just as it is heart-felt.

"I esteem it an invaluable privilege," he says, "to have been introduced to the study of the New Testament under the clear and able guidance of Mr. Norton. How fully did he realize the idea of a true instructor, not standing still and pointing out our way for us over a beaten path, but ascending every height, descending into every depth, with his whole attention and heart, and carrying the hearts of his pupils along with him. The remembrance of those days, when a rich and powerful mind, animated by the spirit of truth, came close to my own mind, renders more vivid my sense of the meaning of the great Teacher of teachers when he described the increase of the power of truth, which was the life of his being, under the figure of a personal coming, and said, 'If any man will keep my commandments, my Father will love him, and we will come unto him and make our abode with him.'"*

"Whatever interest I have felt in the study of the Bible," says another of the most eminent of our Unitarian divines, "or whatever knowledge I have gained of the proper way of pursuing that study, I owe in great measure to him, certainly more to him than to all other men. And when I look back to the three years spent under his kind and faithful instruction, I seem to return to one of the happiest as well as most profitable periods of my life."

It has been said, that the awe which he unconsciously inspired was sometimes unfavorable to the free action and free expression of thought in those who sat under his instructions; and that the severity of his taste, and his known dislike, openly or silently expressed, of everything which bordered on what is theatrical in manner, or over-florid in style, or extravagant in sentiment, had a tendency to repress too much the exuberance of youthful imagination and the warmth of youthful feeling. Certainly the danger was on that side. But for

* Furness's Jesus and his Biographers, p. 212.

one who may perchance have suffered from this cause, many, we are sure, will thank him through life for the restraining, improving, and elevating influence which he exerted on their minds and hearts.

But the field of Mr. Norton's labors and usefulness extended far beyond the bounds of the theological institution with which he was for a time connected, and of the religious body to which he belonged. He became known and widely respected through the writings, chiefly of a religious, partly of a literary character, which through various channels he gave to the press. He was too careful of truth, and too careless of present fame,—like his great neighbor-artist painting for immortality and giving the last touches to his work till death found him still waiting to finish it,—too deeply impressed with the sense of an author's responsibleness in the publication of his opinions on important subjects, too anxious that his offerings at the altar of Christian science should be without blemish and without spot, to be a rapid or voluminous writer. *Non multa sed multum.* He has left enough to lay us under a lasting debt of gratitude. Whenever we hear a contrast suggested between him and others in this respect, implying some defect on his part, we are always reminded of the old fable, in the school-book, of the Cony and the Lion. "See my troop of little ones! and how many hast thou?" "One, but a *lion*." One such work as that on the "Genuineness of the Gospels" is more honorable to a man, than a score of imperfectly prepared, roughly finished, loosely jointed productions, soon to die and be forgotten. Besides, each one must work in his own way, and not in another's; and each subject must have its own mode of treatment. The inquiries on which Mr. Norton spent his strength demand of a conscientious man all the thought, labor, long circumspection, and minuteness of investigation which he can give them. He held his place, he did his part,—a high and peculiar one,—in the confirmation and advancement of Christian truth. Let others be as faithful to theirs. A survey, however, of Mr. Norton's actual labors, both as a theologian and a man of letters, will show that his life was a continuously industrious one;—and even on the point to which we have referred, the amount of his published writings, some injustice may have been done him from the fact that many of them appeared in the periodical literature of his day, and stand somewhat out of sight.

Mr. Norton's earliest contributions to the press appeared in the Literary Miscellany, a periodical published in Cambridge in the style of the day, in 1804-5. They are a notice of Cowper, a short review of a sermon by Rev. Henry Ware, his pastor, and one or two short poetical translations. They are of little interest, except as indicating the turn of his mind at the age of eighteen or nineteen, and as dimly foreshadowing to us in their subjects the future career of the theologian, the man of letters, and the poet. He wrote some years after this for the Monthly Anthology. To some of its volumes his contributions, we believe, were frequent.

It was not, however, till he assumed the editorship of the General Repository, that his full power as a thinker and a writer was publicly developed and understood. The first article of that work, a very clear and powerful, and, as it was then considered, a very bold article, entitled " A Defence of Liberal Christianity," was written by him, and attracted much notice. Its sentiments, then new, or not before so openly expressed, drew down severe animadversion from the orthodox pulpit and press. This was followed by his masterly review, continued through several numbers of the same periodical, of the " Controversy between Dr. Priestley, Dr. Horsley, and others," evincing the most thorough learning and the most patient research. Other minor contributions of his, literary and poetical, are scattered through the work.

With the New Series of the Christian Disciple, commenced in 1819, Mr. Norton resumed his public literary labors, which appear to have been suspended for a time in consequence of the discontinuance of the General Repository, and the want of an appropriate organ for the utterance of his views. Besides some smaller articles of a general character, he contributed several critical and doctrinal dissertations of great value and interest, and full of that marked power which placed him at the head of the theological and controversial writers of his day. Among these are his Review of

Stuart's Letters to Channing, by far the most able, complete, and at the same time condensed confutation of the doctrine of the Trinity which has yet appeared,—his "Thoughts on True and False Religion,"—and his "Views of Calvinism." The earlier volumes of the Christian Examiner were also enriched by his pen. The articles on the Poetry of Mrs. Hemans, and one on Pollok's Course of Time, will be remembered among those of a purely literary character. Besides these and several religious essays in the first and second volumes of the Examiner, on the "Future Life of the Good," the "Works of God," the "Punishment of Sin," the "Duty of Continual Improvement," &c., he contributed some critical dissertations and reviews. His articles on the Epistle to the Hebrews, in the fourth, fifth, and sixth volumes, form the most valuable and instructive discussion which has appeared in the English language, or perhaps in any language, on that subject. We wish they might be republished, as a separate work, for wider circulation. His last contribution to the Christian Examiner appeared, in September, 1849, in the shape of a letter to his friend, Mr. George Ticknor, on the "Origin and Progress of Liberal Christianity in New England, and on Mr. Buckminster's Relations to them." He wrote also for the North American Review, though not often. His most noticeable articles in that publication are those on "Franklin," in January, 1818, on "Byron," in October, 1825, on Rev. William Ware's "Letters from Palmyra," in October, 1837, and a "Memoir of Mrs. Grant of Laggan," in January, 1845. His severe strictures on the character of Lord Byron, and the immoral tendency of some of his poems, although he allowed him all the praise justly due to his remarkable genius, were highly unpalatable to the idolatrous admirers of that great poet. But they were seasonable and true, and will commend themselves to every mind of pure taste and high principle, that is not dazzled and blinded by the intellectual splendor which, like the silver veil of Mokanna, may hide from his votaries the deformity beneath. In this, as in all Mr. Norton's critiques on the poetry and literature of the times, the influence which he exerted was of the highest and most salutary kind, laboring as he did with all his earnestness and strength to bring the literary judgments of the community into harmony with Christian morals and a Christian taste, and fearlessly opposing himself to the popular current, when, either in theology or in letters, it was running, or in danger of running, the wrong way.

The Select Journal contains also much original matter by him. The longest articles in this work from his pen are upon "Goethe" and "Hamilton's Men and Manners in America."

Mr. Norton's withdrawal for the last twenty years from very active and prominent service may have created a false impression in some minds respecting the amount of his labors. It will be seen from the survey that has been given of his contributions to the religious and other periodicals of his time, that his life — especially when we take into consideration the important occupations of his Professorship, the nature of his studies, and the engagements of various kinds which fall upon a man in his position — was not only laboriously industrious, but an abundantly productive one. He was so little ambitious of shining before the world, and so independent, both in mind and in circumstances, of any outward pressure, — he was so careful and conscientiously thorough in all that he undertook, besides being always so far from robust, and, latterly, so much of an invalid, — that we ought rather to be grateful that he did so much, than to wonder that he did not do more. He was not a man to be hurried by the false expectations of others. He wrought " as in his great Taskmaster's eye," not for theirs. He knew best when his work was finished, and then, and not till then, it came forth.

The last years of Mr. Norton's life were chiefly devoted to the preparation and the completion of important works, long planned in the hope of rendering permanent service to the religion which he loved with all his mind and heart and strength, as his own and the world's most precious treasure and hope. One, his great work on the " Genuineness of the Gospels," will be a lasting monument of his intellectual ability and his patient, conscientious research, and one of the standard contributions to the evidences of our Christian faith, which will go down to posterity in company with those of the greatest names in this department of Christian study. It is an honor to our country, of which we have quite as much reason to be proud, as of other illustrious achievements by other pens in more popular and better appreciated fields of mental labor. The historian, the poet, the orator, rise at once into the upper sky of a nation's admiration, and their names become world-renowned. The great theologian, the profound thinker, the retired scholar, elaborating in his study the noblest products of thought, and establishing truths of the most vital importance to the highest interests of man, must, like Kepler, wait his time. Sooner or later that time will come, and the tardy verdict of the world will crown him with its laurel wreath.

The three volumes of the work just mentioned contain an elaborate exposition — finished with all that minute accuracy for which Mr. Norton was so remarkable, and with all that logical acuteness and strength for which he was equally distinguished — of the historical evidence of the genuineness of the Gospels. It was his intention, if his life and health had been continued, to add another volume concerning the internal evidences of their genuineness; which he wished, however, to appear simultaneously with a new translation of the Gospels, accompanied by explanatory notes, on which he had been long engaged. He did not live to complete, as we fondly hoped he might, the former part of his plan; but we rejoice, and all who knew him will rejoice with us, to learn that the translation of the Gospels with critical and explanatory notes, the work which we believe he had most at heart, is entirely finished, and in a state of preparation for the press. Consecrated to us as it is by his long labor upon it, and bearing to us the last messages of his pen, we shall look forward to its publication with an eager interest, believing that it will afford important aid to every class of readers in the interpretation of the New Testament, bring out with new force the evidences of its truth, and present in a clearer and fuller light the beauty and power of our Saviour's character, the sublime import of his teachings, and the divine greatness of his life.* We hope, also, that a dissertation, prepared by him, as is understood, within a recent period, on the theory of Strauss and its kindred vagaries, and forming a part of his contemplated volume on the internal evidences of the Gospels, may be in some form given to the world. It may interest our readers also to know,

* Since the above was written, this important and instructive work — the precious legacy of the Christian scholar, laboring to the last for the truth as it is in Jesus, the matured fruit of long years of patient and conscientious study — has been issued from the press (in May, 1855), under the editorship of his son, Mr. Charles Eliot Norton, and Mr. Ezra Abbot, Jr., in two volumes octavo, the first volume containing the Translation, and the second, the Notes. Simultaneously with this, in accordance with the plan proposed to himself by Mr. Norton, they published another volume of his writings, entitled "Internal Evidences of the Genuineness of the Gospels," containing "Remarks on Christianity and the Gospels, with particular reference to Strauss's 'Life of Jesus,'" and "Portions of an Unfinished Work" on the general subject which forms the title of the book. The publication of these volumes has added largely to the debt of gratitude and reverence which is justly due to him, as one of the most accomplished interpreters of the Christian records, and one of the ablest, acutest, and most earnest defenders of the Christian revelation in our own or in any age.

that he has left behind him a complete translation of the Epistle to the Romans, and of the First Epistle to the Corinthians, and translations of the obscure portions of other Epistles, with a body of notes, critical and exegetical, which must be of great value to the student of the Scriptures. We cannot help expressing our earnest wish that these also may, if possible, be published at some future time, in connection, perhaps, with the articles of which we have already spoken, on the Epistle to the Hebrews. Even the fragmentary products of so clear and penetrating a mind, consecrated through life to the study of the Christian Scriptures and the Christian revelation, and filled with so devout a spirit, will be gladly welcomed.

Mr. Norton's writings are all impressed with the same strongly marked qualities, bearing the image of the man; the same calm but deep tone of religious feeling; the same exalted seriousness of view, as that of a man in sight of God and on the borders of eternity; the same high moral standard; the same transparent clearness of statement; the same logical closeness of reasoning; the same quiet earnestness of conviction; the same sustained confidence in his conclusions, resting as they did, or as he meant they should, on solid grounds and fully examined premises; the same minute accuracy and finish; the same strict truthfulness and sincerity, saying nothing for mere effect. And the style is in harmony with the thought, — pure, chaste, lucid, aptly expressive, unaffected, uninvolved, English undefiled, scholarly, yet never pedantic, strong, yet not hard or dry; and, when the subject naturally called for it, clothing itself in the rich hues and the beautiful forms of poetic fancy, that illumined, while it adorned, his thought.

The works of this eminent man will be always valuable, not only for the treasures of learning which they contain, and the light which they throw on questions of the deepest importance to every thinking man and every Christian theologian, but for the instructive example which they present of rare virtues, never more needed than in this age of hurry and excitement. They furnish lessons to the scholar and the student which he will do well to ponder and profit by; — lessons of patience, of persevering research, of scrupulous accuracy, of thorough and independent investigation, and of a conscientious slowness in the publication of facts and opinions which can be properly established only by long and diligent inquiry. He did not believe in any intuitional knowledge,— knowledge snatched up in a day and by hasty glances into the written or the unwritten page of truth. He did not believe that there is any royal road to solid and trustworthy learning, — any road to it except the old one, as old as man,—the beaten path of patient study, toiling on day after day, year after year. He believed with Newton, himself the example of what he said, that it is by concentration and fixedness of thought, by intent devotion to its subject, more than by native genius, that the best and greatest results are to be wrought out.

He thought it much better to do a little, and to do it well and thoroughly, than to do a great deal poorly. He was therefore in no hurry to throw off into the seething world a multitude of books. He had no ambition to shine as a writer and to keep himself in the world's eye. Apparently, he was quite indifferent to the kind of fame to which so many aspire. He had nobler aims. He cherished a wiser ambition. He cared little for present popularity, he wrote for permanent effect and lasting usefulness. And thus year after year passed away in the faithful endeavor to give greater completeness to the work before him, or to verify its statements, or to supply some missing link in the argument, or to correct some minor blemish that might have crept in, until he could in some degree satisfy his severe taste, his high sense of responsibility, and his conscientious love of the perfect truth. It is easy enough to make a book; but he wished to make a book worth making and worth keeping. And this to one of so high a standard, of so fastidious a taste, of so self-exacting a love of accuracy and completeness, and of so conscientious a purpose, was not easy. But the slow ripening of his mental harvests was amply compensated by the final richness of the product. It would be well, in this surfeiting age of half-made books, if more would follow the example.

Mr. Norton's position as a theologian has already been intimated, in the general account which we have given of his writings and labors. But it claims a more distinct and extended notice. It is an extremely interesting one; and one too for which, judged by its motives, even those who stood in opposition to him on either side must yield him their respect, as we do our grateful admiration. The true key to that position is found in his strong faith, beating through every pulse of his life, in the divine mission of Jesus Christ, and in his profound conviction of the supreme importance of the Christian revelation to all the best hopes of mankind. Misname him who will, if ever there was a believer in Christ, it was he. He was a believer with the head and with the heart too. He was as fully persuaded of the truth of Christianity as of his own existence. The Gospel,—the Gospel of Christ, and not the Gospel of Calvin,—the Gospel, as it came fresh from heaven in its own native beauty and power, was in his eyes the most precious gift of the Good Father. And under this conviction, he felt it to be the work of his life, the work to which God called him, to defend the Christian revelation, and to set forth its heavenly character, with all the power which his Maker had given him, not only against the assaults of infidelity and scepticism without, but against the undesigned yet perilous treachery within. He, with a jealous care for the safety of the priceless treasure, stood on the watch to keep it intact, on which side soever the enemy might approach; and by his words of wisdom, not always heeded as they should have been, he threw new bulwarks around the faith that he loved with a strength of feeling proportioned to his strength of mind.

With this intense faith, shining through his powerful intellect, burning in his pure heart, and ever urging him on with a calm but mighty impulse, he entered on his career, and pursued it consistently, through all the different phases of his life, to the end; whether, as he best liked, he quietly labored by himself in the mine of truth, seeking goodly treasure and pearls for his Master, or, at his Master's call, girded on his armor for the battle, and fearlessly laid siege to the intrenched errors of the past, or with equal chivalry went out to meet the novel errors, home-born or of foreign race, that he saw springing up among us under the very walls of the temple of Christ. He was both a Reformer and a Conservative, as every wise and good man must be, who in the spirit of Paul resolves to prove all things, but to hold fast that which is good and true. At his very first appearance in the theological arena, he was a bold, zealous, uncompromising assailant of the Orthodoxy of the time. He as fearlessly maintained his views, as he had carefully and conscientiously espoused them. "*Nec temere nec timide,*" was the motto which he placed over the opening article of his first editorial work, and which he bore upon his banner through life. He stood ready to avow and to defend what he believed; and he proved himself as able as he was ready, uniting all the courage of Luther with all the scholarship of Erasmus. While others, from love of peace, or fear of giving offence, chose to maintain what seemed to them a justifiable and prudent reserve, he spoke out boldly and fully the conclusions to which he had deliberately come. In his doctrinal views he was no half-way man, — no double-minded one; and in his phraseology there was a studious avoidance of that vague mistiness of language, which is sometimes used as a reconciling veil, and is sometimes the cover of confused and cloudy ideas. Whenever he had occasion to express his opinions, he expressed them without obscurity and without reservation.

As a champion of Liberal Christianity, Mr. Norton stands, as a writer, unquestionably foremost in the field. In the important controversy under which its battles were fought at the commencement of this century, his was the leading *mind.* He furnished the strong weapons of argument and learning by which it best maintained its ground. Others who stood at his side had more of the gift of popular speech: his was the word of knowledge and of wisdom. He was the Moses in the Exodus from the orthodox realm; Dr. Channing, the Aaron. The one was the eloquent rhetorician and advocate; the other, the profound scholar and thinker and sure interpreter of the sacred word. But this zealous Reformer for Christ and the Gospel's sake was a no less zealous Conservative for Christ and the Gospel's sake, when the time called. And there was no inconsistency in his course, any more than in that of the leader of old, when, having shaken off the bondage of Pharaoh, he withstood the innovations of Korah. In one case, he fought against ancient errors; in the other, against the new. In both, he was contending, as he believed, for the eternal truth, the truth as it is in Jesus. When at a more recent period he wrote and published his views concerning the modern rationalism and infidelity whose seeds, imported from the Old World, had struck root and were springing up in the New, — when he strove to tear up the poisonous root, hidden under the perfumed flowers, and to put the Church and the community on their guard against it, — he was animated by the same spirit which had moved him from the beginning. He made no bigot's war upon liberty of thought and speech, but he had a right, and he felt himself bound, to unmask and to resist those doctrines and speculations which were leading, as he thought, to infidelity. As his hostility to Calvinism was the side-growth of his love to Christ and his love to God, so his severity against Straussism and Spinozism was but one of the offshoots of his reverence for the Saviour and his faith in the Gospel. It was the severity of an honest conviction, as honestly expressed, of the pernicious tendency of the views which he opposed. He believed them to be, not only wholly unsound, but, whether so intended or not, hostile to Christianity, betraying it, like Judas, with a kiss, and in their tendencies finally destructive of all religious faith. Without entering at all into the question of the soundness or unsoundness of the views against which Mr. Norton uttered his sincere and solemn warning, we think that all must admit the long-sighted sagacity with which he foresaw the results of the tone of thinking then beginning to show itself in various forms, — the wisely prophetic ken with which he announced the direction and final developments of the new school of German speculation. Just what he predicted came to pass.

But in all his labors and conflicts, in his attack on the "Latest Form of Infidelity," as well as in his "Defence of Liberal Christianity," in his laborious, life-continued study and exposition of the "Evidences of the Genuineness of the Gospels," and in his faithful, never-satisfied endeavors, persevered in to the very last, to unfold the true meaning of those Gospels, and to clothe them in our own language in a form in which their beauty and power may be best seen, and the majesty of the Saviour's life shine out in its own undimmed light, he pursued a nobly consistent career. His profound faith in the Christian revelation, his intense conviction of its inestimable value, was, we repeat, the harmonizing key of his life.

But Mr. Norton was not only an accomplished theologian, a powerful controversialist, a learned and indefatigable critic, a most able and zealous defender of the Christian revelation, a profound and original expositor both of the meaning of its records and the evidences of their truth; he was also one of the pioneers of literary progress in this country, a man of letters, interested in the advancement of all good learning. He was a strong and graceful writer on other subjects besides those which formed the chief occupation of his life. He had a vein of fine poetic talent also, occasionally exercised in his earlier days and in his intervals of leisure, but only enough to open a glimpse of the wealth within. The few specimens which he has left behind are gems of rare lustre, finished of their kind. Apart from their beauty of thought and expression, they have a higher value derived from a higher source. The well-known "Lines written after a Summer Shower," which originally appeared in the first volume of the Christian Disciple, are among the most beautiful in the language. The hymn of resignation, beginning with the words,

> "My God, I thank thee! may no thought
> E'er deem thy chastisements severe,"

is a favorite one in our churches, and has soothed many a grief-stricken spirit. He did a good greater than he could know when he wrote it out of his own experience to be as angel music to the mourner. Another, written by him to a friend in bereavement, beginning,

> "Oh, stay thy tears! for they are blest,
> Whose days are past, whose toil is done,"

is in a similar spirit and of similar beauty.

Whenever we read the scattered effusions of his Christian muse,* we are tempted to lament that he has left us so few of these polished diamonds of thought, till we remember that he was in quest of other and larger treasures, hidden in the mine. He had but one life to work with; and it must select its prize, leaving the rest, however bright and sparkling, unsought, or with now and then a

* These were collected into a small volume in 1853, and a few copies printed for private distribution among his friends.

passing glance and touch. And yet the little that he did in this way shows how much good even a little well done may do, when it is cast in beautiful forms.

But we pass on to what is much greater in God's eye than any work of genius, however brilliant, or any product of thought, however elaborate and mature. Mr. Norton's character and life were marked by the high virtues, the fruits of a Christian faith, whose rich aroma breathes through his written works.

To say that he had none of "those infirmities which," to use his own words, "have clung to the best and wisest," would be ascribing to him a perfection which has belonged to but one who has lived on the earth. To say that he never erred in opinion or in action, would be to say what no man can venture to say of himself or of any other. Certainly he, who was truth itself, would claim no such exemption from human frailty. But towering above these errors and infirmities, whatever they were, which, however magnified to the fault-finding eye, disappeared from the friend's, there were virtues which the world will not willingly let die, and which will make him still a blessing to it in death, as he was a benefactor to it in life. And that which we think would be first and above all remembered by those who had the happiness to enjoy his friendship and to listen to his wise discourse, whether in the lecture-room or in his delightful home, was the peculiar devoutness of his spirit, — the profoundly religious tone of thought and of sentiment which seemed to form the atmosphere in which he lived, — the unformal, unostentatious, but deep piety, so perfectly sincere and unaffected, that made his presence like the air of a temple, — the ever-present sense of those higher relations in which we stand to God and to eternity, springing naturally out of that strong faith in Christ and in his truth which had struck down its roots into his whole being.

No man could be at all intimate with him, or be brought into near communication with him, either as a friend or a pupil, without receiving religious impressions such as few men whom we have known have the power to impart. There was something mightier than any common eloquence, which entered into the hearer's soul and led it by a calm and spiritual force into the presence of God and of things unseen and eternal. And this high religiousness of spirit — born of his vital Christian faith — was seen in union with other virtues which are the proper fruits of that faith. Purity of heart, singleness of purpose, devotion to duty, integrity of dealing, perfect openness and honorableness in all the affairs of life, marked his whole career. Truth — truth in thought, truth in speech, truth in manner, truth in conduct — shone through his life. He especially honored it in others; it made a vital part of his own being. All shams and falsehoods, all equivocations and manœuvring, all forms of cant and hypocrisy, and all affectations of every kind, were therefore peculiarly offensive to his sincere and upright spirit. And in close union, as it commonly is, with his perfect truthfulness, was that Christian courage which dares always to choose its own course and to carry it out without asking leave except of conscience. He held decided opinions upon every important subject that bears upon human life and duty in all a man's public and private relations, and he acted upon them. He did not fear to differ from others, or to walk apart from others; —

> "Nor number nor example with him wrought
> To swerve from truth, or change his constant mind,
> Though single."

Without any false pride of singularity, he cherished a self-relying independence of thought and of action. As in his religious views and his religious course, so in all other things he judged and acted for himself: and judged and acted from high principles fearlessly applied. He sought to try each case at the tribunal of a thoroughly Christianized reason, and to follow out what he accepted as its final decisions. We need not say that he always did what was best, but we may say, what is in truth greater praise, that he always did what he thought was right.

But his independence was not a selfish or cold-hearted independence. It was united with the truest and warmest kindness, when that kindness was called for. His retired habits, the habits of a student and scholar, — the individuality of his character and life, — his slowness and reserve of manner, — his occasional severity of speech, — the flashes of a pure and just indignation against some act of folly, meanness, or misconduct, — his decided and stern condemnation of opinions which he held to be false and dangerous, — were not connected with any want of Christian tenderness or Christian sympathy. It was a part of his creed, and one of the first lessons which his pupils in the Christian ministry learned from him, that timely reproof is often the truest friendship; that the exposure of error, and the cure of it by the needed caustic of sharp and plain-spoken truth, may be the highest charity. But those who knew him best knew the real warmth of his heart and the real kindness — the kindness both of feeling and of principle — which were sometimes hidden from a stranger's eye by the peculiarities of his manner. He was no ascetic, no declaimer against the innocent festivities of the world, no morose hater or proud scorner of its pleasant triflings, no misanthrope, shunning converse with men. If he mingled little in the gayer scenes of society, it was more from his engrossment in the studies that occupied his thoughts, and from the want of a quick flow of animal spirits, than from any unsocial feeling. As a friend, a neighbor, a citizen, he was ever prompt to do his part. His hand was always open to every work of charity. He knew the Christian blessedness of giving. His generous consideration of others, his readiness to help whenever his help was needed, his benevolence to the poor, ever guided by his strong good-sense, his judicious and thoughtful kindness in all the varied occasions of life, his quiet and unostentatious charities, will be remembered by many who shared in them. They were much better known to himself than to the world. His alms were not done to be seen of men.

But it was on the nearer circle around him, on the Christian home in which he lived, that his strong and tender affections beamed out most brightly and warmly. What he was there, where the true character most fully shows itself, they know whose loss is the greatest, and whose grief will be ever mingled with gratitude for the great blessings which they have enjoyed in the privileges of his society, in the tenderness of his love, in the wisdom of his counsels, in the Christian influence of his conversation and his life. To them his memory will be peculiarly blessed, for it will be associated, not only with the tenderest, most delicate, most sympathizing love, but with the highest, holiest, happiest influences, — influences that do not end at the grave. No man had more exalted views than he of the duties and the happiness of domestic life, and of the place which Christianity should hold in it.

We know how difficult it is to draw an unbiassed portrait, in all points true to the life, of one in whom we have a personal interest, or whose name is identified with the religious faith which is as father and mother to our hearts. In that which we have attempted, we have at least wished to avoid the exaggeration which in everything the subject of it so greatly disliked. But it seems to us, as we look upon it again, that a word more may be necessary to place it in its full light, and to give its features their true and best expression. We believe that, on certain points of character, a false impression exists in the minds of some who did not know him intimately. He was on some accounts in danger of being misunderstood and misjudged. In this, however, he shared the lot of many others, whom the world sees through a glass darkly. Every virtue has its shadow mocking it. The near friend sees the virtue; the distant or the fault-seeking eye may catch only the distorted shadow. A man of strong thoughts and strong feelings, Mr. Norton spoke strongly the truth that was in his heart. When he aimed a blow at an unsound doctrine or a dangerous error, he did not strike with the sword in the sheath. He did not attack it with roundabout phrases or with soft innuendo. What he said, he said in plain English, never coarse indeed, but sometimes caustic, always open and sincere. He was "a good hater"; not of persons, however, but of the false opinions with which those persons were identified, of which they were in his mind the living exponents. He was a man of very decided convictions, and not a man given to compromises in important matters. What he thought right to be done or to be said, he went forward to do or to say; alone, if necessary. He was not at all studious of the arts of popularity. From the course and habits of his life he was secluded from that free personal intercourse with others of opposite opinions, which is necessary to a perfect understanding on either side. Hence, those who came into collision with him, and those who saw him at a distance in those situations in which the strong and sharp points of his character were made to protrude, would be likely to do him injustice. A stranger or an opponent might sometimes, from their point of view, imagine him to be deficient in the softer and meeker virtues. The friend at his side, seeing him as he was, *knew* that nothing could be farther from the truth. Under the constitutional coldness and restraint of his manner, and the stateliness and occasional sternness of his speech, there was a deep enthusiasm of character, a sincere warmth of feeling, the truest and most considerate tenderness. A person living with him or in intimate connection with him would be particularly struck with his gentleness, indulgence, and quick human sympathies; he would see as much in him of the John, as others had seen of the Paul. If he was ever severe towards any, it was from the love which he bore to religion and to truth. If he erred, in word or in deed, his errors were the errors of a true-hearted and true-spoken man.

A most pure and gifted spirit has gone from us to join the host that "have crossed the flood." He has ascended from the study of God's word and works in this lower world, where, with all his knowledge, he could know but in part, to the study of God's word and works in that more glorious sphere, where, with Buckminster and Eliot, he will know even as he is known.

The hymn,* little known, we believe, which he composed many years ago for the Christian's dirge, was written unconsciously for his own funeral. It now chants for us, as we stand in spirit at his grave, the farewell of many hearts that honor and bless his memory.

"He has gone to his God; he has gone to his home;
No more amid peril and error to roam.
His eyes are no longer dim,
His feet no more will falter;
No grief can follow him,
No pang his cheek can alter.

"There are paleness, and weeping, and sighs below,
For our faith is faint, and our tears will flow:
But the harps of heaven are ringing;
Glad angels come to greet him;
And hymns of joy are singing,
While old friends press to meet him.

"O honored, belovéd! to earth unconfined,
Thou hast soared on high, thou hast left us behind;
But our parting is not for ever:
We will follow thee, by heaven's light,
Where the grave cannot dissever
The souls whom God will unite."

* His first contribution to the Christian Examiner, and the first of its poetical articles. Vol. I. p. 39.

STATEMENT OF REASONS.

PREFACE.

In the year 1819, I published an article in a periodical work,* of which a number of copies were struck off separately under the title that I have given to this volume. I have since been requested to reprint it, and some years ago undertook to revise and make some additions to it for that purpose. Being, however, interrupted, I laid by my papers, and had given up the intention, at least for an indefinite time. But having lately received an application from a highly esteemed friend, strongly urging its republication, I resumed the task; and the result has been, that I have written a new work, preserving indeed the title of the former, and embodying a great part of its contents, but extending to three times its size.

I have said, "I resumed the task"; and the

* [The Christian Disciple. See Vol. I. New Series, pp. 370-431. The article referred to was occasioned by Professor Stuart's Letters to Dr. Channing.]

expression is appropriate, for the discussion is one in which no scholar or intellectual man can, at the present day, engage with alacrity. To the great body of enlightened individuals in all countries, to the generality of those who on every subject but theology are the guides of public opinion, it would be as incongruous to address an argument against the Trinity, as an argument against transubstantiation, or the imputation of Adam's sin, or the supremacy of the Pope, or the divine right of kings. These doctrines, once subjects of fierce contention, are all, in their view, equally obsolete. To disprove the Trinity will appear, to many of whom I speak, a labor as idle and unprofitable as the confutation of any other of those antiquated errors; and to engage in the task may seem to imply a theologian's ignorance of the opinions of the world, and the preposterous and untimely zeal of a recluse student, believing that the dogmas of his books still rule the minds of men. It would be difficult to find a recognition of the existence of this doctrine in any work of the present day of established reputation, not professedly theological. All mention of it is by common consent excluded from the departments of polite literature, moral science, and natural religion; and from discussions, written or oral, not purely sectarian, intended to affect men's belief, or conduct. Should an allusion to it occur in any such production, it would be regarded as a trait of fanaticism, or as discovering a mere secular respect for some particular church. It is scarcely adverted to, except in works professedly theological; and theology, the noblest and most important branch of philosophy, has been brought into disrepute, so far, at least, as it treats of the doctrines of revealed religion, by a multitude of writers, who have seized upon this branch of it as their peculiar province, and who have been anything but philosophers.

Why, then, argue against a doctrine, which among intelligent men has fallen into neglect and disbelief? I answer, that the neglect and disbelief of this doctrine, and of other doctrines of like character, has extended to Christianity itself. It is from the public professions of nations calling themselves Christian, from the established creeds and liturgies of different churches or sects, and from the writings of those who have been reputed orthodox in their day, that most men derive their notions of Christianity. But the treaties of European nations still begin with a solemn appeal to the

"Most Holy Trinity"; the doctrine is still the professed faith of every established church, and, as far as I know, of every sect which makes a creed its bond of communion; and if any one should recur to books, he would find it presented as an all-important distinction of Christianity by far the larger portion of divines. It is, in consequence, viewed by most men, more or less distinctly, as a part of Christianity. In connection with other doctrines, as false and more pernicious, it has been moulded into systems of religious belief, which have been publicly and solemnly substituted in the place of true religion. These systems have counteracted the whole evidence of divine revelation. The proof of the most important fact in the history of mankind, that the truths of religion have not been left to be doubtfully and dimly discerned, but have been made known to us by God himself, has been overborne and rendered ineffectual by the nature of the doctrines ascribed to God. Hence it is, that in many parts of Europe scarcely an intelligent and well-informed Christian is left. It has seemed as idle to inquire into the evidences of those systems which passed under the name of Christianity, as into the proof of the incarnations of Vishnu, or the divine mission of Mahomet. Nothing of the true character of our religion, nothing attesting its descent from Heaven, was to be discovered amid the corruptions of the prevailing faith. On the contrary, they were so marked with falsehood and fraud, they so clearly discovered the baseness of their earthly origin, that, when imposed upon men as the peculiar doctrines of Christianity, those who regarded them as such were fairly relieved from the necessity of inquiring, whether they had been taught by God. The internal evidence of Christianity was annihilated; and all other evidence is wasted, when applied to prove that such doctrines have been revealed from Heaven.

It is true that in England, in some parts of Continental Europe, and in our own country, a large majority still desire the name of Christians, and have a certain interest in what they esteem Christianity. Notwithstanding much infidelity and skepticism, more or less openly avowed, and notwithstanding that many, who call themselves Christians, regard the teaching of Christ only as containing, when rightly understood, an excellent system of doctrines and duties, without ascribing to it more than human authority, yet there still exists much sincere and enlightened, as well as much traditionary faith in Christianity, as a revelation from God. In the Protestant countries to which I have referred, there has been great freedom of inquiry into its character; wise and good men have labored to vindicate it from misrepresentations; its evidences have been forcibly stated; the more obnoxious doctrines connected with it in the popular creeds have not of late, except in this country, been zealously obtruded upon notice; the moral character required by it has been partially at least understood and inculcated; and imperfectly and erroneously as our religion may have been taught, it has still been a main support of public order and private morals. Many enlightened men, therefore, who have taken only a general view of the subject, and have never given their time or thoughts to determine what Christianity really is, regard the prevailing form of religion with a certain degree of respect. Though they may disbelieve many of its doctrines, and have never separated in their own minds what is true from what is false, they think it, notwithstanding, the part of a prudent and benevolent man to let the whole pass in silence. They either do not advert to Christianity at all; or if they do, it is in ambiguous, though respectful terms, and they refrain from implying either their belief or their disbelief of what are represented as its characteristic doctrines. There is also another class of able and intellectual men, who, perceiving the value of religion in general, sincerely embrace the popular religion as they find it in the creed of their church or sect; being bound to it, perhaps, by strong sentiments and early associations, and believing that he who quits this harbor must embark upon a sea of uncertainties. They form a small exception to the remarks with which I commenced, respecting the prevalent disbelief of the doctrine of the Trinity, and other similar doctrines, by the more intelligent classes of society; — an exception which does not extend to the ignorant, or bigoted, or mercenary defenders of a church or sect.

But admitting these facts, what, after all, is the prevailing state of opinion and feeling respecting Christianity in Protestant countries? It is indicated by their literature. With some considerable exceptions, the productions of the English periodical press may be divided into two great classes. In one of them, you rarely find anything implying a sincere belief and interest in Christianity; you find much that an intelligent Christian could not have written; and in some of the publications to be arranged in this class, you find many thinly veiled or naked expressions of scorn and aversion for what passes under its name, and especially for the established religion and its ministers. In the other class, you observe a party and political zeal for religion, the religion established by law, "the religion of a gentleman," to borrow an expression from Charles the Second, — a zeal for the church and its dignities and emoluments, a zeal that accommodates itself easily to a lax system of morals, and which rarely displays itself more than in its contempt for those who regard religion as something about which our reason is to be exercised. But beside these two classes of publications, there is still another, extensively circulated, below the notice, perhaps, of those who belong to the aristocracy of literature, but which is sapping the foundations of society; a class of publications addressed to the lower orders, in which Christianity is openly attacked, being made responsible for all the wickedness, fraud, oppression, and cruelty that have been perpetrated in its name, and for all the outrages upon reason that have appeared in the conduct of its professors, or been embodied in creeds. There are other proofs equally striking of the very general indifference that is really felt toward Christianity; of the little hold it has upon men's inmost thoughts and affections. The most popular English poet of the day, who has been the object of such passionate and ill-judged admiration, appeared, not merely as a man, but as a writer, under every aspect the most adverse to the Christian character; yet the time has been, when his tide of fashion was at its height, that one could hardly remark upon his immorality or profaneness without exposing himself to the charge of being narrow-minded or hypocritical. I observed not long since, in a noted journal, the editor of which is said to be a Professor of Moral Philosophy at Edinburgh, that he was spoken of by a writer, fresh from the perusal of his life by Moore, as having been throughout his whole course "a noble being," "morally and intellectually," as all but "the base and blind" must feel.* The patriarch of German literature has just left the world amid a general chorus of applause from his countrymen, to which a dissentient voice has for some time scarcely been tolerated among them. His popularity may be compared with that which Voltaire enjoyed in France during the last century.

* The passage may be found in Blackwood's Magazine for February, 1830, p. 417.

There may be different opinions respecting his genius. He has nothing of the brilliant wit of Voltaire, nor of his keenness of remark; and nothing of the truly honest zeal in the cause of humanity, which is sometimes discovered by that very inconsistent writer. No generous sentiment ever prompted Goethe to place himself in imprudent opposition to any misuse of power. The principles which are the foundation of virtue and happiness, were to him as though they were not. His strongest sympathies were not with the higher feelings of our nature. In his mind Christianity was on a level with the Pagan mythology, except as being of a harsher and gloomier character, and possessing less poetical beauty. In the Prologue to his Faust, he introduces in a scene, meant to be ludicrous, the Supreme Being as one of his *dramatis personæ*, with as little reverence as Lucian shows toward Jupiter. I cannot say what there may be in his voluminous works; but in those of the most note I have never met with the strong, heartfelt expression of a high moral truth or noble sentiment. In reading some of his more popular productions, it may be well to recollect the words of one incomparably his superior: *Cynicorum vero ratio tota est ejicienda; est enim inimica verecundiæ, sine quâ nihil rectum esse* *potest, nihil honestum.** As regards the productions of such writers, it has become the cant of a certain class of critics to set aside the consideration of their influence upon men's principles and affections and to consider them merely as productions of genius. In this mode of estimation it is forgotten that there can be no essential beauty opposite to moral beauty, and that a work which offends our best feelings can have no power over the sympathies of a well-ordered mind.

The same absence of religious principle and belief which characterizes so much of the popular literature of the day, appears also in the speculations of men of a high order of intellect. It is but a few years since, that the author of the "Academical Questions"† was praised as a profound thinker, in the most able and popular of modern journals, with scarcely a remark upon the fact that his speculations conducted directly to the dreary gulf of utter skepticism. That work had its day, and is forgotten. I have just been turning over the leaves of another, "On the Origin and Prospects of Man," by one of the most powerful writers of our

* "The whole system of the Cynics is to be rejected, as at war with modesty, without which there can be nothing right, nothing honorable." CICERO. [De Officiis, Lib. I. c. 41.]

† [Sir William Drummond.]

times, the author of "Anastasius."* To me it appears only a system of virtual atheism. It excludes all idea of God, according to the conceptions formed of him by a Christian. The Father of the Universe equally disappears from the later systems of the most celebrated German metaphysicians. That which affects to be regarded as the higher philosophy of the age, is as intelligible upon this point, though upon few others, as the system of Spinoza. Though *all-seeing in its mists*, it does not discern the God who MADE the world and all things therein, and whose mercy is over all his works. In a large proportion of writings which touch upon the higher topics of philosophy, we perceive more or less disbelief or disregard of what a Christian must consider as the great truths of religion. No one can read without interest the work which, just as he was terminating his brilliant career, Sir Humphry Davy left as a legacy, containing the last thoughts of a philosopher. Yet in this work, written as life was fast receding, instead of the Christian doctrine of the immortality of the conscious individual, we find that his imagination rested on a dream, borrowed from Pagan philosophy, of the pre-existence and future glories of the think-

* [Thomas Hope.]

ing principle, assuming new modes of being without memory of the past. It is not simply to the appearance of such speculations that we are to look as characteristic of the age, but to the fact that their appearance excites so little attention, that they blend so readily with the prevailing tone of its literature. I should not be surprised if some intelligent readers of the work last mentioned should even have forgotten the passage referred to.

Such being the state of things, we are led to inquire, Who are the expositors and defenders of religion, and what influence do they exert upon public sentiment? In England the science of theology, so far as it is connected with revealed religion, has fallen into general neglect. Of those who treat its subjects, few deserve a hearing, and the few who deserve cannot obtain it. A few professedly learned works have of late appeared; but for the most part they are mere compilations, made without judgment or accuracy, and conformed to the creed of the Church. There have been some bulky republications of old divines little suited to the wants of the age. Most other religious works that appear are evidently intended only for "the religious public"; a phrase that has become familiar, and marks in some degree the character of the times. Should they pass beyond this narrow circle, they would, I fear, contribute nothing to render Christianity more respected. A very different class of writers is required to assert for religion its true character and authority. In Germany there is a large body of theologians, of whom the most eminent have been able and learned critics. They have thrown much light upon the history, language, and contents of the books of the Old and New Testament. They have released themselves from the thraldom of traditionary errors. But they have, in many cases, substituted for these errors the most extravagant speculations of their own. Nor, with some exceptions, does the power of Christianity show itself in their writings. On the contrary, many of them, being infected with the spirit of infidelity that prevails over the continent of Europe, have regarded Christianity, not as a divine revelation, but merely as presenting a system of doctrines and precepts, for the most part probable and useful, when relieved from the mass of errors that have been added to what was originally taught by its founder. Christianity thus becomes only a popular name for a certain set of opinions. Its authority and value are gone. The whole proof of the doctrines of religion, as taught by Christ, consists solely in the fact that he was a teacher from God. He did not reason; he affirmed. He adduced no arguments but his miracles. Considered as a self-taught philosopher, he did nothing to advance human knowledge, for he brought no new evidence for any opinion. But considered as a teacher from God, he has provided the authority of God for the foundation of our faith.

In our country, if I am not deceived by feelings of private friendship, true Christianity has found some of its best defenders. But the forms in which it is presented throughout a great part of our land, and the feelings and character of many who have pretended to be its exclusive disciples, are little adapted to procure it the respect of intelligent men. They are producing infidelity, and preparing the way for its extensive spread. They are giving to many a distaste for the very name of religion, and leading them to regard all appearance of a religious character with distrust or aversion. In no other country is the grossest and most illiberal bigotry so broadly exhibited as among ourselves. Nowhere else, at the present day, have so many partisans of a low order of intellect risen into notice, through a spurious zeal, not for doctrines, for these are changed as convenience may require, but for the triumph of a sect; and no other region has of late been ravaged by such a moral pestilence as, under the name of religion, has prevailed in some parts of our land, — an insane fanaticism, degrading equally the feelings and intellect of those affected by it.*

In past times, the false systems of religion that have assumed the name of Christianity, and ruled in its stead, have had a certain adaptation to the ignorance, the barbarism, the low state of morals, and the perverted condition of society, existing contemporaneously with them. They were some restraint upon vice. They led man to think of himself as something more than a mere perishing animal. Mixed up with poison as they were, they served as an antidote to other poisons more pernicious. Though Christianity was obscured by thick clouds, yet a portion of its light and heat reached the earth. But the time for those systems has

* If any one should think these expressions too strong, let him make himself acquainted with the transactions which not long since were taking place in the western part of the State of New York. Authentic documents respecting them exist; but such scenes have not been confined to that part of our country. [Some information on this subject may be found in the Christian Examiner for May and June, 1827, Vol. IV. pp. 242-265; and for March, 1829, Vol. VI. pp. 101-130.]

wholly passed. A wilder scheme could not be formed than that of re-establishing the Catholic religion in France, or calling a new Council of Dort to sanction Calvinism in Holland, or giving to Lutheranism its former power over men's minds in Germany. Their vitality is gone, except that it now and then manifests itself in a convulsive struggle. Yet zealots are still claiming for them the authority which belongs of right to true religion; and to the inquiry what Christianity is, the public, official answer, as it may be called, is still returned, that it is to be found in the traditionary creed of some established church, or of some prevalent sect; that it is to be identified with the grim decrepitude of some obsolete form of faith. We are referred back to some one of those systems that have dishonored its name, counteracted its influence, perverted its sanctions, inculcated false and inadequate conceptions of the religious character, and formed broods of hypocrites, fanatics, and persecutors; that have been made to minister to the lust of power, malignant passions, and criminal self-indulgence; and that have striven, if I may so speak, to retard the intellectual and moral improvement of men, seeing in it the approach of their own destruction.

What, then, is to be done to give new power to the great principles of religion? What is to be done to vindicate its true influence to Christianity? We must vindicate its true character. It must be presented to men such as it is. The false doctrines connected with it, in direct opposition to the truths which it teaches, must be swept away. It is not enough that they should be secretly disbelieved; they must be openly disavowed. It must be publicly acknowledged that they are utterly foreign from Christianity. It is not enough that those who defend them should be disregarded or confuted. They must be so confuted as to be silenced. Those who would procure for Christianity its due supremacy in the hearts of men should feel that their first object is so to operate upon the convictions and sentiments of men, that the public sanction which has been given to gross misrepresentations of it shall be as publicly withdrawn. In promoting the influence of Christianity, the main duty of an enlightened Christian at the present day is to labor that it may be better understood. Till this be effected, all other exertions, it may be feared, if not ineffectual, will be mischievous, as prolonging the authority of error, rather than establishing the truth.

But what interest can a philosopher or a man of intellect be expected to take in the squabbles of controversial divines? What impression is to be produced upon indifference, ignorance, traditionary faith, bigotry, and self-interest, by one who has nothing to conjure with but his poor reason? Why be solicitous to cure men of one folly on the subject of religion, since it is sure to be replaced by another? To him who should propose such questions, I might answer, that I do not so despair of mankind. I compare the nineteenth century with the fifteenth, and I perceive that many hard victories have been won, and much has been permanently secured in the cause of human improvement. Truth and Reason, though they work slowly, work surely. An abuse or an error, after having been a thousand times confuted or exposed, at last totters and falls, abandoned by its defenders; and then

> "One spell upon the minds of men
> Breaks, never to unite again."

The disputes of controversial divines, however mean the intellect, or vile the temper, of many who have engaged in them, do in fact concern the most important truths and the most pernicious errors. Having given these answers, I might then ask in return: Why should a Christian, with a deep-felt conviction of the efficacy of his religion to promote the best interests of mankind, be earnestly desirous that its influence may not be superseded and opposed by any of those false systems of doctrine that have been substituted in its place? Why should one, not devoid of common sympathy with his fellow-men, care whether they believe the most ennobling truths, or some pernicious creed, respecting their God and Father, their nature and relations as immortal beings, their duty, motives, consolations, and hopes?

We know the efforts that are making by enlightened men in Europe, particularly in England, to spread intellectual cultivation among the uneducated classes of the Old World. So far as the knowledge thus communicated is what may be called secular, it is beneficial in enlarging and exercising the mind, affording innocent entertainment, and, in some cases, furnishing the means of advancement in life. But to the poor, as to every other class, it is not the knowledge of most value. Without the equal diffusion of religious truth, it may become an instrument of evil rather than of good. Mere intellectual cultivation is as likely to be a source of discontent and disquietude as of happiness. An access of knowledge may tend little to reconcile a man to his situation. The new power it affords will be used according to the disposition of him who possesses it. But you can impress no truth, you can remove no error, respecting the duties and hopes of man as an immortal creature of God, you can impress no truth, you can remove no error, concerning religion, without surely advancing men in morals and happiness. This is the instruction most needed for all classes, but especially for the least informed. Among the highly educated, and those accustomed to the refinements of life, there are certain partial substitutes for religious principle; — the feeling of honor, the desire of reputation, delicacy of taste, the force of public opinion, and a more enlarged perception of the sentiments of their fellow-men, which, when they act on the conduct of others, are generally on the side of virtue. The levities or the business of life, a ceaseless round of trifling or serious occupation, which hurries them on with little leisure to think or feel deeply, may have prevented them from becoming acquainted with the essential wants of our nature. But in preaching to the poor, not the heartless, revolting, debasing absurdities of some established creed, but the doctrines of Jesus Christ, we may give them consolations and hopes to be most intimately felt, new views of their nature, new motives and principles. It is on the diffusion of this sort of instruction among all classes, that the prospects of society now depend. Changes are coming fast upon the world. In the violent struggle of opposite interests, the decaying prejudices that have bound men together in the old forms of society are snapping asunder one after another. Must we look forward to a hopeless succession of evils, in which exasperated parties will be alternately victors and victims, till all sink under some one power whose interest it is to preserve a quiet despotism? Who can hope for a better result, unless the great lesson be learned, that there can be no essential improvement in the condition of society without the improvement of men as moral and religious beings; and that this can be effected only by religious TRUTH? To expect this improvement from any form of false religion, because it is called religion, is as if, in administering to one in a fever, we were to take some drug from an apothecary's shelves, satisfied with its being called medicine.

That a people may be happy in the enjoyment of civil liberty, a certain degree of knowledge and culture must be spread through the community. A general system of education must be established. Self-restraint must supply the place of external coercion. The legitimate purpose of government is to guard the rights of individuals and the community from injury; and the best form of government is that which effects this purpose with the least power, and is least likely therefore to afford the means of misrule and oppression. But the power not conceded to the government must be supplied by the force of moral principle and sentiment in the governed. What education, then, is required; what knowledge is to be communicated; what culture is necessary? I answer, not alone, nor principally, that education which the schoolmaster may give; but moral culture, the knowledge of our true interests and relations. There may be much intellectual culture which will not tend even indirectly to form men to the ready practice of their duties, or to bind them together in mutual sympathy and forbearance, unless it be united with just conceptions of our nature and the objects of action. Let us form in fancy a nation of mathematicians like

La Place or La Lande, ostentatious of their atheism; naturalists as irreligious and impure as Buffon; artists as accomplished as David, the friend of Robespierre; philosophers, like Hobbes and Mandeville, Helvetius and Diderot; men of genius, like Byron, Goethe, and Voltaire; orators as powerful and profligate as Mirabeau; and having placed over them a monarch as able and unprincipled as the second Frederic of Prussia, let us consider what would be the condition of this highly intellectual community, and how many generations might pass before it were laid waste by gross sensuality and ferocious passions. So far only as men are impressed with a sense of their relations to each other, to God, and to eternity, are they capable of liberty and the blessings of social order. The great truths that most concern us are those on which our characters must be formed. But religion is the science that treats of the relations of man as a responsible, immortal being, the creature of God. By teaching the truth concerning them, religion, properly so called, discloses to us the ends of our being, preparing men, by virtue and happiness here, for eternal progress in virtue and happiness hereafter. So far as what bears the name of religion teaches falsehoods concerning them, it becomes the ally of evil, counteracting the improvement of our race. False religion has been the common sign, and often the most efficient cause, of the corruption and misery of nations. All great changes in the constitution of society for the purpose of delivering men from traditionary abuses, must be accompanied with a correspondent advance in religious knowledge, or they will be made in vain. Where the principles of Christianity are operative, there only can men be released from the strong control of some superior power; which, however profligately exercised, may find its own interest in preserving quiet among its subjects. True Christianity urges the performance of the duties of man to man, by the noblest and most effectual motives; and in a community where its influence were generally felt, how little would there be to apprehend from public oppression or private wrong? *Where the spirit of the Lord is, there is liberty.* I apply the words of the Apostle in a different sense from that in which he used them; but in one, the truth of which he would have recognized. In regarding the condition and changes of societies and nations, we are apt to look rather to the immediate occasions of events, than to their radical and efficient causes. A mere worldly politician, for instance, might think it scarcely worth consideration, that the established church should impose a creed which a majority of its clergy do not believe; or that oaths, not meant to be regarded, but enforced as a traditionary ceremony, and subscriptions, to which the conscience can hardly be cheated into assenting, should stand in the path of advancement in church and state. To a philosopher it may appear of far greater moment. Other topics, more exciting to the generality, he might deem of secondary importance. This he might view as a deep-seated evil, working at the core, the natural progress of which would leave but a false and hollow show of religion and morals. Who is there that will deny the influence of true religion to promote the happiness of individuals and the good order of society? Who is there that will deny the mischiefs of superstition, false notions of God and our duty, bigotry, and what is produced as their counterpart, irreligion and atheism? Why is it, then, that many are so little solicitous to discriminate, on this most important subject, truth from falsehood, that they fancy they are giving their countenance to the former, while supporting the latter; and that, if they aid the cause of what is called religion, they do not stop to inquire whether it be the religion that exalts, or the religion that degrades?

In the present state of information and public sentiment, it will be vain to attempt to give authority to false religion. The zeal of partisans, or the power of the state, will be equally ineffectual. The only important consequence of such attempts will be to disgust men with all religion. The experiment has, in one instance, been carried through. In France the forcing of the Roman Catholic faith upon the nation ended in the overthrow of all belief in Christianity. The consequences that ensued had the effect, elsewhere, of frightening infidels into hypocrites and bigots; and a sudden show of religion followed the French Revolution. But from this, had it continued, as little was to be hoped, as from a procession with relics and images going forth to stop a stream of lava in its course. It is only to true religion that we must look for aid in the cause of human happiness. This alone, being in accordance with reason and with our natural sentiments, will find its way to the hearts of men.

The tract which follows in relation to some

of those false doctrines that have prevailed, though it will give no new conviction to the great body of enlightened men, may perhaps awaken the attention of some to the grossness of those corruptions that have been connected with Christianity, and to the necessity of presenting it in a purer form, if its influence is to be preserved. It may tend a little to swell the flood of public sentiment by which they must be swept away. It may perhaps serve to convince some who have looked with offence upon the absurdities taught as Christian doctrines, and mistaken them for such, that one may be a very earnest believer, whose respect for such doctrines is as little as their own. But, especially, it may serve to spread a knowledge of the truth among those who, from their habits of life, have wanted leisure to think and examine for themselves upon subjects of this nature; and who are obliged, as all of us are in a greater or less degree, to take many opinions upon authority, till they see reason to distrust the authority on which they have relied. In addressing myself to such readers, I may take the credit (it is but small) of having avoided a fault common in theological writings intended for popular use. I have not presumed upon their ignorance of the subject; I have not made statements which in a more learned discussion I should be ashamed to urge; I have given no explanations that I knew to be unsatisfactory, because they might seem plausible; I have made no propositions which I do not fully believe; I have urged no arguments but what have brought conviction to my own mind; I have written as one who, being fully persuaded himself, and regarding his subject as free from all doubt and difficulty, is satisfied that nothing more is to be done than to explain to others in intelligible language the views which are present to his own mind.

I have given one reason why it is little to my taste to discuss this doctrine of the Trinity. Whoever treats of the subject is liable to be confounded with a class of writers with whom an intelligent Christian would not willingly be thought to have anything in common. By many who look with indifference on the whole discussion, he who contends for the truth will be placed on a level with those who defend error. Others will think that he is agitating questions which might better be left at rest; and those who hold the traditionary belief will regard him as a disturber of the Christian community. It may, however, be a consolation to him to remember, that even Socrates — the great opposer of the sophists and false teachers of his day — was called λάλος καὶ βίαιος, *prating and turbulent*,* and that the very same epithets, by a singular coincidence, were applied to Locke,† the most enlightened theologian of his age and nation. The feeling, however, naturally arising from the causes I have mentioned, might prevent one from engaging in this controversy, were it not for the deep sense which a sincere Christian must have of the value of true Christianity, and of the necessity of redeeming it from the imputations to which it has been exposed. "'*Love*,' says one of our old poets, '*esteems no office mean*,' and, with still more spirit, '*Entire affection scorneth nicer hands*.'" ‡

But there are other causes which make this an unpleasant subject. It presents human nature under the most humiliating aspect. The absurdities that have been maintained are so gross, the zeal in maintaining them has been so ferocious, there is such an absence of any redeeming quality in the spectacle presented, that it spreads a temporary gloom over our whole view of the character and destiny of

* V. Plutarch. in Catone. [Cat. Maj. c. 23.]

† By Wood, in his "Athenæ Oxonienses."

‡ These quotations from Spenser have thus been brought together by Burke.

man. We seem ourselves to sink in the scale of being, and it demands an effort to recollect the glorious powers with which God has endued our race. While inquiring concerning the truths of religion, we appear to have descended to some obscure region where folly and prejudice are the sole rulers. We may remember, with a feeling of painful oppression, the mortifying language of Hume, in one of those tracts in which he speculates as coldly upon the nature and hopes of mankind as if he were a being of another sphere, bound to us by no common sympathies. "All popular theology, especially the scholastic, has a kind of appetite for absurdity and contradiction. If that theology went not beyond reason and common sense, her doctrines would appear too easy and familiar. Amazement must of necessity be raised; mystery affected; darkness and obscurity sought after; and a foundation of merit afforded to the devout votaries, who desire an opportunity of subduing their rebellious reason by the belief of the most unintelligible sophisms." "To oppose the torrent of scholastic religion by such feeble maxims as these, that *it is impossible for the same thing to be and not to be*, that *the whole is greater than a part*, that *two and three make five*, is pretending to stop the ocean with a bulrush." * And is this all that mankind have to hope? Must this dreary prospect for ever lie before us? Is this all that religion has been, and all that it is to be? We trust not. Still, in the confutation of such doctrines as have been taught, the triumph, if it may be so called, is humbling. It is a triumph over our common nature reduced to imbecility. We discover not how strong human reason is, but how weak. That it can confute them implies no power; that it has been enslaved in their service makes us feel, almost with apprehension, how far it may be debased. But the hold which the doctrines of false religion have had upon the hearts of men has never been proportioned to the extent in which they have been professed. The truths of Christianity have maintained a constant struggle with the opposite errors that have been connected with them. At the present time there are many who acquiesce in these errors, and who even regard them with traditionary respect, in whose minds they lie inert and harmless.

But the very circumstance last mentioned adds to the unpleasant character of the discussion that follows. Every one in his writ-

* [Natural History of Religion, Sect. XI.]

ings sometimes turns his thoughts to those individuals whose approbation would give him most pleasure, and whose good opinion he would most desire to confirm. Among those to whom my thoughts recur, there are friends from whom I can hope for no sympathy in my present task. A difference of opinion upon this or any other subject cannot lessen my respect or love for them; and should the present work chance to fall in their way, I could almost wish to know, that this were the only paragraph that had fixed their attention. I beg them to believe that I am no zealot, no partisan of a sect, no disturber of social intercourse by a spirit of proselytism; and that where I see the fruits of true religion, I have no wish to conform the faith from which they proceed to the standard of my own. The same opinions, true or false, may be held in a very different temper, with very different associations, and with very different effects upon character. The doctrines most pernicious in their general results may be innoxious in many particular cases. The same system of faith which established its *autos de fe* in Spain, numbering its victims by tens of thousands, and sinking that country to the lowest debasement, may have been consistent in Fénelon with every virtue under heaven.

I have but a few words more to say in this connection. The tract that follows relates only to one class of those false doctrines that have been represented as doctrines of Christianity. There are others equally or more important. To re-establish true Christianity must be a work of long and patient toil, to be effected far more by the general diffusion of religious knowledge, than by direct controversy. The views and results to which a few intelligent scholars may have arrived, must be made the common property of the community. Essential and inveterate errors present themselves in every department of Christian theology. False religion has thrown its veil over the character, and perverted the meaning, of the books of the Old and New Testament. Of the immense mass of volumes concerning revealed religion, there is but a scanty number in which some erroneous system does not form the basis of what is taught. In many of the most important branches of inquiry, a common Christian can find no trustworthy and sufficient guide. Of the multitude of topics more immediately connected with Christianity, there is scarcely one which does not require to be examined anew from its foundation, and discussed in a manner very different from what it has been. Religion must be taken, I will not say out of the hands of priests, — that race is passing away, — but out of the hands of divines, such as the generality of divines have been; and its exposition and defence must become the study of philosophers, as being the highest philosophy. Some degree of attention to the fact is necessary, to be aware of the general and gross ignorance that exists concerning almost every subject connected with our faith. But they who would communicate the instruction which is so much needed, must expect to be continually impeded and resisted by prejudice and misapprehension. Let them, however, understand their task and qualify themselves for it. In the present state of opinion in the world, it is evident that he is assuming a responsibility for which he is wholly unfit, who comes forward as a teacher or defender of Christianity, without having prepared himself by serious thought and patient study. The traditionary believer, if he have taken this responsibility upon himself, should stop in his course, till he has ascertained whether he is doing good or evil. A conflict between religion and irreligion has begun, which may not soon be ended; and in this conflict, Christianity must look for aid, not to zealots, but to scholars and philosophers. Our age is not one in which there can be an esoteric doctrine for the intelligent, and an exoteric for the uninformed. The public profession of systems of faith by Christian nations and churches, which are not the faith of the more enlightened classes of society, has produced a state of things that, it would seem, cannot long continue. We may hope that in Protestant countries its result will not be, as it was in France, general infidelity. We may hope that it will not end in a mere struggle between fanaticism and irreligion, as seems to be the tendency of things in some parts of our own country. But these results can be prevented only by awakening men's minds to inquire, What Christianity is? How far it has been misrepresented? What are its evidences? What is its value? And what is to be done to remove those errors which now deprive it of its power?

[Cambridge, 1833.]

A

STATEMENT OF REASONS.

SECTION I.

PURPOSE OF THIS WORK.

I PROPOSE, in what follows, to give a view of the doctrines of Trinitarians respecting the nature of God and the person of Christ; to state the reasons for not believing those doctrines; and to show in what manner the passages of Scripture urged in their support ought to be regarded.

SECTION II.

THE PROPER MODERN DOCTRINE OF THE TRINITY CONTRADICTORY IN TERMS TO THAT OF THE UNITY OF GOD. — FORMS IN WHICH THE DOCTRINE HAS BEEN STATED, WITH REMARKS. — THE DOCTRINE THAT CHRIST IS BOTH GOD AND MAN, A CONTRADICTION IN TERMS. — NO PRETENCE THAT EITHER DOCTRINE IS EXPRESSLY TAUGHT IN THE SCRIPTURES. — THE MODE OF THEIR SUPPOSED PROOF WHOLLY BY WAY OF INFERENCE.

The proper modern doctrine of the Trinity, as it appears in the creeds of latter times, is, that there are three persons in the Divinity, who equally possess all divine attributes; and the doctrine is connected with an explicit statement that there is but one God. Now, this doctrine is to be rejected, because, taken in connection with that of the unity of God, it is essentially incredible; one which no man, who has compared the two doctrines together with right conceptions of both, ever did or ever could believe. Three persons, each equally possessing divine attributes, are three Gods. A person is a being. No one who has any correct notion of the meaning of words will deny this. And the being who possesses divine attributes must be God or a God. The doctrine of the Trinity, then, affirms that there are three Gods. It is affirmed at the same time, that there is but one God. But no one can believe that there are three Gods, and that there is but one God.

This statement is as plain and obvious as any which can be made. But it is not the less forcible because it is perfectly plain and obvious. Some Trinitarians have indeed remonstrated against charging those who hold the doctrine with the "ABSURDITIES consequent upon the language of their creed";* and have asserted that in this creed the word *person* is not used in its proper sense. I do not answer to this, that, if men will talk absurdity, and insist that they are teaching truths of infinite importance, it is unreasonable for them to expect to be understood as meaning something wholly different from what their words express. The true answer is, that these complaints are unfounded; and that the proper doctrine of the Trinity, as it has existed in latter times, is that which is expressed by the language used taken in its obvious sense. By *person*, says Waterland, than whom no writer in defence of the Trinity has a higher reputation, "I certainly mean a *real* Person, an *Hypostasis*, no *Mode*, *Attribute*, or *Property*. . . . . . Each divine Person is an individual, intelligent Agent; but as subsisting in one undivided substance, they are all together, in that respect, but one undivided intelligent Agent. . . . . . The church never professed three *Hypóstases* in any other sense, but as they mean

* The words quoted are from Professor Stuart's Letters to the Rev. W. E. Channing, p. 23, 2d ed.

three Persons."* There is, indeed, no reasonable pretence for saying, that *the great body of Trinitarians*, when they have used the word *person*, have not meant to express proper personality. He who asserts the contrary, asserts a mere extravagance. He closes his eyes upon an obvious fact, and then affirms what he may fancy ought to have been, instead of what there is no doubt really has been maintained. But on this subject there is something more to be said; and I shall remark particularly, not only upon this, but upon the other evasions which have been resorted to, in order to escape the force of the statement which has just been urged

I WISH, however, first to observe, that the ancient opinions concerning the Trinity, before the Council of Nice (A. D. 325), were VERY DIFFERENT from the modern doctrine, and had this great advantage over it, that, when viewed simply in connection with the unity of God, they were not *essentially* incredible. According to that form of faith which approached nearest to the modern Orthodox doctrine, the Father alone was the Supreme God, and the Son and Spirit were beings deriving their existence from him, and far inferior, to whom the title of God could be properly applied only in an inferior sense. The subject has been so thoroughly examined, that the correctness of this statement will not, I think, be questioned, at the present day, by any respect-

* Vindication of Christ's Divinity, pp. 350, 351, 3d ed.

able writer. The theological student, who wishes to see in a small compass the authorities on which it is founded, may consult one or more of the works mentioned in the note below.* I have stated that form of the doctrine which approached nearest to modern Orthodoxy. But the subject of the personality and divinity of the Holy Spirit, it may be observed, was in a very unsettled state before the Council of Constantinople (A. D. 381). Gregory Nazianzen, in his Eulogy of Athanasius, has the following passage, respecting that great father of Trinitarian Orthodoxy. "For when all others who held our doctrine were divided into three classes, the faith of many being unsound respecting the Son, that of still more concerning the Holy Spirit (on which subject to be least impious was thought to be piety), and a small number being sound in both respects; he first and alone, or with a very few, had the courage to profess in writing, clearly and explicitly, the true doctrine of the one

* Petavii Dogmata Theologica, Tom. II. De Trinitate; *particularly* Lib. I. cc. 3, 4, 5. — Huetii Origeniana [appended to Tom. IV. of De la Rue's edition of Origen], Lib. II. Quæst. 2. — Jackson's edition of Novatian, with his annotations. — Whitby, Disquisitiones Modestæ in Cl. Bulli Defensionem Fidei Nicænæ. — Whiston's Primitive Christianity, Vol. IV. — Clarke's Scripture Doctrine of the Trinity. — Priestley's History of Early Opinions, Vol. II. — Münscher's Dogmengeschichte, I. §§ 85 - 111. — [Martini, Versuch einer pragmatischen Geschichte des Dogma von der Gottheit Christi in den vier ersten Jahrhunderten. — Christian Examiner, Jan. 1830, Vol. VII. p. 303, seqq.; Sept. 1831, Vol. XI. p. 22, seqq.; July, 1832, Vol. XII. p. 298, seqq.; and July, 1836, Vol. XX. p. 343, seqq. The articles referred to were written by the Rev. Alvan Lamson, D. D.]

Godhead and nature of the three persons. Thus that truth, a knowledge of which, as far as regards the Son, had been vouchsafed to most of the Fathers before, he was fully inspired to maintain in respect to the Holy Spirit." *

So much for the original doctrine of the Trinity. I shall now proceed to state the different forms which the modern doctrine has been made to assume, and in which its language has been explained, by those who have attempted to conceal or remove the direct opposition between this and the doctrine of the unity of God.

I. MANY Trinitarian writers have maintained a modification of the doctrine, in some respects similar to what has just been stated to be its most ancient form. They have considered the Father as the "fountain of divinity," whose existence alone is underived, and have regarded the Son and Spirit as deriving their existence from him and subordinate to him; but, at the same time, as equally with the Father possessing all divine attributes. Every well-informed Trinitarian has at least heard of the Orthodoxy and learning of Bishop Bull. His Defence of the Nicene Creed is the standard work as regards the argument in support of the doctrine of the Trinity from Ecclesiastical History. But one whole division of this famous book is employed in maintaining the *subordination* of the Son. "No one can doubt," he says, "that the

* Orat. XXI. Opp. I. 394.

Fathers who lived before the Nicene Council acknowledged this subordination. It remains to show that the Fathers who wrote after this Council taught the same doctrine." * Having given various quotations from different writers to this effect, he proceeds: "The ancients, as they regarded the Father as the beginning, cause, author, fountain, of the Son, have not feared to call Him the one and only God. For thus the Nicene Fathers themselves begin their creed: *We believe in one God, the Father omnipotent;* afterwards subjoining: *and in one [Lord] Jesus Christ,— God of God.* And the great Athanasius himself concedes, that the Father is justly called the only God, because he alone is without origin, and is alone the fountain of divinity." † Bishop Bull next proceeds to maintain as the catholic doctrine, that though the Son is equal to the Father in nature and every essential perfection, yet the Father is greater than the Son even as regards his divinity; because the Father is the origin of the Son; the Son being from the Father, and not the Father from the Son. Upon this foundation, he appears to think that the doctrine of the divine unity may be preserved inviolate, though at the same time he contends that the Son, as a real person, distinct from the Father, is equally God, possessing equally all divine perfections, the only difference being that the perfections as they exist in the Son are derived, and as they exist in the Father are underived.

* Defensio Fidei Nicænæ, Sect. IV. c. 1. § 3.

† Ibid., § 6.

The same likewise, according to him, is true of the Spirit.*

But in regard to all such accounts of the doctrine, it is an obvious remark, that the existence of the Son, and of the Spirit, is either *necessary*, or it is *not*. If their existence be necessary, we have then three beings *necessarily existing*, each possessing divine attributes; and consequently we have three Gods. If it be not necessary, but dependent on the will of the Father, then we say, that the distance is infinite between underived and independent existence, and derived and dependent; between the supremacy of God, the Father, and the subordination of beings who exist only through his will. In the latter view of the doctrine, therefore, we clearly have but one God; but at the same time the modern doctrine of the Trinity disappears. The form of statement too, just mentioned, must be abandoned; for it can hardly be pretended that these derived and dependent beings possess an equality in divine attributes, or are equal in nature to the Father. Beings whose existence is dependent on the will of another cannot be equal in power to the being on whom they depend. The doctrine, therefore, however disguised by the mode of statement which we are considering, must, in fact, resolve itself into an assertion of three Gods; or must, on the other hand, amount to nothing more than a form of Unitarianism. In the latter case, however objec-

* Ibid., Sect. IV. cc. 2 - 4.

tionable and unfounded I may think it, it is not my present purpose to argue directly against it; and in the former case, it is pressed with all the difficulties which bear upon the doctrine as commonly stated, and at the same time with new difficulties, which affect this particular form of statement. That the Son and the Spirit should exist necessarily, as well as the Father, and possess equally with the Father all divine attributes, and yet be subordinate and inferior to the Father, — or, in other words, that there should be two beings or persons, each of whom is properly and in the highest sense God, and yet that these two beings or persons should be subordinate and inferior to another being or person, who is God, — is as incredible a proposition as the doctrine can involve.

II. OTHERS again, who have chosen to call themselves Trinitarians, profess to understand by the word *person* something very different from what it commonly expresses; and regard it as denoting neither any *proper personality*, nor any *real distinction*, in the divine nature. They use the word in a sense equivalent to that which the Latin word *persona* commonly has in classic writers, and which we may express by the word *character*. According to them, the Deity considered as existing in three different persons is the Deity considered as sustaining three different characters. Thus some of them regard the three persons as denoting *the three relations* which he bears to men, as their Creator (the Father), their Redeemer (the Son), and their Sanctifier (the Holy Spirit). Others found the distinction maintained in the doctrine on three attributes of God, as his goodness, wisdom, and power. Those who explain the Trinity in this manner are called *modal* or *nominal* Trinitarians. Their doctrine, as every one must perceive, is nothing more than simple Unitarianism, disguised, if it may be said to be disguised, by a very improper use of language. Yet this doctrine, or rather a heterogeneous mixture of opinions in which this doctrine is conspicuous, has been, at times, considerably prevalent, and has almost come in competition with the proper doctrine.

III. There are others, who maintain, with those last mentioned, that, in the terms employed in stating the doctrine of the Trinity, the word *person* is not to be taken in its usual sense; but who differ from them, in maintaining that those terms ought to be understood as affirming a real threefold distinction in the Godhead. But this is nothing more than a mere evasion, introduced into the general statement of the doctrine for the purpose of rescuing it from the charge of absurdity, to which those who thus explain it allow that it would be liable, if the language in which it is usually expressed were to be understood in its common acceptation. They themselves, however, after giving this general statement, immediately relapse into the common belief. When they speak particularly of the Father, the Son, or the Spirit, they speak of each unequivocally as a person in the proper sense of the word. They ascribe to them *personal* attributes. They speak of each as sustaining *personal* relations peculiar to himself, and performing *personal* actions, distinct from those of either of the others. It was the Son who was sanctified and sent into the world; and the Father by whom he was sanctified and sent. It was the Son who became incarnate, and not the Father. It was the Son who made atonement for the sins of men, and the Father by whom the atonement was received. The Son was in the bosom of the Father, but the Father was not in the bosom of the Son. The Son was the Logos who was with God, but it would sound harsh to say that the Father was with God. The Son was the first-born of every creature, the image of the Invisible God, and did not desire to retain his equality with God. There is no one who would not be shocked at the thought of applying this language to the Father. Again, it was the Holy Spirit who was sent as the "Comforter" to our Lord's Apostles, after his ascension, and not the Father nor the Son. All this, those who assert the doctrine of three distinctions, but not of three persons, in the divine nature, must and do say and allow; and therefore they do in fact maintain, with other Trinitarians, that there are three divine persons, in the proper sense of the word, distinguished from each other. They have adopted their mode of stating the doctrine merely with a view of avoiding those obvious objections which overwhelm it as commonly expressed; without any regard to its consistency with their real opinions, or with indisputable and acknowledged truths. The God and Father of our Lord Jesus Christ is an intelligent being, a person. There may seem something like irreverence in the very statement of this truth; but in reasoning respecting the doctrine of the Trinity, we are obliged to state even such truths as this. The Son of God is an intelligent being, a person. And no Christian, one would think, who reflects a moment upon his own belief, can doubt that these two persons are not the same. Neither of them, therefore, is a mere distinction of the divine nature, nor the same intelligent being regarded under different distinctions. Let us consider for a moment what sort of meaning would be forced upon the language of Scripture, if, where the Father and the Son of God are mentioned, we were to substitute the terms, "the first distinction in the Trinity," and "the second distinction in the Trinity"; or, "God considered in the first distinction of his nature," and "God considered in the second distinction of his nature." I will not produce examples, because it would appear to me like turning the Scriptures into burlesque.

If you prove that the person who is called the Son of God possesses divine attributes, you prove that there is another divine person beside the Father. In order to complete the Trinity, you must proceed to prove, *first*, THE PERSONALITY, and then the divinity, of the Holy Spirit. This is the only way in which the doctrine can be established. No one can pretend that there is any passage in the

Scriptures, in which it is expressly taught, that there is a threefold distinction of any sort in the divine nature. He who proves the doctrine of the Trinity from the Scriptures, must do it by showing that there are three persons, the Father, the Son, and the Holy Spirit, who are respectively mentioned in the Scriptures as each possessing divine attributes. There is no other medium of proof. There is no other way in which the doctrine can be established. Of course, it is the very method of proof to which, in common with other Trinitarians, those resort, who maintain that form of stating the doctrine which we are considering. It follows from this, that their real opinions must be in fact the same with those of other Trinitarians. Indeed, the whole statement appears to be little more than a mere oversight, a mistake, into which some have fallen in their haste to escape from the objections which they have perceived might be urged against the common form of the doctrine.

The remarks that have been made appear to me plain, and such as may be easily understood by every reader. I have doubted, therefore, whether to add another, the force of which may not be at once perceived, except by those who are a little familiar with metaphysical studies. But as it seems to show decisively, that the statement which we are considering is untenable by any proper Trinitarian, I have thought, on the whole, that it might be worth while to subjoin it.

In regard to the personality of the divine nature,

the only question is, whether there are three persons, or but one person. Those with whom we are arguing deny that there are three persons. Consequently they must maintain that there is but one person. They affirm, however, that there is a threefold distinction in the divine nature; that is, in the nature of this one person. But of the nature of any being, we can know nothing but by the attributes or properties of that being. Abstract all the attributes or properties of any being, and nothing remains of which you can form even an imagination. These are all that is cognizable by the human mind. When you say, therefore, that there is a threefold distinction in the nature of any being, the only meaning which the words will admit (in relation to the present subject) is, that the attributes or properties of this being may be divided into three distinct classes, which may be considered separately from each other. All, therefore, which is affirmed by the statement of those whom we are opposing is, that the attributes of that ONE PERSON who is God may be divided into three distinct classes; or, in other words, that God may be viewed in three different aspects in relation to his attributes. But this is nothing more than a *modal* or *nominal* Trinity, as we have before explained these terms. Those, therefore, whose opinions we are now considering, are, in fact, *nominal* Trinitarians in their statement of the doctrine, and *real* Trinitarians in their belief. They hold the proper doctrine, with an implicit acknowledgment in the very statement which they have adopted, that the proper doctrine is untenable; and have involved themselves, therefore, in new difficulties, without having effected an escape from those with which they were pressed before.

IV. But a very considerable portion of Trinitarians, and some of them among the most eminent, have not shrunk from understanding the doctrine as affirming the existence of *three equal divine minds*, and consequently, to all common apprehension, of three Gods; and from decidedly rejecting the doctrine of the unity of God, in that sense which is at once the popular and the philosophical sense of the term. All the unity for which they contend is only such as may result from those three divinities being inseparably conjoined, and having a mutual consciousness, or a mutual *in-being:* which last mode of existence is again expressed in the language of technical theology by the terms *perichoresis* and *circumincession.* "To say," says Dr. William Sherlock, "they are three divine persons, and not three distinct infinite minds, is both heresy and nonsense."* "The distinction of persons cannot be more truly and aptly represented than by the distinction between three men; for Father, Son, and Holy Ghost are as really distinct persons as Peter, James, and John."† "We must allow the Divine persons to be real, substantial beings."‡ There are few names of higher authority among Calvinists than that of Howe. The

* Vindication of the Doctrine of the Trinity, p. 66. London, 1690.
† Ibid., p. 105. ‡ Ibid., p. 47.

mode of explaining the doctrine to which he was inclined is well known. He was disposed to regard the three divine persons as "three distinct, individual, necessarily existent, spiritual beings," who formed together "the most delicious society." * Those who give such accounts of the doctrine may at least claim the merit of having rendered their opinions in some degree consistent with each other. They have succeeded, at a dear purchase to be sure, in freeing their creed from intrinsic absurdity, and have produced a doctrine to which there is no decisive objection, except that it contradicts the most explicit declarations of the Scriptures, and the first principles of natural religion; and is, therefore, irreconcilable with all that God has in any way taught us of himself.

After the Council of Nice, that which we have last considered became gradually the prevailing form of the doctrine, except that it was not very clearly settled in what the divine unity consisted. The comparison of the three persons in the Trinity to three different men was borrowed by Sherlock from the Fathers of the fourth century. Gregory Nazianzen, who himself maintained zealously this form of Orthodoxy, says that "those who were too Orthodox fell into polytheism," † i. e. tritheism. It might have been difficult to determine the precise distance from tritheism of those who were not *too* Orthodox.

* Howe's Calm Discourse of the Trinity in the Godhead. Works, Vol. II. p. 537, seqq., particularly pp. 549, 550.

† Orat. I. Opp. I. 16.

THIS, then, is the state of the case. The proper modern doctrine of the Trinity is, when viewed in connection with that of the unity of God, a doctrine essentially incredible. In endeavoring to present it in a form in which it may be defended, *one class of Trinitarians* insist strongly upon the supremacy of the Father, and the subordination of the Son and the Spirit. These, on the one hand, must either affirm this distinction in such a manner as really to maintain only a very untenable form of Unitarianism; or, on the other hand, must in fact retain the common doctrine, encumbered with the new and peculiar difficulty which results from declaring that the Son and Spirit are each properly God, but that each is a subordinate God. *Another class*, the nominal Trinitarians, explain away the doctrine entirely, and leave us nothing in their general account of it with which to contend, but a very unjustifiable use of language. *A third class*, those who maintain three distinctions, and deny three persons, have merely put a forced meaning upon the terms used in its statement; and have then gone on to reason and to write, in a manner which necessarily supposes that those terms are used correctly, and that the common form of the doctrine, which they profess to reject, is really that in which they themselves receive it. And *a fourth class* have fallen into plain and bald tritheism, maintaining the unity of God only by maintaining that the three Gods of whom they speak are inseparably and most intimately united. To these we may add, as *a fifth class*, those who receive, or profess to receive, the common doctrine, without any attempt to modify, explain, or understand it. All the sects of Trinitarians fall into one or other of the five classes just mentioned. Now we may put the nominal Trinitarians out of the question. They have nothing to do with the present controversy. And if there be any, who, calling themselves Trinitarians, do in fact hold such a subordination of the Son and Spirit to the Father, that their doctrine amounts only to one form of Unitarianism, we may put these out of the question likewise. After having done this, it will appear from the preceding remarks that the whole body of real Trinitarians may be separated into two great divisions; namely, those who, in connection with the divine unity, hold the proper doctrine, either with or without certain modifications,— which modifications, though intended to lessen, would really, if possible, add to its incredibility; and those who, maintaining the unity only in name, are in fact proper believers in three Gods. Now we cannot adopt the doctrine of those first mentioned, because we cannot believe what appears to us a contradiction in terms; nor the doctrine of those last mentioned, because neither revelation nor reason teaches us that there are three Gods. If there be any one who does not acquiesce in the conclusion to which we have arrived, I beg him to read over again what precedes, and to satisfy himself, either that there is, or that there is not, some error in the statements and reasonings. The subject is not one with which we are at liberty to trifle, and arbitrarily assume opinions without reason. It behooves every one to attend well to the subject; and to be sure that he holds the doctrine with no ambiguous or unsteady faith, before he undertakes to maintain, or professes to believe it, or in any way gives countenance to its reception among Christians.

WITH the doctrine of the Trinity is connected that of the HYPOSTATIC UNION, as it is called, or *the doctrine of the union of the divine and human natures in Christ, in such a manner that these two natures constitute but one person.* But this doctrine may be almost said to have pre-eminence in incredibility above that of the Trinity itself. The latter can be no object of belief when regarded in connection with that of the Divine Unity; for these two doctrines directly contradict each other. But the former, without reference to any other doctrine, does in itself involve propositions as clearly self-contradictory as any which it is in the power of language to express. It teaches that Christ is both God and man. The proposition is very plain and intelligible. The words *God* and *man* are among those which are in most common use, and the meaning of which is best defined and understood. There cannot (as with regard to the terms employed in stating the doctrine of the Trinity) be any controversy about the sense in which they are used in this proposition, or, in other words, about the ideas which they are intended to express. And we perceive that these ideas are wholly incompatible with each other. Our idea of God is of an infinite being; our idea of man is of a finite being; and we perceive that the same being cannot be both infinite and finite. There is nothing clear in language, no proposition of any sort can be affirmed to be true, if we cannot affirm this to be true, — that it is impossible that the same being should be finite and infinite; or, in other words, that it is impossible that the same being should be man and God. If the doctrine were not familiar to us, we should revolt from it, as shocking every feeling of reverence toward God; and it would appear to us, at the same time, as mere an absurdity as can be presented to the understanding. No words can be more destitute of meaning, *so far as they are intended to convey a proposition which the mind is capable of admitting*, than such language as we sometimes find used, in which Christ is declared to be at once the Creator of the universe, and a man of sorrows; God omniscient and omnipotent, and a feeble man of imperfect knowledge.*

I know of no way in which the force of the statement just urged can appear to be evaded, except by a sort of analogy that has been instituted between the double nature of Christ, as it is called, and the complex constitution of man, as consisting of soul and body. It has been said or implied, that the doctrine of the union of the divine and human natures in Christ does not

* [See Professor Stuart's Letters, p. 48.]

involve propositions more self-contradictory than those which result from the complex constitution of man; — that we may, for instance, affirm of man, that he is mortal, and that he is immortal; or of a particular individual, that he is dead, and that he is living (meaning by the latter term, that he is existing in the world of spirits). The obvious answer is, that there is NO analogy between these propositions and those on which we have remarked. The propositions just stated belong to a very numerous class, comprehending all those in which the same term is at once affirmed and denied of the same subject, *the term being used in different senses;* or in which terms apparently opposite are affirmed of the same subject, *the terms being used in senses not really opposed to each other.* When I say that man is mortal, I mean that his present life will terminate; when I say that he is immortal, I mean that his existence will not terminate. I use the words in senses not opposed, and bring together no ideas which are incompatible with each other. The second proposition just mentioned is of the same character with the first, and admits, as every one will perceive, of a similar explanation. In order to constitute an analogy between propositions of this sort and those before stated, Trinitarians must say, that, when they affirm that Christ is finite and not finite, omniscient and not omniscient, they mean to use the words "finite" and "omniscient" in different senses in the two parts of each proposition. But this they will not say; nor do the words admit of more than one sense.

A being of a complex constitution like man is not a being of a double nature. The very term *double nature*, when one professes to use it in a strict, philosophical sense, implies an absurdity. The nature of a being is ALL which constitutes it what it is; and when one speaks of a double nature, it is the same sort of language as if he were to speak of a double individuality. With regard to a being of a *complex constitution*, we may, undoubtedly, affirm that of a part of this constitution which is not true of the whole being; as we may affirm of the body of man, that it does not think, though we cannot affirm this of man;—or, on the other hand, we may affirm of the being itself what is not true of a part of its constitution, as by reversing the example just given. This is the whole truth relating to the subject. Of a being of a complex constitution, it is as much an absurdity to affirm contradictory propositions, as of any other being.

According to those who maintain the doctrine of the two natures in Christ, Christ speaks of himself, and is spoken of by his Apostles, sometimes as a man, sometimes as God, and sometimes as both God and man. He speaks, and is spoken of, under these different characters indiscriminately, without any explanation, and without its being anywhere declared that he existed in these different conditions of being. He prays to that being whom he himself was. He declares himself to be ignorant of what (being God) he knew, and unable to perform what (being God) he could perform. He affirms that he could do nothing of himself, or by his own power, though he was omnipotent. He, being God, prays for the glory which he had with God, and declares that another is greater than himself.* In one of the passages QUOTED IN PROOF OF HIS DIVINITY, he is called the image of the invisible God; in another of these passages, he, the God over all, blessed for ever, is said to have been anointed by God with the oil of gladness above his fellows; and in a third of them, it is affirmed that he became obedient to death, even the death of the cross.† If my readers are shocked by the combinations which I have brought together, I beg them to do me the justice to believe that my feelings are the same with their own. But these combinations necessarily result from the doctrine which we are considering. Page after page might be filled with inconsistencies as gross and as glaring. The doctrine has turned the Scriptures, as far as they relate to this subject, into a book of riddles, and, what is worse, of riddles admitting of no solution. I willingly refrain from the use of that stronger language which will occur to many of my readers.

The doctrine of the Trinity, then, and that of the union of two natures in Christ, are doctrines which, when fairly understood, it is impossible, from the nature of the human mind, should be be-

* [See John xvii.; Mark xiii. 32; John v. 30; xiv. 28.]

† [Colossians i. 15, seqq.; Hebrews i. 8, 9; Philippians ii. 5–8.]

lieved. They involve manifest contradictions, and no man can believe what he perceives to be a contradiction. In what has been already said, I have not been bringing arguments to disprove these doctrines; I have merely been showing that they are intrinsically incapable of any proof whatever; for a contradiction cannot be proved; — that they are of such a character, that it is impossible to bring arguments in their support, and unnecessary to adduce arguments against them.

Here, then, we might rest. If this proposition have been established, the controversy is at an end, as far as it regards the truth of the doctrines, and as far as it can be carried on against us by any sect of Christians. Till it can be shown that there is some ESSENTIAL mistake in the preceding statements, he who chooses to urge that these doctrines were taught by Christ and his Apostles must do this, not as a Christian, but as an unbeliever. If Christ and his Apostles communicated a revelation from God, these could make no part of it, for a revelation from God cannot teach absurdities.

But here I have no intention of resting. If I were to do so, I suppose that the old, unfounded complaint would be repeated once more, that those who reject these doctrines oppose reason to revelation; for there are men who seem unable to comprehend the possibility that the doctrines of their sect may make no part of the Christian revelation. What pretence, then, is there for asserting that the doctrines in question are taught in the

Scriptures? Certainly they are nowhere *expressly* taught. It cannot even be pretended that they are. There is not a passage from one end of the Bible to the other on which one can by any violence force such a meaning as to make it affirm the proposition, "that there are three persons in the Godhead, the Father, the Son, and the Holy Ghost; and these three are one God, the same in substance, equal in power and glory"; or the proposition that Christ "was and continues to be God and man in two distinct natures and one person for ever."* There was a famous passage in the First Epistle of John (v. 7), which was believed to affirm *something like* the first-mentioned proposition; but this every man of tolerable learning and fairness, at the present day, acknowledges to be spurious. And now this is gone, there is not one to be discovered of a similar character. THERE IS NOT A PASSAGE TO BE FOUND IN THE SCRIPTURES WHICH CAN BE IMAGINED TO AFFIRM EITHER OF THOSE DOCTRINES THAT HAVE BEEN REPRESENTED AS BEING AT THE VERY FOUNDATION OF CHRISTIANITY.

What pretence, then, is there for saying that those doctrines were taught by Jesus Christ and are to be received upon his authority? What ground is there for affirming that he, being a man, announced himself as the infinite God, and taught his followers also that God exists in three persons? But I will state a broader question. What pretence is there for saying that those doctrines were

* [Westminster Assembly's Shorter Catechism, Answers 6 and 21.]

taught by any writer, Jewish or Christian, of any book of the Old or New Testament? None whatever; — if, in order to prove that a writer has taught a doctrine, it be necessary to produce some passage in which he has affirmed that doctrine.

What mode of reasoning, then, is adopted by Trinitarians? I answer, that, in the first place, they bring forward certain passages, which, they maintain, prove that Christ is God. With these passages they likewise bring forward some others, which are supposed to intimate or prove the personality and deity of the Holy Spirit. It cannot but be observed, however, that, for the most part, they give themselves comparatively little trouble about the latter doctrine, and seem to regard it as following almost as a matter of course, if the former be established. Now there is no dispute that the Father is God; and it being thus proved that the Son and Spirit are each also God, it is *inferred*, not that there are three Gods, which would be the proper consequence, but that there are three persons in the Divinity. But Christ having been proved to be God, and it being at the same time regarded by Trinitarians as certain that he was a man, it is *inferred* also that he was both God and man. The stress of the argument, it thus appears, bears upon the proposition that Christ is God, the second person in the Trinity.

Turning away our view, then, for the present, from the absurdities that are involved in this proposition, or with which it is connected, we will proceed to inquire, as if it were capable of proof, what Christ and his Apostles taught concerning it.

SECTION III.

THE PROPOSITION, THAT CHRIST IS GOD, PROVED TO BE FALSE FROM THE SCRIPTURES.

Let us examine the Scriptures in respect to the fundamental doctrine of Trinitarianism; I mean, particularly, the Christian Scriptures; for the evidence which they afford will render any consideration of the Old Testament unnecessary.

I. In the first place, then, I conceive, *that, putting every other part of Scripture out of view, and forgetting all that it teaches, this proposition is clearly proved to be false by the very passages which are brought in its support.* We have already had occasion to advert to the character of some of these passages, and I shall now remark upon them a little more fully. They are supposed to prove that Christ is God in the highest sense, equal to the Father. Let us see what they really prove.

One of them is that in which our Saviour prays: "And now, Father, glorify thou me with thyself, with that glory which I had with thee before the world was." John xvii. 5.

The being who prayed to God to glorify him, CANNOT be God.

The first verse of John needs particular explanation, and I shall hereafter recur to it. I will here only observe, that if by the term *Logos* be meant, as Trinitarians believe, an intelligent being, a person, and this person be Christ, then the person who was WITH God could not have been God, except in a metaphorical or secondary acceptation of the terms, or, as some commentators have supposed, in an inferior sense of the word Θεός (*God*), —it being used not as a proper, but as a common name.

In John v. 22, it is said, according to the common version, "The Father judgeth no man; but hath committed all judgment unto the Son." "*The Father judgeth no man*, that is, without the Son," says a noted Orthodox commentator, Gill, "which is a proof of their equality." A proof of their equality! What, is it God to whom all judgment *is committed* by the Father?

We proceed to Colossians i. 15, &c., and here the first words which we find declare, that the being spoken of is "the image of the Invisible God." Is it possible that any one can believe, that God is affirmed by the Apostle to have been the *image* of God?

Turn now to Philippians ii. 5–8. Here, according to the modern Trinitarian exposition,* we are told, that Christ, who was God, as the passage is brought to prove, did not regard his equality with God as an object of solicitous desire, but humbled himself, and submitted to death, even

* [The exposition and translation of Professor Stuart are here referred to. See his Letters to Dr. Channing, p. 93.]

the death of the cross. Can any one imagine, that he is to prove to us by such passages as these, that the being to whom they relate is the Infinite Spirit?

There is no part of the New Testament in which the language concerning Christ is more figurative and difficult, than that of the first four verses of the Epistle to the Hebrews. But do these verses prove that the writer of the Epistle believed Christ to be God? Let us take the common version, certainly as favorable as any to this supposition, and consider how the person spoken of is described. He is one *appointed* by God to be heir of all things, one *by* whom *God made* the worlds, the *image* of his person, one *who hath sat down at the right hand of God*, one who *hath obtained* a more excellent name than the angels. Is it not wonderful that the person here spoken of has been believed to be God? And, if the one thing could be more strange than the other, would it not be still more wonderful that this passage has been regarded as a main proof of the doctrine?

Look next at Hebrews i. 8, 9, in which passage we find these words: "Therefore God, even thy God, hath anointed thee with the oil of gladness above thy fellows." Will any one maintain that this language is used concerning a being who possessed essential divinity? If passages of this sort are brought by any one to *establish* the doctrine, by what use of language, by what possible statements, would he expect it to be *disproved?*

There are few arguments on which more stress

has been laid by Trinitarians, than on the application of the title "Son of God" to Christ. Yet one who had for the first time heard of the doctrine would doubt, I think, whether a disputant who urged this argument were himself unable to understand the meaning of language, or presumed on the incapacity of those whom he addressed. To prove Christ to be God, a title is adduced which clearly distinguishes him from God. To suppose the contrary, is to suppose that Christ is at once God and the Son of God, that is, his own son, unless there be more than one God.

I think it evident, that the conclusion of the fifth verse of the ninth chapter of Romans, and the quotation, Heb. i. 10–12, do not relate to Christ. I conceive that they relate to God, the Father. Putting these, for the present, out of the question, the passages on which I have remarked are among the principal adduced in support of the doctrine. They stand in the very first class of proof texts. Let any man put it to his conscience what they do prove.

Again, it is inferred that Christ is God, because it is said that he will judge the world. To do this, it is maintained, requires omniscience, and omniscience is the attribute of divinity alone. I answer, that, whatever we may think of the judgment of the world spoken of in the New Testament, St. Paul declares that God will judge the world by A MAN* (not a God) whom HE has APPOINTED.

* "*A* man," so the original should be rendered, not "*that* man":

Again, it is argued that Christ is God, because supreme dominion is ascribed to him. I do not now inquire what is meant by this supreme dominion; but I answer, that it is nowhere ascribed to him in stronger language than in the following passage. "Then will be the end, when he will deliver up the kingdom to God, even the Father; after destroying all dominion, and all authority and power. For he must reign till He [that is, God] has put all his enemies under his feet. . . . . . And when all things are put under him, then will the Son himself be subject to Him who put all things under him, that God may be all in all." *

No words, one would think, could more clearly discriminate Christ from God, and declare his dependence and inferiority; and, of necessity, his infinite inferiority. I say, as I have said before, infinite inferiority; because an inferior and de-

ἐν ἀνδρὶ ᾧ ὥρισε. Acts xvii. 31. [Compare Acts x. 42; John v. 22, 27; Rom. ii. 16.]

* 1 Cor. xv. 24 – 28. [Compare Matthew xxviii. 18; Ephesians i. 17 – 23; Philippians ii. 9 – 11; John iii. 35; Acts ii. 36. — As an illustration of the sort of reasoning which we often find in Trinitarian writings, it may, perhaps, be worth while to mention, that the first three passages just referred to, or rather fragments of them, are quoted in a publication of the American Tract Society, as incontrovertible proofs that Christ is God. See Tract No. 214, entitled "More than One Hundred Scriptural and Incontrovertible Arguments for believing in the Supreme Divinity of our Lord and Saviour Jesus Christ." The 21st of these "Arguments," for example, runs thus: — Christ is God, "because it is said he has a name that is *above every name.* Phil. ii. 9." The whole verse, of which a few words are thus quoted, reads: "Wherefore *God also hath highly exalted him,* and GIVEN him a name which is above every name." See also Arg. 1, 40, 72.]

pendent must be a finite being, and finite and infinite do not admit of comparison.

It appears, then, that the doctrine under consideration is overthrown by the very arguments brought in its support.

II. BUT further; *it contradicts the express and reiterated declarations of our Saviour.* According to the doctrine in question, it was THE SON, or the second person in the Trinity, who was united to the human nature of Christ. It was HIS words, therefore, that Christ, as a divine teacher, spoke; and it was through HIS power that he performed his wonderful works. But this is in direct contradiction to the declarations of Christ. He always refers the divine powers which he exercised, and the divine knowledge which he discovered, to the Father, and never to any other person, or to the Deity considered under any other relation or distinction. Of himself, AS THE SON, he always speaks as of a being entirely dependent upon the Father.

"If of myself I assume glory, my glory is nothing; it is my Father who glorifies me." John viii. 54.

"As the Father has life in himself, so HAS HE GRANTED to the Son also to have life in himself." John v. 26.

This is a verbal translation. A more intelligible rendering would be: "As the Father is the source of life, so has he granted to the Son also to be the source of life."

" The works which the Father HAS GIVEN ME TO PERFORM [i.e. has enabled me to perform], the very works which I am doing, testify of me, that the Father has sent me." John v. 36.

" As the living Father has sent me, and I LIVE BY THE FATHER," &c. John vi. 57.*

" I have not spoken from myself; but He who sent me, the Father himself, has given me in charge what I should enjoin, and what I should teach. . . . . . What, therefore, I teach, I teach as the Father has directed me." John xii. 49, 50.

" The words which you hear are not mine, but the Father's who sent me." John xiv. 24.

" If I do not the works of my Father, believe me not." John x. 37.

" The words which I speak to you, I speak not from myself; and the Father, who dwells in me, himself does the works." John xiv. 10.

" THE SON can do NOTHING OF HIMSELF, but only what he sees his Father doing." John v. 19.

" When you have raised on high the Son of Man [i. e. crucified him], then you will know that I am He [i. e. the Messiah], and that I do nothing of myself, but speak thus as the Father has taught me. And He who sent me is with me." John viii. 28, 29.

I do not multiply passages, because they must

* " In quoting the words as given above, I have followed the Common Version; but the verse should be rendered thus: " As the ever-blessed Father sent me, and I am blessed through the Father, so he, whose food I am, shall be blessed through me." Ζάω, in this verse, is used in the secondary signification which it so often has, denoting, *I am blessed, I am happy.*

be familiar to every one. From the declarations of our Saviour, it appears that he constantly referred the divine power manifested in his miracles, and the divine inspiration by which he spoke, to the Father, and not to any other divine person such as Trinitarians suppose. According to their hypothesis, it was the divine power and wisdom of the Son which were displayed in Jesus; to him, therefore, should the miracles and doctrine of Jesus have been referred; which they never are. No mention of such a divine person appears in his discourses. But of himself, as the Son of God, he speaks as of a being entirely dependent upon his Father and our Father, his God and our God. These declarations are *decisive* of the controversy. Every other argument might be laid aside.

III. But, in the third place, the doctrine that Christ is God *is opposed to the whole tenor of the Scriptures, and all the facts in the history of Christ.* Though conceived by a miracle, he was born into the world *as* other men are, and *such* as other men are. He did not come, as some of the Jews imagined their Messiah would come, no man knew whence.* He was a helpless infant. Will any one, at the present day, shock our feelings and understanding to the uttermost, by telling us that Almighty God was incarnate in this infant, and

* "We know whence this man is; whereas when the Messiah comes, no one will know whence he is." John vii. 27.

wrapped in swaddling-clothes?* He grew in wisdom, and in stature, and in favor with God and men. Read over his history in the Evangelists, and ask yourselves if you are not reading the history of a man; though of one indeed to whom God had given his spirit without measure, whom he had intrusted with miraculous powers, and constituted a messenger of the most important truths. He appears with all the attributes of humanity. He discovers human affections. He is moved even to tears at the grave of Lazarus. He mourns over the calamities about to overwhelm his country. While enduring the agony of crucifixion, he discovers the strength of his filial affection, and consigns his mother to the care of the disciple whom he loved. He was sometimes excited to indignation, and his soul was sometimes troubled by the sufferings which he endured, and which he anticipated. "Now is my soul troubled; and what shall I say? Father, save me from this hour? But for this I came,—for this very hour."† Devotion is the virtue of a created and dependent being. But our Saviour has left us not less an example of piety than of benevolence. His ex-

* Dr. Watts in one of his hymns says:

> "This infant is the MIGHTY GOD,
> Come to be *suckled* and *adored*." — B. I., H. 13.

The language is almost too horrible to be quoted. — Dr. Watts was a man of piety, and of very considerable intellectual powers; yet to this extreme point could his mind be debased by a belief of the doctrine against which we are contending.

† John xii. 27.

pressions of dependence upon his Father and upon our Father, are the most absolute and unequivocal. He felt the common wants of our nature, hunger, thirst, and weariness. He suffered death, the common lot of man. He endured the cross, despising the shame, and he did this for THE JOY SET BEFORE HIM.* "Therefore God has HIGHLY EXALTED HIM." † But it is useless to quote or allude to particular passages, which prove that Christ was a being distinct from, inferior to, and dependent upon God. You may find them on every page of the New Testament. The proof of this fact is, as I have said, imbedded and ingrained in the very passages brought to support a contrary proposition.

But it is useless, for another reason, to adduce arguments in proof of this fact. It is conceded by Trinitarians explicitly and fully. The doctrine of the humanity of Christ is as essential a part of their scheme as the doctrine of his divinity. They allow, or, to speak more properly, they contend, that he was a man. But if this be true, then the only question that need be examined is, whether it be possible for Christ to have been at once God and man, infinite and finite, omniscient and not omniscient, omnipotent and not omnipotent. To my mind, the propositions here supposed are as if one were to say, that to be sure astronomers have correctly estimated the size of the earth; but that it does, notwithstanding, fill infinite space.

* Hebrews xii. 2. † [Philippians ii. 9.]

IV. In the next place, the doctrine is proved to be false, because *it is evident from the Scriptures that none of those effects were produced which would necessarily have resulted from its first annunciation by Christ, and its subsequent communication by his Apostles.* The disciples of our Saviour must, at some period, have considered him merely as a man. Such he was, to all appearance, and such, therefore, they must have believed him to be. Before he commenced his ministry, his relations and fellow-townsmen certainly regarded him as nothing more than a man. "Is not this the carpenter, the son of Mary, and brother of James and Joses and Judas and Simon? And are not his sisters here with us?"* At some particular period, the communication must have been made by our Saviour to his disciples, that he was not a mere man, but that he was, properly speaking, and in the highest sense, God himself. The doctrines with which we are contending, and other doctrines of a similar character, have so obscured and confused the whole of Christianity, that even its historical facts appear to be regarded by many scarcely in the light of real occurrences. But we *may* carry ourselves back in imagination to the time when Christ was on earth, and place ourselves in the

* Mark vi. 3. I have retained the words "brother" and "sisters," used in the Common Version, not thinking it important, in the connection in which the passage is quoted, to make any change in this rendering; but the relationship intended I believe to be that of cousins. [See the note on Matthew xiii. 55, in the author's Notes on the Gospels.]

situation of the first believers. Let us, then, reflect for a moment on what would be the state of our own feelings, if some one with whom we had associated as a man were to declare to us that he was really God himself. If his character and works had been such as to command any attention to such an assertion, still through what an agony of incredulity, and doubt, and amazement, and consternation must the mind pass, before it could settle down into a conviction of the truth of his declaration! And when convinced of its truth, with what unspeakable astonishment should we be overwhelmed! With what extreme awe, and entire prostration of every faculty, should we approach and contemplate such a being! if indeed man, in his present tenement of clay, could endure such intercourse with his Maker. With what a strong and unrelaxing grasp would the idea seize upon our minds! How continually would it be expressed in the most forcible language, whenever we had occasion to speak of him! What a deep and indelible coloring would it give to every thought and sentiment in the remotest degree connected with an agent so mysterious and so awful! But we perceive nothing of this state of mind in the disciples of our Saviour; but much that gives evidence of a very different state of mind. One may read over the first three Evangelists, and it must be by a more than ordinary exercise of ingenuity, if he discover what may pass for an argument that either the writers, or the numerous individuals of whom they speak, regarded our

Saviour as their Maker and God; or that he ever assumed that character. Can we believe, that, if such a most extraordinary annunciation as has been supposed had ever actually been made by him, no particular record of its circumstances, and immediate effects, would have been preserved? — that the Evangelists in their accounts of their Master would have omitted the most remarkable event in his history and their own? — and that three of them at least (for so much must be conceded) would have made no direct mention of far the most astonishing fact in relation to his character? Read over the accounts of the conduct and conversation of his disciples with their Master, and put it to your own feelings whether they ever thought that they were conversing with their God. Read over these accounts attentively, and ask yourself if this supposition do not appear to you one of the most incongruous that ever entered the human mind. Take only the facts and conversation which occurred the night before our Saviour's crucifixion, as related by St. John. Did Judas believe that he was betraying his God? Their Master washed the feet of his Apostles. Did the Apostles believe — but the question is too shocking to be stated in plain words. Did they then believe their Master to be God, when, surprised at his taking notice of an inquiry which they wished to make, but which they had not in fact proposed,* they thus addressed him? "Now

* See John xvi. 17 – 19.

we perceive that you know all things, and need not that any one should question you. By this we believe that you came from God."* Could they imagine that he who, throughout his conversation, spoke of himself only as the minister of God, and who in their presence prayed to God, was himself the Almighty? Did they believe that it was the Maker of heaven and earth whom they were deserting, when they left him upon his apprehension? But there is hardly a fact or conversation recorded in the history of our Saviour's ministry which may not afford ground for such questions as have been proposed. He who maintains that the first disciples of our Saviour did ever really believe that they were in the immediate presence of their God, must maintain at the same time that they were a class of men by themselves, and that all their feelings and conduct were immeasurably and inconceivably different from what those of any other human beings would have been under the same belief. But beside the entire absence of that state of mind which must have been produced by this belief, there are other continual indications, direct and indirect, of their opinions and feelings respecting their Master, wholly irreconcilable with the supposition of its existence during any period of his ministry, or their own. Throughout the New Testament, we find nothing which implies that such a most extraordinary change of feeling ever took place in the disciples

* John xvi. 30.

of Christ as must have been produced by the communication that their Master was God himself upon earth. Nowhere do we find the expression of those irresistible and absorbing sentiments which must have possessed their minds under the conviction of this fact. With this conviction, in what terms, for instance, would they have spoken of his crucifixion, and of the circumstances with which it was attended? The power of language would have sunk under them in the attempt to express their feelings. Their words, when they approached the subject, would have been little more than a thrilling cry of horror and indignation. On this subject they did indeed feel most deeply; but can we think that St. Peter regarded his Master as God incarnate, when he thus addressed the Jews by whom Christ had just been crucified? "Men of Israel, hear these words: Jesus of Nazareth, proved to you TO BE A MAN FROM GOD, by miracles and wonders and signs, which God did by him in the midst of you, as you yourselves know, him, delivered up to you in conformity to the fixed will and foreknowledge of God, you have crucified and slain by the hands of the heathen. Him has God raised to life." *

But what have been stated are not the only consequences which must necessarily have followed from the communication of the doctrine in question. It cannot be denied by those who hold the doctrine of the deity of Christ, that, however satis-

* Acts ii. 22 - 24.

factorily it may be explained, and however well it may be reconciled with that fundamental principle of religion to which the Jews were so strongly attached, the doctrine of the Unity of God, yet it does, or may, at first sight, appear somewhat inconsistent with it. From the time of the Jew who is represented by Justin Martyr as disputing with him, about the middle of the second century, to the present period, it has always been regarded by the unbelieving Jews with abhorrence. They have considered the Christians as no better than idolaters; as denying the first truth of religion. But the unbelieving Jews, in the time of the Apostles, opposed Christianity with the utmost bitterness and passion. They sought on every side for objections to it. There was much in its character to which the believing Jews could hardly be reconciled. The Epistles are full of statements, explanations, and controversy relating to questions having their origin in Jewish prejudices and passions. With regard, however, to this doctrine, which, if it had ever been taught, the believing Jews must have received with the utmost difficulty, and to which the unbelieving Jews would have manifested the most determined opposition, — with regard to this doctrine, there is no trace of any controversy. But if it had ever been taught, it must have been the main point of attack and defence between those who assailed and those who supported Christianity. There is nothing ever said in its explanation. But it must have required, far more than any other doctrine, to be explained, illustrated, and enforced; for it appears not only irreconcilable with the doctrine of the Unity of God, but equally so with that of the humanity of our Saviour; and yet both these doctrines, it seems, were to be maintained in connection with it. It must have been necessary, therefore, to state it as clearly as possible, to exhibit it in its relations, and carefully to guard against the misapprehensions to which it is so liable on every side. Especially must care have been taken to prevent the gross mistakes into which the Gentile converts from polytheism were likely to fall. Yet, so far from any such clearness of statement and fulness of explanation, the whole language of the New Testament in relation to this subject is (as I have before said) a series of enigmas, upon the supposition of its truth. The doctrine, then, is never defended in the New Testament, though unquestionably it would have been the main object of attack, and the main difficulty in the Christian system. It is never explained, though no doctrine could have been so much in need of explanation. On the contrary, upon the supposition of its truth, the Apostles express themselves in such a manner, that, if it had been their purpose to darken and perplex the subject, they could not have done it more effectually. And still more, this doctrine is never insisted upon as a necessary article of faith; though it is now represented by its defenders as lying at the foundation of Christianity. With a few exceptions, the passages in which it is imagined to be taught are introduced incidentally, the attention of the writer being principally directed to some other topic; and can be regarded only as accidental notices of it. It appears, then, that while other questions of far less difficulty (for instance, the circumcision of the Gentile converts) were subjects of such doubt and controversy that even the authority of the Apostles was barely sufficient to establish the truth, this doctrine, so extraordinary, so obnoxious, and so hard to be understood, was introduced in silence, and received without hesitation, dislike, opposition, or misapprehension. There are not many propositions, to be proved or disproved merely by moral evidence, which are more incredible.

I WISH to repeat some of the ideas already suggested, in a little different connection. The doctrine that Christ was God himself, appearing upon earth to make atonement for the sins of men, is represented, by those who maintain it, as a fundamental doctrine of Christianity, affecting essentially the whole character of our religion. If true, it must indeed have affected essentially the whole character of the writings of the New Testament. A truth of such awful and tremendous interest, a fact "at which reason stands aghast, and faith herself is half confounded,"* a doctrine so adapted

* Such is the language of Bishop Hurd in defending the doctrine. "In this awfully stupendous manner, at which REASON STANDS AGHAST, AND FAITH HERSELF IS HALF CONFOUNDED, was the grace of God to man at length manifested." Sermons preached at Lincoln's Inn, Vol. II. p. 287. London, 1785.

to seize upon and possess the imagination and the feelings, and at once so necessary and so difficult to be understood, must have appeared everywhere in the New Testament in the most prominent relief. Nobody, one would think, can seriously imagine it any answer to this remark, to say that "the Apostles doubtless expected to be believed when they had *once* plainly asserted anything"; or to suggest that their veracity might have been suspected, if they had made frequent and constant asseverations of the truth of the doctrine.* What was the business of the Apostles but to teach and explain, to enforce and defend, the fundamental doctrines of Christianity? I say to *defend* these doctrines; for he who reads the Epistles with any attention, will not think that the mere authority of an Apostle was decisive in bearing down at once all error, doubt, and opposition among believers. Even if this had been the case, their converts must still have been furnished with some answer to those objections with which the unbelieving Jews would have assailed a doctrine so apparently incredible, and so abhorrent to their feelings. From the very nature of the human mind, if the minds of the Apostles at all resembled those of other men, the fact that their Master was the Almighty, clothed in flesh, must have appeared continually in their writings, in direct assertions, in allusions, in the strongest possible expressions of feeling, in a thousand different forms. The intrin-

* See Professor Stuart's Letters, p. 128.

sic difficulty of the doctrine in question is so great, and such was the ignorance of the first converts, and their narrowness of conception, that the Apostles must have continually recurred to it, for the purpose of explaining it, and guarding it against misapprehension. As a fundamental doctrine of our religion, it is one which they must have been constantly employed in teaching. If it were a doctrine of Christianity, the evidence for it would burst from every part of the New Testament in a blaze of light. Can any one think that we should be left to collect the proof of a fundamental article of our faith, and the evidence of incomparably the most astonishing fact that ever occurred upon our earth, from some expressions scattered here and there, the greater part of them being dropped incidentally; and that really one of the most plausible arguments for it would be found in the omission of the Greek article in four or five texts? Can any one think that such a doctrine would have been so taught, that, putting out of view the passages above referred to, the whole remaining body of the New Testament, the whole history of our Saviour, and the prevailing and almost uniform language of his Apostles, should appear, at least, to be thoroughly irreconcilable with it? I speak, it will be remembered, merely of the proposition that Christ is God. With regard to the doctrine of his double nature, or the doctrine of the Trinity, it cannot, as I have said, be pretended that either of these is anywhere directly taught. The whole New Testament, the Gospels and the

Epistles, present another aspect from what they must have done, if the doctrines maintained by Trinitarians were true. If true, it is incredible that they should not have appeared in the Scriptures in a form essentially different from that in which alone it can be pretended that they do at present.

V. In treating of the argument from Scripture, I have thus far reasoned *ad hominem;* as if the doctrine that Christ is God, in the Trinitarian sense of the words, were capable of proof. But I must now advert to the essential character of the doctrine. *It admits of being understood in no sense which is not obviously false; and therefore it is impossible that it should have been taught by Christ, if he were a teacher from God.*

From the nature of the Trinitarian doctrines, there is a liability to embarrassment in the whole of our reasoning from Scripture against them; it being impossible to say *definitely* what is to be disproved. I have endeavored, however, to direct the argument in such a manner as to meet those errors in any form they may assume. That so many have held, or professed to hold them, (a phenomenon one of the most remarkable in the history of the human mind,) is principally to be explained by the fact, that the language in which they are stated, taken in its obvious sense, expresses propositions so utterly incredible. Starting off from its obvious meaning, the mind has recourse to conceptions of its own, obscure, undefined, and unsettled; which, by now assuming one shape and then another, elude the grasp of reason. In disproving from the Scriptures the proposition that Christ is God, the arguments that have been urged, I trust, bear upon it in any Trinitarian sense which it may be imagined to express. But what does a Trinitarian mean by this proposition? Let us assume that the title "Son of God," applied to Christ, denotes, in some sense or other, proper essential divinity. But the Son is but *one* of *three* who constitute God. You may substitute after the numerals the word *person*, or *distinction*, or any other; it will not affect the argument. God is a being; and when you have named Christ or the Son, you have not, according to the doctrine of the Trinity, named all which constitutes this being. The Trinitarian asserts that God exists in three persons; or, to take the wholly unimportant modification of the doctrine that some writers have attempted to introduce, that "God is three in a certain respect." But Christ, it is also affirmed, is God, the Son is God. Does he, then, exist in three persons? Is he three in a certain respect? Unquestionably not. The word "God" is used in two senses. In one case, as applied to the Supreme Being, properly, in the only sense which a Christian can recognize as the literal sense of the term; in the other case, as applied to Christ, though professedly in the same, yet clearly and necessarily in a different signification, no one can tell what.

Again: the Father is God. Nothing can be

added to his infinity or perfections to complete our idea of God. Confused as men's minds have been by the doctrine we are opposing, there is no one who would not shrink from expressly asserting anything to be wanting to constitute the Father God, in the most absolute and comprehensive sense of the term. His conceptions must be miserably perplexed and perverted, who thinks it possible to use language on this subject too strong or too unlimited. In the Father is all that we can conceive of as constituting God. And there is but one God. In the Father, therefore, exists all that we can conceive of as constituting the One and Only God. But it is contended that Christ also is God. What, however, can any one mean by this proposition, who understands and assents to the perfectly intelligible and indisputable propositions just stated? Is the meaning, that Christ as well as the Father — or, if the Father be God, we must say, as well as God — is the One and Only God? Is it that we are in error about the unity of God, and that Christ is another God? No one will assent to either of these senses of the proposition. Does it imply, then, that neither the Father nor the Son is the One and Only God, but that together with another, the Holy Spirit, they constitute this mysterious Being? This seems at first view more conformed to the doctrine to be maintained; but it must be observed, that he who adopts this sense asserts, not that Christ is God, but that he is not God; and asserts at the same time that the Father is not God.

Once more: if Christ be God, and if there be but one God, then all that is true of God is true of Christ, considered as God; and, on the other hand, all that is true of the Son is true of God. This being so, open the Bible, and where the name of God occurs, substitute that of the Son; and where the name of the Son occurs, that of God. "The Son sent his beloved Son"; "Father, the hour is come; glorify *thy Son* that *thy Son* also may glorify Thee." I will not, for the sake of confuting any error, put a change on this most solemn and affecting passage. I have felt throughout the painful incongruity of introducing conceptions that ought to be accompanied with very different feelings and associations into such a discussion, and I am not disposed to pursue the mode just suggested of exemplifying the nature of the errors against which I am contending. But one who had never seen the New Testament before would need but to read a page of it to satisfy himself that "the Son of God" and "God" are not convertible terms, but mean something very different.

But a Trinitarian may answer me, that the word "God" in the New Testament almost always denotes either the Trinity or the Father; and that he does not suppose it to be applied to the Son in more than about a dozen instances. One would think that this state of the case must, at the first view of it, startle a defender of the doctrine that Christ is God. It is strange that one equal to the Father in every divine perfection should so rarely be denoted by that name to which he is equally entitled. But passing over this difficulty, what is the purport of the answer? You maintain that Christ is God, that the Son is God. If so, are not all the acts of God his acts? Is not all that can be affirmed of God to be affirmed of him? You hesitate, perhaps; but there is no reason why you should. If there be any meaning in the New Testament, these questions must be answered in the negative. It is clear, then, that, whatever you may imagine, you do not use the term "God" in the same sense when applied to the Son, as when applied by you to what you call the Trinity, or to the First Person of the Trinity; or as when applied either by you or us to the Supreme Being. But, as regards the question under discussion, the word admits of no variety of signification. The proposition, then, that Christ is God, is so thoroughly irreconcilable with the New Testament, that no one could think of maintaining it except through a confused misapprehension of its meaning.

HERE, then, I close the argument from Scripture; not because it is exhausted, but because it must be useless to pursue it further.* I will only add a few general remarks, founded in part on what has been already said concerning the pas-

* [The reader who wishes to pursue it further is referred to Wilson's "Scripture Proofs and Scriptural Illustrations of Unitarianism," 3d ed., 1846, 8vo, — a work which gives a fuller view than can easily be found elsewhere, not only of the Scripture proofs of Unitarianism, but of the *alleged* Scripture evidence for Trinitarianism.]

sages adduced by Trinitarians in support of their doctrines.

In the first place, it is to be recollected that the passages urged to prove that Christ is God are alone sufficient evidence against this proposition. A large portion of them contain language which cannot be used concerning God, which necessarily distinguishes Christ from God, and which clearly represents him as an inferior and dependent being.

In the next place, I wish to recall another remark to the recollection of my readers. It is, that the doctrines maintained by Trinitarians, upon the supposition of their possibility and truth, must have been taught very differently from the manner in which they are supposed to be. Let any one recollect, that THERE IS NO PRETENCE THAT ANY PASSAGE IN SCRIPTURE AFFIRMS THE DOCTRINE OF THE TRINITY, OR THAT OF THE DOUBLE NATURE OF CHRIST; and then let him look over the passages brought to prove that Christ is God; let him consider how they are collected from one place and another, how thinly they are scattered through the New Testament, and how incidentally they are introduced; let him observe that, in a majority of the books of the New Testament, there is not one on which a wary disputant would choose to rely; and then let him remember the general tenor of the Christian Scriptures, and the undisputed meaning of far the greater part of their language in relation to this subject. Having done this, I think he may safely say, before any critical examination of the meaning of those passages, that their meaning must have been mistaken; that the evidence adduced is altogether defective *in its general aspect;* and that it is not by such detached passages as these, taken in a sense opposed to the general tenor of the Scriptures, that a doctrine like that in question can be established. We might as reasonably attempt to prove, in opposition to the daily witness of the heavens, that there are three suns instead of but one, by building an argument on the accounts which we have of parhelia.

Another remark of some importance is, that, as Trinitarians differ much in their modes of explaining the doctrine, so are they not well agreed in their manner of defending it. When the doctrine was first introduced, it was defended, as Bishop Horsley tells us, "by arguments drawn from Platonic principles."* To say nothing of these, some of the favorite arguments from Scripture of the ancient Fathers were such as no Trinitarian at the present day would choose to insist upon. One of those, for instance, which was adduced to prove the Trinity is found in Ecclesiastes iv. 12, "A threefold cord is not soon broken." Not a few of the Fathers, says Whitby, explain this concerning the Holy Trinity.† Another passage often adduced, and among others by Athanasius, as declarative of the generation of the Son from the substance of the Father, was discovered in the

* Charge, IV. § 2, published in Horsley's Tracts in Controversy with Dr. Priestley.

† Dissertatio de S. Scripturarum Interpretatione secundum Patrum Commentarios, pp. 95, 96.

first verse of the 45th Psalm. The argument founded upon this disappears altogether in our common version, which renders it: "My heart is inditing a good matter." But the word in the Septuagint corresponding to *matter* in the common version is *Logos;* and the Fathers understood the passage thus: My heart is throwing out a good Logos.* A proof that the second person in the Trinity became incarnate, was found in Proverbs ix. 1: "Wisdom hath builded her house"; † for the second person, or the Son, was regarded in the theology of the times as the Wisdom of the Father. These are merely specimens taken from many of a similar character, a number more of which may be found in the work of Whitby just referred to in the margin. Since the first introduction of the doctrine, the mode of its defence has been continually changing. As more just notions respecting the criticism and interpretation of the Scriptures have slowly made their way, one passage after another has been dropped from the Trinitarian roll. Some which are retained by one expositor are given up by another. Even two centuries ago, Calvin threw away or depreciated the value of many texts, which most Trinitarians would think hardly to be spared. ‡

* Dissertatio de S. Scripturarum Interpretatione secundum Patrum Commentarios, p. 75.

† Ibid., p. 92.

‡ [Thus, for example, in his note on John x. 30, "I and my Father are one," Calvin says: "The ancients improperly used this passage to prove that Christ is of the same substance with the Father. For

There are very few of any importance in the controversy, the Orthodox exposition of which has not been abandoned by some one or more of the principal Trinitarian critics among Protestants.* Among Catholics, there are many by whom it is rather affirmed than conceded, that the doctrine of the Trinity is not to be proved from the Scriptures, but rests for its support upon the *tradition of the Church.*

WHENCE, then, was the doctrine of the Trinity derived? The answer to this question is important. Reason and Scripture have borne their testimony against the doctrine; and I am now about to call another witness, Ecclesiastical History.

he is not speaking of a unity of substance, but of his agreement (*consensu*) with the Father; implying that whatever he does will be confirmed by the Father's power." — Opp. VI. P. II. 103.

It may be observed, that the *earlier* Christian Fathers who treat of this passage do not explain it in the manner which is censured by Calvin. They understood the word "one," which is in the neuter gender in the original, as denoting, not a unity of nature, but of will and affection, a moral unity; referring for this use of language to other passages of Scripture, as John xvii. 11, 21 - 23; Acts iv. 32; 1 Cor. iii. 8, &c. So Tertullian, Advers. Praxeam, c. 22; Novatian, De Trinitate, c. 27; Origen, Cont. Celsum, Lib. VIII. c. 12, Opp. I. 750, 751; Comm. in Joannem, Tom. xiii. c. 36, Opp. IV. 245; and elsewhere. See also the citations from Hippolytus, Alexander of Alexandria, and Eusebius, in Jackson's notes on Novatian, pp. 368, 369. The passage is understood in a similar manner by Erasmus, Grotius, Bp. Pearce, Abp. Newcome, Bp. Middleton, Knapp, Rosenmüller, Kuinoel, Stuart, Schleusner, Wahl, and Robinson.]

* [For abundant proof of this fact, see Wilson's "Concessions of Trinitarians," Manchester, Eng., and Boston, U. S., 1845. 8vo.]

SECTION IV.

ON THE ORIGIN OF THE DOCTRINE OF THE TRINITY.

We can trace the history of this doctrine, and discover its source, not in the Christian revelation, but in the Platonic philosophy; * which was the prevalent philosophy during the first ages after the introduction of Christianity, and of which all the more eminent Christian writers, the Fathers as they are called, were, in a greater or less degree, disciples. They, as others have often done, blended their philosophy and their religion into one complex and heterogeneous system; and taught the doctrines of the former as those of the latter. In this manner, they introduced errors into the popular faith. "It is an old complaint of learned men," says Mosheim, "that the Fathers, or teachers of the ancient church, were too much inclined to the philosophy of Plato, and rashly confounded what was taught by that philosopher with the doctrines of Christ, our Saviour; in consequence of which, the religion of Heaven was greatly corrupted, and

* I state the proposition in this general form, in which the authorities to be adduced directly apply to it. But it is to be observed, that the doctrine of the personality of the Logos, and of his divinity, in an inferior sense of that term, which was the germ of the Trinity, was immediately derived from Philo, the Jewish Plato as he has been called, which fact I shall hereafter have occasion to advert to.

the truth much obscured." * This passage is from the Dissertation of Mosheim, *Concerning the Injury done to the Church by the Later Platonists.* In the same Dissertation, after stating some of the obstructions thrown in the way of Christianity by those of the later Platonists who were its enemies, he proceeds to say: "But these evils were only external, and although they were injurious to our most holy religion, and delayed its progress, yet they did not corrupt its very nature, and disease, if I may so speak, its vitals. More fatal distempers afflicted Christianity, after this philosophy had entered the very limits of the sacred city, and had built a habitation for herself in the minds of those to whom the business of instruction was committed. There is nothing, the most sacred in our faith, which from that time was not profaned, and did not lose a great part of its original and natural form." † "Few of the learned," he adds in another place, "are so unacquainted with ecclesiastical history, as to be ignorant what a great number of errors, and most preposterous opinions, flowed in from this impure source." ‡ Among the false doctrines thus introduced from the Platonic philosophy is to be reckoned, pre-eminently, that of the Trinity. Gibbon says, with a sneer, that "the Athenian sage [Plato] marvellously anticipated one of the most surprising discoveries of the

* Mosheim, De turbatâ per recentiores Platonicos Ecclesiâ Commentatio, § vi.

† Ibid., § xxxiii.

‡ Ibid., § xlviii.

Christian revelation."* In making this assertion, Gibbon adopted a popular error, for which there is no foundation. Nothing resembling the doctrine of the Trinity is to be found in the writings of Plato himself.† But there is no question that, in different forms, it was a favorite doctrine of the later Platonists, equally of those who were not Christians as of those who were. Both the one and the other class expressed the doctrine in similar terms, explained it in a similar manner, and defended it, as far as the nature of the case allowed, by similar arguments; and both appealed in its support to the authority of Plato. Clement of Alexandria, one of the earliest of the Trinitarian and Platonizing Fathers, (he flourished about the commencement of the third century,) endeavors to show, that the doctrine was taught by that philosopher. He quotes a passage from one of the epistles ascribed to him,‡ in which mention is made of a second and third principle, beside the "King of all things." In this passage, he observes, he "can

* [Decline and Fall of the Roman Empire, Ch. xxi.]

† Mosheim says, ironically: "Certainly the three famous hypostases of the later Platonists may be discovered in the Timæus of Plato, as easily and readily as the three principles of the chemists, salt, sulphur, and mercury." "Certe tres illas celeberrimas hypostases Platonicorum in Timæo Platonis ostendere, æque facile et promptum est, atque tria chymicorum principia, sal, sulphur, et mercurium ex hoc Dialogo eruere." (See his Notes to his Latin Translation of Cudworth's Intellectual System, 2d ed., Tom. I. p. 901.) The doctrine of the Trinity is as little to be discovered in any other genuine writing of Plato as in the Timæus.

‡ The second epistle to Dionysius; which, with all the other epistles ascribed to Plato, is now generally regarded as spurious.

understand nothing to be meant but the Sacred Trinity; the third principle being the Holy Spirit, and the second principle being the Son, by whom all things were created according to the will of the Father." * A similar interpretation of the passage is referred to by Eusebius; † and in the oration which he ascribes to Constantine, as addressed "To the Assembly of Saints," Plato is eulogized as teaching, conformably to the truth, that "there is a First God, the Father, and a Second God, the Logos or Son." ‡ Augustine tells us in his Confessions, that he found the true doctrine concerning the Logos in a Latin translation of some Platonic writings, which the providence of God had thrown in his way.§ Speaking of those ancient philosophers who were particularly admired by the later Platonists, he says: "If these men could revive, and live over again their lives with us, with the change of a few words and sentences they would become Christians, as very many Platonists of our own time have done." || Theodoret gives the following account of the Platonic Trinity as compared with the Christian: "Plotinus and Numenius, explaining the opinion of Plato, represent him as teaching the existence of three principles which are beyond time and eternal, The

* Stromat. Lib. V. c. 14. p. 710, ed. Potter.

† Præparatio Evangelica, Lib. XI. c. 20.

‡ Cap. 9.

§ "Tu, Domine . . . . . procurasti mihi . . . . . quosdam Platonicorum libros," &c. [Confess. Lib. VII. cc. 8, 9.] Opp. I. col. 128. Basil. 1556.

|| Lib. de Verâ Religione. [Cap. 4, al. 7.] Opp. I. col. 704.

Good, Intellect, and the Soul of the World. He gives the name of The Good to the being whom we call Father; of Intellect, to him whom we name Son and Logos; and the power which animates and gives life to all things, which the Divine Word names Holy Spirit, he calls Soul. But these doctrines, as I have said, have been stolen from the philosophy and theology of the Hebrews." * Basnage had good reason for observing, that the Fathers almost made Plato to have been a Christian, before the introduction of Christianity. Immediately after this remark, Basnage quotes a writer of the fifth century, who expresses with honest zeal his admiration at the supposed fact, that the Athenian sage should have so marvellously anticipated the most mysterious doctrines of revelation.†

I will produce a few passages from modern *Trinitarian* writers, to show the near resemblance between the Christian and Platonic Trinity. The very learned Cudworth, in his great work on the Intellectual System, has brought together all that antiquity could furnish to illustrate the doctrine. He institutes a long and minute comparison between the forms in which it was held by the Heathen Platonists, and that in which it was held by the Christian Fathers. Toward the conclusion of this, we find the following passages: —

"Thus have we given a true and full account, how, according to Athanasius, the three divine

* Græc. Affect. Curat. Serm. II. Opp. IV. 500, ed. Sirmond.

† Basnage, Histoire des Juifs, Liv. IV. ch. 4. § 20.

hypostases, though not *monoousious*, but *homoousious* only, are really but one God or Divinity. In all which doctrine of his, there is nothing but what a true and genuine Platonist would readily subscribe to." *

"As the Platonic Pagans after Christianity did approve of the Christian doctrine concerning the Logos, as that which was exactly agreeable with their own; so did the generality of the Christian Fathers, before and after the Nicene Council, represent the genuine Platonic Trinity as really the same thing with the Christian, or as approaching so near to it, that they differed chiefly in circumstances, or the manner of expression." †

In proof of this, Cudworth produces many passages similar to those which I have quoted from the Fathers. Athanasius, he observes, "sends the Arians to school to the Platonists." ‡

Basnage was not disposed to allow such a resemblance between the Christian and Platonic Trinity as that which Cudworth maintains, and has written expressly in refutation of the latter. It is not necessary to enter into this controversy. The sentence with which he concludes his re-

* Ch. IV. § 36. p. 620. [Vol. II. p. 15, Andover edit.]

† Page 621. [al. II. 17.]

‡ Page 623. [al. II. 19, 20.] The study of Cudworth is strongly recommended by Bishop Horsley for the information which his work contains respecting the tenets of the Platonists. See his Charge, before quoted, V. § 5. I would recommend it also, with particular reference to the subject before us; for I know no other work from which so much information can be derived concerning the origin of the Christian doctrine of the Trinity.

marks on the subject, is enough for our purpose. "Christianity, in its triumph, has often reflected honor on the Platonists; and as the Christians took some pride in finding the Trinity taught by a philosopher, so the Platonists were proud in their turn to see the Christians adopt their principles." *

I quote the authorities of learned Trinitarians, rather than adduce the facts on which they are founded, because the facts could not be satisfactorily stated and explained in a small compass. It is to be observed, that Trinitarians, in admitting the influence of the Platonic doctrine upon the faith of the early Christians, of course do not regard the Platonic as the original source of the Orthodox doctrine, but many of them represent it as having occasioned errors and heresies, and particularly the Arian heresy. Such was the opinion of Petavius, who in his Theologica Dogmata,† after giving an account of the Platonic notions concerning the Trinity, thus remarks.

"I will now proceed to consider the subject on account of which I have entered into so full an investigation of the opinions of the Platonists concerning the Trinity; namely, in what manner this doctrine was conceived of by some of the ancients, and how the fiction of Plato concerning the Trinity was gradually introduced into Christianity by those of the Platonists who had become converts to our religion, or by others who had been

* Histoire des Juifs, Liv. IV. ch. 3, 4.

† De Trinitate, Lib. I. c. 3. § 1.

in any way indoctrinated in the Platonic philosophy. They are to be separated into two classes. One consists of such as, properly speaking, were unworthy the name of Christians, being heretics. The other, of those who were true Christians, Catholics, and saints; but who, through the circumstances of their age, the mystery not yet being properly understood, threw out dangerous propositions concerning it."

The very Orthodox Gale, in his Court of the Gentiles, says: "The learned Christians, *Clemens Alexandrinus*, *Origen*, &c., made use of the *Pythagorean* and *Platonic* philosophy, which was at this time wholly in request, as a *medium* to illustrate and prove the great mysteries of faith, touching the Divine λόγος, *word*, mentioned John i. 1, hoping by such *symbolisings*, and claiming kindred with these philosophic notions and traditions (originally Jewish) touching the Platonic λόγος, νοῦς, and τριάς, [the Platonic trinity,] they might gain very much credit and interest amongst these *Platonic Sophistes*."*

Beausobre, in his History of Manichæism, adverts to this subject. His opinion concerning the resemblance of the Platonic and Christian Trinity appears in the following passage.

"Such, according to Chalcidius,† was the Platonic Trinity. It has been justly regarded as defective. 1. It speaks of a *first*, a *second*, and a

* Part III. B. II. c. 1. § 9.

† Chalcidius was a Platonic philosopher, who lived before the close of the fourth century.

third God; expressions which Christianity has banished. Still, as appears from what I have said, Plato really acknowledged but a single God, because he admitted, properly speaking, but a single First Cause, and a single Monarch. 2. This theology is still further censured for the division of the Divine Persons, who are not only distinguished, but separated. The objection is well grounded. But this error may be pardoned in a philosopher; since it is excused in a great number of Christian writers, who have had the lights of the Gospel. 3. In the last place, fault is found with this theology on account of the inequality of the Persons. There is a supreme God, to whom the two others are subject. There was the same defect in the theology of the Manichæans. They believed the consubstantiality of the Persons, but they did not believe their equality. The Son was below the Father, and the Holy Spirit below the Father and Son. But if we go back to the time when Manichæus lived [about the middle of the third century], we shall be obliged to pardon an error which was then very general. . . . . . Huet, who acknowledges that Origen has everywhere taught that the Son is inferior to the Father, excuses him on the ground that this was the common doctrine of those writers who preceded the Council of Nice. And Petavius not only does not deny it, but proves it at length in his First Book on the Trinity."*

* Histoire du Manichéisme, Tom. I. pp. 560, 561.

There has been no more noted defender of the doctrine in modern times than Bishop Horsley. The following is a quotation from his Letters to Dr. Priestley.

"I am very sensible that the Platonizers of the second century were the Orthodox of that age. I have not denied this. On the contrary, I have endeavored to show that their Platonism brings no imputation upon their Orthodoxy. The advocates of the Catholic faith in modern times have been too apt to take alarm at the charge of Platonism. I rejoice and glory in the opprobrium. I not only confess, but I maintain, not a perfect agreement, but such a similitude as speaks a common origin, and affords an argument in confirmation of the Catholic doctrine [of the Trinity], from its conformity to the most ancient and universal traditions." *

In another place he says: "It must be acknowledged, that the first converts from the Platonic school took advantage of the resemblance between the Evangelic and Platonic doctrine on the subject of the Godhead, to apply the principles of their old philosophy to the explication and confirmation of the articles of their faith. They defended it by arguments drawn from Platonic principles; they even propounded it in Platonic language." †

The celebrated Bentley, upon taking his degree of Doctor of Divinity in 1696 at Cambridge, defended "the identity of the Christian and Platonic

* Letters to Dr. Priestley, Letter 13. † Charge, IV. § 2.

Trinity," together with "the Mosaic account of the Creation and the Deluge," and "the proof of divine authority by the miracles recorded in Scripture." Nor does it appear that the first-mentioned position was regarded with surprise or obloquy, any more than the last two.*

I might produce more authorities in support of the facts which have been stated. But I conceive it to be unnecessary. The fair inference from these facts every reader is able to draw for himself. The doctrine of the Trinity is not a doctrine of Christ and his Apostles, but a fiction of the school of the later Platonists, introduced into our religion by the Fathers, who were admirers and disciples of the philosophy taught in this school. The want of all mention of it in the Scriptures is abundantly compensated by the ample space which it occupies in the writings of the heathen Platonists, and of the Platonizing Fathers.

But what has been stated is not the only evidence which Ecclesiastical History affords against this doctrine. The conclusion to which we have just arrived is confirmed by other facts. But these, however important, I will here but barely mention. They are the facts *of its gradual introduction; of its slow growth to its present form; of the strong opposition which it encountered; and of its tardy reception among the great body of common Christians.*†

* See Monk's Life of Bentley, p. 57.

† On these subjects, see Dr. Priestley's History of Early Opinions concerning Jesus Christ. [Compare Mr. Norton's "Account of the

CUDWORTH, after remarking "that not a few of those ancient Fathers, who were therefore reputed Orthodox because they zealously opposed Arianism," namely, Gregory Nyssen, Cyril of Alexandria, and others, entertained the opinion that the three persons in the Trinity were three distinct individuals, "like three individual men, Thomas, Peter, and John," — the divine nature being common to the former as the human nature is to the latter, — observes that "some would think that the ancient and genuine Platonic Trinity, taken with all its faults, is to be preferred before this Trinity." He then says: "But as this Trinity came afterwards to be decried for tritheistic, so in the room thereof started there up that other Trinity of persons numerically the same, or having all one and the same singular existent essence, — a doctrine which seemeth not to have been owned by any public authority in the Christian Church, save that of the Lateran Council only." *

This is the present Orthodox form of the doctrine of the Trinity. Cudworth refers to the fourth general Lateran Council, held in 1215, under Pope Innocent the Third. The same Council which, in the depth of the Dark Ages, established the modern doctrine of the Trinity, established, likewise, that of Transubstantiation;

Controversy between Dr. Priestley, Dr. Horsley, and others," in the General Repository and Review (Cambridge, 1812, 1813), Vols. I.-III.]

* Intellectual System, Ch. IV. § 36. pp. 602-604. [I. 791-793, Andover edit.]

enforced with the utmost rigor the persecution of heretics, whom it ordered to be sought out and exterminated; and prepared the way for the tribunals of the Inquisition, which were shortly after established.*

* See Fleury, Histoire Ecclésiastique, An. 1215.

SECTION V.

CONCERNING THE HISTORY OF THE DOCTRINE OF THE HYPOSTATIC UNION.

It may throw some further light upon the human origin of the doctrine of the Trinity, briefly to notice the history of that of the Hypostatic Union.

By Trinitarians it is represented as a doctrine of fundamental importance, that Christ was at once God and man, the two natures being so united as to constitute but one person. It is this, indeed, which is supposed to give its chief interest to the doctrine of the Trinity; since only he who was at once God and man could, it is said, have made for men that infinite atonement which the justice of God, or rather the justice of the Father, required. But in the minds of most of those who profess the doctrine, it exists, I conceive, merely as a form of words, not significant of any conceptions, however dim or incongruous. They have not even formed an imagination, possible or impossible, of what is meant by the Hypostatic Union. It is a remarkable fact, that while new attempts to explain the doctrine of the Trinity, new hypotheses and illustrations of it, have been abundant, this other doctrine has, in modern times, been generally left in the nakedness of its verbal statement; that "the Godhead and manhood being joined together in one person never to be divided, there is one Christ, very God and very man, who truly suffered, was crucified, dead, and buried."

It was in the fifth century that the doctrine assumed its present form. The Fathers of the second century believed in the incarnation of the Logos, or the Son of God; they believed that he became a man, that is, they believed that he manifested himself in a human body; but their conceptions concerning the particular nature of the relation between the divinity and humanity of Christ were obscure and unsettled. Their general notions respecting the Incarnation may more easily be ascertained, though they have not till of late been made the subject of much critical inquiry.

In Justin Martyr there is, I think, but one passage concerning the mode and results of the connection between the two natures in Christ, which has been regarded as of much importance; and that has been differently explained, and, as the text now stands, is, I believe, unintelligible.* What,

* Justin (Apologia Sec. p. 123, ed. Thirlb.) [c. 10, p. 48, C. ed. Morel.] is speaking of the superiority of Christ to all other lawgivers. These, he admits, possessed a portion of the Logos, that is, were enlightened, in a certain degree, by the Wisdom of God; but Christ was the Logos himself; therefore the doctrines he taught and Christians believed (τὰ ἡμέτερα) were far higher than all which had been taught before. The passage in question, by the insertion of a comma and a letter, may receive a certain meaning, but one which throws little light on the subject. — Μεγαλειότερα . . . . φαίνεται τὰ ἡμέτερα διὰ

however, is more important, it appears from the general tenor of his language on this subject, that Justin regarded the Logos alone as, properly speaking, Christ himself. His notions of the *incarnation* of the Logos were essentially those which we usually connect with that word as denoting the assumption of a body by a spiritual being, and not as implying any union or combination of a superior nature with the human. Though he uses the term "man" in reference to the animate body of Christ, yet the real agent and sufferer whom he seems always to have had in view is the Logos; for the conceptions of Justin concerning the Logos were not such as to exclude the idea of his suffering. Speaking of the agony of Christ in the garden of Gethsemane, he says it was recorded, "that we might know that it was the will of the Father that his Son should truly thus suffer for our sakes; and that we might not say that he being the Son of God had no feeling of what was done to him or what befell him."* In later times, indeed, language was used, and its use has continued to our own day,—language not utterly intolerable only because it is utterly without meaning,—in

τοῦτο [,] λογικὸν τὸ [f. τὸν] ὅλον τὸν φανέντα δι' ἡμᾶς Χριστὸν γεγονέναι, καὶ σῶμα, καὶ λόγον, καὶ ψυχήν. "It appears that our doctrines are far superior, for this reason, that the whole Christ who appeared for us, body, Logos, and animal soul, pertained to the Logos (λογικὸν γεγονέναι).

Perhaps the use of such language may be illustrated by a passage of Origen (Cont. Cels. Lib. III. § 41, Opp. I. 474), which will be quoted hereafter. See also Lib. II. § 51. Opp. I. 426.

* Dial. cum Tryph. pp. 361, 362. [al. c. 103, p. 331, D.]

which God is spoken of as having suffered and been crucified. But Justin, and other early Fathers, when they spoke of the sufferings of the Logos, meant what they said. This is evident, not merely from passages as explicit as that just quoted, but from the manner in which they regarded the doctrine of those who denied the personality of the Logos, and maintained that the divinity in Christ was the divinity of the Father. Such opinions, it was affirmed, necessarily led to the belief that the Father himself had suffered. Those who held them were charged with this belief, and hence denominated Patripassians. The charge, without doubt, was unjust; but it shows that the doctrine of those who made it was, that the Logos, the divine nature of the Son, had suffered in Christ. If they had not held this belief concerning the Logos, or Son, there would have been no pretence for charging their opponents with holding a corresponding belief concerning the Father; especially as their opponents maintained, what they themselves did not maintain, that Christ was properly and in all respects a man; and this being so, had no occasion to turn their thoughts to any other sufferer than the man Christ.

The opinions of Irenæus were similar to those of Justin. He regarded the Logos as supplying in Christ the place of the *intelligent soul* or *mind* of man. I use these expressions, because Irenæus, in common with other ancient philosophers, distinguished between the mind, intellect, or spirit, and the principle of life, or animal soul, which was also considered as the seat of the passions. The vagueness with which the names were used, denoting these two principles in man, is one cause of obscurity in the present inquiry. But Irenæus, it appears, conceived that the Logos in becoming incarnate assumed only a body and an animal soul, the place of the human intellect being supplied by the Logos himself.* In holding this doctrine, he, though the champion of the church against the heretics of his own day, was himself a precursor both of the Arian and the Apollinarian

* See the passages quoted by Münscher, in his Handbuch der christlichen Dogmengeschichte. Band II. § 181. Münscher, however, is incorrect in representing Irenæus as having supposed the Logos to have assumed a human BODY only. According to Irenæus, *an animal soul* (anima, ψυχή) was also conjoined with the Logos. In opposition to the Gnostics, who denied that Christ had a proper human body, he says (Lib. III. c. 22. § 2): "If the Son of God had received nothing from Mary, ... he would not have said, My soul (ἡ ψυχή μου) is exceedingly sorrowful." Dr. Priestley, on the other hand, contends (Hist. of Early Opinions, Vol. II. p. 203, seqq.) that, according to Irenæus, Christ had a proper human soul. His error arises from his not adverting to the distinction above mentioned, between the intellect or spirit and the animal soul. This distinction is stated and illustrated by Irenæus, Lib. V. c. 6. § 1. The latter passage is to be compared with that quoted by Dr. Priestley, of which his rendering is erroneous.

It may be observed that the mistake of Münscher is followed by Neander (Geschichte der christ. Relig. u. Kirche, Band I. s. 1063), who says, speaking of the early opinions concerning Christ: "The assumption of the human nature was conceived of merely as the assumption of a human body, as we find it clearly expressed by Irenæus." [This statement of Neander's was modified in the second edition of this part of his work, published in 1843. See Torrey's Translation, I. 634.]

heresies concerning the Incarnation; for the error of both consisted in regarding the Logos as having supplied the place of the human intellect in Christ.

In opposition to those Gnostics who maintained that the Æon, as they denominated him, or the divine being, Christ, at the time of the crucifixion, departed from the man, Jesus, and left him to suffer alone, Irenæus often speaks of the proper sufferings of the Logos.*

Of the opinions of Clement of Alexandria concerning the mode of connection between the two natures, nothing, I think, can be affirmed definitely and with assurance.† Of the passages adduced

* See many passages to this effect collected by Jackson in his Annotations to Novatian, pp. 357, 358. On this subject, and on the opinions of the earlier Fathers generally respecting the Incarnation, see also Whiston's Primitive Christianity, Vol. IV. pp. 272-321.

Dr. Priestley (History of Early Opinions, Vol. II. pp. 205, 215, 216) produces a single passage from Irenæus (Lib. III. c. 19. § 3), on which he relies for proof that Irenæus did not conceive of the Logos as suffering. The Greek of this passage is quoted by Dr. Priestley. It is preserved by Theodoret, who may probably have somewhat altered the expressions to conform them to his own opinions, as they do not agree with those of the old Latin version, which is here the better authority. Nor does Dr. Priestley's translation correspond even with the Greek. He renders: "The Logos being quiescent in *his* temptation, crucifixion, and death"; thus separating the Logos from Christ, and representing Christ as a distinct person by the use of the personal pronoun, *his*. The Greek is, ἡσυχάζοντος μὲν τοῦ Λόγου ἐν τῷ πειράζεσθαι καὶ σταυροῦσθαι καὶ ἀποθνήσκειν; which should be rendered: "The Logos being quiescent (i. e. suspending his powers) when tempted, when crucified, and at death."

† See the quotations from and references to him in Münscher. *Ibid.*, § 183.

from him, one of the principal has, I think, no relation to the subject; but refers throughout to the indwelling of the Logos in all true believers. It is, however, so remarkable, as showing how loosely language was used, on which, in the writings of the earlier Fathers, too much stress has often been laid, that it deserves quotation. "That man," he says, "with whom the Logos abides, does not assume various appearances, but preserves the form of the Logos; he is made like to God; he is beautiful, not adorned with factitious beauty, but being essential beauty; for such God is. That man becomes a god, because God so wills it. It has been well said by Heraclitus, 'Men are gods and the gods are men'; for the Logos himself, a conspicuous mystery, is God in man, and man becomes a god; the Mediator accomplishing the will of the Father; for the Mediator is the Logos common to both; being the Son of God and the Saviour of men, being his minister and our instructor." *

* The following is the original of the passage. See Potter's edition of Clement, p. 251. I have altered his pointing, as the sense seems to me to require, and in one instance, in the last sentence, *θεός* is printed with a small initial letter where he has used a capital.

Ὁ δὲ ἄνθρωπος ἐκεῖνος, ᾧ σύνοικος ὁ Λόγος, οὐ ποικίλλεται, οὐ πλάττεται· μορφὴν ἔχει τὴν τοῦ Λόγου· ἐξομοιοῦται τῷ Θεῷ· καλός ἐστιν, οὐ καλλωπίζεται· κάλλός ἐστι τὸ ἀληθινόν, καὶ γὰρ ὁ Θεὸς ἐστίν. Θεὸς δὲ ἐκεῖνος ὁ ἄνθρωπος γίνεται, ὅτι βούλεται ὁ Θεός. Ὀρθῶς ἄρα εἶπεν Ἡράκλειτος, Ἄνθρωποι, θεοί· θεοί, ἄνθρωποι. Λόγος γὰρ αὐτός, μυστήριον ἐμφανές, Θεὸς ἐν ἀνθρώπῳ, καὶ ὁ ἄνθρωπος, θεός· καὶ τὸ θέλημα τοῦ Πατρὸς ὁ μεσίτης ἐκτελεῖ· μεσίτης γὰρ ὁ Λόγος, ὁ κοινὸς ἀμφοῖν, Θεοῦ μὲν υἱός, σωτὴρ δὲ ἀνθρώπων, καὶ τοῦ μὲν διάκονος, ἡμῶν δὲ παιδαγωγός. Pædagog. Lib. III. c. 1.

Archbishop Potter, in the notes to his edition of Clement, observes, "that Clement often says, that men through piety and virtue are not only assimilated to God, but as it were transformed into the divine nature, and become gods." *

But the opinions of Clement respecting the Incarnation appear perhaps with sufficient distinctness in what he says of the body of Christ. According to him, "It would be ridiculous to suppose that the body of our Saviour required the aliments necessary to others for his support. He took food not for the sake of his body, which was sustained by a holy power, but that he might not give occasion to those with whom he was conversant to form a wrong opinion concerning him; — as, in fact, some [the Docetæ] afterward supposed, that he had been manifested with only the appearance of a body. But he was wholly impassible; liable to be affected by no motions either of pleasure or pain." † It would seem that Clement here excludes all conception even of an *animal soul* in Christ; and that he regarded the appearance of the Logos on earth as merely the manifestation of him to the senses of men in a body, answering in form and substance to a human body, but not subject to the same necessities and accidents.

* See note 11, p. 71, and note 7, p. 88. In the latter he produces remarkable examples of this use of language. See also numerous examples from other early Christian writers, in Sandii Interpretationes Paradoxæ, p. 227, seqq. [and Whiston's Primitive Christianity, Vol. IV. p. 100, seqq.]

† Stromat. VI. § 9. p. 775.

The language of Tertullian is vacillating and self-contradictory. His conceptions on the whole subject of the Logos were unsteady; and no form of words had as yet been settled which might serve as a guide to one without ideas of his own. He rejected the philosophical distinction of his day between the intellect (*mens*, *animus*), and the animal soul (*anima*), and maintained, in conformity with our modern belief, the proper unity of the soul (*anima*), of which he regarded the intellect as a part. But this soul, in common with many of the ancient philosophers, he conceived of as corporeal. He regarded it as diffused through the body, possessing its shape, and constituting its principle of life.* A living body he probably considered as essentially united with a soul; and in believing the Logos to have assumed a living body, he represents him as having assumed also a human soul. The soul being, in his view, corporeal as well as the body, the conception or the imagination thus became more easy to be apprehended. But that, in assigning a human soul to Christ, he assigned to him likewise a human intellect, is not, I think, to be proved. This part of the soul, he may have thought was supplied by the Logos; and there is much in his writings which favors the supposition. It appears, I think, to have been his *prevalent* conception, in common with the other Fathers of his time, that the Logos alone was the proper agent in Christ. I will pro-

* See his treatise *De Animâ*.

duce only two passages, to which there are many more or less analogous. In arguing against the Gnostics, who denied that Christ had a fleshly body, he compares the assumption of such a body by Christ to the appearances of angels related in the Old Testament. "You have read, and believed," he says, "that the angels of the Creator were sometimes changed into the likeness of men, and bore about so true a body, that Abraham washed their feet, and Lot was drawn away from Sodom by their hands; an angel also wrestled with a man, the whole weight of whose body was required to throw him down and detain him. But that power which you concede to the angels, who may assume a human body and yet remain angels, do you take away from a divine being more powerful than they? (hoc tu potentiori deo aufers?) As if Christ could not continue a divine being (deus) after having put on humanity." * He often speaks, though, I think, not with clear or consistent conceptions, of the sufferings of the Logos. He represents him as the agent in all those operations referred to God in the Old Testament, which the Gnostics regarded as unworthy of the Supreme Being. They are ignorant, he says, that, though not suitable to the Father, they were suitable to the Son; and proceeds to express conceptions very different from those which, as we have seen, were entertained by Clement of Alexandria. "They are ignorant that those things

* De Carne Christi, c. 3.

were suitable to the Son, who was about to submit to the accidents of humanity, thirst, and hunger, and tears, to be born, and even to die." *

THUS far, the loose general notion of most of those who speculated on the subject seems to have been, that the incarnation of the Logos was analogous to the appearance of angels in human shapes; and to the supposed incarnations of heathen deities, with the imagination of which a great majority of Christians were familiar, as converts from Gentilism. † One of the latest writers on the history of Christian doctrines, Münter, late Bishop of Zealand, observes, that "The Catholic Fathers, who maintained in opposition to the Gnostics the reality of the body of Christ, appear in part to have placed the human nature of Christ in this body; and their common expressions and representations show clearly, that they had very imperfect conceptions concerning this nature, corresponding to those entertained by the heathen, by the learned Jews, and by all parties of Christians, concerning the appearances of God or of gods in the ancient world." — "The well-known error of Apollinaris, that Jesus had only an animal soul, the principle of life; and that the Divine Logos

* Advers. Praxeam, c. 16. [See, further, Norton's Evidences of the Genuineness of the Gospels, Vol. II. p. 252, seqq., and Vol. III. p. 174, seqq.]

† "Alia sunt quæ Deus in æmulationem elegerit sapientiæ secularis. Et tamen apud illam facilius creditur Jupiter taurus factus aut cygnus, quam vere homo Christus penes Marcionem." Tertullian, De Carne Christi, c. 4.

performed in him all the functions of an intelligent soul, was by no means so new as it was represented to be in the fourth century." Among the Fathers, according to Münter, Tertullian was perhaps the first who affirmed Jesus to have a proper human soul; although he adds, that some passages may be adduced from him which appear to favor the contrary opinion.* Similar remarks to those quoted from Münter are made by Neander in his Ecclesiastical History. †

Such, we may conclude, was the state of opinion respecting the Incarnation from the time of Justin Martyr, about the middle of the second century, to that of Origen, in the third century. It is a remarkable fact, that the foundations of the doctrine of the deity of Christ were laid in the virtual rejection of the truth of his being, properly speaking, a man; a truth at the present day almost undisputed. This fact was admitted only in words; the sense of which was nearly the same, as when angels assuming a human shape are spoken of as men in the Old Testament. It may be observed, also, that in this, as in other doctrines, the ancient Fathers had a great advantage over those who in later times have been denominated Orthodox; as their doctrine, which represented the Logos as constituting the whole of the intelligent nature of Christ, or, in other words, made the Logos and Christ identical, was

* Dogmengeschichte, Band II. H. I. 269 – 274.

† Band I. 1063, 1064; II. 905. [See Torrey's Translation, I. 635: II. 425.]

neither absurd in its statement, nor abhorrent to our natural feelings. But there is another remark, which, though not immediately to our present purpose, is still more important. When we find that in the second century Christ was no longer considered as a man, properly speaking, but as the incarnate Logos of God, we perceive how imperfect a knowledge had been preserved by unwritten tradition, not merely of the doctrines of our religion, but of the impression which its historical facts must have made upon the first believers; for if Christ were a man in the proper sense of the word, those who were conversant with him while on earth undoubtedly believed him to be so. In the passage of our religion from the Jews to whom it had been taught, to the Gentiles through whom it has been transmitted to us, the current of tradition was interrupted. Hence followed, even in the second century, a state of opinion respecting the facts and doctrines of Christianity, which renders it evident, that neither Christianity itself, nor those writings from which we derive our knowledge of it, had their origin, or received their character, in that age. The Christianity of the Gospels is not that of the earliest Christian Fathers. Though they had departed but little from the spirit of our religion, or from its essential doctrines; and though their works, (I speak of the Fathers of the first three centuries,) notwithstanding the disrespect and unjust prejudices of many in modern times, are monuments of noble minds; yet it is equally true, that we find in their writings the doctrines of Christianity intimately blended with opinions derived either from the philosophy of the age, or from the popular notions of Jews and Gentiles, or having their source in the peculiar circumstances in which they themselves were placed.

We come now to Origen, in the first half of the third century, and with him new opinions open upon us. Origen fully and consistently maintained the doctrine of a human soul in Jesus. Imbued with the principles of Platonism, he believed this soul, in common with all other souls, to have pre-existed, and in its pre-existent state to have, through its entire purity and moral perfection, become thoroughly filled and penetrated by the Logos, of whom all other souls partake in proportion to their love toward him. It thus became one with the Logos, and formed the bond of union between the body of Jesus and the divinity of the Logos; in consequence of which both the soul and body of the Saviour, being wholly mixed with and united to the Logos, partook of his divinity and were transformed into something divine.* But from the illustrations which Origen

* Εἰς θεὸν μεταβεβηκέναι. Cont. Cels. Lib. III. § 41. p. 474. The words should not be rendered, as they are by Münscher, "transformed into God" (in Gott übergegangen). Origen, here, as often elsewhere, uses θεός (God), not in our modern sense, as a *proper* name, but as a *common* name. This use of the term, which was common to him with his contemporaries, and continued to be common after his time, is illustrated by his remarks upon the passage, "and the Logos was God" (Opp. IV. p. 48, seqq.); in which he contends, that the Logos was "god" in an inferior sense; — not, as we should say, *God*,

uses, respecting the connection between the Logos and the human nature of Christ, it is clear that he had no conception of that form of the doctrine which prevailed after his time. "We do not," he says, "suppose the visible and sensible body of Jesus to have been God, nor yet his soul, of which he declared, *My soul is sorrowful even unto death.* But as he who says, *I the Lord am the God of all flesh*, and, *There was no other God before me and there shall be none after me*, is believed by the Jews to have been God using the soul and body of the prophet as an organ; and as, among the Gentiles, he who said,

> 'I know the number of the sands and the measure of the deep,
> And I understand the mute and hear him who speaks not,'

is understood to be a god, addressing men by the voice of the Pythoness;—so we believe that the divine Logos, the Son of the God of all, spoke in Jesus when he said, *I am the way and the truth and the life; . . . . . I am the living bread which has descended from heaven;* and when he uttered other similar declarations." A little after, Origen compares that union of the soul and body of Jesus

but a *god*, or rather, not *the* Divine Being, but *a* divine being; and in which he maintains that "beside the True God, many beings, by participation of God, become *divine*," literally, "become gods."

The full illustration of the use of the term *god* as a *common* name would, I think, throw much light upon the opinions both of the ancient Heathens and Christians. But this is not the place to enter upon it. [On this subject see the author's Evidences of the Genuineness of the Gospels, Vol. III. Additional Note D, "On the Use of the words Θεός and *Deus*." Compare also the quotation before given from Clement of Alexandria, p. 113, and p. 114, note *.]

with the Logos, by which they are made one, to the union of all Christians with their Lord as described by St. Paul (1 Cor. vi. 17), "He who is joined to the Lord is one spirit with him," though he represents it as a union of a far higher character, and more divine.*

In this unsettled state the doctrine of the Incarnation continued till the fourth century. It is remarked by Münscher, when he comes to treat of the controversies which then arose, that "Most of the earlier Fathers spoke simply of a human body, which the Logos or Son of God had assumed. Origen, on the contrary, ascribed to Christ an intelligent human soul, and considered this as the bond of union between his divine nature and his human body. Some Fathers had also spoken occasionally of a union or commingling of man with God; but their propositions concerning it were indefinite and incidental, and had obtained no authority in the Church; and the opinion of Origen was far from being an hypothesis generally received."† I quote this as the statement of a respectable writer; without assenting to all the expressions, as may appear from what precedes.

In the fourth century, the doctrine of Athanasius concerning the Trinity being established by the Council of Nice, and its partisans, in opposition

* Origen, Cont. Cels. Lib. II. § 9. Opp. I. 392-394.

† Dogmengeschichte, Band IV. § 77.

to the Arians, zealously using the strongest language concerning the divinity of the Son as *consubstantial* with that of the Father, the Orthodox faith was now verging to such a profession of their equality, that to represent the Logos as suffering in his divine nature began to appear an error, like that of representing the Father as suffering. On the other hand, the Arians, viewing the Logos as a created being, found no difficulty in retaining the ancient doctrine concerning his simple incarnation in a human body, and his having suffered in the proper sense of the words. Among their opponents, likewise, Apollinaris, who had been the friend of Athanasius, and distinguished for his zeal in asserting the Orthodox faith concerning the Trinity, undertook, with a less fortunate result, to define the doctrine of the Incarnation. He, with the Arians and the ancient Fathers, maintained that the Logos supplied in Christ the place of the human intellect. He also freely used the language, which has since become common, concerning the sufferings of the Divinity in Christ; and his opponents, in consequence, represented him as believing the Divine Nature to be passible. But it seems most probable that he, like others, used this language without meaning. His doctrine was condemned by the second general council, that of Constantinople (A. D. 381), in which it was decreed that Christ was not only "the perfect Logos of God," but also "a perfect man possessed of a rational soul"; and the latter doctrine was thus at last established as Orthodox.

The Deity being impassible, it would seem, indeed, if Christ really suffered, that it was necessary to regard him as a perfect man, capable of suffering. But, on the other hand, if the sufferings of Christ were those of a man only, it might seem to follow that Christ was only a man, and the whole mystery of the Incarnation would disappear.

In this state of things recourse was had to a doctrine which has been denominated the Communication of Properties.* It was maintained that, the divine and human natures in Christ being united in one person, what was true of either nature might be asserted of Christ. Christ then being God, it might be affirmed with truth that God was born, hungered, thirsted, was crucified, and died. It was maintained, at the same time, that the Divine Nature was impassible and unchangeable. The last proposition annihilated all meaning in the former, not leaving it even the poor merit of being the most offensive mode of expressing some conception that might be apprehended as possible. What sense those who have asserted the sufferings of God have fancied that the words might have, is a question which, after all that has been written upon the subject, is left very much to conjecture. I imagine that it is, at the present day, the gross conception of some who think themselves Orthodox on this point, that the divine and human natures being united in Christ as the Mediator, a compound nature, different from either and capable of suffering, was thus formed.

* Ἀντιδόσις. — Κοινωνία ἰδιωμάτων.

THE doctrine of the Communication of Properties, says Le Clerc, "is as intelligible as if one were to say that there is a circle which is so united with a triangle, that the circle has the properties of the triangle, and the triangle those of the circle."* It is discussed at length by Petavius, with his usual redundance of learning. The vast folio of that writer containing the history of the Incarnation, is one of the most striking and most melancholy monuments of human folly which the world has to exhibit. In the history of other departments of science, we find abundant errors and extravagances; but Orthodox theology seems to have been the peculiar region of words without meaning; of doctrines confessedly false in their proper sense, and explained in no other; of the most portentous absurdities put forward as truths of the highest import; and of contradictory propositions thrown together without an attempt to reconcile them. A main error running through the whole system, as well as other systems of false philosophy, is, that words possess an intrinsic meaning, not derived from the usage of men; that they are not mere signs of human ideas, but a sort of real entities, capable of signifying what transcends our conceptions; and that when they express to human reason only an absurdity, they may still be significant of a high mystery or a hidden truth, and are to be believed without being understood.

* Ars Critica, P. II. S. I. c. 9. § 11.

In the fifth century, the doctrine of the Hypostatic Union was still further defined. Before this time, says Mosheim, "it had been settled by the decrees of former councils [those of Nice and Constantinople] that Christ was truly God and truly man; but there had as yet been no controversy and no decision of any council concerning the mode and effect of the union of the two natures in Christ. In consequence, there was a want of agreement among Christian teachers in their language concerning this mystery." * The controversy which now arose had its origin in the denial of Nestorius, patriarch of Constantinople, that Mary could in strictness of speech be called "the Mother of God," a title which had been applied to her by Athanasius himself. Though we are accustomed to expressions more shocking, yet this title may perhaps sound harshly in the ears of most Protestants. Mosheim, however, who is solicitous to pass some censure upon Nestorius, finds but two faults or errors to impute to him, the first of which is, that "he, rashly, and to the offence of many, wished to set aside an *innocent title* which had been long in common use." † The other is, that he presumptuously employed unsuitable expressions and comparisons in speaking of a mystery transcending all comprehension. Cyril was at this time patriarch of Alexandria, and the rival of Nestorius, — a turbulent, ambitious, unprincipled man. He took advantage of the opinions of Nes-

* Hist. Eccles. Sæc. V. Pars II. c. 5. § 5.

† "—— vocabulum dudum tritum et innocens." Ibid., § 9.

torius to charge him with heresy, and procured the calling of the third general council, that of Ephesus, A. D. 431. In this council Cyril presided, and the heresy of Nestorius was anathematized, and Nestorius himself deposed, and denounced as a "second Judas." On a subject concerning which the parties understood neither each other nor themselves, it has been found by modern inquirers hard to determine in what particulars the heresy of the "new Judas" differed from the Orthodoxy of Cyril, except in the denial that Mary could in strictness of speech be called "the Mother of God." In general, Nestorius was charged with making so wide a distinction between the human and divine natures in Christ, as to separate Christ into two persons. There is, however, no ground for supposing that Nestorius maintained so heretical and so rational an opinion, as that God was one person, and the inspired messenger of God another. Whatever was meant by the accusation of his dividing Christ into two persons, he himself earnestly denied its truth; while, on the other hand, it appears that Cyril, in his eagerness to widen the distance between himself and his rival, either fell into the snare of the Apollinarian heresy, or at least grazed its limits. Cyril prevailed in his factious contest, through his influence with the officers of the imperial household, and the bribes which he lavished upon them; for what was Orthodoxy was to be determined in the last resort by the Emperor Theodosius, or rather by the women and eunuchs of his court. "Thanks to the purse of St. Cyril," says

Le Clerc, "the Romish Church, which regards councils as infallible, is not, at the present day, Nestorian."* The creeds of Protestants are equally indebted to St. Cyril for their purity.

But notwithstanding the decision of the Council of Ephesus, the contest still raged. The *monophysite* doctrine, as it was called, that is, the doctrine of but a single nature in Christ, the heresy of Apollinaris, on the very borders of which lay the Orthodoxy of Cyril, was maintained by Eutyches, who had been a friend of Cyril and a bitter opponent of the Nestorians. Eutyches was condemned and deposed by Flavian, patriarch of Constantinople. But though Cyril was dead, his party still predominated. A council was called at Ephesus, the proceedings of which were determined by the will and the violence of Dioscurus, who had succeeded him as patriarch of Alexandria. The opinions of Eutyches were sanctioned by it; and Flavian, who was present, suffered such personal outrages from his theological opponents, that he only escaped to die on the third day following. This council, however, the Church of Rome does not regard as œcumenical and entitled to authority. Leo, then pope, joined the party opposed to Dioscurus, which through his aid finally prevailed; and the Council of Ephesus received a name, of which we may best perhaps express the force in English by calling it a Council of Banditti.†

* Biblioth. Univers., Suite du Tome XXI. p. 27.

† Συνοδὸς λῃστρική.

So far, however, as its authority was acknowledged, the Church had been plunged by it into the monophysite heresy. But a new council was called, which is reckoned as the fourth general council, that of Chalcedon, A. D. 451. The majority of this council was composed of monophysites; but the Emperor and the Pope favored the opposite party. Their authority prevailed; and the result may be given in the words of Gibbon. "The Legates threatened, the Emperor was absolute. . . . . . In the name of the fourth general council, the Christ in one person, but in two natures, was announced to the Catholic world: an invisible line was drawn between the heresy of Apollinaris and the faith of St. Cyril, and the road to paradise, a bridge as sharp as a razor, was suspended over the abyss by the master hand of the theological artist."* "This council," says Mosheim, "decided that all Christians should believe that Jesus Christ is one person in two distinct natures without any confusion or mixture, which has continued to be the common faith." † It has continued to be the doctrine of creeds; what is now the faith of those who consider themselves as believers in the Incarnation, is probably a question which the greater number have never thought of answering.

Of the language, however, that has been used in modern times concerning this doctrine, it may

* [Decline and Fall, &c., Ch. XLVII.]
† Hist. Eccles. Sæc. V. P. II. c. 5. § 15.

be worth while to produce one or two specimens.

Lord Bacon gives us this account of the belief of a Christian: —

"He believes a Virgin to be a Mother of a Son; and that very Son of hers to be her Maker. He believes him to have been shut up in a narrow room, whom heaven and earth could not contain. He believes him to have been born in time, who was and is from everlasting. He believes him to have been a weak child carried in arms, who is the Almighty; and him once to have died, who only hath life and immortality in himself."*

The following passage is from a sermon by Dr. South: —

"But now was there ever any wonder comparable to this! to behold Divinity thus clothed in flesh! the Creator of all things humbled not only to the *company*, but also to the *cognation*, of his creatures! It is as if we should imagine the whole world not only represented *upon*, but also contained *in*, one of our little artificial globes; or the body of the *sun* enveloped in a *cloud* as big as a *man's hand;* all which would be looked upon as astonishing impossibilities; and yet as short of the other, as the greatest Finite is of an Infinite, between which the disparity is immeasurable. For that God should thus in a manner transform Himself, and subdue and master all his glories to a possibility of human

* Characters of a Believing Christian.

apprehension and converse, the best reason would have thought it such a thing as God could *not do*, had it not seen it *actually done*. It is (as it were) to cancel the essential distances of things, to remove the bounds of nature, to bring heaven and earth, and (which is more) both ends of the *contradiction*, together." *

To one wholly ignorant of theological controversy, these passages might have the air of malicious irony. But a little further acquaintance with creeds and theological systems would satisfy him that such language may be used in earnest.

It is with some hesitation that I adduce another passage from the same sermon of South, which occurs a few pages after what has been quoted. When thus treating, as it were, of the morbid anatomy of the human mind, it is often a question how far one ought to proceed in exhibiting to common view the more disgusting cases of disease. The reverence due to the subjects which are profaned, and an unwillingness to shock the feelings of his readers, should restrain a writer from any unnecessary display. But it is not a little important that the character of the doctrine under consideration, and the monstrous extravagances to which it leads, should be well understood. In reading, then, the following words, it is to be recollected that the author was a man distinguished as a fine writer, whose uncommon natural talents

* South's Sermons, 6th ed., 1727, Vol. III. p. 299. Sermon on Christmas Day, 1665.

16

had been cultivated by learning. From the works of grosser minds, it would be easy to produce many passages more intolerable.

"Men," says South, "cannot persuade themselves that a *Deity* and *Infinity* should lie within so narrow a compass as the contemptible dimensions of an human body; that Omnipotence, Omniscience, and Omnipresence should be ever wrapt in swaddling-clothes, and abased to the homely usages of a stable and a manger; that the glorious Artificer of the whole universe, *who spread out the heavens like a curtain, and laid the foundations of the earth*, could ever turn carpenter, and exercise an inglorious trade in a little cell. They cannot imagine that *He who commands the cattle upon a thousand hills, and takes up the ocean in the hollow of his hand*, could be subject to the meannesses of hunger and thirst, and be afflicted in all his appetites. That he who once *created*, and at present *governs*, and shall hereafter *judge*, the world, shall be abused in all his concerns and relations, be *scourged, spit upon, mocked, and at last crucified.* All which are passages which lie extremely cross to the notions and conceptions that reason has framed to itself, of that high and impassible perfection that resides in the divine nature."

There is a short poem written by Watts after the death of Locke,* in which, on account of "the wavering and the cold assent" which that great

* On Mr. Locke's Annotations, left behind him at his death. [See Watts's Works, IV. 396, 397.]

man was supposed by him to have given to "themes divinely true," he invokes the aid of Charity that he may see him in heaven. What were these "themes divinely true," appears in the following verses: —

> "Reason could scarce sustain to see
> The Almighty One, the Eternal Three,
> Or bear the infant Deity;
> Scarce could her pride descend to own
> Her Maker stooping from his throne,
> And dressed in glories so unknown.
> A ransomed world, a bleeding God,
> And Heaven appeased by flowing blood,
> Were themes too painful to be understood."

The Eternal Three! The Deity an infant! God bleeding! The Maker of the universe appeasing Heaven by his flowing blood! These are not doctrines to be trifled with. Consider what meaning can be put upon these words; take the least offensive sense they can be used to express, and then let any one ask himself this question: If these doctrines are not doctrines of Christianity, what are they? It is a question that deserves serious consideration. There is but an alternative. If they are not doctrines of Christianity, then they are among the most insane fictions of human folly: the monstrous legends of Hindoo superstition present nothing more revolting, or more in contrast with the truths of our religion.

But, in fact, some of the most portentous of these expressions are used utterly without meaning. They can express nothing which an intelligent man will admit that he intends to express.

Attempt to give a sense to the propositions, God was an infant; God poured out his blood; God died. Even he whom familiarity has rendered insensible to language really equivalent, may shudder at so naked a statement of what he professes to believe. Let him attempt to give a sense to these words, and just in proportion as he approaches toward the shadow of a meaning, will he approach toward a conception, from which, if he have the common sentiments of a man and a Christian, he will shrink back with abhorrence.

Since Christianity, then, has been represented as teaching such doctrines, and even as suspending the salvation of men upon their belief, is it wonderful that it has had, and that it has, so little power over men's minds and hearts? Could means more effectual have been devised for destroying its credit and counteracting its efficacy? If TRUE RELIGION be the great support of the moral virtues, and essential to the happiness of individuals and the well-being of society, is it strange that there has been so little virtue, happiness, or peace in the world? And what, then, are our duties as Christians, and as friends of human kind? What is the duty of all enlightened men, — of all qualified to inquire into the character and history of these doctrines, — of all who profess or countenance them with an uncertain faith? Of such as are fitted to think and act upon subjects of this nature, there is but one class to whom a solemn appeal may not be made. It consists of those who, after a thorough examination, have felt themselves compelled to receive these doctrines — if the thing be possible — as doctrines taught by Christ and his Apostles.

SECTION VI.

DIFFICULTIES THAT MAY REMAIN IN SOME MINDS RESPECTING THE PASSAGES OF SCRIPTURE ALLEGED BY TRINITARIANS.

As I have endeavored to express myself as concisely as possible, I shall not recapitulate what I have written. If any one should think the arguments that have been urged deserve consideration, but yet not be fully satisfied of their correctness, it will be but the labor of an hour or two to read them over again. The time will be well spent, should it contribute toward freeing his faith from an essential error, and giving him clearer, more correct, and consequently more ennobling and operative conceptions of Christianity.

Here, then, as I have had occasion to say before, I might close the discussion. But even if the truth for which I am contending be fully established, still difficulties may remain in some minds which it is desirable to remove. Like a great part of Scripture, the passages adduced in support of the Trinitarian doctrines have been interpreted upon no general principles, or upon none which can be defended. But many persons have been taught from their childhood to associate a false meaning with words and texts of the Bible. This meaning, borrowed from the schools of technical theology, is that which immediately presents itself to their minds, when those words and texts occur. They can hardly avoid considering the expositions so familiar to them, as those alone that could be obvious to an unprejudiced reader. He who would break the associations which they have between certain words and a certain meaning, and substitute the true sense for that to which they are accustomed, appears to them to be doing violence to the language of Scripture.

Now these prejudices, so far as they are capable of being removed, can be removed only by establishing correct principles of interpretation, applying them to the subject in hand, and pointing out the true or the probable meaning of the more important passages that have been misunderstood. This, therefore, I shall endeavor to do in the sections that follow.

SECTION VII.

ON THE PRINCIPLES OF THE INTERPRETATION OF LANGUAGE.

SUPPOSING the doctrines maintained by Trinitarians to be capable of proof, the state of the case between them and their opponents would be this. They quote certain texts, and explain them in a sense which, as they believe, supports their opinions. We maintain that the words were intended to express a very different meaning. How is the question to be decided? We do not deny that there are certain expressions in these texts, which, nakedly considered, *will bear* a Trinitarian sense; how is it then to be ascertained, whether this sense or some other was intended by the writer?

In order to answer this question, it is necessary to enter into some explanation concerning the nature of language and the principles of its interpretation. The art of interpretation derives its origin from the *intrinsic ambiguity of language.* What I mean to express by this term is the fact, that a very large portion of sentences, *considered in themselves*, that is, *if regard be had merely to the words of which they are composed*, are capable of expressing not one meaning only, but two or more different meanings; or (to state this fact in other terms) that in very many cases, the same sentence, like the same single word, may be used to express various and often very different senses. Now in a great part of what we find written concerning the interpretation of language, and in a large portion of the specimens of criticism which we meet with, especially upon the Scriptures, this fundamental truth, this fact which lies at the very bottom of the art of interpretation, has either been overlooked, or not regarded in its relations and consequences. It may be illustrated by a single example. St. John thus addresses the Christians to whom he was writing, in his First Epistle, ii. 20: —

"*You have an anointing from the Holy One, and know all things.*"

If we consider these words in themselves merely, we shall perceive how uncertain is their signification, and how many different meanings they may be used to express. The first clause, "You have an anointing from the Holy One," may signify, —

1. *Through the favor of God, you have become Christians or believers in Christ;* anointing being a ceremony of consecration, and Christians being considered as consecrated and set apart from the rest of mankind.

2. Or it may mean, *You have been truly sanctified in heart and life:* a figure borrowed from outward consecration being used to denote inward holiness.

3. Or, *You have been endued with miraculous powers:* consecrated as prophets and teachers in the Christian community.

4. Or, *You have been well instructed in the truths of Christianity.**

I forbear to mention other meanings, which the word *anointing* might be used to express. These are sufficient for our purpose.

The term *Holy One*, in such a relation as it holds to the other words in the present sentence, may denote either God, or Christ, or some other being.

You know all things, literally expresses the meaning, *You have the attribute of omniscience.* Beside this meaning it may signify, *You are fully acquainted with all the objects of human knowledge;* or, *You know every truth connected with Christianity;* or, *You have all the knowledge necessary to form your faith and direct your conduct;* or the proposition may require some other limitation; for *all things* is one of those terms, the meaning of which is continually to be restrained and modified by a regard to the subject present to the mind of the writer.

This statement may afford some imperfect notion of the various senses which the words before us may be used to express; and of the uncertainty that must exist about their meaning, when they are regarded without reference to those considerations by which it ought to be determined. I say, imperfect, because we have really kept one very important consideration in mind, that they were written by an Apostle to a Christian community.

* See Wetstein's notes on this passage, and on 1 Tim. iv. 7.

Putting this out of view, it would not be easy to fix the limit of their possible meanings. It must be remembered that this passage has been adduced merely by way of illustration; and that, if it were necessary, an indefinite number of similar examples might be quoted.

I will mention, and I can barely mention, some of the principal causes of the intrinsic ambiguity of language. 1. Almost every word is used in a variety of senses; and some words in a great variety. Now, as we assign one or another of these senses to different words in a sentence, we change the meaning of the whole sentence. If they are important words, and the different senses which we assign vary much from each other, we change its meaning essentially. 2. But beside their common significations, words may be used in an undefined number of figurative senses. A large proportion of sentences may, therefore, be understood either figuratively or literally. Considered in themselves, they present no intrinsic character that may enable us to determine whether they are literal or figurative. They may often be understood in more than one literal, and in more than one figurative sense; and a choice is then to be made among all these different senses. 3. A very large portion of sentences which are not what rhetoricians call figurative, are yet not to be understood strictly, not to the letter, but with some limitation, and often with a limitation which contracts exceedingly their literal meaning. "I do not," says Mr. Burke, addressing the friend to whom he is writing, in his

Reflections on the French Revolution,—"I do not conceive you to be of that sophistical, captious spirit, or of that uncandid dulness, as to require for every general observation or sentiment an explicit detail of the correctives and exceptions, which reason will presume to be included in all the general propositions which come from reasonable men." Sentences that are general or universal in their terms, are often to be regarded merely in relation to the subject treated of, or the persons addressed; and their meaning is often to be greatly limited by a regard to one or another of these considerations. 4. In eloquence, in poetry, in popular writing of every sort, and not least in the Scriptures, a great part of the language used is the language of emotion or feeling. The strict and literal meaning of this language is, of course, a meaning which the words may be used to express; but this is rarely the true meaning. The language of feeling is very different from that of philosophical accuracy. The mind, when strongly excited, delights in general, unlimited propositions, in hyperboles, in bold figures of every sort, in forcible presentations of thought addressed indirectly to the understanding through the medium of the imagination, and in the utterance of those temporary false judgments which are the natural result, and consequently among the most natural expressions, of strong emotion. Different senses in which such language may be understood often present themselves; and it is sometimes not easy to determine which to adopt.

But further, language is conventional; and the use of it varies much in different ages and nations. No uniform standard has existed by which to measure the expressions of men's conceptions and feelings. In one state of society, language assumes a bolder character, more unrestrained, and more remote from its proper sense; in another, the modes of speech are more cool and exact. The expressions of compliment and respect, for instance, in France or Italy, and the expressions of the Orientals generally, are not proportional to our own. A sentence translated verbally from one language into another will often convey a stronger or more unlimited meaning than was intended by him who uttered it. "John," says our Saviour, "came neither eating nor drinking." * These words, as spoken by him, had nothing of the paradoxical character which would belong to them if now uttered for the first time in our own language. They meant only that John, leading an ascetic life, refrained from taking food after the common fashion, at regular meals. — "Work out your salvation," says St. Paul, "with fear and trembling." † The Apostle, who elsewhere exhorts Christians to "rejoice always," did not here intend that their life should be one of anxious dread; and we may express his purpose by saying, "with earnest solicitude." He tells the Corinthians that they had received Titus with "fear and trembling," ‡ by which words, in this place, he means what we

* Matthew xi. 18. † Philippians ii. 12. ‡ 2 Cor. vii. 15.

might call "respect and deference." — Christ says, that he who would be his follower must "hate father and mother."* The genius of our language hardly admits of so bold a figure, by which, however, nothing more was signified, than that his followers must be prepared to sacrifice their dearest affections in his cause. — But even where there is no peculiar boldness or strength of expression in the original, we are liable to be deceived by a want of analogy to our modes of speech. Figures and turns of expression familiar in one language are strange in another; and an expression to which we are not accustomed strikes us with more force, and seems more significant, than one in common use, of which the meaning is in fact the same. We are very liable to mistake the purport of words which appear under an aspect unknown or infrequent in our native tongue. The declaration, "I and my Father are one,"† may seem to us at first sight almost too bold for a human being to use concerning God, merely because we are not accustomed to this expression in grave discourse. But in familiar conversation no one would misunderstand me, if, while transacting some business as the agent of a friend, I should say, "I and my friend are one"; meaning that I am fully empowered to act as his representative. The passage quoted is to be understood in a similar manner; and the liability to mistake its meaning arises only from our not being familiar with its

* Luke xiv. 26. † John x. 30.

use on solemn occasions. — "The Son of Man came to give his life a ransom for many." * We do not express the intended figure in this particular form, the *noun* "ransom" being commonly employed by us only to denote a price paid to him who has had power over the ransomed. The passage has, consequently, been misunderstood; but the *verb* "ransom" has a wider significancy, corresponding to the sense of our Saviour; and by a very slight change in the mode of expression, the occasion of mistake is removed: "The Son of Man came to give his life to ransom many"; that is, to deliver them from the evils of ignorance, error, and sin. — "Whatever," said our Saviour to St. Peter, "thou shalt bind on earth will be bound in heaven, and whatever thou shalt loose on earth will be loosed in heaven." † This passage and another corresponding to it, in which the same authority is extended to the Apostles generally, ‡ have been perverted to the worst purposes. The figure in which our Saviour expressed his meaning is not found in modern languages, but was familiar to the Jews. "To bind" with them signified "to forbid," and "to loose" signified "to permit"; § and the meaning of Christ was, "I appoint you to preach my religion, by which what is forbidden is forbidden by God, and what is permitted is permitted by God." As its minister, you will speak in his name and with his authority, forbidding or permitting on

* Matthew xx. 28. † Matthew xvi. 19. ‡ Matthew xviii. 18.

§ See Wetstein's note on Matthew xvi. 19.

earth what is forbidden or permitted in heaven. — It is further to be remarked, that, in some cases where there is this want of correspondence between languages, the verbal rendering of a passage may be unintelligible, and even offensive; as in the address of St. Paul to the Corinthians, thus translated in the Common Version: "Ye are not straitened in us, but ye are straitened in your own bowels."* The meaning of St. Paul, which a reader of those words might hardly conjecture, is this: "You do not suffer from any deficiency in us, but you are deficient in your own affections." — Sometimes a verbal rendering gives a sense altogether false: "Now I beseech you, brethren, that ye all speak the same thing."† So St. Paul is represented as addressing the Corinthians in the Common Version. But "to speak the same thing" was a phrase used in Greek in a sense unknown in English, to denote "agreeing together"; and the exhortation in fact was, that they should "all agree together." — These examples, few as they are, may serve to illustrate the mistakes to which we are exposed from the want of analogy between languages; and to show that the true meaning of a passage may be very different from the sense which, without further in-

* 2 Cor. vi. 12. — To one acquainted with the French language, the character of the rendering in the Common Version may be illustrated, by supposing a verbal translation of the following account of a tragic actress: "Elle sait émouvoir et toucher; jamais comédienne n'eut plus d'entrailles."

† 1 Cor. i. 10.

quiry, we should receive from a verbal rendering of it into English. A verbal rendering of an ancient author must be often false, ambiguous, or unintelligible, and when not exposed to graver charges, will commonly fail in preserving the full significancy, the spirit and character, of the original.

Those which have been mentioned are some of the principal causes of the ambiguity of language; or, as we may say in other terms, they are some of the principal modes in which this ambiguity manifests itself. But a full analysis of the subject, accompanied by proper examples, would fill many pages. From what has been already said, the truth of the propositions maintained will, I think, appear, at least sufficiently for our present purpose.

It is, then, to the intrinsic ambiguity of language, that the art of interpretation owes its origin. If words and sentences were capable of expressing but a single meaning, no art would be required in their interpretation. It would be, as a late writer,* thoroughly ignorant of the subject, supposes, a work to be performed merely with the assistance of a lexicon and grammar. The object of the art of interpretation is to enable us to solve the difficulties presented by the intrinsic ambiguity of language. It first teaches us to perceive the different meanings which any sentence may be used to express, as the different

* Dr. Thomas Chalmers. See the conclusion of the article *Christianity*, in the Edinburgh Encyclopædia.

words of which it is composed are taken respectively in one sense or another; as it is understood literally, or figuratively; strictly and to the letter, or popularly and in a modified sense; as the language of emotion, or as a calm and unimpassioned expression of thoughts and sentiments; as the language of one age or nation, or that of another; and it then teaches us (which is its ultimate purpose) to distinguish, among *possible* meanings, the *actual* meaning of the sentence, or that meaning which, in the particular case we are considering, was intended by the author. And in what manner does it enable us to do this? Here, again, a full and particular answer to this question is not to be comprised in the compass of a few pages. The general answer is, that it enables us to do this *by directing our attention to all those considerations which render it probable that one meaning was intended by the writer rather than another.*

Some of these considerations are, the character of the writer, his habits of thinking and feeling, his common style of expression, and that of his age or nation, his settled opinions and belief, the extent of his knowledge, the general state of things during the time in which he lived, the particular local and temporary circumstances present to his mind while writing, the character and condition of those for whom he wrote, the opinions of others to which he had reference, the connection of the sentence, or the train of thought by which it is preceded and followed, and, finally, the manner in which he was understood by those for whom he wrote, — a consideration, the importance of which varies with circumstances. The considerations to be attended to by an interpreter are here reduced to their elements. I cannot dwell long enough upon the subject, to point out all the different forms and combinations in which they may appear. But where the words which compose a sentence are such, that the sentence may be used to express more than one meaning, its true meaning is to be determined SOLELY by a reference to EXTRINSIC CONSIDERATIONS, such as have been stated. In the case supposed (a case of very frequent occurrence), all that we can learn from the mere words of the sentence is the different meanings which the sentence is capable of expressing. It is obvious that the words, considered in themselves, can afford no assistance in determining which of those different meanings was that *intended by the author*. This problem is to be solved solely by a process of reasoning, founded upon such considerations as have been stated.

I will illustrate this account of the principles of interpretation by an example of their application.

Of MILTON, Dr. Johnson says, that

"He had considered creation in its whole extent, and his descriptions are therefore learned." *

"But he could not be always in other worlds, he must sometimes return to earth, and talk of things visible and known." †

* [Life of Milton. Works, IX. 167.] † [Ibid., p. 168.]

Addison tells us, that "he knew all the arts of affecting the mind."*

Bentley, in the Preface to his edition of the Paradise Lost, speaks of him thus: —

"He could spatiate at large through the compass of the whole universe, and through all heaven beyond it; could survey all periods of time from before the creation to the consummation of all things."

"Milton's strong pinion now not heaven can bound," are the words of Pope.†

"He passed," says Gray, "the flaming bounds of place and time, and saw the living throne" of God.‡

In the age subsequent to his own, "he continued," says Aikin, "to stand alone, an insulated form of unrivalled greatness." §

Why do we not understand all this language strictly and to the letter? Why, without a moment's hesitation, do we put upon the expressions of all these different authors a sense so very remote from that which their words are adapted to convey, when viewed independently of any extrinsic consideration by which they may be explained? The answer is, because we are satisfied (no matter how) that all these writers believed Milton to be a man, and one not endued with supernatural powers. This consideration determines us at once to

* [Spectator, No. 333.]

† [Imitations of Horace, Book II. Ep. I. 99.]

‡ [Ode on the Progress of Poesy, III. 2.]

§ [Letters to a Young Lady on English Poetry, Letter XI.]

regard their language as figurative, or as requiring very great limitation of its verbal meaning.

Let us attend to another example of the application of those principles which have been laid down. Our Saviour says, "Whoever lives and has faith in me will never die";* and similar declarations, as every one must remember, were often repeated by him. I recollect to have met with a passage in an infidel writer, in which it was maintained that these declarations were to be understood literally; and that Christ meant to assure his disciples that they should not suffer the common lot of man. Why do we not understand them literally? Because we are satisfied that our Saviour's character was such that he would not predict a falsehood. An infidel, likewise, might easily satisfy himself that his character was such that he would not predict what the next day's experience might prove to be a falsehood.

I will give one more example: "Unless you eat the flesh of the Son of Man, and drink his blood, you have not life within you."† He who will turn to the context of the passage may see that this declaration is repeated and insisted upon by our Saviour, in a variety of phrases and in different relations. The Roman Catholics understand this passage, when viewed in connection with the words used in instituting our Lord's supper, as a decisive argument for the doctrine of transubstantiation. If either doctrine were capable of proof,

* John xi. 26.

† John vi. 53.

I should certainly think that there was no passage in Scripture which went so far to prove the doctrine of the Trinity, as this does to prove the doctrine of transubstantiation. Why, then, do we not understand the words in the sense of the Roman Catholics? Why do we suppose a figure so bold, and to our ears so harsh, as we are compelled to suppose, if we do not understand them literally? Solely because we have such notions of the character and doctrines of our Saviour, that we are satisfied that he would not teach anything irrational or absurd; and that the declaration in question would be very irrational, if understood literally without reference to the doctrine of transubstantiation; and altogether absurd, if supposed to imply the truth of this doctrine. It is upon the same principle that we interpret a very large proportion of all the figurative language which we meet with. We at once reject the literal meaning of the words, and understand them as figurative, because, if we did not do this, they would convey some meaning which contradicts common sense; and it would be inconsistent with our notions of the writer, to suppose him to intend such a meaning. But this principle, which is adopted unconsciously in the interpretation of all other writings, has been grossly disregarded in the interpretation of Scripture. If one should interpret any other writings (except those in the exact sciences) in the same manner in which the Scriptures have been explained, he might find as many absurdities in the former as there are pretended mysteries in the latter.

Upon the principle just stated, we may reject the literal meaning of a passage, when we cannot pronounce with confidence what is its true meaning. The words of our Saviour just quoted are an example in point. One may be fully justified in rejecting their literal meaning, who is wholly unable to determine their true meaning. To do this is certainly no easy matter. Similar difficulties, that is, passages about the true meaning of which we can feel no confidence, though we may confidently reject some particular meaning which the words will bear, are to be found in all other ancient writings as well as the Scriptures.

If the facts and principles respecting interpretation which have been stated are correct, any one who will examine what has been written concerning this subject may perceive how little it has been understood by a large proportion of those who have undertaken to lay down rules of exposition, and how much it has been involved in obscurity and error. There are many writers who appear, neither to have had any distinct conception of the truth, that sentences are continually occurring which may severally express very different senses *when we attend only to the words of which they are composed*, nor, of consequence, any just notions of the manner in which the actual meaning of such sentences is to be determined. Yet it is to such sentences that the art of interpretation is to be applied; and its purpose is, to teach us in what manner their ambiguity may be resolved.

We are now, then, prepared to answer the question formerly proposed. Certain passages are adduced by Trinitarians in support of their opinions. We do not deny that there are expressions in some of these passages, which, the words alone being regarded, *will bear* a Trinitarian sense. How is it to be ascertained whether this sense, or some other, was intended by the writer?

Now this is a question which, as we have shown, is to be determined solely by extrinsic considerations; and all those considerations that have been brought into view in the former part of this discussion bear directly upon the point at issue. My purpose has been to prove that the Trinitarian doctrines were not taught by Christ and his Apostles. If this has been proved, it has been proved that they were not taught by them in any particular passage. All the considerations that have been brought forward apply directly to the interpretation of any words that may be adduced; and if these considerations are decisive, then it is certain that the Trinitarian exposition of every passage of the New Testament must be false. Their force can be avoided but in one way; not by proving, positively, that certain words will bear a Trinitarian meaning,—that is conceded; but by proving, negatively, that it is impossible these words should be used in any other than a Trinitarian meaning,—that they admit of but one sense, which, under all circumstances, they must be intended to express. But this no man of common information will maintain. If, then, there be not some gross error in the preceding reasonings, the controversy respecting the Trinitarian exposition of those passages is decided. Whatever may be their true sense, the Trinitarian exposition must be false.

But I will now recur to the essential character of the Trinitarian doctrines, for the purpose of showing, that, though there are words in the New Testament which, abstractly considered, will bear some one or other Trinitarian sense, yet that this sense can be ascribed to them only in violation of a fundamental principle of interpretation.

SECTION VIII.

FUNDAMENTAL PRINCIPLE OF INTERPRETATION VIOLATED BY TRINITARIAN EXPOSITORS. — NO PROPOSITION CAN BE INCOMPREHENSIBLE, IN ITSELF CONSIDERED, FROM THE NATURE OF THE IDEAS EXPRESSED BY IT.

THE principle of interpretation to which I refer is so constantly present to the mind of every one, and is acted upon so unconsciously in reading all other books but the Scriptures, that, except in reference to them, it is scarcely necessary to announce it or advert to it. It has been already mentioned. In many cases, as I have said, we at once reject the literal meaning of words, and understand them as figurative, because if we did not do this they would convey some meaning which contradicts common sense; and it would be inconsistent with our notions of the writer to suppose him to intend such a meaning. Men's minds being constituted alike, so that, when a subject is clearly understood, what appears an absurdity to one will appear an absurdity to another, we do not ascribe an absurd meaning to the language of any writer, except upon the special consideration of some well-known peculiarity of belief, or defect or cloudiness of intellect. Yet a great part of all language diverted in any way from its literal sense *will bear* an absurd meaning, that is, admits of being so interpreted when the words alone are regarded.

We may take as instances of this the examples of the use of language quoted in the preceding section. But I will produce a few more passages, from which it may appear to those not familiar with the subject how absurd or false the literal meaning of language often is, and how instantly and unconsciously it is rejected upon the principle I have stated. I give them without comment, for none is required. My purpose is merely to call attention to a fact respecting the use of language, which, though frequently overlooked, must be acknowledged as soon as it is pointed out.

Speaking of the conciliatory measures toward the American colonies adopted by the Rockingham administration just before its dissolution, Mr. Burke says: "The question of the repeal [of the Stamp Act] was brought on by ministry in the committee of this house, in the very instant when it was known that more than one court negotiation was carrying on with the heads of the opposition. Everything upon every side was full of traps and mines. Earth below shook; heaven above menaced." *

Speaking of the rapid increase of numbers in these colonies, he says: "Such is the strength with which population shoots in that part of the world, that, state the number as high as we will, whilst the dispute continues, the exaggeration

* [Speech on American Taxation.]

ends. Whilst we are discussing any given magnitude, they are grown to it."*

"A strong and habitually indulged imagination," says Foster, "has incantations to dissolve the rigid laws of time and distance, and to place a man in something so like the presence of his object, that he seems half to possess it; and it is hard, while occupying the verge of paradise, to be flung far back in order to find or make a path to it, with the slow and toilsome steps of reality."†

Remarking upon the responsibility of writers of fictitious narratives, in regard to the characters they delineate, the same author has the following passage: "They create a new person; and in sending him into society, they can choose whether his example shall tend to improve or pervert the minds that will be compelled to admire him."‡

I will quote a few more sentences, from Young.§

> "The death-bed of the just . . . .
> Is it his death-bed? No; it is his shrine:
> Behold him there just rising to a god."

> "Shall we this moment gaze on God in man;
> The next, lose man for ever in the dust?"

> "A Christian dwells, like Uriel, in the sun."

Speaking of the beauty of the material world, as relative to our perceptions, and existing only so far as it is perceived by the eye of man:—

* [Speech on Conciliation with America.]

† [Essay on the Application of the Epithet Romantic, Letter III.]

‡ [On the Aversion of Men of Taste to Evangelical Religion, Letter VIII.]

§ [Night Thoughts, II. 629; VII. 222, 1354; VI. 429.]

"But for, the magic organ's powerful charm,
Earth were a rude, uncolored chaos still. . . . . .
Ours is the cloth, the pencil, and the paint,
Which Nature's admirable picture draws. . . . . .
Like Milton's Eve, when gazing on the lake,
Man makes the matchless image man admires.
Say then, shall man, his thoughts all sent abroad, ...
His admiration waste on objects round,
When Heaven makes him the soul of all he sees?"

Any person in his common reading may find numberless similar passages, of which we reject without hesitation the verbal meaning, simply because it is absurd or evidently false. But this principle has not been regarded in the interpretation of Scripture. The believer in transubstantiation contends that we are to understand verbally the declaration: "Unless you eat the flesh of the Son of Man, and drink his blood, you have not life within you."* The sect of the Antinomians would have us take to the letter the words of St. Paul, as rendered in the Common Version: "But to him that worketh not, but believeth on him that justifieth the ungodly, his faith is counted for righteousness."† And of the believers in the doctrine of Atonement, some contend, that, when the Apostle speaks of the church as being "purchased by the blood of Christ," or, as they would have it read, "by the blood of God," we are to regard the blood of the Son as being paid, as it were, to the Father to deliver us from his wrath. All the errors connected with Christianity have appealed for support to such verbal misinterpretations of particular

* [John vi. 53.]

† [Romans iv. 5.]

passages. Hence it has been said, that anything may be proved from the Scriptures. And it is true, that, if we proceed in so erroneous a method, and neglect every fact and principle which ought to be attended to in the interpretation of language, there is no meaning too false, too absurd, or too ridiculous, to be educed from the words of Scripture, or, equally, from those of any popular writing. An experiment may be made upon the passages just quoted in the preceding paragraphs.*

* "Quæ lex, quod senatûs-consultum, quod magistratûs edictum, quod fœdus, aut pactio, quod (ut ad privatas res redeam) testamentum, quæ judicia, aut stipulationes, aut pacti et conventi formula non infirmari, aut convelli potest, si ad verba rem deflectere velimus; consilium autem eorum, qui scripserunt, et rationem, et auctoritatem relinquamus? Sermo mehercule et familiaris et quotidianus non cohærebit, si verba inter nos aucupabimur. Denique imperium domesticum nullum erit, si servulis hoc nostris concesserimus, ut ad verba nobis obediant; non ad id, quod ex verbis intelligi possit, obtemperent."

"What law, what decree of the Senate, what ordinance of a magistrate, what treaty or convention, or, to return to private concerns, what testament, what judicial decision, what stipulation, what form of agreement, may not be invalidated or annulled, if we insist on bending the meaning to the words, and neglect the intent, purport, and will of the writer? Truly, our familiar and every-day discourse would have little coherence, if we lay in wait for each other's words. There would be no domestic government, if we allowed our slaves to obey our commands in their verbal meaning, and not in that sense in which the words are to be understood."

Cicero, Orat. pro A. Cæcinâ, § 18.

A late writer, however, to whom I have before adverted, p. 147, Dr. Chalmers (in the article there mentioned), contends earnestly that the verbal method of interpreting the Scriptures is the true method. "The examination of the Scriptures," he says, "is a pure work of grammatical analysis. It is an unmixed question of language." "We admit of no other instrument than the vocabulary and the lexi-

It is in the verbal manner spoken of, that the passages brought to prove the Trinitarian doctrines have been interpreted. But in order to withdraw the propositions thus resulting, from the jurisdiction of reason, they have been called incomprehensible mysteries. A certain obscurity has thus been thrown over the subject, by which some minds are perplexed. I will now, therefore, attempt to show, what, I think, may be shown clearly, that no proposition can be incomprehensible from the nature of

con." "The mind and meaning of the author who is translated is purely a question of language, and should be decided upon no other principles than those of grammar or philology." But this principle "has been most glaringly departed from in the case of the Bible; ..... the meaning of its author, instead of being made singly and entirely a question of grammar, has been made a question of metaphysics, or a question of sentiment: ..... instead of the argument resorted to being, Such must be the rendering, from the structure of language, and the import and significancy of its phrases; it has been, Such must be the rendering, from the analogy of the faith, the reason of the thing, the character of the Divine mind, and the wisdom of all his dispensations." There are Christians "who in addition to the word of God talk also of the reason of the thing." "Could we only dismiss the uncertain fancies of a daring and presumptuous theology, sit down like a school-boy to his task, and look upon the study of divinity as a mere work of translation, then we would expect the same unanimity among Christians, that we meet with among scholars and literati about the system of Epicurus, or philosophy of Aristotle."

The illustration is particularly unhappy, at least so far as regards the philosophy of Aristotle. But I do not insist on this, nor on the looseness and uncertainty of some of the language which I have quoted. The main ideas are sufficiently apparent. We are to come to the study of the Scriptures merely with our grammar and lexicon. Having done so, let us consider how we shall proceed. Our lexicon will exhibit to us ten or twenty different meanings, perhaps, of some of the most important words in a sentence. Our grammar, beside

the ideas expressed; that there can be no meaning conveyed in words, which is not perfectly intelligible, I do not say by this or that individual, but by the human understanding.

Words are only human instruments for the expression of human ideas; and it is impossible that they should express anything else. The meaning of words is that idea or aggregate of ideas which men have associated with certain

teaching us the relations of words to each other, will discover to us the various and often numerous modifications of meaning, which some alteration in the form of a word renders it capable of expressing. If it happen to have an appendix treating of the rhetorical figures, we may also learn something from it concerning the many changes of signification to which words are subjected according to established modes of speech; though our knowledge, if derived merely from this source, may not be extensive. But as yet we are furnished only with objects of choice among a variety of meanings, without anything to decide us how to choose. We have only learned, and that but very imperfectly, what the words *may* signify; our business is to learn what they *do* signify. Take a sentence, which in different relations may be used to express different meanings with equal propriety, — and such sentences are constantly occurring, — what assistance will our grammar or lexicon afford, to determine in any particular case its actual meaning? Certainly none at all.

But in the process of interpretation, we are to have recourse to no other instruments. We are expressly enjoined, for instance, to exclude all consideration of the reason of the thing. By this must be meant, that we are not to consider what may reasonably be said upon any subject; or, in other words, what a reasonable man, with no false opinions, would say concerning it. Let us try, then, how we shall succeed in interpreting Scripture, after having excluded this and every other extrinsic consideration. St. Luke ascribes these words to our Saviour: "Blessed are you poor, for yours is the kingdom of God." Shall we exclude all consideration of the reason of the thing, and, taking the word *poor* in its most common and obvious sense, understand our Saviour as asserting for a universal truth, that

sounds or letters. They have no other meaning than what is given them by men; and this meaning must be always such as the human understanding is capable of conceiving; for we can associate with sounds or letters no idea or aggregate of ideas which we have not. Ideas, therefore, with which the human understanding is conversant, are all that can be expressed by words. If an angel have faculties of a different

all men destitute of property are blessed? But these words, it will be said, are explained by the parallel passage in St. Matthew. Explained by a parallel passage! We are, then, very soon obliged to have recourse to something beside our grammar and lexicon. But how are they explained by the passage in St. Matthew? "Blessed are the poor in spirit." Without taking any extrinsic consideration into view, but confining ourselves to the mere words before us, in which of the many meanings of the word *spirit* shall we here understand it? Shall we receive it in a sense which occurs repeatedly in the New Testament, according to which it denotes the temper and virtues of a Christian, and understand the words as meaning: "Blessed are they who are poor in the temper and virtues of a Christian"? But leaving these difficult passages, he who chooses to put out of view the reason of the thing, and all those other circumstances which ought to determine our judgment, may proceed with his grammar and lexicon to the next beatitude of our Saviour, and then to the next; and then he may open at random upon any passage of the New Testament, till he has satisfied himself respecting the practicability of his method.

If the opinions on which I have remarked were the extravagances of an individual writer alone, so long a notice of them would hardly be justifiable. But the assertions, I cannot say the arguments, of Dr. Chalmers, are intended to maintain a system of interpretation in which the false doctrines that have been connected with Christianity have found their main support. It is to be observed, however, that the verbal method of interpretation is, in fact, principally confined to passages brought in proof of those doctrines, and is abandoned in regard to other portions of Scripture, to which its application would produce some unsanctioned error or absurdity.

nature from those which we possess, he can make no use of our language to convey to our minds the results of their exercise. If any being have more senses than we have, he can find no words of ours to express to us his new perceptions. It being impossible, therefore, that words should be employed to denote anything but human ideas; whenever they have a meaning, this meaning, though liable to be mistaken, must in its own nature be capable of being fully understood.

To talk of an incomprehensible meaning, if we use the word "incomprehensible" in a strict sense, is to employ terms which in themselves express an absurdity. It is the same sort of language, as if we were to speak of an invisible illumination. The meaning of a sentence is the ideas which it is adapted to convey to the mind of him who reads or hears it. But if it be capable of conveying any ideas, that is, if it have any meaning, it is merely stating the same fact in other terms, to say that those ideas are capable of being received and understood.

No one, indeed, will deny, that there are many truths incomprehensible by us; which are above reason, or, in other words, which are wholly out of the grasp of our present faculties. But these truths cannot be expressed in human language. Nor, while our faculties remain what they are, can they be in any way revealed to us. To reveal is to make known. But what cannot be comprehended cannot be made known, and therefore cannot be revealed.

This very plain subject has been obscured by a oose and ambiguous use of language. It is said, that we believe truths which we do not comprehend; — that we believe that the grass grows; but do not know how it grows; — that we believe that some things are infinite; but that we do not comprehend infinity; — that we believe that God knows all things; but that we cannot form a conception of omniscience. Let us examine these propositions. *The grass grows:* do we not know what we mean when we use these words? It is as intelligible a proposition as can be stated. We affirm, and we intend nothing more than to affirm, that certain well-known, sensible phenomena take place. It is true that we do not know *how* it grows, that is to say, we do not know the proximate causes of its growth; and it is equally true, that we affirm nothing about those causes in the proposition stated. Our affirmation does not extend beyond our knowledge. The fact that there are many phenomena of which we cannot assign the causes, does not tend to prove that, when we affirm those phenomena to exist, we utter incomprehensible propositions.

But we say of many things, that they are or may be infinite; that space and duration are infinite; that the attributes of God are infinite; that our own existence will be infinite or without termination; and we do not understand what is meant by infinity; we do not comprehend these truths. I answer, that if we do not understand those propositions, — if they are unintelligible, — it is very idle to make them. We do not comprehend infinity in itself considered; but we comprehend our own idea of infinity, with the knowledge, as in very many other cases, that it is an inadequate idea. Our ideas of things infinite are, as that word implies,* essentially negative ideas. They consist in the conception of certain things, accompanied with the belief of the absence of all limit or termination. We not only have an idea of infinity, but it is impossible we should not have. The very constitution of our minds is such that we cannot, for instance,.imagine a period when time began, or when it may end. It is true that we are unable to conceive of infinity positively, we do not understand all its nature; and we can reason about it therefore but very partially. It belongs to the class of inadequate ideas, which includes far the greater portion of all our ideas; and the propositions relating to it are no more unintelligible than the propositions which relate to other ideas of this class. I affirm, that the same person who called on me to-day visited me yesterday; and there is no one, I think, who will maintain that this is an incomprehensible proposition. Yet there are few who will pretend to have a perfectly adequate idea of identity, the notion of which is involved in the proposition just stated; and many questions may be raised respecting this subject, as well as respecting infinity, by which most minds would be perplexed. I say that the sun is the

* From the Latin *in* negative, and *finitus*.

principal source of light and heat; and the proposition is perfectly intelligible. But I have not an adequate idea of the sun; there are many things concerning it, as well as concerning infinity, which I can neither affirm nor deny. I cannot say, for instance, whether, as some have imagined, it be adapted to the support of animals and vegetables, in any respect similar to those which exist upon the earth. Our idea of infinity differs from most other ideas of the class to which I have referred it, only in this respect, — that its inadequacy is occasioned by the fact, that the subject is beyond the grasp of our faculties; while the inadequacy of most other ideas seems to arise from the deficiency of our means of information. But this is a difference which does not in any degree affect the nature of the propositions made concerning it, so as to distinguish them from other propositions relating to inadequate ideas.

But it will be said, that we have no conception of omniscience; and yet that we make propositions concerning it, which have a meaning and a very important one. I answer, that they have not only an important, but a perfectly intelligible meaning; and that this subject is of a similar kind to many others, of the nature and relations of which the *understanding* has distinct ideas, though they are subjects of which the *imagination* cannot form distinct conceptions. Fix on any particular object of knowledge, and I can *conceive*, in every sense of the word, that this should be known to God. But when these objects are infinite, or when they are multiplied beyond very narrow limits, my imagination fails and is altogether confounded. But the same is the case with regard to much humbler subjects. No ideas can be more definite, considered as objects of the understanding, than those which relate to number and quantity; yet it is principally collective and aggregate ideas involving the notion of great numbers or vast quantity, that the imagination is thus unable to embrace. When I am told that there are more than six hundred millions of inhabitants upon the earth, I *understand* the proposition as perfectly, as when I am told that there are six individuals in a certain room. But of the latter my imagination can form a distinct conception, of the former it cannot. I have no images in my mind which correspond in any considerable degree to the immense number of individuals mentioned; or to that vast mass of matter with all its various modifications which constitutes the earth. Still less can one form distinct images of what astronomy has made known to us respecting the universe. But who will pretend that man cannot comprehend the truths which man has discovered? We need not, however, go so far for examples. I can form no image of a figure with twenty equal sides,—none which shall distinguish it from a similar figure of nineteen or twenty-one. But I am surely able to comprehend propositions respecting such a figure with twenty sides; and I have a very clear idea of it as an object of the understanding. The fact therefore that our imaginations cannot conceive of omniscience, has no bearing to prove that our reason cannot comprehend the propositions which we make concerning it. When indeed we regard omniscience as infinite knowledge, then our ideas respecting it, however clear, must be inadequate. But, as I have just shown, propositions relating to inadequate ideas may be altogether intelligible.

Language then cannot be formed into propositions having a meaning, which meaning is not, in itself considered, fully to be comprehended. This is merely saying, in other terms, that the human mind is capable of comprehending the ideas of the human mind, for no other ideas are associated with, or can be expressed by, language. What then is the character of those propositions, said to be derived from the Scriptures, which are called incomprehensible; and which, it is affirmed, express mysteries above human reason? I answer, that so far as they have a meaning, they are intelligible; and that many of them are, in fact, propositions which are perfectly intelligible. When I am told that the same being is both God and man, I recognize, as I have before said,* a very *intelligible*, though a very absurd proposition, that is, I know well all the senses which the words admit. When it is affirmed that "the Father is God, and the Son is God, and the Holy Ghost is God; and yet there are not three Gods, but one God"; no words can more clearly convey any meaning,

* See pp. 57, 58.

than those propositions express the meaning, that there are three existences of whom the attributes of God may be predicated, and yet that there is only one existence of whom the attributes of God may be predicated. But this is not an incomprehensible mystery; it is plain nonsense.

It seems to me in one respect a most futile, and in another a most irreverent, sort of discussion, to inquire, what would be, or what ought to be, our state of mind, if such propositions were found in revelation; or had been taught us by any being performing miracles in evidence of his mission from God. It is a thing impossible, and not to be imagined. When we have once settled the real nature of those propositions, all controversy about their making a part of Christianity is at an end; unless, indeed, we urge this controversy, not as Christians, but as unbelievers.

The propositions, then, of which we speak, are altogether intelligible, and are not mysteries. It is only in violation of that fundamental rule of criticism, which continually prevents us from misunderstanding the words of other books in an irrational or absurd meaning, that any support has been found for them in the writings of the New Testament. These writings have been explained in a manner, in which if any other work were explained, we should think that its author was regarded by his expositor as destitute of common sense; unless we ascribed this character to the expositor himself. It may give us some idea of the extent to which the misinterpretation of the

Scriptures has been carried, and of the degree to which the religion of Christians has been corrupted, to recollect that the creed attributed to Athanasius, but which is in fact a spurious work of some unknown author, which Athanasius himself would have regarded with abhorrence, — a creed which seems to have been formed in a delirium of folly, — was for ages the professed faith of the whole Western Church; and is still the professed faith of a great portion of Protestants.

I have said, "the *professed* faith"; for although the propositions which it embodies, considered in themselves, may have one or more distinct meanings, they have no meaning in the mind of him who proposes them as religious truths. The words cannot be understood in any sense which he will acknowledge to be what he intends to express. He may have obscure, unsettled, and irrational notions, which appear to him to answer in some sort to the proposition affirmed; but he can have no belief that really corresponds to it; for though men may, and often do, believe contradictory propositions which they have never compared together, yet no man can believe an obvious contradiction. While he is maintaining these propositions, he may, perhaps, hold a doctrine which might properly be expressed in different words; and which does not in fact differ from the doctrine of those to whom he fancies himself most opposed. But whatever he does in fact believe, that he may express distinctly and fully, in words which carry no contradiction upon their face. The obscurity of the subject cannot be made a plea for the want of the utmost propriety and perspicuity of language; for it is not the subject which he is required to explain, but only his own belief concerning it. But what one man believes may be made perfectly intelligible to another of equal capacity and information.

ARCHBISHOP TILLOTSON said of the Athanasian creed, that he wished the Church of England "were well rid of it." * There are other parts of her service which it is even more desirable that church should be well rid of. Familiarity may reconcile us to what is most offensive. But let us imagine it as possible that one should be ignorant of the errors prevailing among Christians, and, at the same time, penetrated with just conceptions of the Divinity. With what inexpressible astonishment and horror would he listen for the first time to an assembly of Christian worshippers, thus addressing their God: —

"By the mystery of thy holy incarnation, by thy holy nativity and circumcision, by thy baptism, fasting, and temptation, — Good Lord, deliver us.

"By thine agony and bloody sweat, by thy cross and passion, by thy precious death and burial, by thy glorious resurrection and ascension, ... Good Lord, deliver us."

How many join in these petitions with an intelligent belief of the propositions implied in them?

* In a letter to Bishop Burnet, about a month before Tillotson's death. See Birch's Life of Tillotson.

I answer, *Not one;* for when understood, they *cannot* be believed. How many fancy that they believe them, having some obscure notions, which they think answer to what is intended? Certainly not a majority of those listeners who have at all exercised their reason upon the subject. But the doctrines implied are not doctrines of the Church of England alone. Other churches and sects are equally responsible for their promulgation. And what must we think of the public sanction thus given to such representations of God and Christianity? What, in the present state of the world, will be the effect upon the religious sentiments of men, if absurdities so revolting are presented to their minds as essential doctrines of our faith? If there be any honor due to God, if Christianity be not a mere vulgar superstition, if there be any worth in religion, if any respect is to be paid to that reason which God gave us when he formed us in his own likeness, if any concern is to be felt for man who has been insulted and degraded, it is a matter of the most serious importance, that this solemn mockery of all that is most venerable, and most essential to human happiness, should cease.

SECTION IX.

EXPLANATIONS OF PARTICULAR PASSAGES OF THE NEW TESTAMENT, ADDUCED BY TRINITARIANS.

I WILL now proceed to examine the principal passages urged by Trinitarians. I do this, not chiefly for the purpose of showing that they do not support their doctrines, — that point, I trust, is already settled, — but in order to assist those who may wish to attain a correct notion of their meaning, and particularly such as are familiar only with the Trinitarian application of them. Most of them present more or less difficulty to a modern reader; otherwise they could not, with any appearance of reason, have been perverted to the support of such doctrines; and one may reasonably desire to know how they are probably to be understood.

But it is to be remarked, that the case is the same with some of these as with many other passages in the New Testament. We may confidently reject a particular sense, as not having been intended by the speaker or writer, while, at the same time, we doubt whether we have ascertained his true meaning. Of different expositions we may sometimes hesitate which to prefer, or question whether any one be correct, though no other that seems preferable occur to us. In the study of ancient authors, we must often content ourselves with an approximation to the thoughts intended to be expressed; and for the most part have not a full and clear view of all that was present to the mind of the writer. It would require a mastery which none can attain over the whole power of an ancient language as used by different individuals, and an intimacy which none can acquire with all the circumstances affecting the conceptions and feelings of an ancient writer and his contemporaries, to determine in every case the exact force and bearing of his words. Our knowledge is not unfrequently so imperfect, that we are unable fully to estimate the relative importance of the different considerations which may incline us to adopt one meaning or another. The explanations, therefore, of some of the passages to be examined may be more or less probable or accurate, without in any degree affecting the force of the preceding arguments. However much those who reject the Trinitarian exposition of certain words may differ among themselves as to their true meaning; there is, in consequence, as little reason for assenting to the Trinitarian exposition, as is furnished by the differences among Protestants for adopting the creed of the Church of Rome, or the differences among Christians for becoming an unbeliever. An equal diversity of opinion has existed among interpreters concerning the meaning of many passages not particularly obnoxious to controversy. Nor is this variety of explanation to be supposed peculiar to the New Testament. In proportion to the attention which has been paid to the ancient philosophers, to Plato and Aristotle, for example, there has been a similar want of agreement concerning their doctrines and sentiments. It may be worth while to illustrate what has been said, and to show the difficulty that may exist in ascertaining the meaning of words, even when the discussion excites no prejudice or party feeling, by attending to a few of the first declarations of our Saviour, which it is probable many readers pass over with scarcely a question as to their sense.

"Reform; for the kingdom of Heaven is at hand."* The Common Version, instead of "Reform," has "Repent." To correct this error, nothing more is necessary than a knowledge of the proper sense of the original word. But what was intended by the words "kingdom of Heaven," as used by Christ? and how were they understood by the Jews, his contemporaries, when first uttered? Both questions are important. The Jews had expected that their Messiah would come to establish a temporal kingdom; and the idea of a temporal kingdom was suggested to their minds by those words when they first heard them. The fact concerning their expectations is ascertained by a process of investigation and reasoning. But such a kingdom was not intended by our Saviour. Under common circumstances, we endeavor to use words in that sense in which they will at once be understood by our hearers. But we learn from an examination of the Gospels, that Christ employed

* Matthew iv. 17.

terms, familiar to his hearers, in new senses, and left his meaning to be gradually ascertained and settled, as the minds of his disciples might open to the truth. What then was his meaning? This is a question to which, I think, many readers may find it more difficult to return a clear and precise answer, than it appears to be at first thought. He who will look into the commentators may perceive how indefinitely and inaccurately it is liable to be understood. For myself, I conceive him to have intended by the "kingdom of Heaven," or, in other words, "the kingdom of God," that state of things in which men should recognize the authority of God as the supreme lawgiver, and submit themselves to his laws, as human subjects to those of a human government. This I suppose to be the radical idea of the term as used by him, an idea which is to be regarded under various relations, is united with different accessory thoughts, and suggests different associations, according to the various connections in which it is presented.*

"Blessed are the poor in spirit; for theirs is the kingdom of Heaven," † — that is, they will enjoy the blessings which God confers upon the subjects of his kingdom, upon those who obey his laws. But are they blessed for what they are, or for the peculiar advantages which they enjoy for becoming what they ought to be? Is the blessing absolute and universal? Or does it refer only to the

* [See also the note on Matthew xiii. 11, in the author's Notes on the Gospels.]

† Matthew v. 3.

favorable circumstances of the class spoken of? Or is it confined to some particular individuals of that class? That these are not idle questions, may appear from the words which St. Luke ascribes to Christ: "Blessed are you poor," the qualification "in spirit" being omitted; "for yours is the kingdom of Heaven";* which we cannot understand as referring without exception to the whole class of the poor. The words given by St. Matthew have been by some critics so constructed as to correspond to those of St. Luke.† Thus Wetstein understands them as addressed particularly to Christ's poor disciples, and as meaning, Blessed in the view of the Spirit, Blessed in the sight of God, are the poor, that is, you poor. It would detain us too long, to enter into the reasons for which, as it seems to me, this interpretation is to be rejected. Let us attend, then, to some other expositions. Many commentators of the Romish Church understand by the "poor in spirit" those who voluntarily submit to poverty. Among Protestants, Whitby and others understand "men of a truly humble and lowly spirit." Paley, apparently led astray by the sound of the words in the Common Version, supposes our Saviour to declare that "the poor-spirited are blessed"; and has, in consequence, misrepresented the character of Christian, that is, of true morality.‡ We may, with some reason, suppose Christ to have meant, that,

* Luke vi. 20.

† By connecting τῷ πνευματι with μακάριοι.

‡ See his Evidences of Christianity, Part II. Ch. 2.

in the existing circumstances of the Jews, the poor were far more likely than the rich to have the dispositions which would lead them to become his followers; and that in consequence he pronounced those blessed who had the spirit of the poor. But I think it most probable that his meaning was still different. The word used in the original is to be distinguished from that which denotes simply the want of wealth. It implies destitution, and was used to denote such as lived by charity. Looking around him upon the multitude, he saw perhaps many who had no earthly goods; and there stood near him the few disciples who had at that time left all to follow him. Borrowing, as was usual with him, a figure from present objects, he speaks of that poverty which is not in external circumstances, but the poverty of the mind, the destitution felt within. The meaning of his words, I believe, was, Blessed are such as feel that they are destitute of all things; and he referred to such as, free from the high pretensions and spiritual pride of the generality of the Jews, might feel that as Jews they had no claims upon God, might recognize their own deficiencies in goodness, and be sensible how much was wanting to their true happiness.

Let us go on a little further. "Blessed are the mourners; for they will be comforted." * Does this intend those who deny themselves the blessings of life and endure voluntary penance, as some Cath-

* Matthew v. 4.

olics explain the passage? You will say not. Does it mean those who mourn for their sins, as many Protestant commentators tell us? I think otherwise. The purpose of our Saviour was, I believe, simply to announce that his religion brought blessed consolation to all who mourned.

"Blessed are the meek; for they shall inherit the earth." So the next words are rendered in the Common Version. I will not go over the different meanings that have been assigned to them, but will only ask my reader, if he have not particularly attended to the subject, in what sense he has understood them? The rendering should be, "Blessed are the mild, for they will inherit the land"; that is, "the promised land." The passage cannot be understood without attention to the conceptions of the Jews. They believed, that, if they obeyed God, they should remain in possession of "the promised land"; if they disobeyed him, that they would be removed from it, and scattered among other nations. Hence "the inheriting of the land" was in their minds but another name for the enjoying of God's favor. In this associated and figurative sense the terms were used by Christ. His meaning was, literally, Blessed are the mild, for they will enjoy the favor of God. In the Psalm (xxxvii. 11) from which he borrowed the words, they are, probably, to be understood literally.

These examples may serve in some measure to show, that it is not always easy to determine the meaning even of passages which may seem at first view to present little difficulty. If, therefore, we may hesitate about the true sense of those quoted by Trinitarians, this circumstance will afford no ground for hesitation in rejecting the Trinitarian sense. We must not assign an absurd meaning to a passage, because we are unable to satisfy ourselves about the meaning intended. He would reason very ill, who, because he was unable to satisfy himself as to what was meant by our Saviour when he spoke of eating his flesh and drinking his blood, should, on that account, adopt the Roman Catholic exposition of his words.

In what follows, I shall confine my remarks to passages of the New Testament. If the doctrines of Trinitarians were not taught by Christ and his Apostles, it would be a superfluous labor to examine the passages of the Old Testament which have been represented as containing indications of them.* There are arguments so futile that one may be excused from remarking upon them. At the present day, it can hardly be necessary to prove that the writer of the first chapters of Genesis was not a Trinitarian; or that there is no evi-

* ["The Old Testament," says Professor Stuart, "does but obscurely (if at all) reveal the doctrine of a Trinity. . . . . . On the supposition that has been made, namely, that the full development of Trinity was not made, and could not be made, until the time of the Saviour's incarnation, it is easy to see why nothing more than preparatory hints should be found in the Old Testament respecting it. He who finds more than these there, has reason, so far as I can see, to apprehend that his speculations in theology have stronger hold upon him than the principles of philology." — Biblical Repository for July, 1835, pp. 105 - 108.]

dence for the doctrine in the words of Isaiah (vi. 3), "Holy, holy, holy is the Lord of Hosts"; though, according to Dr. William Lowth, a standard commentator on the Prophets, "the Christian Church hath always thought that the doctrine of the blessed Trinity was implied in this repetition." Another expositor of equal note, Bishop Patrick, tells us, that "many of the ancient Fathers think there is a plain intimation of the Trinity in these words, 'The Lord our God is one Lord'"; yet it cannot be expected that one should go into an explanation of this proposition, for the sake of removing any difficulty in comprehending it. The passage of the Old Testament which is most relied upon by Trinitarians is found in Isaiah ix. 6. It has been often explained. There is, I think, no evidence that it relates to Christ; and if it do, the common version of it is incorrect. It may be thus rendered: —

> "For unto us a child is born,
> Unto us a son is given;
> And the government shall be upon his shoulder;
> And he shall be called
> Wonderful, counsellor, mighty potentate,
> Everlasting father, prince of peace." *

* I quote the translation given by the Rev. George R. Noyes in his Sermon upon Isaiah ix. 6, lately published, and refer to the same discourse for its explanation and defence. I do so the more readily, as it gives me an opportunity of expressing my respect for that able and accurate scholar, and my strong interest in those labors by which he is contributing so much toward a better understanding of the Hebrew Scriptures.

[The sermon here referred to was republished in No. 78 of the Tracts of the American Unitarian Association. See also, on this

I proceed, then, to remark upon the principal passages adduced by Trinitarians professedly from the New Testament in support of their doctrines; and in doing so shall distribute them into several different classes, according to the different errors which have led to their misuse. The sources of misinterpretation and mistake will thus appear, and in regard to the texts of less importance which I shall omit to notice, it will in general be easy to determine to what head they are to be referred, and in what manner understood.

CLASS I.

To the first class we may refer *Interpolated and Corrupted Passages.* Such are the following.

passage, the remarks of the Rev. Dr. Noyes in the Christian Examiner for January, 1836, Vol. XIX. pp. 292-295. The article just cited examines the question, "Whether the Deity of the Messiah be a doctrine of the Old Testament," with particular reference to the statements and reasonings of Hengstenberg, in his Christology. In connection with two others by which it was followed, on the "Meaning of the Title *Angel of Jehovah*, as used in Scripture," and "The *Angel of Jehovah* mentioned in the Old Testament, not identical with the Messiah," (see the Christian Examiner for May and July, 1836,) it presents, probably, the ablest and most satisfactory discussion of the subject of which it treats that is to be found in the English language. — It may be mentioned, that the translation given above, "mighty potentate," instead of "the mighty God," as in the Common Version, is supported, substantially, by the authority of Luther, Gesenius, De Wette, and Maurer.]

Acts xx. 28. Here in the Common Version, we find these words: "To feed the church of GOD, which he hath purchased with his own blood." Instead of "the church of God," the true reading is "the church of the Lord." *

1 Timothy iii. 16. "GOD was manifested in the flesh." The reading Θεός (*God*) is spurious; but it has been doubted whether we should read ὅς (*who* or *he who*) or ὅ (*which*).

1 John v. 7. The famous text of the *three heavenly witnesses.*† The value that has been formerly attached to this passage, though unquestionably

* [Among the critics and commentators who regard this as the genuine or as the most probable reading, may be mentioned the names of Grotius, Wetstein, Michaelis (Anmerk. in loc.), Bp. Marsh, Griesbach, Schott, Heinrichs, Rosenmüller, Kuinoel, Lachmann, Tischendorf, Meyer, De Wette, Olshausen, Baumgarten, Adam Clarke, John Pye Smith, Stuart (Bibl. Repos. for April, 1838, p. 315), Barnes, Hackett, Davidson, Tregelles.]

† [This text is generally referred to, for conciseness, as "1 John v. 7," though in fact the spurious words form a part of the 7th and 8th verses. It would hardly be worth while to notice this, had not some who have written on the subject been so ignorant as to argue the genuineness of the seventh verse from the assumed genuineness of the first part of the eighth; though the latter, equally with the spurious portion of the former, is wanting in all known Greek manuscripts written before the invention of printing, in all the ancient versions but the Latin Vulgate, and even in the oldest manuscripts of that; is quoted by *no* ancient Greek Father, and by no Latin Father before the latter part of the fifth century. The following are the verses in question, as translated in the Common Version, the spurious portion being enclosed in marks of parenthesis: —

"For there are three that bear record (in heaven, the Father, the Word, and the Holy Ghost; and these three are one. 8. And there are three that bear witness in earth), the spirit, and the water, and the blood: and these three agree in one."]

interpolated, may be estimated from the obstinacy with which it has been contended for, from its still retaining its place as genuine in the editions of the Common Version, and even in editions of the original professedly formed on the text of Griesbach, from the lingering glances cast toward it by such writers as Bishop Middleton, and from the pertinacity with which the more ignorant or bigoted class of controversialists continue to quote and even defend it.

After all that has been written concerning these texts, no one of them requires particular notice except that from the First Epistle to Timothy. Of this the true reading and proper explanation are both doubtful. In respect to the reading, the question is, as I have mentioned, between ὅς (*who* or *he who*) and ὅ (*which*). Griesbach gives the preference to the former, but it has been shown, I think, that he is incorrect in the citation of his authorities.* The original reading, I believe to have

* See Laurence's Remarks upon Griesbach's Classification of Manuscripts, pp. 71 – 83. According to Griesbach, of the Versions (which as regards this text afford by far the most important evidence to be adduced), the Arabic of the Polyglot, and the Slavonic, alone support the reading Θεός; in all the others, a pronoun is used answering to ὅς or to ὅ. That is to say, the Coptic, the Sahidic, and the Philoxenian Syriac *in its margin*, express the pronoun ὅς; the Vulgate, and the older Latin versions, ὅ, *quod;* and the Peshito or vulgar Syriac, the Philoxenian Syriac *in its text,* the Erpenian Arabic, the Æthiopic, and the Armenian, use a pronoun which may be translated indifferently "who" or "which."

But according to Dr. Laurence, whose statements I see no reason to distrust, "the Coptic, the Sahidic, and the Philoxenian versions do not necessarily read ὅς, but most probably ὅ," and "the Peshito or

been ὅ (*which*). For this the external evidence, when fairly adjusted, seems greatly to preponderate; and it may have been altered by transcribers first into ὅς, and afterwards into Θεός, in consequence of the theological interpretation of the passage, according to which the mystery spoken of was Christ,—an interpretation that appears to

vulgar Syriac, the Erpenian Arabic, and the Æthiopic, do not indifferently read ὅς or ὅ, but indisputably ὅ." "The Armenian reads neither ὅς nor ὅ, but, in conjunction with the Byzantine text, Θεός." Of all these versions, therefore, Griesbach's account is incorrect; and the number and importance of those which favor the reading ὅ, taken in connection with the fact of its having been, from the first, the reading of the whole Western Church, produce a preponderating weight of evidence in its favor.

In regard to the Philoxenian version, Dr. Laurence, as may appear from what is quoted, expresses himself with some obscurity. But I presume his opinion was, that both in the text and in the margin it probably reads ὅ. See White's note in his edition of this version.

[Later investigations have shown that the statements of Dr. Laurence here relied on are in several respects erroneous. But before pointing out their inaccuracy, it may be well, for the better understanding of the subject, to mention the dates generally assigned by scholars to the ancient versions which contain this passage. The Old Latin or Italic, and the Peshito Syriac, are supposed to have been made in the second century; the Coptic and Sahidic, in the third, or the latter part of the second; the Æthiopic, Gothic, and Latin Vulgate, in the fourth; the Armenian, in the fifth; the Philoxenian or Harclean Syriac was completed A. D. 508, and revised A. D. 616. Later versions are the Georgian, of the sixth century, but since altered from the Slavonic, made in the ninth; and the Arabic versions, one edited by Erpenius, supposed to be made from the Syriac, another published in the Paris and London Polyglots, made from the Greek,—both of uncertain date and very little value,—and still another of the ninth century, made from the Greek at Emesa in Syria by one Daniel Philentolos, a manuscript of which is preserved in the Vatican Library.

In regard to the reading of the present passage in these versions,

have been given it at an early period. But the passage, I believe, has no reference to Christ personally.

The words translated "mystery of godliness," as if purposely to obscure the sense, should be rendered "the new doctrine of piety," or "concerning piety"; and in order to avoid an awkward collo-

the following is believed to be a correct account of the facts which may now be considered as established. The Old Latin or Italic version, and the Latin Vulgate, read *quod*, corresponding to ὅ, *which*; — the Gothic, as edited by Gabelentz and Loebe, has the masculine relative, answering to ὅς, *who*, though the word corresponding to μυστήριον, *runa*, is feminine; — the Peshito Syriac, the Coptic, the Sahidic, the Æthiopic, the Armenian, the Philoxenian Syriac both in the text and in the margin, the Erpenian Arabic, and the Arabic of Philentolos (see Hug's Introd. to the N. T., § 107, 3d ed.), use a pronoun which may here be indifferently translated *who* or *which*; — the Arabic of the Polyglot, the Slavonic, and the Georgian, support the reading Θεός, *God*. In most of the ambiguous versions, the relative pronoun has the same form for all the genders; in the Coptic and Sahidic it is masculine, but the word answering to μυστήριον being also masculine, we have no means of determining whether the translators had before them ὅς or ὅ. In respect to the Armenian version, the Eclectic Review for January 1831, p. 48, gives a quotation, apparently from a later edition of Dr. Laurence's Essay, according to which he no longer claims it as supporting the reading Θεός, but leaves its testimony doubtful. The Eclectic Reviewer himself, Dr. Henderson, and Dr. Tregelles, for whom a special collation of Zohrab's edition of this version has been made by a competent scholar, represent it as reading a pronoun equivalent to either ὅς or ὅ, as stated above. As to the Philoxenian Syriac, see the note of White, referred to by Mr. Norton.

The evidence of the ancient versions is particularly important in regard to this passage, on account of the slight difference between the three readings as written in the ancient Greek manuscripts. In the uncial or more ancient manuscripts, Θεός, ὅς, and ὅ were written nearly as follows: $\overline{\Theta C}$, OC, O. The change from one of these readings to another could therefore be much more easily made in the

cation of words in English, we may connect the epithet "great" with the substantives "pillar and foundation"; an arrangement which, though contrary to the construction of the original, sufficiently expresses the sense. The following rendering, then, I believe, gives the meaning of the Apostle.

"I thus write to you, hoping to come to you

Greek manuscripts than in those of the ancient versions. The more important of these versions represent the text of manuscripts far older, probably, than any that have come down to us. They represent, moreover, the text of manuscripts found in countries widely separated from each other. Their testimony has therefore not only the weight of the highest antiquity, but is far more independent, than that of the great mass of modern manuscripts. A large majority of these were written in the eleventh and twelfth centuries, or later, within the narrow limits of the patriarchate of Constantinople, and under influences which tended to produce a uniformity of text. (See Norton's Genuineness of the Gospels, Vol. I., Additional Note A, pp. xxx.-xxxii.) In many passages the reading which the great body of them present differs from that which is proved to be genuine by the agreement of the most ancient witnesses combined with internal evidence. It is accordingly a well-established principle of criticism, to use the words of Tregelles, that "the mass of recent documents possesses no determining voice, in a question as to what we should receive as genuine readings." When, therefore, we find that the evidence of the *nine oldest versions* in favor of a relative pronoun as the original reading in this passage is confirmed by the *five oldest and best manuscripts* which we possess (the Alexandrine, Ephrem, Augian, and Boernerian reading ὅς, the Clermont ὅ), and also by *the earliest Fathers* to whose testimony we can appeal with any confidence, we can have little doubt that the reading Θεός, though found in all but three of the cursive, and in two of the later uncial manuscripts, is a corruption of the original. It is perhaps worth noting, that one of the more recent manuscripts which read ὅς, the Codex Colbertinus 2844 (numbered 17 in the Epistles by the critical editors), is of peculiar value. . Eichhorn, as quoted by Tregelles, speaks of it as "full of the most excellent and oldest readings"; and styles it "the Queen of the manuscripts in cursive letters."

shortly; but should I be delayed, that you may know how you ought to conduct yourself in the house of God, that is, the assembly of the living God. Beyond doubt, the great pillar and foundation of the true religion is the new doctrine concerning piety, which has been made known in human weakness, proved true by divine power, while

We are left then to decide between ὅς and ὅ. The question which of these readings is to be preferred is rendered more difficult of solution by the ambiguous evidence of most of the versions, and, it may be added, of many of the Fathers. It is not necessary to discuss it here. Among modern critics, ὅς is regarded as the most probable reading by Benson, Griesbach, Schott, Vater, Rosenmüller, Heinrichs, Meyer, De Wette, Olshausen, Wiesinger, Huther, Lachmann, Tischendorf, Davidson, and Tregelles; ὅ is preferred by Erasmus, Grotius, Sir Isaac Newton, Wetstein, and Professor Porter.

One who wishes to pursue the subject further, and to examine the authorities for the statements which have here been made, may consult, in addition to the notes of Wetstein, Griesbach, Scholz, and Tischendorf, in their editions of the Greek Testament, the Eclectic Review for January 1831, Art. III.; Porter's Principles of Textual Criticism, (London, 1848,) pp. 482-493; Davidson's Biblical Criticism, (London, 1853,) Vol. II. pp. 382-403; Tregelles's Account of the Printed Text of the Greek New Testament, (London, 1854,) pp. 227-231; and the able reviews of Porter and Davidson, by the Rev. Dr. Noyes (who prefers the reading ὅς), in the Christian Examiner for January 1850, and May 1853. The note of Wetstein deserves particularly to be studied. — Of the earlier defenders of the common reading of this passage, the ablest, perhaps, is Berriman, whose "Critical Dissertation upon 1 Tim. iii. 16" appeared in 1741. Among its later champions, the most prominent is Dr. Ebenezer Henderson, whose essay on the subject, entitled "The Great Mystery of Godliness Incontrovertible," &c., was published in London in 1830, and reprinted, with additional observations by Professor Stuart, in the Biblical Repository for January 1832. The remark of Dr. Davidson, that "Henderson's reasoning to show that the Old Syriac version may have had Θεός equally well as ὅ, is a piece of special pleading undeserving of notice," may be applied with justice

angels were looking on, which has been proclaimed to the Gentiles, believed in the world, and has obtained a glorious reception."

In the beginning of the second chapter of this Epistle, St. Paul speaks earnestly, and at length, of the prayers to be offered by Christians in their public assemblies. The main object of their thus

to many other parts of this essay. The careful inquirer will find that it abounds in misstatements and false assumptions; and will be astonished at the *suppression* of important facts, of which it hardly seems possible that the author can have been ignorant. Some of Dr. Henderson's errors are pointed out in the article in the Eclectic Review before referred to, and in the Christian Examiner for January 1850, p. 29, note. There are other important mistakes and omissions not there noted, particularly in his account of the evidence of the Fathers.

Professor Stuart, in the new edition of his Letters to Dr. Channing contained in his "Miscellanies," published in 1846, has some remarks on this passage, in which he has repeated many of Dr. Henderson's errors, and added others of his own. After the statements and references which have been made, it is not worth while to point these out in detail. But though the accuracy of Professor Stuart cannot be relied on, he has shown his candor in the following honest concession, which is quoted with approbation by Dr. Davidson, himself a Trinitarian.

"I cannot feel," he says, in concluding his remarks supplementary to Dr. Henderson's essay, "that the contest on the subject of the reading can profit one side so much, or harm the other so much, as disputants respecting the doctrine of the Trinity have supposed. Whoever attentively studies John xvii. 20-26, 1 John i. 3, ii. 5, iv. 15, 16, and other passages of the like tenor, will see that 'God might be manifest' in the person of Christ, without the necessary implication of the proper divinity of the Saviour; at least, that the phraseology of Scripture does admit of other constructions besides this; and other ones, moreover, which are not forced. And conceding this fact, less is determined by the contest about ὅς and Θεός, in 1 Tim. iii. 16, than might seem to be at first view."—Biblical Repository for January, 1832, p. 79.]

associating together was to excite their feelings of piety by mutual sympathy. Then follow directions respecting the well-ordering of a Christian community or church, and the proper character of its officers; and, in conclusion, the Apostle recurs to the great distinctive character of Christianity, its new doctrine of piety to God, that state of mind which their assemblies were particularly intended to cherish. Thus we have a connected train of thought. But if the conclusion of the passage be explained of the manifestation of Christ, or of God, in the flesh, a new subject is abruptly introduced, having but a remote connection with what precedes; and one which we perceive no reason for the Apostle's adverting to in this place.*

CLASS II.

Passages relating to Christ which have been mistranslated.

To this class belongs Philippians ii. 5, seqq. Here the Common Version makes the Apostle say of Christ, that he "thought it not robbery to be equal with God." This has been considered a decisive argument that Christ is God; though

* [For a notice of the various readings of some other passages supposed to have a bearing on the doctrine of the Trinity, see Appendix, Note C.]

it is an absurdity to say of any being, that he "thought it not robbery to be equal with himself." Perhaps no text, however, has been more frequently quoted or referred to.* But it now seems to be generally conceded that the words have been mistranslated. In the verses that follow, the verbal rendering of ἐν μορφῇ Θεοῦ is, "in the form of God," and that of μορφὴν δούλου, "the form of a servant." But as these phrases do not correspond to our modes of expression, they can hardly convey a distinct meaning to most readers. "To be in the form of another," as here used, means "to appear as another," "to be as another." In a translation it is better to substitute one of these equivalent, but more intelligible phrases. The whole passage may be thus rendered: —

"Let the same disposition [Let the same humility and benevolence] be in you which was in Jesus Christ, who being as God did not think that his equality with God was to be eagerly retained; but divested himself of it, and made himself as a servant and was as men are, and being in the common condition of man, humbled himself, and was submissive, even to death, the death of the cross."

Christ was "in the form of God," or "the image of God," or "as God"; he was "like God,"

* Thus Dr. Watts in one of his hymns: —

"Yet there is one of human frame,
Jesus arrayed in flesh and blood,
Thinks it no robbery to claim
A full equality with God.
Their glory shines with equal beams," &c.

Book II., H. 51.

or he was "equal with God" (the latter words being correctly understood); because he was a minister in the hands of God, wholly under his direction; because his words were the words of God, his miracles, the works of the Father who sent him, and his authority as a teacher and legislator, that of the Almighty, not human, but divine. Yet notwithstanding that he bore the high character of God's messenger and representative to men, with all the powers connected with it, he was not eager to display that character, or exercise those powers, for the sake of any personal advantage, or of assuming any rank or splendor corresponding to his pre-eminence over all other men. "Being rich, for our sakes he became poor."* He divested himself as it were of his powers, lowered himself to the condition of common men, lived as they live, exposed to their deprivations and sufferings, and voluntarily, as if weak as they, submitted to an ignominious and torturing death. — When it is affirmed that Christ made himself as a servant, these words are illustrated by those which he himself used, while inculcating, like the Apostle, the virtues of humility and benevolence, with a like reference to his own example: "The Son of Man came not to be served, but to serve."† It is in imitation of this example, that he directs him, "who would be chief among his disciples, to become the servant of all."‡

* [2 Cor. viii. 9.] † Matthew xx. 28. ‡ [Mark x. 44.]

I PROCEED to another example. It is the mistranslation of the word αἰῶνες by the English word "worlds," in the commencement of the Epistle to the Hebrews.* For giving this sense to the original term, there is not, I think, any authority to be found either in Hellenistic or classic Greek. It was not so used till long after the composition of this Epistle. In the theological dialect of Christians, this sense was assigned to it in reference to the present passage and to another in this Epistle (Ch. xi. 3.); and the corresponding Latin word *sæculum* acquired the same meaning. The Greek word αἰών was used to denote a space of time of considerable length, leaving its precise limits undefined. Hence it denotes, secondarily, the state of things existing during such a period. In this sense it often occurs in the New Testament. We use the word *age* in a like signification, employing it to denote the men of a particular period, considered in reference to their circumstances and character, as when we speak of the "manners of an age," "the learning of an age," &c. So, likewise, the word *time* is used, though, by an idiom of our language, rather in the plural than the singular, as in the phrase, "the times of the Messiah." Shakespeare, however, says in the singular, "the time is

* There can be no reason for not explaining the passages in the Epistle to the Hebrews which I believe to have been misunderstood, though I do not regard the Epistle as the work of St. Paul or any other Apostle. My reasons for this opinion I have formerly given in the Christian Examiner (Vols. IV., V., VI.), in a series of articles which I may, perhaps, at some time republish.

out of joint,"* meaning, "the present state of things is in disorder."

In the passage under consideration, αἰῶνες, "ages," most probably, I think, denotes the "different states of things which, in successive periods, would result from Christianity." In the Epistle to the Ephesians, it is used, I suppose, in the same sense, Ch. iii. ver. 11, κατὰ πρόθεσιν τῶν αἰώνων ἣν ἐποίησεν ἐν Χριστῷ Ἰησοῦ τῷ κυρίῳ ἡμῶν, "conformably to a disposition of the ages which he has made by Christ Jesus our Lord"; † and probably also in the same Epistle (ii. 7) where the Apostle speaks of the favor of God that will be manifested "in the ages to come." In these passages, as well as in that from the Epistle to the Hebrews, the reference, I presume, extends beyond this life to the future condition of Christians, to "the ages" after death. ‡ Thus, then, I would render and explain the meaning of the writer to the Hebrews in the first five verses of this Epistle: —

"God, who at different times and in different ways formerly spoke to our fathers by the Prophets, has at last spoken to us by his Son, whom

* [Hamlet, Act I. Sc. V.]

† Not, as in the Common Version, "according to the eternal purpose, which he purposed in Christ Jesus our Lord."

‡ In Hebrews xi. 3, αἰῶνες is again translated "worlds." Here we may render thus: "Through faith we understand that the ages have been so ordered by the power of God, that what is seen had not its origin in what was conspicuous." The meaning of the writer I conceive to have been, that through faith we believe that Christianity with all its results is to be referred to the power of God, not having had its origin in any state of things previously existing.

he has appointed heir of all,* through whom also he has given form to the ages,† who being a reflection of his glory, and an image of his perfections, and ruling all things with authority from him,‡ after having cleansed us from our sins by himself alone, § has sat down at the right hand of the Majesty on high; being as much greater than the angels, as the title which he has obtained is preeminent above theirs. For to which of the angels did God ever say, *Thou art my Son, this day have I made thee so?* And again, *I will be to him a Father, and he shall be to me a Son?*"

ANOTHER passage which may be mentioned is the conclusion of the First Epistle of St. John, thus rendered in the Common Version: —

"And we know that the Son of God is come, and hath given us an understanding, that we may know him that is true; and we are in him that is true, *even* in his Son Jesus Christ. This is the

* We may suppose that, the preceding dispensations of God being intended to prepare the way for Christianity, Christ is represented as "heir of all" which has been accomplished by them; or the figurative term *heir* may be used with reference to the title of *Son* immediately before given to Christ, and "heir of all" may be equivalent to "Lord of all," denoting that Christ has been appointed "head over all" in the Christian dispensation.

† Or, in other words, "has given form to what exists and is to exist," as the results of Christianity.

‡ Read *αὑτοῦ*, and not *αὐτοῦ*, as is suggested, and almost required, by the occurrence of *αὐτοῦ* in the preceding clause, and by the use of *ἑαυτοῦ* immediately after without the insertion of *καί*.

§ That is, without the intervention of the sacrifices of the Jewish law.

true God and eternal life. Little children, keep yourselves from idols."

According to the Trinitarian exposition of these words, the true God is the Son of God, and the two persons, who are so clearly distinguished by St. John, are one being. But the appearance of a Trinitarian meaning is the result of a false translation, particularly of the improper insertion of the word "even." The passage may be thus rendered. Its sense may be made clearer by going back a little, and beginning at verse 18.

"We know that whoever is born of God avoids sin; the child of God guards himself, and the Wicked One cannot touch him. We are assured that we are of God, and that the whole world is subject to the Wicked One. And we are assured that the Son of God has come, and has given us understanding to know Him who is True. And we are with Him who is True through his Son Jesus Christ. He is the True God, and eternal life. Children, keep yourselves from idols."

The meaning is, that He with whom Christians are, He who is True, is the True God, and the giver of eternal life.* In the former part of the

* [Compare verse 11. The pronoun translated "He" by Mr. Norton, or "This" in the Common Version, is regarded as referring to "Him who is True" by the most unprejudiced interpreters, whether Trinitarian or Unitarian; among others, by Erasmus, Grotius, Wetstein, Michaelis, Morus, Abp. Newcome, Rosenmüller, Jaspis, Schott, Winer (Gram. § 23. 1), Lücke, De Wette, Neander, Huther, Meyer (on Rom. ix. 5, 2d ed.), and Hofmann (Schriftbeweis, I. 128). The pronoun οὗτος often refers not to the nearest preceding noun, but to a remoter antecedent, more prominent in the mind of the writer. See 2 John 7, Acts iv. 11, and the Lexicons of the N. T. *sub voce.*

passage St. John expresses the Jewish conception of the personality and power of Satan. To him, the Wicked One, he regarded the heathen world as subject; while believers were through Christ with Him who is True, the True God. They were, therefore, to keep themselves from idols.

Should it be said that these ideas are not happily expressed, I answer, it is evident that the author of this Epistle was as unskilful a writer as we might expect to find one originally a Galilæan fisherman; and should it be brought as an objection against his being an inspired Apostle, that he adopted a popular error of his countrymen respecting the existence and power of a being, the supposed author of evil, I would ask in return, how, if he were not an inspired Apostle, one thus exposed in common with others to the errors of his age, rose so high above his contemporaries in his comprehension of the ESSENTIAL truths of religion?

With the passage quoted from St. John may be compared the words of his Master, which he had previously recorded: "And this is eternal life, to know thee, the only true God, and Jesus Christ whom thou hast sent."* After having recorded these words, with what amazement would he have been seized, had it been revealed to him that an epistle of his own would be interpolated in one place, and its meaning perverted in another, for the sake of proving a doctrine, about to be generally received by Christians, that he who thus ad-

* John xvii. 3.

dressed the only true God, that he whom God had sent, was himself the only true God!

To the class of mistranslations are likewise to be referred those passages which, on account of the omission of the Greek article, have been so rendered as to apply to Christ the title of "God." These, however, are in this particular correctly translated in the Common Version. As the question is purely a critical one, I will place the remarks to be made upon it in a note.*

* The argument for the deity of Christ founded upon the omission of the Greek article was revived and brought into notice in the last century by Granville Sharp, Esq. He applied it to eight texts which will be hereafter mentioned. The last words of Ephesians v. 5 may afford an example of the construction on which the argument is founded:

ἐν τῇ βασιλείᾳ τοῦ Χριστοῦ καὶ Θεοῦ.

From the article being inserted before Χριστοῦ and omitted before Θεοῦ, Mr. Sharp infers that both names relate to the same person, and renders, "in the kingdom of Christ our God." Conformably to the manner in which he understands it, it might be rendered, "in the kingdom of him who is Christ and God." The proper translation I suppose to be that of the Common Version, "in the kingdom of Christ and of God," or "in the kingdom of the Messiah and of God."

The argument of Sharp is defended by Bishop Middleton in his Doctrine of the Greek Article. By attending to the rule laid down by him, with its limitations and exceptions, we shall be able to judge of its applicability to the passages in question. His rule is this: —

"When two or more attributives, joined by a copulative or copulatives, are assumed of [relate to] the same person or thing, before the first attributive the article is inserted, before the remaining ones it is omitted." (pp. 79, 80.)

By attributives, he understands adjectives, participles, and nouns which are significant of character, relation, and dignity.

The limitations and exceptions to the rule stated by him are as follows: —

To the class of mistranslations might strictly be referred a very large part of all the passages adduced by Trinitarians, as will appear from what

I. There is no similar rule respecting "names of substances *considered as substances.*" Thus we may say ὁ λίθος καὶ χρυσός, without repeating the article before χρυσός, though we speak of two different substances. The reason of this limitation of the rule is stated to be that "distinct real essences cannot be conceived to belong to the same thing"; or, in other words, that the same thing cannot be supposed to be two different substances. — In this case, then, it appears that the article is not repeated, *because its repetition is not necessary to prevent ambiguity.* This is the true principle which accounts for all the limitations and exceptions to the rule that are stated by Bishop Middleton and others. It is mentioned thus early, that the principle may be kept in mind; and its truth may be remarked in the other cases of limitation or of exception to be quoted.

II. No similar rule applies to proper names. "The reason," says Middleton, "is evident at once; for it is impossible that *John* and *Thomas*, the names of two distinct persons, should be predicated of an individual." (p. 86.) This remark is not to the purpose; for the same individual may have two names. The true reason for this limitation is, that proper names, when those of the same individual, are not connected by a copulative or copulatives, and therefore that, when they are thus connected, no ambiguity arises from the omission of the article.

III. "Nouns," says Middleton, "which are the names of abstract ideas, are also excluded; for, as Locke has well observed, 'Every distinct abstract idea is a distinct essence, and the names which stand for such distinct ideas are the names of things essentially different.'" (*Ibid.*) It would therefore, he reasons, be contradictory to suppose that any quality were at once ἀπειρία and ἀπαιδευσία. But the names of abstract ideas are used to denote personal qualities, and the same personal qualities, as they are viewed under different aspects, may be denoted by different names. The reason assigned by Middleton is therefore without force. The true reason for the limitation is, that *usually* no ambiguity arises from the omission of the article before words of the class mentioned.

IV. The rule, it is further conceded, is not of universal application as it respects *plurals;* for, says Middleton, "Though *one* individual

follows; but my purpose under the present head has been to remark only on a few, in which the error is more gross than usual, or the misuse of

may act, and frequently does act, in several capacities, it is not likely that a *multitude* of individuals should all of them act in the *same* several capacities: and, by the *extreme improbability* that they should be represented as so acting, we may be forbidden to understand the second plural attributive of the persons designed in the article prefixed to the first, however the usage in the singular might seem to countenance the construction." (p. 90.)

V. Lastly, "we find," he says, "in very many instances, not only in the plural, but even in the singular number, that where attributives are in their nature *absolutely incompatible*, i. e. where the application of the rule would involve a contradiction in terms, there the first attributive only has the article, *the perspicuity of the passage not requiring the rule to be accurately observed.*" (p. 92.)

Having thus laid down the rule, with its limitations and exceptions, Bishop Middleton applies it to some of the passages in the New Testament adduced by Mr. Sharp in proof of the divinity of Christ. These were Acts xx. 28 (supposing the true reading to be τοῦ κυρίου καὶ Θεοῦ); Ephes. v. 5; 2 Thess. i. 12; 1 Tim. v. 21 (if κυρίου should be retained in the text); 2 Tim. iv. 1 (if we read τοῦ Θεοῦ καὶ κυρίου); Titus ii. 13; 2 Peter i. 1; Jude 4 (supposing Θεόν to belong to the text). In four of these eight texts, the reading adopted to bring them within the rule is probably spurious, as may be seen by referring to Griesbach; and they are in consequence either given up, or not strongly insisted upon, by Middleton. In one of the remaining, 2 Thess. i. 12, the reading is κατὰ τὴν χάριν τοῦ Θεοῦ ἡμῶν καὶ κυρίου Ἰησοῦ Χριστοῦ. Of this Middleton is "disposed to think that it affords no certain evidence in favor of Mr Sharp," because he "believes that κύριος in the form of Κύριος Ἰησοῦς Χριστός became as a title so incorporated with the proper name as to be subject to the same law." (pp. 554, 564.) The three remaining texts are those on which he principally relies.

By the application of the rule to the passage last mentioned, it is inferred that Christ is called "God," and "the great God"; and it is affirmed that the rule requires us to understand these titles as applied to him. The general answer to this reasoning is as follows.

It appears by comparing the rule with its exceptions and limita-

which has principally arisen from their being incorrectly rendered. As may readily be supposed, the different classes of texts that I have formed

tions, that it in fact amounts to nothing more than this: that when substantives, adjectives, or participles are connected together by a copulative or copulatives, if the first have the article, it is to be *omitted* before those which follow, when they relate to the same person or thing; and is to be *inserted*, when they relate to different persons or things, EXCEPT when this fact is sufficiently determined by some other circumstance. The same rule exists respecting the use of the definite article in English.

The principle of exception just stated is evidently that which runs through all the limitations and exceptions which Middleton has laid down and exemplified, and is in itself perfectly reasonable. When, from any other circumstance, it may be clearly understood that different persons or things are spoken of, then the insertion or omission of the article is a matter of indifference.

But if this be true, no argument for the deity of Christ can be drawn from the texts adduced. With regard to this doctrine, the main question is, whether it were taught by Christ and his Apostles, and received by their immediate disciples. Antitrinitarians maintain that it was not; and consequently maintain that no thought of it was ever entertained by the Apostles and first believers. But if this supposition be correct, the insertion of the article in these texts was wholly unnecessary. No ambiguity could result from its omission. The imagination had not entered the minds of men, that God and Christ were the same person. The Apostles in writing, and their converts in reading, the passages in question, could have no more conception of one person only being understood, in consequence of the omission of the article, than of supposing but one substance to be meant by the terms *ὁ λίθος καὶ χρυσός*, on account of the omission of the article before *χρυσός*. These texts, therefore, cannot be brought to disprove the Antitrinitarian supposition, because this supposition must be proved false, before these texts can be taken from the exception and brought under the operation of the rule. The truth of the supposition accounts for the omission of the article.

[On the subject of this note, one may further consult the able tract of the Rev. Calvin Winstanley, entitled "A Vindication of certain

run into each other; the misinterpretation of a passage not unfrequently having its origin in more than one cause.*

CLASS III.

Passages relating to God, which have been incorrectly applied to Christ.

THE first which I shall mention belongs likewise to the head of mistranslations. It is Romans ix. 5, thus rendered in the Common Version: "Whose

Passages in the Common English Version of the New Testament. Addressed to Granville Sharp, Esq."; published in 1805, and reprinted, with additions, at Cambridge (Mass.) in 1819. See also an essay by Professor Stuart, entitled "Hints and Cautions respecting the Greek Article," in the Biblical Repository for April 1834; and the Rev. T. S. Green's "Grammar of the New Testament Dialect," (London, 1842,) p. 205, seqq., — a work containing many acute observations. Winer, in his Grammar of the New Testament Idiom, § 18. 5, shows that there is no ground for the inference which Middleton and others would draw from the omission of the article in Titus ii. 13 and Jude 4.]

* [It may here be proper to notice the gross mistranslation of Hebrews ii. 16, which reads, "For verily he took not on *him the nature of* angels; but he took on *him* the seed of Abraham." The Italics are those of the Common Version, the words thus printed being a wholly unauthorized addition of the translators. The verse should be rendered: "For he, truly, does not give aid to angels [i. e. is not the Saviour of angels]; but he gives aid to the offspring of Abraham." The passage is thus understood by all modern interpreters of any note. — It may also be remarked, that in the 14th verse of the same chapter "took part of" is improperly used for "partook of," "shared."]

are the fathers, and of whom as concerning the flesh Christ came, who is over all, God blessed for ever. Amen."

It must, one would think, strike a Trinitarian, who maintains the correctness of this construction and rendering, as a very extraordinary fact, that the title of "God over all blessed for ever," which is nowhere else given to Christ, should be introduced thus incidentally and abruptly, without explanation or comment, and without any use being made of the doctrine. The supposed fact appears still more extraordinary and unaccountable, when we recollect that one main purpose of the Epistle to the Romans was to meet the prejudices and errors of the unbelieving Jews respecting Christianity; and that the doctrine which the Apostle is imagined to have asserted so briefly and explicitly, and then to have left without attempting to clear it from a single objection, must have been in the highest degree obnoxious to them; and one, therefore, which, in consistency with the design of the Epistle, required the fullest illustration and defence. In the second century, Justin Martyr, though far indeed from affirming that Christ was "God over all," maintained that he was "another god," the Logos of the Supreme. In the Dialogue which he represents himself as having held with an unbelieving Jew, Trypho, in defence of Christianity, he brings forward views and arguments similar to those in the Epistle to the Romans; but in addition to these we find a new topic, the deity of Christ, occupying a great part of the discussion.

If the doctrine had been maintained by St. Paul, as it was by Justin, one would think that, in answering the objections of the Jews, it would have been as necessary for the Apostle, as for Justin, to explain and defend it. The sentiments of the Jews concerning it, which undoubtedly would have been as strong in the time of St. Paul as they were a century later, appear from the words which Justin ascribes to Trypho: "You undertake to prove an incredible and almost impossible thing, — that a god submitted to be born and to become a man." * "As for what you say, that this Christ existed as a god before time was, and afterwards becoming a man, submitted to be born, and that he was born out of the common course of nature, it seems to me not only paradoxical, but foolish." † "All we [Jews]," says Trypho in another place, "expect that the Messiah will be a man born of human parents." ‡ The whole argument of St. Paul in opposition to the prejudices of the unbelieving Jews must have been incomplete and unsatisfactory, if he asserted this "incredible and almost impossible" doctrine in the clause of a sentence without attempting any vindication of its truth.

The passage has, I believe, no bearing whatever upon the doctrine which it has been adduced to prove. The fact is well known, that the present pointing of the New Testament is of no authority;

* Dial. cum Tryph., p. 283, ed. Thirlb. [c. 68. p. 292, D. ed. Morel.]
† Ibid., p. 233. [al. c. 48. p. 267, B.]
‡ Ibid., p. 235. [al. c. 49. p. 268, A.]

the more ancient manuscripts having been unpointed; and the points which we now find having been introduced by later transcribers and by editors. Let any one, then, turn to the passage in his Greek Testament, and put a dot at the top of the line (equivalent to a semicolon) after σάρκα instead of a comma, as at present, and a comma after πάντων, and he will perceive that the following meaning immediately results: "He who was over all was God blessed for ever."

"He who was over all," that is, over all which has just been mentioned by the Apostle. The rapidity of expression in the original, however, does not fully appear in such a rendering; because in our language we are obliged to supply the ellipsis of the substantive verb. It may be imitated, however, by employing the participle instead of the verb. Doing this, I will give what seems to me a more correct translation of the passage, and of its context, than that in the Common Version: —

"— My brothers, my natural kinsmen; who are Israelites, whose was the glory of being adopted as sons, whose were the covenants, and the Law, and the service of the temple, and the promises; whose were the fathers, and from among whom the Messiah was to be born; he who was over all being God blessed for ever. Amen."

This conclusion, as every one must perceive, is in the highest degree proper and natural. Among the privileges and distinctions of the Jews, it could not be forgotten by the Apostle, that God had presided over all their concerns in a particular manner. With regard to the ellipsis of the substantive verb, which we have supposed, nothing is more common. In the five verses, including the verse we are considering, between the 3d and 9th, it occurs at least six times.*

* The following texts, to which many others might be added, afford examples of a similar ambiguity of construction in the writings of St. Paul from the omission of the substantive verb: Romans viii. 33, 34; x. 12; 1 Cor. i. 26; 2 Cor. iii. 14 (μὴ ἀνακαλυπτόμενον for ἔστι γὰρ μὴ ἀνακαλυπτόμενον); 2 Cor. v. 5; Ephes. iv. 4 (comp. 5); Coloss. ii. 17.

[Considering the importance which has been attached to this passage, and the different explanations which have been given of it by distinguished scholars, a few additional remarks will perhaps be pardoned.

The *past* privileges of the Jews being referred to by the Apostle, Mr. Norton has used the past tense in supplying the ellipsis of the substantive verb. So Conybeare and Howson, in their recent work on St. Paul, with Locke, Taylor, Wakefield, our countryman Charles Thomson, Semler, Stolz, and other translators and commentators. The past tense of the verb should similarly be supplied in 1 Cor. xv. 47, 48, though the authors of the Common Version have improperly used the present. As the present participle denotes present time not absolutely, but relatively to the time of the leading verb of the sentence, or to the time, whatever it may be, which the writer has in mind, there can of course be no objection, if this view of the ellipsis is correct, to rendering ὁ ὢν ἐπὶ πάντων "he who was over all." (See John xii. 17, and Winer, Gram. des neutest. Sprachidioms, § 46. 6.) It has, indeed, been contended by some critics, as Noesselt and Flatt, that ὁ ὢν *must* refer to Χριστός as the antecedent, and be rendered "who is"; as if the article ὁ with ὢν or any other participle could not form the subject of an independent proposition. It can hardly be necessary to refer to such passages as John iii. 31, vi. 46, viii. 47, Rom. viii. 5, 8, etc., to prove a fact which belongs to the elements of Greek grammar.

In the first part of the fifth verse, Mr. Norton has translated ἐξ ὧν ὁ Χριστὸς τὸ κατὰ σάρκα, "from among whom the Messiah was to be

The passage was at an early period applied to Christ, particularly by the Latin Fathers. With the notions, however, of the earlier Christians, respecting the inferiority of the Son to the Father, the passage, when thus constructed, presented a difficulty as well as an argument. Hippolytus,*

born." The verbal rendering is, "from whom [was] the Messiah as to the flesh." It has been urged by many Trinitarians that the phrase "as to the flesh," which they would render "as to his human nature," implies that Christ possessed also a higher nature, namely, the divine; and that it is necessary to understand the last part of the verse as referring to him, to complete the antithesis. Let us examine these points. In the third verse of this chapter Paul speaks of his "kinsmen *as to the flesh*." Did Paul or his countrymen have also a divine nature? In 1 Cor. x. 18 we find the words, "Behold Israel *as to the flesh*"; or, to translate more freely, "Look at those who are Israelites by natural descent"; that is, in distinction from Christians, the spiritual Israel, the true people of God. See also Galatians iv. 23, 29, and compare the eighth verse of the present chapter. The phrase κατὰ σάρκα is a common one in the Epistles of St. Paul in reference to natural descent, or to other outward circumstances and relations, in distinction from what is spiritual. It certainly suggests an antithesis; but it does not follow that the antithesis must be *expressed*, as is manifest from the first two passages quoted above. It was not to the Apostle's purpose, in this enumeration of the peculiar distinctions of the Jews, to supply the antithesis. It was only "as to the flesh" that Christ belonged peculiarly to the Jews. This view is confirmed by a passage in the Epistle of Clement of Rome to the Corinthians, cited by Yates in his "Vindication of Unitarianism." Ἐξ αὐτοῦ γὰρ ἱερεῖς καὶ Λευῖται πάντες οἱ λειτουργοῦντες τῷ θυσιαστηρίῳ τοῦ Θεοῦ· ἐξ αὐτοῦ ὁ κύριος Ἰησοῦς τὸ κατὰ σάρκα· ἐξ αὐτοῦ βασιλεῖς καὶ ἄρχοντες καὶ ἡγούμενοι, κατὰ τὸν Ἰούδαν. "For from him [Jacob] were all the priests and Levites who served at the altar of God; from him was the Lord Jesus *as to the flesh;* from him were kings and rulers and leaders, in the line of Judah." (Cap. 32. Patr. Apost. Opp. ed. Hefele, p. 98, ed. tert.) If Clement,

* Contra Noëtum, § 6. Opp. I. 237.

or some writer under that name, explains it in reference to the declaration of Christ rendered in the Common Version, "All things are delivered unto me of my Father"; conceiving the dominion over all things not to have been essentially inherent in Christ as properly the Supreme God, but

in a passage so similar to the present, did not think it necessary to express the antithesis implied in τὸ κατὰ σάρκα, St. Paul may not have thought it necessary here.

In another place, however, the Apostle *has* supplied the antithesis suggested by the words in question; but there, instead of describing Christ as "God over all, blessed for ever," he clearly distinguishes him from God. See the beginning of this Epistle, where he speaks of himself as "set apart to preach the gospel of God," "the gospel concerning his Son, who was *of the race of David by natural descent* [verbally, *as to the flesh*], but clearly shown to be *the Son of God, as to his holy spirit*, by his resurrection from the dead." (I quote from the unpublished translation of Mr. Norton.) Though this passage has also been brought to prove the Son of God to be God himself, it does not appear to call for any remark, except perhaps this: that if any doctrine is unequivocally taught by St. Paul, it is, that the divine power displayed in the resurrection of Christ from the dead was not his own, but the power of God, the Father. See Acts xiii. 30-37; xvii. 31; Rom. iv. 24; vi. 4; viii. 11; x. 9; 1 Cor. vi. 14; xv. 15; 2 Cor. iv. 14; xiii. 4; Galat. i. 1; Ephes. i. 19, 20; Coloss. ii. 12; 1 Thess. i. 10.

But to return to our text. Among the examples of the ellipsis of the substantive verb referred to in Mr. Norton's note, we find one in which the construction is strikingly similar to that here supposed, as will be seen on placing the passages in juxtaposition: —

Romans ix. 5. ὁ ὢν ἐπὶ πάντων Θεός, εὐλογητός, κ. τ. λ.
2 Cor. v. 5. ὁ δὲ κατεργασάμενος ἡμᾶς εἰς αὐτὸ τοῦτο Θεός.

To this may be added,

2 Cor. i. 21. ὁ δὲ βεβαιῶν ἡμᾶς ..... καὶ χρίσας ἡμᾶς Θεός· and
Heb. iii. 4. ὁ δὲ πάντα κατασκευάσας Θεός.

The construction of the passage thus illustrated, though apparently first suggested by Mr. Norton, not only seems to be liable to no well-as assigned to him by the Father. It was, perhaps, understood in a similar manner by Novatian, who has twice quoted the passage,* but who clearly did not believe Christ to be the Supreme Being. Tertullian says: "We never speak of two Gods or two Lords, but, following the Apostle, if the

grounded philological objection, but agrees admirably with the rapid, earnest style of the Apostle Paul. The ellipsis of the substantive verb when Θεός forms the predicate of the sentence, is certainly in accordance with his usual manner.

There is another method, however, of understanding the passage, proposed by Erasmus, and since adopted by many distinguished scholars, according to which the last part of the sentence in question forms a doxology, a period or colon being placed after σάρκα, as by Mr. Norton. It may be observed, that, although in a question of punctuation manuscripts are of no authority, we actually find a point placed after σάρκα in this passage in several Greek manuscripts, among them the celebrated Codex Ephræmi. This punctuation is also followed by two of the most eminent critical editors, Lachmann and Tischendorf. The words may then be rendered, "He who is over all (or, He who was over all), God, be blessed for ever!" or, "God, who is over all, be blessed for ever! Amen." This construction is adopted by Whiston, Semler, Böhme, Paulus, Reiche, Glöckler, Winzer, Köllner, Meyer, Fritzsche, Rückert (in his second edition, though strongly opposing it in his first), Schrader, and Krehl. (Many of these names are given on the authority of Meyer and De Wette.)

It has been very confidently asserted by Stuart and others, that this construction is forbidden by the laws of grammar, and wholly inadmissible, on the ground that, in forms of doxology in the New Testament and the Septuagint, the word εὐλογητός always *precedes* the subject, as we commonly say in English, "Blessed be God!" and not, "God be blessed!" The answer to this is, in the first place, that the usage referred to is not invariable in the Septuagint. In Psalm lxvii. 20 (al. lxviii. 19), in the first instance in which it occurs the subject precedes: Κύριος ὁ Θεὸς εὐλογητός, εὐλογητὸς Κύριος

* [De Trinitate, cc. 13, 30.]

Father and Son are to be named together, we call the Father, God, and Jesus Christ, Lord." "But when speaking of Christ alone, I may call him God, as does the same Apostle: *Of whom is Christ, who is God over all blessed for ever.* For speaking of a ray of the sun by itself, I may call it the sun;

ἡμέραν καθ' ἡμέραν. See also Genesis xxvii. 29, ὁ καταρώμενός σε ἐπικατάρατος, ὁ δὲ εὐλογῶν σε εὐλογημένος, "Cursed be he that curseth thee, and blessed be he that blesseth thee." Attempts have indeed been made to get rid of the passage in Psalm lxvii., by asserting that the reading is corrupt. But for this there is no critical authority. See Holmes and Parsons's edition of the Septuagint. All that can be said is, that the Septuagint here, as often elsewhere, does not literally correspond with the Hebrew, which in this passage the translator probably misunderstood.—In the second place, the question whether the predicate or subject shall precede in Greek is determined, not by any arbitrary rule, but by the comparative emphasis which the writer intends to give the one or the other, and by its connection with other words in the sentence. To write in Greek, εὐλογητὸς ὁ Θεὸς ὁ ὢν ἐπὶ πάντων εἰς τοὺς αἰῶνας, as Koppe and others assert would be necessary if Paul had intended to close the sentence with a doxology, would be as unnatural as to say in English, "Blessed be God who is over all for ever," to say nothing of the ambiguity thus created. On a grammatical point like this there is no higher authority than Winer, who, after mentioning the fact that in the doxologies of the Old Testament the predicate usually precedes, goes on to remark: "But only empirical interpreters could regard this position as an unalterable rule; for where the subject forms the leading idea, particularly where it stands in contrast with another subject, the predicate may and will be placed after it, comp. Ps. lxvii. 20. And so also in Romans ix. 5, if the words ὁ ὢν ἐπὶ πάντων Θεὸς εὐλογητός, etc. are referred to God, the position of the words is altogether suitable, and even necessary." (Gram. des neutest. Sprachidioms, § 65. 3, p. 636, 5te Aufl.) The Trinitarian Olshausen also says: "Rückert's remark, that εὐλογητός, when applied to God, must, according to the idiom of the Old and New Testament, always precede, is of no importance. Köllner rightly observes, that the position of the words is altogether [everywhere] not a mechanical thing,

but when I mention at the same time the sun, from which this ray proceeds, I do not then give that name to the latter." *

But it is to be observed that some of the earlier Fathers, especially the Greek Fathers, expressly denied that Christ is "the God over all." This title was applied to him by the Sabellians, and was considered as a distinguishing mark of their

but is rather determined, in each particular conjuncture, by the connection, and by the mind of the speaker." (Comm. on Romans, p. 326, note, Engl. Transl. published in Clark's Foreign Theol. Libr.)

It may be mentioned that some critics, placing the colon or period after πάντων instead of σάρκα, refer the words "who is over all" to Christ, and make the remainder of the verse a doxology. So Locke, Wetstein, Oertel, Justi, Stolz, Ammon, Baumgarten-Crusius, and De Wette in his German translation (3d ed., 1839), though in his Commentary (4th ed., 1847) he appears more inclined to the construction just remarked upon. But this latter mode of understanding the passage seems to make the doxology too abrupt, and is exposed to other objections.

It is not the purpose of this note to discuss the question of the comparative merits of Mr. Norton's interpretation, and that which regards the words ὁ ὢν ἐπὶ πάντων, etc., as forming a doxology. It is enough if it has been shown that neither is open to any valid philological objection, and that the pretence that the "laws of grammar" require us to understand the latter part of the verse as referring to Christ is groundless. The impartial reader will place a proper estimate on the language of such writers as Haldane, who speaks of "the awful blindness and obstinacy of Arians and Socinians in their perversions of this passage" as "more fully manifesting the depravity of human nature, and the rooted enmity of the carnal mind against God, than the grossest works of the flesh." (Exposition of the Epistle to the Romans, Amer. reprint of the 5th Edinb. ed., p. 454.)]

* "Solum autem Christum potero deum dicere, sicut idem Apostolus, *Ex quibus Christus; qui est*, inquit, *deus super omnia, benedictus in ævum omne.* Nam et radium solis seorsum, solem vocabo; solem autem nominans cujus est radius, non statim et radium solem appellabo." — Advers. Praxeam, c. 13.

heresy. There is no one of the Fathers more eminent than Origen. "Supposing," says Origen in his work against Celsus, "that some among the multitude of believers, likely as they are to have differences of opinion, rashly suppose that the Saviour is the God over all; yet we do not, for we believe him when he said, 'The Father who sent me is greater than I.'"* Even after the Nicene Council, Eusebius, in writing against Marcellus, says: "As Marcellus thinks, He who was born of the holy virgin, and clothed in flesh, who dwelt among men, and suffered what had been foretold, and died for our sins, was the very God over all; for daring to say which, the church of God numbered Sabellius among atheists and blasphemers." † Now it is incredible that the text in question should have been overlooked. But the early Fathers, in making these, and a multitude of other similar declarations, concerning the inferiority of the Son to the Father, never advert to it. It evidently follows from this, that they had not the same conception as modern Trinitarians have of the meaning of the passage. They had read the words of the Apostle in which he speaks of "the God and Father of our Lord Jesus Christ, who is

* Origen. cont. Cels., Lib. VIII. § 14. Opp. I. 752.

† Euseb. Eccles. Theol., Lib. II. c. 4. This, and the passage from Origen, are given by Wetstein in his critical remarks on the text, with other authorities to the same purpose. See also Whitby, Disquisitiones Modestæ, *passim*, but particularly pp. 26, 27, p. 122, and p. 197, ed. secund.—For placing a period after σάρκα, Griesbach quotes the authority of "many Fathers who denied that Christ could be called 'the God over all.'"

blessed for evermore";* and the mystery of the Trinity being as yet but ill understood, they had not made such an advance in Orthodoxy as to believe that Jesus Christ was the same being as his God and Father.

We pass to Hebrews i. 10–12. It is unnecessary to give the words at length. This passage belongs to the present class. The words were originally addressed by the Psalmist (Psalm cii. 25) not to Christ, but to God, and are so addressed by the author of the Epistle.†

* 2 Cor. xi. 31.

† The following are the remarks of Emlyn: — "Here we may observe, that the tenth verse, *And thou Lord*, &c., (though it is a new citation,) is not prefaced with, *And to the Son he saith*, as ver. 8, or with an *again*, as ver. 5, 6, and so chap. ii. 13, but barely, *And thou Lord.* Now the God last mentioned was Christ's God, who had anointed him; and the author thereupon, addressing himself to this God, breaks out into the celebration of his power, and especially his unchangeable duration; which he dwells upon, as what he principally cites the text for; in order, I conceive, to prove the stability of the Son's kingdom, before spoken of: *Thy throne, O God, is for ever and ever; God, thy God, has anointed thee; and thou, Lord,* i. e. thou who hast promised him such a throne, *art he who laid the foundation of the earth,* and *by thy hands* made the heavens, which, though of long and permanent duration, yet will at length perish; *but thou remainest, thou art the same, thy years shall not fail.* So that it seems to be a declaration of God's immutability made here, to ascertain the durableness of Christ's kingdom, before mentioned; and the rather so, because this passage had been used originally for the same purpose in the 102d Psalm, viz. to infer thence this conclusion, ver. ult.: *The children of thy servants shall continue, and their seed be established before thee.* In like manner it here proves the *Son's* throne should be established *for ever and ever*, by the same argument, viz. by God's immutability; and so was very pertinently alleged of God, without being applied to the Son; to show how able *his God*, who had anoint-

CLASS IV.

Passages that might be considered as referring to the doctrine of the Trinity, supposing it capable of proof and proved, but which in themselves present no appearance of any proof or intimation of it.

Such is the case with some of those urged with the most confidence; as the form of baptism recorded in Matthew (xxviii. 19), and thus rendered in the Common Version: —

"Go ye therefore, and teach all nations, baptizing them in the name of the Father, and of the Son, and of the Holy Ghost."

Here, as in many other passages, the error and obscurity of the version have favored the imposition of a sense upon the passage which the original does not suggest. "To baptize *in the name* of another" is to baptize by authority from him, as his representative. But this every scholar knows is not the sense of our Saviour's direction. The Greek word rendered "name" is in this passage, as often in the Scriptures, redundant. It is used pleonastically, by an idiom of the Hebraistic Greek, in which

ed him, was to make good and maintain what he had granted him, viz. a durable kingdom *for ever*." — *Emlyn's Examination of Dr. Bennet's New Theory of the Trinity.* Works, Vol. II. pp. 340, 341. London, 1746.

Beside the purpose pointed out by Emlyn, the author of the Epistle may have had another in view, which was to declare, that while the throne of Christ, being upheld by God, should endure for ever, the heavens, the local habitation, as they were considered, of angels, should, on the contrary, perish, be rolled up as a garment and changed.

the Septuagint and New Testament are written. We have not the same turn of expression in our own language. In the original, it adds nothing to the sense of the passage. When literally rendered into another language in which the same idiom does not exist, it tends only to obscure the meaning. It should not therefore appear in a translation into English.

But even if the term "name" be retained, there is no ground for the rendering, "baptizing them *in* the name." The Greek preposition εἰς should here be rendered *to*. The whole passage may be thus translated: —

"Go ye, therefore, and make disciples of all nations; baptizing them to the Father, and to the Son, and to the holy spirit."

The meaning of which is, Go and make converts of men of all nations, dedicating them by baptism, through which they are to make a solemn public profession of their faith, to the worship of the Father, the only true God, to the religion which he has taught men by his Son, and to the enjoyment of those holy influences and spiritual blessings which accompany its reception.

One may easily understand how this passage has appeared to Trinitarians to convey so clear a notice of the Trinity, since they have adopted its terms as technical in their theology, and imposed upon them new and arbitrary senses, which have become strongly associated with the words, Father, Son, and Holy Ghost. But he who contends that any proof of the doctrine is to be derived from it, must proceed altogether upon assumptions obviously false. Let us state them clearly.

In the first place, to prove the personality of the holy spirit from this passage, it must either be assumed, —

That when three objects are mentioned together in a sentence, and two of them are persons, the third must be a person also;* that is, the Father and Son being persons, the holy spirit must be a person also:

Or, the personality and deity of the holy spirit, and the deity of the Son, may all be rested upon the assumption, —

That baptism was a rite of such a character, that to be baptized "in the name of," or "to the name of," or "to" any person or object, necessarily implies, that such person or object possesses the character of God: †

Or, it may be assumed, —

That when three persons or objects are thus

* [As to the tenableness of this assumption, see 1 Samuel xxv. 32, 33: "Blessed be the LORD God of Israel, who sent thee this day to meet me; and *blessed be thy advice;* and blessed be thou." Acts xx. 32: "I commend you to God, and *to the word of his grace,* which is able to build you up, and to give you an inheritance among all them which are sanctified." Tobit xi. 13: "Blessed art thou, O God, and *blessed is thy name* for ever; and blessed are all thine holy angels." See also Psalm lxxii. 18, 19; cv. 4; Hosea iii. 5; Ephesians vi. 10.]

† [See 1 Corinthians x. 2: The Israelites "were all baptized *unto Moses* in the cloud and in the sea." Ch. i. 13: "Were ye baptized *in the name of Paul?*" Romans vi. 3: "Know ye not, that so many of us as were baptized into Jesus Christ were baptized *into his death?*" See also Matthew iii. 11; 1 Corinthians xii. 13.]

mentioned together, they must all be of equal dignity;* so that, in the present case, the Father being God, the same character must also belong to the Son and holy spirit.

These are the only grounds on which the deity of the Son and of the holy spirit can be inferred from the passage before us. But at this point of the reasoning, if we have arrived at any doctrine, it is the doctrine of the existence of three Gods. In order, therefore, to conclude the proof of the Trinity from this passage, it is necessary further to assume, —

That when three persons are thus mentioned together in a sentence, they must be regarded as constituting but one Being.

UNDER this head may be explained the title "SON OF GOD" as applied to Christ; on which I have before had occasion to remark.† The Trinitarian supposes it to be evidence of the deity of Christ; because as the son of a man has the nature of a man, so the Son of God must have a divine nature.

* [See 1 Timothy v. 21: "I charge thee before God, and the Lord Jesus Christ, and *the elect angels*." Revelation i. 4, 5: "Grace be unto you and peace from Him who is, and was, and will be; and *from the seven spirits which are before his throne;* and from Jesus Christ, the faithful witness." 1 Chronicles xxix. 20: "And all the congregation ..... bowed down their heads, and worshipped the LORD *and the king*." See also Luke ix. 26; Exod. xiv. 31; 1 Samuel xii. 18; Prov. xxiv. 21; Acts xv. 28; and the passages quoted in the first note on the preceding page.]

† See p. 68.

If the doctrine of the deity of Christ involved no absurdity, the title in question might, without doubt, be used according to the analogy supposed; but the proof of the doctrine must still be derived from other sources. No evidence of it could be drawn from this title alone; because the title is one in common use, and its significancy in every other application of it is wholly different from the meaning ascribed to it by Trinitarians when applied to Christ. For this entire difference, they must necessarily contend; and in doing so virtually acknowledge that there is no usage to justify them in understanding the title in the sense which they assign to it, and consequently that no inference can be drawn from this title alone in proof of the deity of Christ.

Nor is there any difficulty in explaining its application to our Saviour. The author of the Epistle to the Hebrews (i. 5) quotes the words which God in the Old Testament is represented to have used concerning Solomon, as applicable to Christ: "I will be to him a father, and he shall be to me a son." * By these words was meant, that God would distinguish Solomon with peculiar favors; would treat him as a father treats a son; and they are to be understood in a similar manner when applied to Christ. "We

* [2 Samuel vii. 14; compare 1 Chronicles xvii. 13; xxviii. 6. The same term is applied to the Israelites collectively, as the chosen people of God. See Exodus iv. 22, "Israel is my son, my first-born"; and Hosea xi. 1, "When Israel was a child, I loved him, and called my son out of Egypt."]

beheld," says St. John in his Gospel (i. 14), "his glory, glory like that of an only son from a father";* that is, we beheld the glorious powers and offices conferred upon him, by which he was distinguished from all others, as an only son is distinguished by his father. It is in reference to this analogy, and probably, I think, to this very passage in his Gospel, that St. John elsewhere calls Christ "the only Son of God," a title applied to him by no other writer of the New Testament.†

But the title was also familiarly used to denote those qualities which recommend moral beings to the favor of God; those which bear such a likeness to his moral attributes as may be compared with the likeness which a son has to his father; those which constitute one, in the Oriental style, to be of the family of God. Thus our Saviour exhorts his disciples to do good to their enemies, that they may be "sons of their Father in heaven." ‡ Nor is this use of the term confined to the Scriptures. Philo urges him who is "not yet worthy to

* Ἐθεασάμεθα τὴν δόξαν αὐτοῦ, δόξαν ὡς μονογενοῦς παρὰ πατρός. These words should not be rendered, as in the Common Version, "We beheld his glory, the glory as of the only begotten of the Father." To justify this rendering, both *μονογενοῦς* and *πατρός* should have the article.

† There is a doubt whether the words, John iii. 16–21, in which this title occurs, are to be considered as the language of Christ or of the Evangelist. If St. John intended to ascribe them to Christ, he has probably clothed the ideas of his Master in his own language; and we may so account for the use of a title in this passage, which Christ never elsewhere applies to himself.

‡ Υἱοὶ τοῦ πατρὸς ὑμῶν, Matthew v. 45; compare Luke vi. 35.

be called a son of God," to aim at higher excellence.*

In reference to both these analogies, the term was pre-eminently applicable to Christ; and he was therefore called by others, and by himself, "THE Son of God," the article being used, as often, to denote pre-eminence.†

THERE are two subjects, that of Prayer to Christ, and that of the Pre-existence of Christ, each involving the consideration of several particular passages, which may properly be treated under the present head. I will first speak

Of Prayer to Christ.

IT has been maintained that Christ is God, for the supposed reason that prayers were addressed to him by the first Christians. But the fact, if admitted, would afford no support for this conclusion.

* De Confusione Linguarum. Opp. I. 427, ed. Mang. — *Διὰ τὴν ὁμοιότητα υἱοὶ ἐκείνου εἶναι λογισθέντες*, "through likeness to God accounted to be his sons," is an expression in the Clementine Homilies, X. § 6.

† The words ascribed (Luke i. 32) to the angel who foretold to Mary the birth of Christ, are sometimes quoted as explanatory of the title "Son of God," with reference to his miraculous conception. I believe, however, these words to mean: "He shall be great; and he shall be [*not* shall be called] a son of the Most High"; *καλεῖσθαι* being equivalent to *εἶναι*, as in other passages. We find the same expression in Psalm lxxxii. 6. In verse 35, *διό*, rendered in the Common Version "therefore," may be understood as meaning, "whence it may be inferred," "conformably to which," "so that."

[It may be remarked, that our Saviour himself has expressly stated the ground which justified him in calling himself "the Son of God." See John x. 36.]

To pray is to ask a favor. In a religious sense, it is to ask a favor of an invisible and superior being. There is nothing in the nature of prayer which renders it improper to be addressed to a being inferior to God. Whether such address be proper or not, must depend upon other considerations. In itself considered, there would be nothing more inconsistent with the great principles of natural religion in our asking a favor of an invisible being, an angel, or a glorified spirit, than in our asking a favor of a fellow-mortal. For anything we can perceive, God might have committed the immediate government of our world, of this little particle of the universe, or the immediate superintendence of the Christian church, to some inferior minister of his power. Such a being might thus have become an object of prayer. Nay, in consistency with all that we know of the character of God, there might have been an intercourse, very different from what now exists, between the visible and the invisible world. The spirits of our departed friends might have become our guardian angels, with power to confer benefits and to answer our petitions. Prayers then might have been addressed to them. If, therefore, it were to appear that God has revealed to us that Christ is an object of prayer, as was believed by Socinus and his followers, this would afford no reason for concluding that Christ is God. What follows respecting prayer to Christ is, consequently, a mere digression; but a digression on a topic so important that it needs no excuse.

Those, at the present day, who reject the doctrine of the Trinity, believe that God * is the only object of prayer. To him alone they believe that Christ taught his followers to pray, by his precepts and example. He nowhere enjoined prayer to himself. And though the subject of prayer, viewed in the abstract, may appear under the aspect just presented; yet, regarded in relation to the actual character and condition of man, we may perceive the goodness of that appointment of God which teaches us to direct our prayers to him alone. We may understand the privilege of raising our undivided thoughts to our God and Father, and reposing our whole trust in him. Man is thus brought into an intimate connection with his Maker, which could hardly have otherwise existed.

Of the passages in the New Testament which have been supposed to favor the doctrine of prayer to Christ, the first that may be noticed is his own declaration to his disciples: "Again, I say to you, If two of you agree on earth concerning everything which they ask, their prayers will be granted by my Father in heaven. For where two or three come together as my disciples, there am I in the midst of them." † By the latter words our Saviour

* To a Trinitarian, I may say that I use the term "God" to denote "the God and Father of our Lord Jesus Christ."

† Matthew xviii. 19, 20: "Concerning *everything* which they ask," περὶ παντὸς πράγματος; not, "concerning *anything*," as in the Common Version. The object of Christ, in the discourse from which the words are taken, was to inculcate upon his disciples perfect concord among themselves, and an entire unity of feeling and purpose as ministers of his religion. The reference is to those prayers which

did not mean to affirm, that he would be present with them to hear their prayers, which would be inconsistent with the words preceding, in which he refers them to his Father in heaven, as him who would grant their requests. His purpose was to declare, that the designs, labors, and prayers in which his followers might unite for the promotion of his cause, would be equally blessed with his own. It would be as if he were praying with them. They might feel the same confidence that his actual presence would inspire.

Another passage commonly adduced in relation to this topic has, I think, no bearing upon it. It is the address of Stephen to Christ at his martyrdom.* Upon this occasion Christ is represented as having been visibly present to Stephen. The prayer of the martyr, therefore, that he would receive his spirit, or, in other words, that he would receive him to himself, is of no force to prove that it is proper to offer prayers to Christ as an invisible being. We might with as much propriety adduce in support of this proposition the requests which were addressed to him when conversant among men, — those, for instance, in which his miraculous aid was implored. There is no evidence that the last words of Stephen, in which he prayed for his murderers, were addressed to Christ.

St. Paul, in his Second Epistle to the Corinthians (xii. 8), speaking of "the thorn in his flesh,"

they might offer as his ministers, and in which they might all accord.

* Acts vii. 59.

says that he thrice besought the Lord, meaning, I think, Christ, that he might be relieved from it. Immediately before, he speaks of the extraordinary nature of the revelations that had been granted him. He was converted by the personal interposition of Christ. He himself mentions a subsequent period when Christ was present with him, and directed his conduct.* Considering the peculiar miraculous intercourse subsisting between him and our Lord, his addressing a request to him cannot be considered as affording any example or authority for prayer to Christ under ordinary circumstances. The request of Paul may have been offered when he had a miraculous sense or perception of his Master's presence.

We have indeed sufficient ground for believing, generally, that after our Saviour's removal from earth there still continued a peculiar connection between him and his Apostles and first followers; that he exercised a *miraculous* superintendence over their concerns, and held *miraculous* intercourse with them. Of the nature and extent of this connection the Apostles were probably ignorant, having never been enlightened on the subject by express revelation. The facts with which we know them to have been acquainted are sufficient to account for their expressions concerning it, in the very few passages that may be supposed to relate to it.

Among these may, perhaps, be reckoned the passages in which St. Paul expresses his wish, that

* Acts xxii. 17, seqq. [See also Acts xix. 9, 10; xxiii. 11; Galatians i. 1, 11, 12.]

the "favor of Christ" may be with those whom he addresses. But it seems to me most probable, that by the favor of Christ the Apostle means principally, if not solely, that favor, those blessings, of which Christ was the minister to man.

The only other passages of importance in which prayer is supposed to be addressed to Christ by a writer of the New Testament, are the following:—

1 Thess. iii. 11, 12. "May our God and Father himself, and our Lord Jesus Christ, direct our way toward you; and may the Lord make you increase and abound in your love toward each other and toward all, as we do toward you."

2 Thess. ii. 16, 17. "May our Lord Jesus Christ himself, and our God and Father who has loved us, and has, through his favor, given us everlasting encouragement and good hope, encourage your hearts and confirm you in every good word and work."

In the former of these passages, we find St. Paul expressing a wish that Christ under God might direct his way to the Thessalonians. It may be explained by the fact of that peculiar and miraculous superintendence over his preaching which was exercised by his Master. We know that he had first preached to the Thessalonians in consequence of a miraculous direction.* In the latter passage,

* "But Paul and Silas having passed through Phrygia and Galatia, and being restrained by the holy spirit from preaching the religion in Asia, came to Mysia, and were preparing to go to Bithynia; but the spirit of Jesus did not permit them. So, passing through Mysia, they went down to Troas. And a vision appeared by night to Paul. A certain man, a Macedonian, was standing by him and entreating him, saying, Pass over to Macedonia and help us. Then,

in his wishes that the Thessalonians might enjoy spiritual blessings from Christ, he may probably refer to the blessings flowing from the gospel which Christ taught. The effects of the gospel are ascribed to its great teacher; and sometimes, in the figurative style of the New Testament, with a turn of expression which, according to our more restrained use of language, might imply an immediate agency in their production which was not intended by the writer. If, however, the Apostle had in view, not the power of the gospel, but a present agency of Christ, we must consider his language as founded upon the conception which he entertained of Christ's extraordinary agency over the concerns of the first Christians.

This agency, as I have said, was miraculous. We have no reason to believe in its continuance after the Apostolic age. A connection of the same nature, a miraculous connection between Christ and his followers, does not exist at the present day; nor have we any ground for believing that God has committed to him a superintendence of their concerns. Though it should, therefore, appear, that, in consequence of the extraordinary and peculiar relation subsisting between Christ and the first Christians, he was, under certain circumstances and conditions, regarded by his Apostles as one to whom requests might be addressed; yet, upon the ceasing of that relation, no reason

immediately after this vision, we endeavored to go to Macedonia, concluding that the Lord [Christ] had directed us to preach the Gospel to them." Acts xvi. 6 – 10.

would remain for his being regarded by common Christians as an object of prayer.

But it has been contended that the first Christians, generally, were accustomed to offer prayers to Christ. This belief is founded upon a few passages in which Christians, according to the rendering of the Common Version, are represented as "calling upon his name." Thus, Acts ix. 14, "He [Saul] hath authority to bind all that call on thy name"; — the address of Ananias to Saul, Acts xxii. 16, "And now why tarriest thou? arise and be baptized, and wash away thy sins, calling on the name of the Lord"; — 1 Cor. i. 2, "To the church of God which is at Corinth, ... with all that in every place call upon the name of Jesus Christ, our Lord." Another passage to the same effect may be found in Acts ix. 21.

The expression in the original, rendered "*to call on the name of*," is one often used in the Septuagint in relation to God, where direct address in prayer to him is intended. But its meaning varies, I believe, when used concerning a different being.

In this, as in many other cases, the term rendered "name" is pleonastic, and should be omitted in a translation. This being premised, it may next be remarked, that the Greek verb ἐπικαλεῖσθαι, rendered "to call upon," does not properly and directly denote religious invocation. In its primary sense, it signifies "to call" or "to call upon" any one; in a secondary meaning, "to call on one for help." By a very easy extension of this meaning, it denotes, I believe, "to look to one for help," "to rely upon one for help, protection, deliverance," "to trust in one." In this use of it, no verbal address is implied; the word is used metaphorically. It literally denotes "calling for help"; it is used to express the state of mind in which we trust in another for help. In this sense, I think, the word ought to be understood, when used concerning Christ. The meaning of the terms rendered "calling on the name of Christ," would, I believe, be properly and fully expressed in English by the words, "looking to Christ for deliverance," that is, through the power of the gospel.

But, it may be asked, why, when the words in question have a meaning in which they are often used in the Septuagint, and according to which they would describe Christians generally as invoking, that is, praying to, Christ, should this meaning be set aside? I repeat what I have said, that the verb ἐπικαλεῖσθαι does not properly and directly denote religious invocation; and that, its object being changed, there is nothing improbable in the supposition that the signification of the verb is changed also. I answer further, that there seem to be insuperable objections to the belief that prayer was offered to Christ by the first Christians. His followers were not commanded by our Saviour to pray to him. Without such a command, they could not have supposed that he whom they had known habitually to offer prayers to his Father and our Father, was himself an object of prayer. Our Saviour referred his Apostles from himself to God, as the invisible being to whom their requests were to be addressed when he should be taken from them,—as the only proper object of prayer: "Then you will have no need to question me.* Truly, truly I tell you, Whatever you may ask the Father in my name, he will grant you."† Conformably to this, we find no precept enjoining prayer to Christ in their writings. But whether Christians were or were not to pray to Christ, could not have been a matter of indifference. It was either to be done, or it was not to be done. If a duty, it differed from other duties, in the circumstance that it must have been founded solely upon revelation and an express command. At the same time, if Christians were to have two objects of prayer, peculiar directions, explanations, and cautions must have been necessary. But nothing appears in the New Testament answering to the suppositions which have been made. There is an entire want of that evidence of the fact which must have existed, if prayer to Christ had been commanded by himself and his Apostles. But if not so commanded, it was not practised by the first Christians. The case was the same with them as with us; if it be not a duty to pray to Christ, it is a duty not to pray to him.

[See John xvi. 17 – 19.]

† John xvi. 23. The words ἐν ἐκείνῃ τῇ ἡμέρᾳ, rendered [in the Common Version] "in that day," are merely equivalent to the adverb "then." The time intended is that following our Saviour's ascension, when, in figurative language, he says that he shall be with his Apostles again, not referring to his personal presence, but to his presence with them in the power and blessings of his gospel, and in the aid afforded them by God as his ministers.

It appears, therefore, from the New Testament, that the first Christians did not offer prayers to Christ. But there is still other evidence of this truth, to which, though of less importance, it may be worth while to advert.

It has been urged that Pliny, in his celebrated letter to Trajan,* states (on the authority of some who said that they had been Christians, but who had deserted the religion) that Christians in their assemblies were "accustomed to sing together a hymn in alternate parts to Christ as to a god," — "carmen Christo, quasi deo, dicere secum invicem."

These words have been alleged to prove, both that Christians prayed to Christ, and that they believed him to be God. But the only fact which appears is, that Christians sung hymns in celebration of Christ. The rest is the interpretation of a heathen, who compared in his own mind these hymns to those which the heathens sung in honor of their gods, who like Christ had dwelt on the earth, and like him, having died, were supposed to be still living in a higher state of being. With his heathen notions, he conceived of the Christians as making a sort of apotheosis of their Master. But there is evidence on the subject before us much more direct and more important than that of Pliny.

It is the evidence of Origen, who wrote a treatise "On Prayer" in the former half of the third century. Of prayer, properly speaking, Origen says: —

* [Plinii Epist. Lib. X. Ep. 96 (al. 97).]

"If we understand what prayer is, it will appear that it is never to be offered to any originated being, not to Christ himself, but only to the God and Father of all; to whom our Saviour himself prayed, and taught us to pray. For when his disciples asked him, *Teach us to pray*, he did not teach them to pray to himself, but to the Father. ..... Conformably to what he said, *Why callest thou me good? there is none good except one, God the Father*, how could he say otherwise than, 'Why dost thou pray to me? Prayer, as you learn from the Holy Scriptures, is to be offered to the Father only, to whom I myself pray.' ..... 'You have read the words which I spoke by David to the Father concerning you; *I will declare thy name to my brethren; in the midst of the assembly will I sing hymns to thee.* It is not consistent with reason for those to pray to a brother, who are esteemed worthy of one Father with him. You, with me and through me, are to address your prayers to the Father alone.' ..... Let us then, attending to what was said by Jesus, and all having the same mind, pray to God through him, without any division respecting the mode of prayer. But are we not divided, if some pray to the Father and some to the Son? Those who pray to the Son, whether they do or do not pray to the Father also, fall into a gross error, in their great simplicity, through want of judgment and examination."*

* De Oratione, cc. 25, 26. Opp. I. pp. 222-224. I quote the last passage principally because it is erroneously rendered by Dr. Priestley (History of Early Opinions, II. 161) in a manner directly adverse to his own argument.

In learning and talents, Origen, during his lifetime, had no rival among Christians. There was none who possessed the same weight of character. The opinions which he expresses in the passages just quoted were undoubtedly the common opinions of the Christians of his time.

Origen himself, indeed, in other passages, asserts or implies that prayer in an inferior sense may be addressed to the Logos or Christ. In his work against Celsus, he says, for instance: "Every supplication, prayer, request, and thanksgiving is to be addressed to Him who is God over all, through the High-Priest, superior to all angels, the living and divine Logos. But we shall also supplicate the Logos himself, and make requests to him, and give thanks and pray, whenever we may be able to distinguish between prayer properly speaking and prayer in a looser sense." * Probably what is here meant may appear from two other passages, in his work against Celsus, in which he says: "We first bring our prayers to the only Son of God, the First-born of the whole creation, the Logos of God, and pray to him and request him, as a High-Priest, to offer up the prayers which reach him to the God over all, to his God and our God." † It is, indeed, most likely that the doctrine of Origen concerning the propriety of offering prayers, in any sense of the term, to the Logos or Christ, had its

* Cont. Cels. Lib. V. § 4. Opp. I. 580. — ἐὰν δυνώμεθα κατακούειν τῆς περὶ προσευχῆς κυριολεξίας καὶ καταχρήσεως.

† Ibid., Lib. VIII. § 13. p. 751, et § 26. p. 761. Compare, however, Lib. V. § 11, ad fin. p. 586. [See also Lib. III. c. 34. p. 469.]

origin rather in his own philosophical opinions, than in the belief and practice of the generality of Christians.

The Trinitarian supposes that the first Christians were taught to pray to Christ or the Son, as God equal to the Father, and that they were distinguished, by the circumstance of offering such prayers, as "those who called upon the name of the Lord." How is it possible to reconcile this supposition with the state of opinion and practice which we find among Christians during the time of Origen, the first half of the third century? The Antitrinitarian believes that the doctrine of the deity of Christ had been making gradual progress. When, therefore, he finds that, at the period just mentioned, Christ was still spoken of, by a writer so eminent as Origen, as not being an object of prayer properly so called, no doubt remains on his mind that he had never been so regarded at any preceding period, that he was not so represented by himself or his Apostles, nor so esteemed by the first Christians.

On the Pre-existence of Christ.

I WILL now turn to the passages which are supposed particularly to assert the pre-existence of Christ. If this doctrine were proved, it would afford no proof of his being God; but the prejudices in favor of the Trinitarian doctrine have, notwithstanding, been strengthened by a misunderstanding of the passages referred to. The figurative language in which several of them are expressed may, I think, be explained by the following considerations.

One of the main objections of the generality of the Jews to Christianity was its being a novelty, an innovation, subverting their former faith. The Pharisees said: "We are disciples of Moses. We know that God spoke to Moses; but as for this man, we know not whence he is."* The doctrine of Christ was in direct opposition to the popular religion of the Jews, which, though a religion of hypocrisy, formalities, superstition, and bigotry, they had identified in their own minds with the Law; — and the Law, their ancient Law, which for fifteen centuries, as they believed, had been their distinguishing glory, they looked upon as an immutable covenant made by God with his chosen people. Were the doctrines of Christ, they might ask, to be opposed to what they believed, and what their fathers had believed, upon the faith of God? Was a teacher of yesterday to be placed in competition with Moses and the Prophets? Was it to be supposed that God would change his purposes, alter the terms of their allegiance, and substitute a new religion for that which he had so solemnly sanctioned?

One mode of meeting these feelings and prejudices of the Jews was by the use of language adapted to their modes of conception, asserting or implying that the sending of Christ, and the establishment of his religion, had always been purposed

* John ix. 28, 29.

by God. This was done in part by figurative modes of speech, conformed to the Oriental style, and more or less similar to many which we find in the Old Testament. Facts connected with the introduction of Christianity were spoken of by Christ and his Apostles — according to the verbal meaning of their language — as having taken place before the world was; the purpose being to express in the most forcible manner, that their existence was to be referred immediately to God, and had from eternity been predetermined by him. What they meant to represent God as having foreordained, they described as actually existing.

Thus St. Paul says in his Epistle to the Romans (viii. 29, 30), "For those whom God foreknew, he predestined should be conformed to the image of his Son, that he might be the first-born among many brethren; and whom he predestined he summoned, and whom he summoned he made righteous, and whom he made righteous he glorified." I refer particularly to the last clause, in which God is spoken of as having already glorified the disciples of Christ, because it is certain that he will.*

Thus also in writing to the Ephesians (i. 3, 4): "Blessed be the God and Father of our Lord Jesus Christ, who, having exalted us to heaven, is blessing us with every spiritual blessing through Christ, he *having in his love chosen us through him before the foundation of the world.*"

To Timothy (2 Ep. i. 8, 9) he says: "Suffer to-

* Compare verses 17 – 25.

gether with me for the gospel, sustained by the power of God, who has delivered us, and summoned us by a sacred call, not in consequence of our works, but conformably to his own purpose, and *the favor bestowed upon us through Christ Jesus before time was.*"

So also to Titus (i. 1, 2): "Paul, a servant of God, and an Apostle of Jesus Christ, to preach the faith of the chosen of God, and to make known the truth which leads to the true worship of God, founded on the expectation of eternal life, which God who cannot deceive *promised before time was.*"

For other passages in which that which is purposed by God is figuratively spoken of as actually existing, see Exodus xv. 13, comp. 17; 1 Samuel xv. 28; Psalm cxxxix. 16; Isaiah xlix. 1; John x. 16; Acts xviii. 10; Galatians i. 15.

When Christianity, after having been preached to the Jews, was, if I may so speak, committed in trust to its Gentile converts, it had to encounter the same objection of its being a novel doctrine; and this objection was met in a similar manner, and by a similar use of language. In his "Exhortation to the Gentiles," Clement of Alexandria says: "Error is ancient, truth appears a novelty." Then, after mentioning some of those nations which made the most extravagant pretensions to antiquity, he adds: "But we [Christians] were before the foundation of the world; through the certainty of our future existence, previously existing in God himself." *

* Πρὸ δὲ τῆς τοῦ κόσμου καταβολῆς ἡμεῖς· οἱ τῷ δεῖν ἔσεσθαι,

We should hardly expect to find in the New Testament a critical explanation of any figurative mode of speech; but something very like such an explanation of that which we are considering is found in St. Paul, when his words are properly translated and understood.

In the book of Genesis (xvii. 4, 5) God is represented as saying to Abraham, "Behold, my covenant is with thee, and thou shalt be a father of many nations. Neither shall thy name any more be called Abram, but thy name shall be Abraham; for *a father of many nations have I made thee.*"

ἐν αὐτῷ πρότερον γεγεννημένοι τῷ Θεῷ, p. 6, ed. Potter. — Thus too in a book which in very early times was in considerable repute among Christians, "The Shepherd of Hermas," Hermas represents himself as being told by an angel in a vision, that "the Church was the first created of all things, and for her sake the world was made." (Lib. I. Vis. 2.)

We find the same figurative use of language in the writings of the later Jews. In the Talmud it is recorded that R. Eliezer said: "Seven things were created before the world; the Garden of Eden, the Law, the Righteous, the Israelites, the Throne of Glory, Jerusalem, and the Messiah, the Son of David." This, in the Book Cosri, is explained as meaning, that "they were prior in the intention of God"; they constituting the end for which the world was created; and the end being *in intention* precedent to the means. (Liber Cosri, ed. Buxtorf. p. 254.) Many similar passages are quoted or referred to by Schoettgen (Horæ Hebr., Tom. II. pp. 436, 437), among which are the following. Sohar Levit., fol. 14, col. 56: "Rabbi Hezekiah sat down in the presence of Eleazar, and asked, How many lights were created before the foundation of the world? He answered, Seven; the light of the Law, the light of Gehenna, the light of Paradise, the light of the Throne of Glory, the light of the Temple, the light of Repentance, and the light of the Messiah." In various other Rabbinical books cited by Schoettgen we find the same enumeration, except that the word "light" is omitted throughout, and "the *name* of the Messiah" is substituted for "the light of the Messiah." But in

Referring to this passage, St. Paul says, in his Epistle to the Romans (iv. 16, 17): "The promise was sure to all the offspring of Abraham, not to those under the Law only, but to those who have the faith of Abraham, who is the father of us all (as it is written, *I have made thee a father of many nations*) in the sight of God in whom he trusted,—of Him who restores life to the dead, and speaks of the things which are not, as though they were." In the view of the Apostle, God, as it were, restored life to the dead, in enabling Abraham and Sarah to have a son;* and, in calling Abraham

Bereshith Rabba, sect. 1, fol. 3, 3, there is a different statement:—"Six things preceded the creation of the world: some of these were created, as the Law and the Throne of Glory; others it was in the mind of God to create, namely, the Patriarchs, Israel, the Temple, and the name of the Messiah." In Midrash Tehillim, fol. 28, 2, it is said that the use of the word קֶדֶם in Psalm lxxiv. 2 "teaches us, that God created Israel before the foundation of the world." The same commentary elsewhere says, that "Repentance preceded the creation of the world"; and in Sohar Levit., fol. 29, col. 113, the following passage occurs: "Before God created the world, he created Repentance, and said to her, It is my will to create man in such a relation to thee, that, when he returns to thee from his transgressions, thou shalt be ready to forgive his transgressions, and to make expiation for them."

* That this was the meaning of the Apostle appears from the verses which immediately follow those quoted above: "For he [Abraham] had confident hope of that which was past hope, that he should be the father of many nations, according to the declaration, *Thus will thy offspring be.* And, not being weak in faith, he did not regard his own body then dead, he being about a hundred years old, nor the deadness of Sarah's womb; nor had he any doubt or mistrust about the promise of God."

Compare also Hebrews xi. 19, where, in reference to the birth of Isaac, Abraham is said to have received him, "figuratively speaking, from the dead."

the father of many nations, spoke of the things which were not, as though they were.

Using language in the manner which has been illustrated, our Saviour spoke, in his last prayer with his disciples, on the night before his death, of the glory which he had with God before the world was.

"When Jesus had thus spoken, he raised his eyes to heaven and said:—

"Father! the hour has come. Glorify thy Son, that thy Son may glorify thee,—through the power that thou hast granted him over all men, to give to all those whom thou hast given him eternal life. And this is eternal life, to know thee, the only true God, and Jesus Christ whom thou hast sent. I have glorified thee on earth. I have finished the work which thou gavest me to do. And now, Father! glorify thou me with thyself, with that glory which I had with thee before the world was." *

Afterwards, in speaking of his disciples, our Saviour says: "The glory which thou hast given me, I have given them"; † words implying that the glory which he had with the Father was such as might be conferred on men; and such as, by constituting them his Apostles, he had enabled them to attain.

"Father!" he continues, "I desire for those whom thou hast given me, that where I am they also may be with me, so that they may behold my

* John xvii. 1-5. † Ibid., verse 22.

glory, which thou gavest me, for thou didst love me before the foundation of the world." *

The character and purport of these expressions of Jesus are explained by what has been said. A principal object of our Saviour in the language of this prayer, as well as throughout the discourse which precedes it, was to strengthen the minds of his Apostles to meet that fearful trial of their faith which was close at hand, and to prepare them for their approaching separation from him. He uses, in consequence, the most forcible modes of speech, in order to produce the deepest impression. He desired, by the whole weight of his authority, by every feeling of affection and awe, by language the most pregnant and of the highest import, and by figures too strong and solemn ever to be forgotten, to make them feel his connection, and their own connection, with God. Their teacher, their master, their friend, was the special messenger of God, distinguished by his favor beyond all other men; and in this favor they shared, as his followers. He was, in the Oriental style, "one with God" in the work in which he had been engaged; and they, in like manner, were to be one with God and him. God had from eternity regarded him with love; and they were like objects of God's love.† They were hereafter to behold in heaven the consummate glory of him, who before the close of another day was to be exposed to the

* John xvii. 24.

† "—that the world may know that thou hast sent me, and hast loved them as thou hast loved me." John xvii. 23.

mockery of the Roman soldiers, to suffer the outrages of an infuriated mob, and to expire by a death as ignominious as it was cruel.

Having furnished the key to passages of this kind, of which there are not many, I will notice particularly but one other. John viii. 52, 53, 56–58: "The Jews said to Jesus, Now we are sure that you are possessed by a dæmon. Abraham died, and the Prophets; and you say, Whoever obeys my teaching will never taste of death. Are you greater than our father Abraham, who died? And the Prophets died. Whom do you make yourself to be? Jesus answered, ... Your father Abraham exulted that he might see my day; and he saw it, and rejoiced. Then the Jews said to him, You are not yet fifty years old; and have you seen Abraham? Jesus said to them, Truly, truly I tell you, Before Abraham was born, I was He."

The rendering of the Common Version, "Before Abraham was, I am," is without meaning, — the present tense, "I am," being connected with the mention of past time, "before Abraham was"; and this circumstance has doubtless assisted in producing the belief that the words express a mystery. But our Saviour says that Abraham saw his day, that is, the times of the Messiah. This declaration no one understands verbally, and there is as little reason for giving a verbal meaning to that under consideration. In the explanation of it two things are to be attended to.

In the first place, after the words ἐγὼ εἰμί, rendered in the Common Version, "I am," we must understand ὁ Χριστός, "the Messiah"; as is evident from two preceding passages in the same discourse. In verse 24, Jesus says, with the same ellipsis, "Unless you believe that *I am* [that is, *that I am the Messiah*], you will die in your sins"; and in verse 28 he tells the Jews, "When you have raised on high [crucified] the Son of Man, then you will know that *I am*," meaning, *that I am the Messiah*. The same ellipsis occurs repeatedly in the Gospels and Acts; as, for instance, in Mark xiii. 6 and Luke xxi. 8 we find the words, "Many will come in my name, saying *I am*"; while in Matthew xxiv. 5 the ellipsis is supplied, "Many will come in my name, saying, I am the Messiah." Other examples are referred to below.*

This apparently strange omission of the predicate of so important a proposition may, I think, be thus explained. The Messiah was expected by the Jews as one who, placing himself at the head of the nation, would deliver them from the tyranny under which they were suffering. Equally to Herod, the ruler of Galilee, and to the Roman procurator of Judæa, an individual, publicly announcing himself as the Messiah, must have appeared a daring rebel, exciting the nation to revolt. The subject was one about which the Jews must have communed together with the feelings of conspirators; and in discussing it, they would use imper-

* Acts xiii. 25 (comp. John iii. 28); John iv. 26; xiii. 19.

fect and ambiguous language, indicating, rather than expressing, their meaning. Even when danger was not feared, a certain degree of secrecy might be affected, and there might be a disposition to employ terms the full significance of which would be understood only by those who felt with the speaker. Upon the appearance of Jesus, the multitude being excited by his miracles and preaching, and the intimations concerning his character, the inquiry arose among them, whether he were the Messiah. The question was often asked, we may suppose, eagerly, but cautiously, "Is it he?" *Οὗτός ἐστι;* — not broadly and rashly, "Is he the Messiah?" and a corresponding answer returned, *'Εστί,* "He is," — *Οὐκ ἔστι,* "He is not." I have adverted to the dangerous nature of the subject, as connected with the purpose of revolt against the Roman power. The mere fact, however, of its being one of universal interest, on which the thoughts of men were strongly bent, may be alone sufficient to account for the use of abbreviated expressions to convey a meaning that every one was ready to apprehend. Still, the predicate of the proposition we are considering being suppressed, and the language, in consequence, being in itself wholly ambiguous, this manner of speaking might be adopted by Christ for the purpose of at once intimating his claims to be the Messiah, and leaving his meaning in some degree uncertain. Thus in the present discourse, when he tells the Jews (verse 24), "Unless you believe that *I am He*, you will die in your sins"; they ask in return,

"Who are you?" The use, therefore, of this mode of expression corresponded to that reserve as to openly and explicitly avowing himself to be the Messiah, which the expectations and feelings of the Jews compelled him to maintain till the closing scenes of his ministry.*

In the next place, the verb εἰμί is here to be understood as having the force of the perfect tense, that is, as denoting, literally or figuratively, a state of being, commenced at a distant time, and continued to the present. It is thus elsewhere used in St. John's Gospel. "Have I been [*verbally*, Am I] so long with you, and yet have you not known me, Philip?"† But such is our use of language, that this meaning is here to be expressed in English by the imperfect tense, "I was." If we should say, "Before Abraham was born, I have been," the idea of uninterrupted continuance of being to the present time is so far from being conveyed, that it is rather excluded.

The full meaning of Jesus, then, was this: Be-

* It may be objected to this account, that the Jews of Jerusalem are represented in the seventh chapter of John's Gospel as explicitly discussing the question, whether Jesus were or were not the Messiah. (See verses 26, 27, 31, 41, 42.) I answer, that it is not necessary to suppose that the caution of the Jews respecting the subject in question was *always* maintained. It might disappear in the heat of controversy, and it gave way, without doubt, to the excitement of strong feelings; as when the multitude wished to compel Jesus to place himself at their head, as their king (John vi. 15); and upon his triumphant entry into Jerusalem, just before his crucifixion. It is sufficient for the purpose of explaining our Saviour's language, if the mode of expression he adopted were common.

† John xiv. 9.

fore Abraham was born, I was the Messiah; that is, I was designated by God as the Messiah. The words cannot be understood verbally, because "the Messiah" was the title of one bearing an office which did not exist till it was assumed by Jesus on earth. Before Abraham, there was no Messiah except in the purpose of God. The language used by Christ is of the same figurative character with that which we find at the commencement of the prophecy of Jeremiah, as addressed to him by God (i. 5): "Before I formed thee in the womb, I knew thee; and before thou camest forth at thy birth, I sanctified thee, and I ordained thee a prophet to the nations."

We will now consider some passages of a different character. In his conversation with Nicodemus, our Saviour says (John iii. 12, 13): "If I tell you earthly things and you believe not, how will you believe should I tell you heavenly things? And no one has ascended to heaven, except him who has descended from heaven, the Son of Man, who is in heaven."

Heaven being considered by the Jews as the local habitation of the Deity, "to ascend to heaven" is here a figure used to denote the becoming acquainted with the purposes and will of God, with things invisible and spiritual, "heavenly things"; "to be in heaven" is to possess such acquaintance; and "to descend from heaven," or "to come from heaven," is to come from God.

In this sense the expression "to descend from heaven" is used by our Saviour in his discourse with the Jews, recorded in the sixth chapter of John's Gospel. The Jews, whom he had disappointed the day before in their attempt "to make him their king," or, in other words, to compel him to assume publicly the character of the Messiah, according to their conception of it, had now collected about him with very different feelings. They were disposed to disparage his miracles in comparison with those of Moses. He had fed five thousand men with a few loaves and fishes; but Moses, they said, quoting the Old Testament, "had given them," the Jews, "bread *from heaven* to eat."* In what follows, this expression is used figuratively by our Saviour, to denote that his doctrine came from God, or, to express the same idea in other words, that he himself came from God. It was usual for him to draw his figures from something which had just been said, or some present object or recent event. "Moses," he says, "gave you not the bread from heaven"; meaning that Moses had not given them a religion like his own, adapted to supply all their spiritual wants; "but my Father," he continues, "is giving you the true bread from heaven; for the bread of God is that which is now descending from heaven and giving life to the world."† By "the bread of God which gives life to the world," our Saviour here means his doctrines, his religion; and with this, by

* John vi. 31.

† Verses 32, 33.

an obvious figure, common in the New Testament, he afterwards identifies himself. "I am the bread of life; he who comes to me will never hunger, and he who has faith in me will never thirst."* "I have descended from heaven, not to do my own will, but the will of Him who sent me";† — that is, I who bring this religion from heaven have no other purpose but to perform the will of God.

The Jews, that is, some of the Jews, his enemies, carped, as usual, at his words. "Then the Jews murmured at him, because he said, I am the bread which has descended from heaven. And they said, Is not this man Jesus, the son of Joseph? one whose father and mother we know? What, then, does he mean by saying, I have descended from heaven?"‡ We have no reason to suppose that they understood him as meaning that he, being a man, had descended from heaven; or that he, being a pre-existent spirit, had assumed a human form. Their objection was to the absolute authority which this man, Jesus, the son, as they called him, of Joseph and Mary, claimed as the delegate of God. They had the same feeling as was shown by his fellow-townsmen of Nazareth, when they asked: "Is not this man the carpenter, the son of Mary, and kinsman of James and Joses and Judas and Simon?"§

In verse 62 of this chapter, there is a passage thus rendered in the Common Version: "What

* John vi. 35.

† Verse 38.

‡ Verses 41, 42.

§ Mark vi. 3.

and if ye shall see the Son of Man ascend up where he was before?" It has been thought to refer to his ascension to heaven, and to imply that he existed in heaven before his appearance on earth. In order to understand it, we must attend to its connection.

In the preceding part of the discourse, our Saviour had spoken of his religion as bread or food descending from heaven, and having figuratively identified himself with his religion, he describes this food as giving eternal life. "Truly, truly I tell you, He who puts his trust in me has eternal life. I am the bread of life; your fathers ate the manna in the desert and died; but if any one eat of this bread which is descending from heaven, he shall not die. I am the bread of life which has descended from heaven; if any one eat of this bread, he shall live for ever."* As food is the means of prolonging the natural life, so the religion of Christ was the means of enjoying eternal life. Metaphors of a similar kind, derived from taking food, and applied to the partaking of what is desirable, the being compelled to endure what is painful, or the experiencing the consequences, good or evil, of our own conduct, occur elsewhere in the Scriptures, and are probably common in most languages. In such metaphors, however, as well as in other figurative modes of speech, the Oriental style passes beyond the limits within which we are confined. Thus in Ecclesiasticus, Wisdom is per-

* John vi. 47-51.

sonified and represented as saying: "Those who eat me shall yet be hungry, and those who drink me shall yet be thirsty."* Thus too in the Talmud, R. Hillel, who asserted that the Messiah had already come, is said to have been opposed by other doctors, who maintained that "the Israelites were yet to eat the days of the Messiah." He, on the contrary, affirmed that "they had eaten their Messiah in the days of Hezekiah."†

But in the words following those last quoted from our Saviour's discourse, there is an accession to the figure. It becomes the vehicle for expressing a new fact. He says: "But the bread which I will give is my body, which I will give for the life of the world." In this language, he refers, I conceive, to his own death. He goes on: "Unless you eat the flesh of the Son of Man, and drink his blood, you have not life within you"; and he repeats and insists upon this strong figure. When he thus describes the food of life, of which his followers were to partake, as his own flesh and his own blood, the only purpose, I believe, of this amplification of the figure is to show that the blessings to be enjoyed through him were to be purchased by his violent death. It was, I think, so understood, at least partially, by those who heard him. His object was to destroy all hope of his establishing a splendid temporal kingdom, such as the Jews had been expecting; and thus to repress

* Chapter xxiv. 21.

† See Wetstein's note on John vi. 51. [See also Noyes's note on Ezekiel iii. 1.]

all worldly motives in those who were inclined to be his followers. Their Master was not to be a conqueror and a monarch, as they might have hoped, dispensing honors and favors to his adherents and countrymen; the sacrifice of his own life was required, a bloody death was to be suffered by him, in order that his followers might enjoy those blessings of which he was the minister. So, as I have said, he appears to have been understood; and many of his followers in consequence deserted him.

"Thus taught Jesus in a synagogue at Capernaum. Then many of his disciples, when they heard him, said, This is hard teaching; who can listen to it? But Jesus, knowing in his own mind that his disciples were murmuring on account of his discourse, said to them, Does this give you offence? What, then, if you should see the Son of Man ascending where he was before?"*

The meaning is, Does it offend you that I speak of my death? What, then, if you shall see me rising from the dead, and appearing where I was before? When Jesus made mention of his death, he on other occasions connected it with the prediction that he should rise from the dead. To his resurrection he alludes as a signal proof to be given of the divinity of his mission, but never elsewhere to his ascension.† After the words

* John vi. 59 – 62.

† See an explanation of this verse in Simpson's Essays on the Language of Scripture. [For a somewhat different explanation, taken from Mr. Norton's Notes on the Gospels, see Appendix, Note A.]

which have been quoted, he goes on, contrary in some degree to his usual custom, to explain in part the figurative language which he had used: "What is spiritual," he says, "gives life. The flesh profits nothing"; — that is, my flesh would profit you nothing; — "the words which I speak to you are spiritual, and give life." *

It has been contended by some modern German divines, who appear themselves to regard Christ merely as a human teacher, that he was believed or represented by his Apostles, if not by himself, to have been a pre-existent being, the Logos of God. They appeal, of course, to some of the same passages which are brought forward by Trinitarians and others in support of this doctrine, and in proof of the deity of Christ in which it is implied. But we may here make the general remark, that if the Apostles had regarded their Master as an incarnation of a great pre-existent spirit, far superior to man, they would not have left us to gather their belief from a doubtful interpretation of a few scattered passages. No fact concerning him, personally, would have been put forward in their writings with more prominence and distinctness. None would have been oftener brought into notice. None would have more strongly affected their imaginations and feelings. None would have been adapted more to affect their disciples. St. Matthew would not have written an account of his Master, as it must be

* John vi. 63.

conceded that he has, without anywhere expressly declaring the fact. The Apostles would have left us in as little doubt concerning their belief of it, as concerning their belief of his crucifixion and resurrection.

CLASS V.

Passages relating to the divine authority of Christ as the minister of God, to the manifestation of divine power in his miracles and in the establishment of Christianity, and to Christianity itself, spoken of under the name of Christ, and considered as a promulgation of the laws of God's moral government,—which have been misinterpreted as proving that Christ himself is God.

For example: there are two passages in the prophecies of the Old Testament which speak of a messenger as going before Jehovah to prepare his way and announce his coming. They are:—

Isaiah xl. 3. "A voice is crying, Prepare ye in the waste the way of Jehovah, make straight in the desert a road for our God."

Malachi iii. 1. "Lo! I will send my messenger, and he shall prepare the way before me."

These passages are in the Gospels applied to John the Baptist, the precursor of Christ.*

* Matthew iii. 3; xi. 10; Mark i. 2, 3; Luke i. 76; iii. 4; vii. 27; John i. 23.

The angel, who, according to the narrative in the first chapter of Luke's Gospel, announced the birth of John, is likewise represented as saying to Zachariah: —

"And many of the sons of Israel will he turn back to the LORD, their God; and he will go before him with the spirit and the power of Elijah."*

From these passages, it is inferred that Christ is Jehovah. But they admit of an easy explanation.

In conformity to the rude apprehensions of the Jews, we often find in the Bible, particularly in the Old Testament, strong, and, in themselves considered, harsh figures applied to God, which are borrowed from the properties, passions, and actions of man, and even of the inferior animals. Among them is the common figure by which God, in giving any peculiar manifestation of his power, is represented as changing his place, and coming to the scene where his power is displayed. But if we except the case of miraculous operations exerted directly upon the minds of men, the power of God must be manifested by means of sensible objects. It is often represented as exerted through the agency of human beings, and other conscious ministers of his will. When thus exerted, its effects, and the circumstances by which its display is attended, are sometimes referred to God as the ultimate cause, and sometimes to the immediate agent. What is said in one case to be done by an angel, or by Moses, or by Christ, or by some other

* Luke i. 16, 17.

instrument of God's will, is in another case said to be done by God. The power displayed is regarded, according to different modes of conceiving the same thing, as appertaining to him or to them. God comes, according to the language of Scripture, when a commissioned instrument of his will appears; and the precursor of the latter is the precursor of God. Thus, too, as the power and goodness of God were displayed in Christ, he might be denominated "Immanuel," a name meaning "God is with us." * [See Matthew i. 23; Isaiah vii. 14.]

* In the usage supposed, there is nothing extraordinary, or foreign from our modes of expression. But in the Pentateuch the agent of God's will, Moses, is confounded with God himself in a very strange and almost inexplicable manner; which at least illustrates the fact, how far we ought to be from insisting upon the bare letter of a passage, picked out here and there, in opposition to common sense and the general tenor of a writing.

In Deuteronomy xi. 13–15, Moses is represented as thus addressing the Israelites: —

"And it shall come to pass, if ye shall hearken diligently to my commandments which I command you this day, to love Jehovah, your God, and to serve him with all your heart and with all your soul, that I will give you the rain of your land in its due season, ... and I will send grass in thy fields."

Instead of "I will give," the Samaritan text, the Septuagint, and the Vulgate here read, "He will give"; but this reading appears obviously to have been introduced to remove the difficulty of the passage.

Again, Deuteronomy xxix. 2, 5, 6: —

"And Moses called together all Israel, and said to them, ... I have led you forty years in the wilderness; your clothes have not waxen old upon you, nor your shoes waxen old upon your feet; ye have not eaten bread, nor drunk wine nor strong drink; that ye may know that I, Jehovah, am your God."

Here the Samaritan text agrees with the Hebrew; the Septuagint in the Alexandrine manuscript, and the Vulgate and Syriac versions,

In the first part of the discourse of our Saviour with the Jews, recorded in the fifth chapter of John's Gospel (verses 16–30), which took place after he had excited their enmity against him by miraculously curing a man on the Sabbath, there are expressions as strong as are anywhere used concerning his authority as a minister of God, and concerning his religion as taught and sanctioned by God, as a promulgation of the laws of God's moral government. The words of Christ were bold and figurative. The style of St. John, who

alter as in the preceding passage, changing the pronoun of the first person for that of the third.

Once more, Deuteronomy xxxi. 22, 23: —

"Moses, then, wrote this song the same day, and taught it the children of Israel.

"And he gave Joshua, the son of Nun, a charge, and said: Be strong and of good courage; for thou shalt bring the children of Israel into the land which I sware unto them, and I will be with thee."

Here, to avoid the difficulty, the Septuagint reads, "which the Lord sware unto them, and he will be with thee"; expressly ascribing the speech to Moses, as the connection requires, and supplying his name, thus: "And Moses charged Joshua." The Vulgate takes a different course, ascribing the whole speech to Jehovah, thus: "And the Lord charged Joshua."

The various readings of the Versions evidently deserve no consideration, as the origin of them is apparent. Whoever may look into a number of commentators, unless he be more fortunate than myself, will be surprised to find, either that these passages are passed over in silence, or that the attempts to explain them are but slight and unsatisfactory. How they are to be explained, or accounted for, is a question which it is not here the place to discuss, and one which it is not easy to answer. But it may be remarked, that if a passage corresponding to them had been found in the discourses of Christ, it must have appeared, I think, to a Trinitarian a much stronger argument than any that can now be adduced in support of the doctrine of the deity of Christ.

has reported them, is in general obscure, except in mere narrative; and the same style appears in his own compositions and in the discourses of our Saviour as recorded by him, which differ in this respect from those given by the other three Evangelists. It appears probable, therefore, that St. John, preserving essentially the thoughts uttered by his Master, conformed the language, more or less, to his own modes of expression. The passage, from these causes, is in the original somewhat difficult to be understood; and in the imperfect and erroneous rendering of the Common Version, its bearing and purpose are scarcely to be discerned. As in similar cases, the obscurity thus spread over it has served to countenance the supposition that it involves some mysterious meaning. Yet, even as rendered in the Common Version, the passage, so far from affording any proof of the deity of Christ, presents only the conception of his entire dependence upon God.

In order to enter into its character and purpose, we must consider that the Jews in general, having little moral desert to recommend them to the favor of God, placed their reliance upon external ceremonies; and among these, there was none to which they attached more importance than a superstitious observance of the Sabbath. The majority of the Jews had that enmity toward Christ, which the bigots of a false religion always feel toward a teacher of the truth, who discloses the nothingness and the falsehood of their pretensions. As the descendants of Abraham, as performing "the works of the Law," which in their view were little more than the ceremonies of the Law, as God's chosen people, they considered themselves as holy, and looked upon Christ as a profane heresiarch. Their feelings toward him were such as in the fifteenth century might have been excited among the members of the Romish Church in any Catholic country, by one openly teaching, I do not say Protestantism, but pure Christianity, the essential truths of religion and morals, and fearlessly reproving the vices, superstitions, and hypocrisy of the age. They regarded him, as such a reformer would have been regarded, as an enemy of God; for if he were not at enmity with God, they were.

In opposition to this state of feeling among them, our Saviour used the strongest expressions to declare, that he was acting wholly under the guidance of God, and that his authority was the authority of God. It is an obvious remark, though it may be worth pointing out, that the expressions of the most absolute dependence upon God, and the boldest assertions of divine authority, amount to the same thing, and occur indiscriminately in his discourses. So far as he was a mere instrument in the hands of God, so far was his authority identical with that of God. These considerations will perhaps explain the general character of the passage we are considering, which may be thus rendered: —

"Upon this the Jews came in pursuit of Jesus, because he had done thus on the Sabbath. But Jesus said to them, As my Father is continually working, so I also work.—Then, for this, the Jews were more bent on killing him, because he had not only broken the Sabbath, but also had spoken of God as particularly his Father, putting himself on an equality with God. Then Jesus said to them, Truly, truly I tell you, The Son can do nothing of himself, but only what he sees his Father doing. But what his Father does, the Son also does in like manner. For the Father loves the Son, and directs him in all that he does, and will direct him in greater works than these, to your astonishment. For as the Father raises the dead and gives them life, so also the Son gives life to whom he will. Nor does the Father condemn any one, but has committed all condemnation to the Son; that all may honor the Son as they honor the Father. He who honors not the Son, honors not the Father who sent him. Truly, truly I tell you, He who hears my words, and puts his trust in Him who sent me, has eternal life, and shall not come under condemnation, but has passed from death to life. Truly, truly I tell you, that the hour is coming, and now is, when the dead shall hear the voice of the Son of God, and those who hear it shall live. For as the Father is the fountain of life, so has he given to the Son to be the fountain of life; and he has intrusted him with authority to pass condemnation also, because he is the Man. Be not astonished at this; for the hour is coming, when all who are in their tombs shall hear his voice, and come forth; those who have done good, to the resurrection of life, and those who have done evil, to the resurrection of condemnation. I can do nothing of myself. I condemn as I am directed, and my condemnation is just; for I regard not my own will, but the will of Him who sent me."

We will now attend to some passages in this discourse, which require or admit further illustration. The Jews, exasperated against Jesus, had represented him to themselves as one who impiously impugned the authority of their Law, having openly manifested his contempt for it by a wanton violation of the Sabbath. The immediate purport of the first address of our Saviour to them may be thus expressed: I am executing the works of God, to whom my relation is like that of a son to a father; and as the immediate works of God are not suspended from a regard to the rest of the Sabbath, neither is there reason that mine should be, — "As my Father is continually working, so I also work." (Verse 17.) The ultimate object of these words was to affirm, in a manner very striking, at once from its indirectness and its brevity, that he was acting as the minister of God with his full approbation and authority. The Jews did not familiarly speak of God as their father; and when Jesus called him "MY Father," they understood him at once as meaning to express, that his relation to God was different from that of all other men. They understood, likewise, that he "put himself on an equality with God," in implying that he was no more bound by a regard to the law of the Sabbath than God, by whose authority he acted.

There is nothing, I think, in what follows, that requires particular explanation, till we come to the words: "As the Father raises the dead and gives them life, so also the Son gives life to whom he will." (Verse 21.) With ζωή, "life," in the New Testament, the idea of happiness is associated. "Eternal life," for example, denotes eternal happiness. The meaning of Christ, then, in these words, may be thus expressed: The Father raises the dead to a new and happy state of being; but in this work he has appointed the Son as his minister, who by his religion affords the means of securing this blessedness, which will be conferred on all his followers without exception, as if by his own act and will.

"Nor does the Father condemn any, but has committed all condemnation to the Son." (Verse 22.) This language, it is obvious, must on any supposition be regarded as figurative. What was meant by it is, that Christ, being the teacher of that religion through which the laws and sanctions of God's moral government are made known, might be regarded as the minister of God appointed to pronounce the sentence of condemnation on all exposed to it. He condemned only those whom God condemned, and he condemned all those whom God condemned. It is as such a minister that he afterward represents himself, when he says, "I condemn as I am directed." At the close of the discourse (verse 45), dropping this figure, he represents God in person as the judge who passes sentence. "Think not," he says, "that

I shall accuse you to the Father. There is one who is accusing you, Moses, in whom you have trusted." In another discourse (ch. xii. 47, 48) he explains what is meant by him when he speaks of judging and condemning men. It signifies that men will be judged and condemned according to those laws and sanctions of moral conduct which he has made known to them in his religion: "If any one who hears my words regards them not, I do not pass sentence on him; for I have not come to pass sentence on the world, but to save the world. There is a judge for him who rejects me and receives not my words; — THE DOCTRINE I HAVE TAUGHT, that will pass sentence on him hereafter."

In the discourse before us, our Saviour used the words on which we are remarking in reference to the Jews, his enemies, who considered themselves as secure of not being condemned by God, however their characters and conduct might be condemned by Jesus. It will be, he gives them to understand, as if all condemnation were committed to the Son.

"Truly, truly I tell you, He who hears my words, and puts his trust in Him who sent me, has eternal life, and shall not come under condemnation, but has passed from death to life." (Verse 24.) The punishment of sin is often represented in the New Testament under the figure of death. Death is regarded as the most severe of human punishments, and commonly apprehended as the greatest of the inevitable evils of our present state; except when this apprehension is done away by the faith and hopes of a Christian. To his view, indeed, it changes its aspect. To him it is a deliverance from the thraldom of this life, and a rapid and glorious advance in that course of progression and blessedness on which he has entered. It is no interruption of that ETERNAL LIFE, which he has commenced. According to the common apprehension of death, "he shall never die." But to the sinner death appears under an opposite aspect. The natural dread of it is not alleviated by any rational hope of a happier life to follow it. On the contrary, it is the commencement of that state in which the tendencies of his evil dispositions will be more fully developed, and their consequences more bitterly felt. Now to the dispensations of the future life Christ always refers as the great sanctions of his religion. Death, then, being the termination of all sinful gratifications, and the commencement of future punishment, for this reason, in connection with those before mentioned, is employed, by an obvious figure, to represent the whole punishment of sin; and those who lie exposed to this punishment are, by a figure equally obvious, spoken of as already "dead"; as the good are spoken of as already in possession of "eternal life." Thus, too, we may perceive why death, presenting itself under such opposite aspects to the one class and to the other, is represented, though common to all, as the punishment of the wicked.

"Truly, truly I tell you, that the hour is coming, and now is, when the dead shall hear the voice of the Son of God, and those who hear it shall live." (Verse 25.) The discourse of our Saviour has been misunderstood, from inattention to the causes why sinners are metaphorically called by him "dead." It has been thought to be on account of the deadness of their moral principles and affections. Hence some commentators have supposed that there is in this discourse a series of harsh transitions, from the literally dead who are raised to life by the Father, to the morally dead spoken of in the words last quoted, and then again to the proper dead "who are in their tombs." Others have explained the words just quoted as referring to the literally dead who were raised to life by our Saviour during his ministry, though no corresponding meaning can be put upon his language immediately preceding, in which he speaks of those who have "passed from death to life," and the explanation is, at the same time, foreign from the purpose and connection of the discourse, and inconsistent with the antithetical opposition which runs through it between the two general classes, of the dead, and of those who have eternal life. Others still, by a far more extravagant interpretation, have understood Jesus, when he speaks of those in their tombs who shall hear his voice and live, to refer only to the morally dead, and consequently to describe only a moral resurrection. The true meaning of the words we are considering I conceive to be, that Christ had come to call sinners to reformation; that those who lay exposed to death *with all its fearful consequences*, "the dead," as they are figuratively called, would hear his voice; and that those who listened to it would be delivered from death as an evil, and have only to look forward to life and blessedness.

"The Father has intrusted him with authority to pass condemnation also, because he is the Man." (Verse 27.) The rendering of the last words needs explanation. In the Oriental languages, the term "son of man" was used simply as equivalent to "man." Of this, as every one knows, there are many examples in the Old and New Testament. In the Syriac version of the New Testament, this periphrasis not unfrequently occurs where only the word ἄνθρωπος, "man," is used in the original. In this, which is, I conceive, the only sense of the term, it was used by Christ concerning himself. "The Son of Man" means nothing more than "the Man." Why he so designated himself has not, I think, been satisfactorily explained. It may be accounted for by the state of things which has been already referred to.* The coming of the Messiah was a dangerous topic of discourse. He would, consequently, be designated by ambiguous titles; and such language would naturally be used as, "When THE MAN [the Son of Man] comes"; "THE MAN will deliver us." Hence this term, I imagine, came to signify the Messiah, but somewhat ambiguously. The uncertainty of its application might be increased, when our Saviour entered on his ministry; for he, simply as an individual exciting such strong and

* See before, pp. 243 - 245.

general interest and curiosity by his miracles and doctrine, would, we may easily suppose, be designated as "the Man."* A term which thus strongly intimated, but did not directly express, his claim to be that great minister of God whom the Jews had been expecting, was well suited to the circumstances in which he was placed; and was, in consequence, adopted by him as a title appropriate to himself. With these views, I would not however object to the common rendering, "the Son of Man," if it be so familiar as to make a change unpleasant, except in passages like that before us, in which, by giving a verbal instead of a true rendering, the sense is obscured. "God," says our Saviour in this passage, "has intrusted me with authority to pass condemnation, because I am the Man"; intending by this to express, in language which somewhat veiled his meaning, that he was that last minister of God whom the Jews had hoped for under the name of "the Messiah," or "the Anointed." *Messiah*, or *Anointed*, it may be observed, is a common name, as well as *Man;* and the former term, equally with the latter, could become the designation of a particular individual only from the manner of its application.†

* We may observe an analogous use of language in the First Epistle of John, in which Christ is designated simply by the pronoun "He," without any previous mention of his name to which the pronoun can refer. See 1 John ii. 12; iii. 5, 7, 16. [Compare Noyes's note on Job v. 1.]

† [Mr. Norton, in his Translation of the Gospels, has given a very different rendering of the 27th and 28th verses of this chapter, as follows: "And he has intrusted him with authority to pass condemna-

"Be not astonished at this; for the hour is coming in which all who are in their tombs shall hear his voice, and come forth; those who have done good, to the resurrection of life, and those who have done evil, to the resurrection of condemnation." (Verses 28, 29.) The meaning of our Saviour may be thus expressed: Be not astonished at what I have told you, that God has appointed me as his minister, to announce whom he approves, and whom he condemns, and to afford to all the means

tion also. Because he is a son of man, marvel not at this; for the hour is coming," &c.

His note on the passage is this: —

"The meaning is, Do not marvel that I, though only a man, claim such connection with God, or that I claim to be charged with such a ministry by him, and to be intrusted with such authority from him, — for the character of my ministry may be announced in a manner still more striking. All men are, as it were, to be called from their tombs by my voice, and to rise to blessedness or to condemnation, as they have obeyed or disobeyed those laws which I teach.

"In connecting the words in the manner shown in the translation which I have given, their meaning is obvious, and suitable to the whole tenor of the discourse. As regards the more common rendering, 'He has given him authority to execute judgment also, because he is the Son of Man,' or 'because he is a son of man,' I know of no satisfactory or probable explanation of the latter clause. The absence of the article in Greek before the words rendered 'son of man' forbids their being rendered '*the* Son of Man.' The connection of the clauses which I have adopted is sanctioned by the Syriac translator of the New Testament, by Chrysostom, Theophylact, and Euthymius Zigabenus.

"John could not have inverted the order of the clauses without producing ambiguity, on account of the recurrenee of ὅτι, and its *common* use after τοῦτο as an explanatory particle."

The paragraph in the text has not been cancelled, it being desirable to retain the remarks on the meaning of the term "Son of Man," which are not affected by the rendering of this particular passage.]

of passing from death to life; — Be not astonished at this, for, in truth, the future condition of all will be determined by their obedience or disobedience to the laws of my religion, which are the laws of God. They shall be judged by this standard, as if they were called from their tombs by my voice to be judged in person by me. This mode of understanding the passage will be still further illustrated by what follows.

It is a common figure in the New Testament to speak of Christ personally, when his religion, under some one of its aspects, effects, or relations, is intended; and this is sometimes done when the expression is such as our use of language does not allow. St. Paul addresses the Colossians, according to a verbal rendering, thus (ii. 6, 7): "As, then, ye have received Christ Jesus the Lord, walk in him, rooted and grounded in him." He exhorts them (iii. 13) to forgive each other, "as Christ had forgiven them"; not referring to any forgiveness from Christ in person, but to the forgiveness of their past sins upon their becoming sincere Christians. He says to the churches addressed in the Epistle to the Ephesians, churches to which Jesus had never preached (iv. 20, 21): "You have not so learned Christ, since you have heard him and been taught by him as the truth is in Jesus." He speaks to the Romans of the "spirit of Christ," that is, "the spirit of Christianity," dwelling in them; and the expression, "that Christ may dwell in your hearts," is elsewhere (Ephesians iii. 17) used by him. He writes to the Corinthians (1 Ep. xv. 18) of those "who have fallen asleep in Christ," meaning, those who have died "being Christians"; for "to be in Christ" is a common phrase in his Epistles for "being a Christian." He tells the Philippians (i. 8), "God is my witness how earnestly I love you all ἐν σπλάγχνοις Χριστοῦ Ἰησοῦ," words which, from the difference in our modes of expression, do not admit of a verbal translation into our language; but the meaning of which is "with Christian tenderness." Again he says to them (i. 21), "For to me life is Christ, and death is gain"; that is, "My life is devoted to the cause of Christ, to the promotion of his religion." In the same Epistle (iii. 8) are these words: "I have suffered the loss of all these things, counting them but as refuse, that I might win Christ"; where the expression, "to win Christ," means "to secure the blessings of Christianity." To the Galatians, he writes (iii. 27, 28), "Whoever of you has been baptized to Christ, has put on Christ"; that is, as appears from the connection, "is entitled to all the privileges of a Christian." The Apostle proceeds: "There is neither Jew nor Gentile, neither slave nor freeman, neither male nor female; but you are all one in Christ Jesus," — "you are all on an equality as Christians." So also the author of the Epistle to the Hebrews speaks of "Jesus Christ, the same yesterday, to-day, and for ever," intending by those words to express the unchangeableness of Christian truth.*

* [Hebrews xiii. 8; compare verse 9.]

I have perhaps brought together more examples than are necessary, of a common form of expression. Our Saviour himself uses language in a similar manner. By a figure of speech, he refers to himself personally the effects of his religion, the divine power exerted in its establishment, and the operation of those laws of God's moral government which it announces. Thus he says (Matthew x. 34): "Think not that I came to bring peace on earth. I came not to bring peace, but a sword." So also in Luke (xii. 49): "I came to cast fire on the earth; and what would I, since it has already been kindled?" In these passages, every one understands that our Saviour speaks of the effects of his religion, and not of anything to be accomplished by his immediate agency. In like manner, when he declares that he has come "to save the world," he refers to the power of his religion in delivering men from ignorance, error, sin, and their attendant evils. "For God," it is said, "did not send his Son into the world to condemn the world, but that through him the world may be saved. He who has faith in him is not condemned; but he who has not faith is already under condemnation, for not having faith in the only Son of God. And the ground of condemnation is this, that, the light having come into the world, men preferred the darkness to the light; for their deeds were evil."* This passage shows how men are to be saved by Christ, namely, by their own act in believing and obeying him; and is

* John iii. 17 – 19.

also one of those which explain what is meant by his figurative language when he speaks of judging and condemning men.

"I am the resurrection and the life."* In what sense our Saviour used these sublime words may appear from what immediately follows. "He who has faith in me, though he die, will live; and whoever lives and has faith in me will never die." Christ is the resurrection and the life, because through faith in him, through a practical belief of the truths which he taught, eternal life is to be obtained. Thus he afterwards says (John xii. 49, 50): "For I have not spoken from myself; but He who sent me, the Father himself, has given me in charge what I should enjoin, and what I should teach; and I know that WHAT HE HAS CHARGED ME WITH is eternal life"; that is, it affords the means of attaining eternal life.

He says to the Jews, in reference to those Gentiles who would embrace his religion (John x. 16): "I have other sheep, which are not of this fold; those too I must bring in, and they will hearken to my voice, and there will be one flock and one shepherd." In these words he does not mean to assert his own personal agency in the conversion of the Gentiles; they were not literally to hear his voice; but they were to be converted by the preaching of his religion. There is a similar figure in the words (John xii. 32), "And I, when I shall be raised up from the earth, shall draw all men to me."

* John xi. 25.

In his most affecting conversation with his disciples, the evening before his crucifixion, he tells them (John xiv. 18, 19), "I will not leave you fatherless. I am coming to you again. A little while only, and the world will see me no more; but you will see me. Inasmuch as I am blessed, you will be blessed also." Here, as I have before had occasion to explain, our Saviour refers, not to any personal presence with his disciples, but to his presence with them in the power of his religion, his presence to their minds and hearts.

In other instances, Jesus uses what may be technically called "an equivalent figure," by which I mean figurative language not intended to correspond to the real state of things except so far as to produce an effect upon the mind equivalent to what that might produce if distinctly apprehended. Thus he tells his disciples (John xiv. 2, 3), "There are many rooms in my Father's house. Were it not so, should I have told you that I am going there to prepare a place for you? And when I have gone and prepared a place for you, I am coming again, and will take you to myself, that where I am, you may be also." When Jesus thus speaks of preparing a place for his disciples, and, after preparation, returning to take them with him, he uses figurative terms which do not admit of being transformed into literal. The general effect of the language, its aggregate significance, if I may so speak, is alone to be regarded. The meaning is, Your future blessedness will be as great, and is as certain, as if it were prepared for you by me, your Master and friend, and you were assured that I should return in person to conduct you to it.

In a similar manner we are to understand another declaration of Jesus, already noticed, which has been erroneously explained (Matthew xviii. 19, 20): "Again, I say to you, If two of you agree on earth concerning everything which they ask, their prayers will be granted by my Father in Heaven. For where two or three come together as my disciples, there am I among them." By this, as I have said,* our Saviour intended that the prayers of his followers for the promotion of his cause, for the guidance and aid necessary to them as his ministers, would be granted as if they were his own, as if he himself were praying with them.

In order to explain some other passages in which our Saviour speaks figuratively of his personal agency, it is necessary to attend to a new consideration. The Jews had been accustomed to designate the dispensation which they expected from their Messiah as "the kingdom of the Messiah," or "the kingdom of God," or "of Heaven." This language, though the conceptions which they had attached to it were erroneous, was such as, taken in a figurative sense, might well describe the Christian dispensation. It was adopted, therefore, by our Saviour, and after him by his Apostles; and to this leading metaphor of a kingdom much of the figurative language throughout the New

* See before, pp. 223, 224.

Testament is conformed. The establishment of Christianity in the world is spoken of by Christ as the establishment of the kingdom or reign of the Messiah, or of God. This event he describes, figuratively, as "his coming to reign," or simply as "his coming," that is, his manifestation to men in his true character.

Thus we find the following language (Matthew xvi. 27, 28): "The Son of Man is coming in the glory of his Father, with his angels; and then will he render to every one according to his deeds. I tell you in truth, There are some here present who will not taste of death, before they see the Son of Man entering on his reign." The literal meaning of these words may be thus given: The kingdom of Heaven, the Christian dispensation, will be established by a glorious display of the power of God; and, being established, men will be rewarded or punished as their actions conform to its laws; every one will be judged by the laws of its king, the Son of Man; and the establishment of Christianity in the world will be made secure and evident during the lifetime of some of those now present.

He is coming "with his angels." Angels were conceived of by the Jews as ministers of God's providence; and Christ, conforming his language to their conceptions, repeatedly speaks of the ministry of angels, figuratively, to denote some manifestation of the power of God. Thus he tells Nathanael (John i. 51), "Ye will see heaven opened, and the angels of God ascending and descending to the Son of Man"; meaning, Ye will witness manifest proof of the relation existing between God and me, his minister. When our Saviour speaks of his coming in the glory of God, with his angels, he does not mean by these figures to express, that he himself will appear in person with some visible and splendid display; his meaning is as has been explained; corresponding to what he elsewhere says (Luke xvii. 20, 21), "The kingdom of God is not coming with any show that may be watched for; nor will men say, Lo! it is here; or, Lo! it is there; for lo! the kingdom of God is within you."

In relation to this subject, there are still other facts to be attended to. With the establishment of Christianity was connected the punishment of the Jews for their rejection of Christ. They, in return, were rejected by God. The peculiar relation which they held toward him was publicly abrogated. As a nation they ceased to exist. Their country was ravaged, they were destroyed, or forced from it into slavery or exile; Jerusalem was laid waste, and the temple burnt and thrown down. How the establishment of Christianity was connected with these events, we shall perceive, if we consider that the Jews had been separated by God from other nations, to be the subjects of a special dispensation, by which he was made known to them and they were called to worship him. They were, in an obvious sense of the words, his chosen people. But in rejecting Christ and refusing to obey him, they had virtually renounced their allegiance to God. They had dissolved by their own act the connection that had existed between Him and them. They had, if one may so speak, put the question at issue, whether they were still in favor with God, still his peculiar people, and Christ were a blasphemous impostor speaking falsely in the name of God, as they had declared him to be; or whether Christ spoke with divine authority, and they consequently had refused to submit to the authority of God. The peculiar relation that had existed between God and them was recognized by Christ himself; to them he was immediately sent; his claims were in the first instance submitted to them; and they had rejected him as a false Messiah. The question thus at issue must, it would seem, receive a public and solemn decision, before the evidence of Christianity could be considered as complete; and this decision was made by God in the rejection and punishment of the nation.

This punishment, it is further to be recollected, had been announced by Christ. He had thus suspended the completion of the full evidence of his divine mission till the accomplishment of his prophecy. When that took place, the series of proofs might be considered as closed, and his religion as established.

Nor is this all. The Jews were the bitter enemies of Christianity; and it was against persecution from them alone that the religion had first to struggle. In their opposition to it they had a vantage-ground which none of its subsequent enemies possessed. They claimed to know the character and purposes of God, and to be the proper judges of a prophet pretending to be sent from him to their nation. In the view of many Gentiles, the question at issue between the Jews and Christ was, without doubt, regarded as "a question of their own superstition,"* which it was for them to decide. Now from this opposition and persecution, of a nature to be so injurious to the growth of the new religion, Christianity was relieved by the destruction of the nation. It no longer appeared as an offshoot from Judaism, but assumed its independent character, not deriving support from the preceding dispensation, but throwing back evidence upon it.

Thus it appears in what manner the establishment of Christianity was connected with the destruction of the Jewish nation; and why our Saviour sometimes speaks of the events as simultaneous. This is the case throughout the prophecy in the twenty-fourth chapter of Matthew, so far as it relates to the calamities coming upon the Jews.† In this there are some passages that strikingly illustrate the modes of expression elsewhere used by Christ. He evidently speaks of his own coming and presence, figuratively, in the Oriental language of poetry and prophecy; and, in the same use of language, refers to his own personal agency

* Acts xxv. 19; compare xviii. 15.

† [For an explanation of the latter part of this chapter (vv. 42 – 51), which relates to a different subject, see Mr. Norton's Notes on the Gospels.]

events which were not to be effected by it, but were to be accomplished in his cause by God.

After warning his disciples against being deceived by those who would falsely claim the character of the Messiah, (his character, I conceive, as a deliverer from the tyranny of the Romans,) he says: "Should they say to you, Lo! he [the Messiah] is in some solitary place; go not forth: Lo! he is in some private chamber; believe it not. For the coming of the Son of Man will be like the lightning which flashes from the east to the west,"* — as apparent and splendid. The meaning is, For the evidence which God will afford for the establishment of my religion will be the most conspicuous and unequivocal.

In what immediately follows, after predicting the extinction of the Jewish nation in language of which we have abundant examples in the Hebrew prophets, that is, in the strongest figures representing a day of utter darkness,† he proceeds: "And

* Matthew xxiv. 26, 27.

† "A day of darkness" is an obvious figure for a "day of distress." Hence, in the Oriental style, a time of utter calamity, the destruction of a nation, is described by the extinction of the sun and the other lights of heaven. Thus Isaiah (ch. xiii. 9, 10), in speaking of the destruction of Babylon, says: —

"Behold, the day of Jehovah is coming, cruel with wrath and fierce anger, to lay the land desolate and to destroy its sinners out of it.

"For the stars of heaven and its constellations shall not give their light, the sun shall be darkened in his going forth, and the moon shall not cause her light to shine."

So also Ezekiel, describing the fall of Egypt (ch. xxxii. 7, 8): —

"And when I shall put thee out, I will cover the heaven, and make its stars dark. I will cover the sun with a cloud, and the moon shall

then THE SIGN of the Son of Man will appear in heaven; and then all the tribes of the land will beat their breasts, when they shall see the Son of Man coming upon the clouds of heaven with power and great glory." The Jews had repeatedly demanded of Christ a sign from heaven; that is, a miracle conspicuous in the heavens, or apparently having its origin there. This, for some reason or other, they pretended to regard as what might afford clear proof of his being the Messiah, such proof as his other works did not furnish. They made the refusal of this sign one main pretext of their unbelief. "The Jews," says St. Paul, "demand signs." * In St. John's Gospel the Jews are represented as comparing Christ with Moses, and asking, "What sign do you show us, that we may give you credit? What do you perform? Our fathers ate the manna in the desert; as it is written, *He gave them bread* FROM HEAVEN *to eat*." † It is in reference, I think, to this demand of the Jews, that our Saviour says, "Then THE SIGN of the Son of Man will appear in heaven"; intending by these words, that the most conspicuous proof would then be given of his divine mission. This proof, he expresses in what follows, would be a display of God's providence in the establishment of his re-

not give her light; all the bright lights of heaven will I make dark over thee, and spread darkness over thy land."

It is unnecessary to quote at length more examples of this figurative language. Others may be found, Isaiah xxxiv. 4; Jeremiah xv. 9; Joel ii. 30, 31; iii. 15; Amos viii. 9.

* 1 Corinthians i. 22.

† John vi. 30, 31.

ligion, which would cause all the inhabitants of the land to lament. It would be his triumph and their desolation. He describes it under the figure of his coming on the clouds of heaven with great power and glory.

This is one of those passages which may teach us how such figurative language is to be understood. There was no visible appearance of our Saviour at the destruction of Jerusalem, nor have we reason to ascribe the punishment of the Jews in any degree to his personal agency. No such visible appearance took place before the generation then living had passed away. Yet all the events which it was his purpose to predict occurred during that period. After what has been quoted, he says (verse 34): "I tell you in truth, that they will all take place before this generation passes away." It is, then, the power of God displayed in his cause, which he speaks of figuratively as his own. Thus, likewise, we are to understand his words when he says, in his last charge to his disciples (Matthew xxviii. 18), "All power is given me in heaven and on earth"; where he ascribes to himself personally the power of God which would be exerted in the support of Christianity.

After the prediction of the destruction of Jerusalem, our Saviour in the next chapter (Matthew xxv.) represents the kingdom of Heaven, or Christianity, as established and in operation. All are to be judged by its laws, the laws of God's moral government. Some will be rewarded, and some punished, all according to their deeds. After his enforcing this truth in two parables, follows that most solemn and impressive description, in which he represents himself personally as the Judge of men. It contains a most important truth enveloped in a most striking figure. It is a scenical representation, adapted powerfully to affect the minds of his immediate hearers, and our own. The naked truth here taught is the most important, the most practical truth of religion, — that which concerns us the most deeply; it is, that our happiness or misery is to be determined by ourselves, by the conformity of our conduct to the will of God, which Christ has revealed. The solemn imagery in which this truth is presented is but an expansion of the figure that our Saviour had before used: "The Son of Man is coming in the glory of his Father, with his angels; and then will he render to every one according to his deeds." What was predicted in these words was to take place while some who heard him were still living: "I tell you in truth, There are some here present who will not taste of death, before they see the Son of Man entering on his reign." While the generation then living continued on earth, the kingdom of Heaven was to be established, the Messiah was to assume his reign, and men were to be judged by his laws.* It may be observed, that the figure which connects his judging in person with his assuming his reign, would be obvious

* [Compare the note on Matthew xxv. in Mr. Norton's Notes on the Gospels; and in regard to the figurative use of language here illustrated, see, further, his note on Matthew xiii. 36 – 43.]

to an Oriental; the ancient custom having been for kings to sit in person as judges. Hence, both in the Old and New Testament, the verb "to judge" is not unfrequently used as equivalent to the verb "to reign" or "to rule."

But this language is highly figurative; and why, it may be asked, was such language used by our Saviour, language of which the purport is liable to be misunderstood? The answer is, that, in the first place, the ESSENTIAL meaning of the words, that meaning which is of the deepest interest to all, may be readily understood. It is clearly taught, that every man will receive according to his deeds; that our condition in the future life will be determined by our character in the present. To account for the imagery in which this truth is presented, we must look to the intellectual habits and culture of those addressed. The contemporaries and countrymen of Christ clothed their conceptions in language very different from that with which we are familiar. To them, Oriental fashions of speech were vernacular. They were to be addressed through their feelings and imagination. The great body of the Jews, unaccustomed to any exercise of the understanding, had scarcely the power of apprehending a truth presented to them as a philosophical abstraction, in its naked and literal form. An array of figures was required to command their attention. It was necessary that the doctrine taught should be incorporated, as it were, in images obvious to sight, in order to affect their minds. The ideas presented were to be conveyed in a manner adapted to their conceptions and associations, to their capacity of comprehending and feeling. A teacher, divine or human, who should have explained the truths of religion in the language of Locke or of Butler, would have found no hearers on the shores of Gennesaret or within the walls of Jerusalem. Our Saviour, had he been addressing a small body of philosophers, would undoubtedly have expressed himself in a manner very different from that in which he spoke to the Jewish multitudes, or even to his own disciples. I say in a very different *manner;* for the essential truths of religion could not have been more distinctly made known by him.

But his language, it may be said, is now liable to be misunderstood by us. Certainly it is so, upon some points of minor importance, if we will not exercise our reason upon the subject; and he is in a great error who supposes that any rule can be laid down for the study of the Scriptures, which shall supersede the exercise of investigation, thought, and judgment. Except in treating of the exact sciences, the very nature of language renders impossible such a use of it as will preclude all liability to be misunderstood. The impression which it makes, the ideas which it excites, in him who hears or reads it, depend upon the previous state of his own mind. In proportion as one is prepared to apprehend a subject as it was apprehended by him who spoke or wrote, he will be more likely to receive the meaning designed. In passing from one age to another, or from one nation to another, the significance of language varies with the ever-varying conceptions of men. Our Saviour often left his words to be explained by subsequent events, or to be rightly apprehended as the minds of his hearers acquired power to accommodate themselves to the truth. During his ministry, his Apostles often misunderstood him; and it was not till many years after his ascension, that they comprehended the purport of the simple direction, "Go and make disciples from all nations"; and then only in consequence of a new miracle.

The language of Christ respecting his future coming and his judgment of men was likewise, I believe, misunderstood by his Apostles. Interpreting it literally, they anticipated a personal and visible return of their Master to earth at no distant period, when he would appear as the Judge of mankind. This is a subject necessary to be explained in connection with the views that have been given of the meaning of Christ, which would be otherwise imperfect and unsatisfactory. At the same time, it is a subject involving considerations of great importance. But its discussion in this place would too much interrupt the train of the present argument; and I shall, therefore, treat of it in an Appendix to this volume.*

I may here take notice, however, of the argument founded by Trinitarians upon the conceptions of the Apostles respecting the judgment of mankind

* [See Appendix, Note B.]

by Christ. It has been contended by them, that what the Apostles expected is still future; that Christ is hereafter to judge all men in person; that, in order to this, he must be acquainted with every thought and action of every individual; that such knowledge supposes omniscience; that omniscience is the attribute of God alone; and that Christ, therefore, is God. Without examining any of the other steps in this argument, one need only remark upon the very limited notion which it implies of omniscience on the one hand, and of the power of God on the other. The knowledge of all thoughts and deeds which have taken place in this world from its creation would be, compared with OMNISCIENCE, less than the acquaintance that a child may have with its nursery, compared with the apprehensions of an archangel. Would it, then, be an act transcending the power of God to communicate that knowledge? Could he not give to one man a perfect acquaintance with one other? And if this be possible, is his power still so bounded, that he could not give to one who had been a man, a perfect knowledge of the thoughts and deeds of *all* other men who have lived?

In urging such obvious arguments as these, there is a humiliating consciousness of the weakness of the cause we are opposing. One may feel as if he were wasting reasoning upon a subject unworthy of it; as if his remarks implied a want of common intelligence in his readers; as if he were exposed to the same ridicule, as he who should gravely and earnestly labor the proof of an undeniable proposition. But the same is the case with all direct reasoning against the doctrine of the Trinity; and one can reconcile himself to the discussion of it only by considering, not what that doctrine is in itself, but how widely and how long it has prevailed, how obstinately it is still professed, and the manifold mischiefs which have flowed and are still flowing from it.

CLASS VI.

Passages misinterpreted through inattention to the peculiar characteristics of the modes of expression in the New Testament.

CORRESPONDING to what has been already said, the modes of expression in the books of the New Testament are often different from those which we should use at the present day to express the same essential meaning. All our habits of life, all the habits of our minds, our conceptions, our modes of apprehension, our associations of thought, are more or less unlike those of their writers, or of the individuals for whom the books were primarily intended. Our imaginations are familiar with different objects; our feelings are excited by other causes; our minds are occupied by other subjects. While the essential truths of religion, as taught by Christ and his Apostles, have remained unchanged and unchangeable, the sphere of human knowledge has widened, and philosophy has made great advances. A gradual change has been taking place in the character of men's ideas; they are combined in different aggregates, they are embodied in other forms of language, they are better defined, they stand in different relations to each other. Let any one recollect and bring together what he may know of the half-civilized inhabitants of Galilee, of the bigoted Jews of Jerusalem, or of the Christian converts from heathenism at Corinth or Ephesus; and he will perceive that they were men, who, in their ways of thinking and feeling, in their opinions and prejudices, in their degree of information, in their power of comprehending truth, in the influences to which they had been subject, and in the circumstances in which they were placed, were very unlike an intelligent reader of the New Testament at the present day. The writers of the New Testament partook of the character of their age and nation. Their circumstances, likewise, were in the highest degree peculiar, and produced corresponding feelings, which we cannot fully apprehend without an effort of thought and imagination. They were Jews, accustomed to strong Oriental modes of speech, and to figurative language of a kind not familiar to us, and the force of which, therefore, we are liable to misapprehend. All these circumstances contributed to produce a style of expression in the New Testament which is not to be judged of by the standard of our own. We may satisfy ourselves that we have ascertained the true meaning of a writer, even when his language varies much from that which the habits of our time might lead us to adopt in conveying the same ideas.

Of passages that bear the stamp of what, in a wide sense of the term, one may call the Oriental style of the New Testament, we have already had many examples under the preceding heads, particularly under the last. I now propose to explain a few passages in the Epistles to the Ephesians and Colossians; two epistles written probably at the same time, having a striking likeness, and serving to illustrate each other. That which goes under the name of the Epistle to the Ephesians was probably a circular epistle sent to different churches in Asia Minor. They were written from Rome late in the life of the Apostle, just about the termination of his first imprisonment in that city. They were addressed to Christians who were principally converts from heathenism. One main object of the Apostle was to impress them with a deep sense of the blessings they had received solely through the favor of God, of the value of their religion, and of the relations in which its teacher stood to God and to his followers; and thus to prevent them from confounding it with any human doctrine, and modifying it, or adding to it, from heathen philosophy or the superstitions of the Jews. He was earnest to make them feel how intimately they were connected with Christ, and to direct their thoughts to him as, under God, the only source of their knowledge, blessings, and hopes.

There was danger that, after the first excitement produced by the promulgation of Christianity had passed away, it would be regarded by many Gentile converts only as a new speculation upon topics which had long engaged the attention of their philosophers, — a system of opinions having its origin in a nation whom they regarded as barbarous (in the ancient sense of the word), which they might adopt in part only, reject, or modify, like other speculations, in their view similar. It was with a feeling of this danger, that St. Paul told the Corinthians that he was sent "to preach, not with wisdom of words, lest the cross of Christ should become of no account";* and that he was "determined to know nothing among them, but Jesus Christ, and him crucified."† In the two Epistles we are considering, he teaches those addressed, that it was through Christ alone that they who were formerly Gentiles had attained to a knowledge of God, and of the truths and hopes of religion. To raise and strengthen their sense of the value of Christianity, he describes its blessings, especially in reference to themselves who had been Gentiles, in the strongest terms; and, to fix their attention on Christ as their great and sole Master, he uses language equally strong in speaking of his relation to God, of the importance and dignity of his office, and of the dependence of all his followers upon him.

To the Colossians he says (i. 9-20):—

"So then we also, since we first heard of your

* 1 Cor. i. 17. † 1 Cor. ii. 2.

faith, cease not to pray for you, and to ask that you may be made perfect in the knowledge of God's will, having all spiritual wisdom and understanding; that you may walk worthily of the Lord to all acceptance, being fruitful in every good work, and increasing in the knowledge of God; being endued with all strength through his glorious power, so as to bear all things patiently and joyfully; giving thanks to the Father, who has qualified us to share the lot of the holy who are in the light, rescuing us from the empire of darkness, and transferring us into the kingdom of his beloved Son; by whom we are delivered, our sins being remitted; who is the image of the invisible God, the first-born of the whole creation; for by him all has been created, the heavenly and the earthly, the seen and the unseen, whether thrones, or principalities, or governments, or powers, all has been created through him and for him, and he is over all, and all exists by him. And he is the head of the body, the community of the holy,* he being the beginning, the first-born from the dead, that he might have pre-eminence in all things. For with him it pleased God that whatever is perfect should be united, and through him to reconcile all to himself, — making peace through the blood of his cross, — all whether in heaven or on earth through him."

In this passage there are some expressions that require explanation. God, says St. Paul, "has

* Or "the church": I use the term given above as more comprehensive and expressive.

transferred us from the empire of darkness into the kingdom of his beloved Son." To this metaphor much of the following language corresponds. It was this kingdom which had been newly *created*, that is, had been newly *formed;* for it is thus that the word rendered *created* is to be understood. We find it, and its correlatives, repeatedly used in a similar sense by St. Paul, namely, to denote the moral renovation of men by Christianity. Thus he says: —

" If any man be in Christ, he is a new creature. *The old things have passed away; behold, all things have become new.*" 2 Cor. v. 17.

" For in Christ Jesus neither is circumcision anything, nor uncircumcision, but a new creature." Gal. vi. 15.

" For we are God's workmanship, created through Christ Jesus for good works." Ephes. ii. 10.

" Put on the new man, who is created in the likeness of God with the righteousness and holiness of the true faith." Ephes. iv. 24.

The language from the Epistle to the Colossians in which Christ is said to have created all things, is to be explained in a corresponding manner. He created all things in the new dispensation, in the kingdom of Heaven. It has been understood as declaring, that the *natural creation* was the work of Christ. But it is obvious, at first sight, that the words used are not such as properly designate the objects of the *natural world;* and not such, therefore, as we should expect to be employed, if these were intended. In speaking of the natural creation, the same Apostle refers it to God in different terms, — to "the living God who made heaven and earth, and the sea, and all things that are in them." *

But what is meant by the Apostle when he speaks of Christ as creating things heavenly, and unseen, thrones, principalities, governments, and powers? I answer, that Christ is here spoken of by him as the founder and monarch of the kingdom of Heaven; and that this kingdom is conceived of, not as confined to earth, but as extending to the blessed in heaven, to those who have entered, or may enter, on their reward. Christ being represented under the figure of a king, and his followers being those who constituted the subjects of his kingdom, their highest honors and rewards are spoken of, in figurative language, as thrones, principalities, governments, and powers. He himself said to his Apostles: "In the regeneration," — that is, "in the new creation," for the terms are equivalent, — "In the regeneration, when the Son of Man shall sit on the throne of his glory, you also shall sit on twelve thrones, judging the twelve tribes of Israel." † "To sit on my right hand and on my left" — to hold the highest places in my kingdom, to attain the highest rewards conferred on my followers — "is not mine to grant, but it will be given to those for whom it has been prepared by my Father." ‡ But the kingdom of Heaven including the seen as well as the unseen,

* Acts xiv. 15. † Matthew xix. 28. ‡ Matthew xx. 23.

the earthly as well as the heavenly, the terms in question are to be understood, not merely as referring to the rewards of the blessed in heaven, but as denoting likewise the highest offices and dignities of this kingdom on earth; the offices of those who were ministers of Christ, its king, — his apostles and teachers. The purpose of St. Paul is to declare, that Christ is the former and master of the whole church on earth and in heaven, of the whole community of the holy; that he is the author of all their blessings; that all authority among them is from him; that all are ruled by his laws; that the whole kingdom on earth and in heaven exists through him, and, figuratively speaking, "for him," as its monarch.

The same leading ideas are somewhat differently expressed in the corresponding passage in the Epistle to the Ephesians (i. 15–23): —

"And therefore I, hearing of your faith in the Lord Jesus, and of your love toward all the holy, do not cease to give thanks for you, praying that the God of our Lord Jesus Christ, the Father of glory, may give you the spirit of wisdom and divine illumination, that you may become acquainted with him, the eyes of your minds being enlightened, that you may know what is the hope to which he has summoned you, and how rich is that glorious inheritance which he has given you among the holy, and how exceedingly great is his power exerted for us believers, corresponding to the operation of his might displayed in raising Christ from the dead; whom he hath seated at his own right hand in heaven, over all rule, and authority, and power, and dominion, and every title of honor in this age or in that to come; putting all things under his feet, and appointing him supreme head of the community of the holy, which is his body, the perfectness of him who is made completely perfect in all things."

In the passage first quoted from the Epistle to the Colossians, there is a clause (verse 19) which I have rendered, " For with him it pleased God, that whatever is perfect should be united." The rendering of the Common Version is, " For it pleased the Father, that in him should all fulness dwell." The word here translated " fulness, πλήρωμα, means "perfectness," "perfection," "completion," "fulness," or "that which perfects," "completes," "fills." In the Epistles to the Ephesians and Colossians, it is used by St. Paul in a peculiar manner; and from the want of a corresponding term which will readily suggest his meaning, there is in some instances a difficulty in expressing it in English. The rendering of the passages where it occurs must be varied according to the circumstances of the case.

The leading idea, I conceive, which St. Paul intended to express by this word in these two Epistles, is the *Perfectness* of Christianity, whether considered as a perfect display of the character of God, as a perfect system of religious truth, or as making its disciples perfect, in the scriptural sense of that word. All perfection, in his view, was combined in it; and his meaning in the clause just referred to is, that it pleased the Father that this whole Perfectness, with all those who were the subjects of it (*πᾶν τὸ πλήρωμα*), should abide with Christ. To him, as their sole master and teacher, his followers were to look. Nothing, to complete his religion, was to be drawn from any other source. Whatever was perfect was in him, that is, in his religion; to him every "perfect" man was united.

Thus he says in the Epistle to the Ephesians (iii. 14–19): —

"For this, I bend my knees to the Father of our Lord Jesus Christ, whose name is borne by every family [of Christ's disciples] in heaven or on earth, that, from his glorious abundance, he may grant you to be powerfully strengthened, through his spirit, within; that Christ may dwell in your hearts through faith; that you may have your root and foundation in love; and thus that you may be able to comprehend, with all the holy, the breadth and the length, the depth and the height, of his goodness,* and to know that Christian love†

* I insert the words "of his goodness" to make what I conceive to be the meaning of the Apostle clear in a translation. The reference of the preceding terms descriptive of magnitude is, I suppose, to *τὸν πλοῦτον τῆς δόξης αὐτοῦ*, verbally, "the richness of his glory," which I have rendered, "his glorious abundance." These words, and others equivalent, — as *ὁ πλοῦτος τῆς χάριτος αὐτοῦ*, *ὁ πλοῦτος τοῦ Χριστοῦ*, — occur often in these Epistles as descriptive of the goodness of God to the Gentiles. With the passage in the text may be compared Romans xi. 33, *Ὦ βάθος πλούτου καὶ σοφίας καὶ γνώσεως Θεοῦ!*

† *Τὴν ἀγάπην τοῦ Χριστοῦ*, "that love which Christ has taught and requires," of which the Apostle so often speaks in these Epistles, that love which, he elsewhere teaches, is better than knowledge.

which is better than knowledge; so that your perfection may correspond to the whole perfect dispensation of God,"—verbally, that "you may be perfected to the whole perfection of God," that is, the whole perfection which has God for its author.

In another passage in the same Epistle (iv. 11–13) he says, that God (to whom, and not to Christ, the preceding verses relate)*

"—gave to some to be apostles, to some to be public teachers, to some to be evangelists, to some to be pastors and private teachers, that they might perfect the holy, execute the work of the ministry, form the body of Christ, till we all attain the same faith, and the same knowledge of the Son of God, becoming full-grown men, reaching the full stature of Christian perfection."

The words of the last clause, verbally rendered, would be, "the measure of the stature of the Perfectness [that is, of the perfect dispensation] of Christ."

In a passage already quoted (Ephesians i. 23), the community of the holy is called "the body of Christ, the perfectness of him who is made completely perfect in all things." The word πλήρωμα, *perfectness*, is not here used in the extent of its signification as I have explained it. It is limited to the subjects of the perfect diepensation of Christ. As it stands, it has a double reference; one figurative to the idea of the perfectness, produced by uniting a body to its head, the church being the

* [See the Christian Examiner for January 1828, Vol. V. pp. 65–67.]

body and Christ the head; the other literal, the church being called the perfectness of Christ, partly because its members are considered as perfect, and partly because its formation was the perfecting of the great design of him, who, as a minister of God and teacher of the truth, was "made completely perfect in all things."

We will now turn to Colossians ii. 1 – 10 : —

"For I wish you to know what earnest care I have for you, and for those of Laodicea, and for all who have not known me in person; that being knit together in love, their minds may be excited to attain to all the riches of a complete understanding, to a full acquaintance with the new doctrine of God, in which are stored all the treasures of wisdom and knowledge. What I would is this, that no one may impose upon you by specious discourses. For I, though I am absent in body, am present with you in spirit, rejoicing at the sight of your well-ordered state, and the firmness of your faith in Christ. As, therefore, you have received Christ Jesus the Lord, so continue to walk in his way, rooted in him, built upon him, and established in the faith as it has been taught you, abounding in thanksgiving. Beware lest any man make a prey of you by a vain and deceitful philosophy, conformed to the doctrines of men, the principles of the world, and not to Christ; for with him abides, as his body, all that is divinely perfect; and you are made perfect through him, who is the head of all rule and authority."

By the words rendered "all that is divinely perfect," I understand the whole divine, perfect dispensation, with all who had become the subjects of it.* In the light in which the passage has been placed, it will be perceived that the leading ideas, and the language in which they are expressed, are both essentially the same with what we find in other passages of these two Epistles, which we have before noticed. These thoughts dwelt upon the mind of the Apostle while writing, and he reiterates them with a slight change of form. They consist in exhortations to unwavering faith, to entire deference to the instructions of Christ alone, and to constant progress in Christian knowledge and love; exhortations founded upon the perfectness of the religion taught by Christ, upon his divine authority, and upon the most intimate connection subsisting between him and all his true followers, he being the head, as it were, and they the body, all their blessings and all their knowledge, all that was perfect in them, being derived from him.

There are two other passages which, perhaps, it may be worth while to notice under the present head. In the twelfth chapter of John's Gospel (verse 40), the Evangelist applies to the Jews of his time words derived from Isaiah (vi. 10), which he thus gives: "He has blinded their eyes, and

* In the original words, τὸ πλήρωμα τῆς θεότητος, the genitive may denote the relation of an attribute to its subject, so that the words may be equivalent to τὸ θεῖον πλήρωμα; or the relation of a cause to its effect, so that they may mean "the perfection which has divinity for its author." The *ultimate* meaning is in both cases the same.

made their minds callous, so that they see not with their eyes, nor understand with their minds, nor turn from their ways, for me to heal them." "These words," he continues, "said Isaiah, when he saw his glory, and spoke concerning him." The primary reference of the passage was to the indirect effects to be produced by the preaching of the Prophet himself upon the Jews of his time.* But the Evangelist regarded it as having a secondary reference to Christ; and supposed Isaiah when uttering those words to have seen, that is, to have foreseen, his glory; the verb *to see* having here the same force as when used concerning Abraham: "Abraham *saw* my day and rejoiced."†

But the words found in Isaiah are represented by the Prophet as having been addressed to himself by Jehovah, when he beheld a vision of him in the temple; and the Trinitarian contends, that the glory seen by Isaiah, to which St. John refers, was this glory of Jehovah, and consequently that Jehovah and Christ are the same. Unquestionably this interpretation might be admitted, if it involved no absurdity and no contradiction to what is elsewhere said by the Evangelist. But if it do, it is equally unquestionable that it cannot be admitted.

An argument has been founded by Trinitarians upon the exclamation of the Apostle Thomas, when convinced of the truth of his Master's resurrection: "And Thomas said to Jesus, My Master!

* [See on this passage Mr. Norton's Notes on the Gospels.]

† [John viii. 56.]

and my God!"* Both titles, I believe, were applied by him to Jesus. But the name "God" was employed by him, not as the proper name of the Deity, but as an appellative, according to a common use of it in his day; or perhaps in a figurative sense, as it sometimes occurs in modern writers, of which the passages before quoted from Young afford examples.† I have already had occasion to remark upon the different significancy of the term "God" in ancient and in modern times, a difference important to be well understood in order to ascertain the meaning of ancient authors.‡ The name "God" is an appellative in the Old Testament;§ and it is a characteristic and peculiar

* [John xx. 28.]

† See p. 158.

‡ [See p. 120, note.]

§ [The Hebrew words commonly translated "God" in the Old Testament are *Elohim* and *El*. The former is applied to Moses, Exodus vii. 1 (comp. iv. 16); — to the apparition of Samuel, 1 Sam. xxviii. 13 (comp. verse 14); — to Solomon, or some other king of Israel, Psalm xlv. 6; — to judges, Exodus xxi. 6; xxii. 8, 9, 28; — and to kings or magistrates, Psalm lxxxii. 1, 6, and perhaps cxxxviii. 1 (comp. verse 4, and Psalm cxix. 46). See also Ezekiel xxviii. 1. Many have supposed the word *Elohim* to denote *angels* in Genesis iii. 5 (comp. verse 22), Psalm viii. 5, and some other passages, as Psalm xcvii. 7, where the Septuagint version has ἄγγελοι. This opinion was entertained by Milton, who accordingly, in his Paradise Lost, very often denominates angels "gods." The title "God of gods" is repeatedly given to Jehovah in the Old Testament: see Deuteronomy x. 17; Joshua xxii. 22; Psalm l. 1 (Heb.); cxxxvi. 2; Daniel xi. 36.

El is the Hebrew word which is translated "God" in Isaiah ix. 6, where it is supposed by most Trinitarian commentators to be a name of Christ. This passage has already been noticed. (See p. 182.) The same word is applied to Nebuchadnezzar in Ezekiel xxxi. 11, where it is rendered in the Common Version "the mighty one"; in

distinction of the *writers* of the New Testament, when compared with those who preceded and followed them, that they used this name as it is used by enlightened Christians at the present day.

But the argument deserves notice as illustrating

the Septuagint, ἄρχων, "ruler." In Ezekiel xxxii. 21, where it is used in the plural, it is translated "the strong." In Isaiah ix. 6, the Septuagint version, according to the Alexandrine manuscript, and also the versions of Aquila, Symmachus, and Theodotion, render the word by ἰσχυρός, "strong."

Our Saviour refers to this use of the word "God," in a lower sense, in the Old Testament. "Is it not written in your Law, *I said, Ye are gods?* If those are called gods to whom the word of God was addressed," &c. See John x. 34-36, and compare Psalm lxxxii. 1, 6.

There is but one passage in the New Testament, besides that now under consideration, in which there is any good reason for supposing the name "God" to be given to Christ. This is in the Epistle to the Hebrews, i. 8, 9, quoted from Psalm xlv. 6, 7,—"Thy throne, O God, is for ever and ever," &c. But here the context proves that the word "God" does not denote the Supreme Being, but is used in an inferior sense. This is admitted by some of the most respectable Trinitarian critics. Thus the Rev. Dr. Mayer remarks: "Here [i. e. in Hebrews i. 8] the Son is addressed by the title *God;* but the context shows that it is an official title, which designates him as a king: he has a kingdom, a throne, and a sceptre; and in ver. 9, he is compared with other kings, who are called his fellows; but God can have no fellows. As the Son, therefore, he is classed with the kings of the earth, and his superiority over them consists in this, that he is anointed with the oil of gladness above them; inasmuch as their thrones are temporary, but his shall be everlasting." (Article on "The Sonship of Christ," in the Biblical Repository for January 1840, p. 149.) So Professor Stuart says: "As to the quotation of Psalm xlv. it seems to me a clear case, that it does not fairly establish the truly divine nature of him to whom it is applied. *Elohim* appears to be here applied as designating an *official capacity*, which is high above that of all other kings." (Biblical Repository for July 1835, pp. 105, 106; compare his Commentary on Hebrews, p. 294, 2d ed.) After these admissions, it is hardly worth while to mention the fact, that such commentators as Calvin and Grotius

the very loose reasoning which has been resorted to in bringing passages from the Old and the New Testament in support of false doctrines. Supposing that Thomas *had* believed, and asserted, that his Master was God himself; in what way should

regard the Psalm in question as relating, in its primary sense, to Solomon.

Such, then, being the use of the word "God" in the Old Testament, Thomas may have applied it to Christ as it is applied to the subject of the forty-fifth Psalm, where it denotes "a divinely-anointed king," regarded as the earthly representative of God. But, without reference to this use of the word, there is no difficulty in conceiving that Thomas, under the circumstances related by the Evangelist, may have applied the term "God" to Christ, not as the Infinite and Unchangeable Being, but as one invested with the authority of God and manifesting his perfections, — his Image and Vicegerent on earth. He had listened to his words of eternal life; he had beheld the manifestations of that supernatural power which stilled the tempest, which gave sight to the blind, which raised the dead; in his Master's resurrection he now recognized, with feelings which we can hardly realize, the immediate interposition of the Almighty; the impression which had been made on his mind and heart by all that was divine in Christ was vivified anew; he felt the truth of the sublime words which but a few days before he had heard from his lips, "He who has seen me has seen the Father"; and, overwhelmed with wonder, reverence, and awe, he exclaims, "My Master! and my God!"

But is it not marvellous that theologians have made of this exclamation a *proof-text*, construing language of the strongest emotion as if it were the language of a creed? A more rational view, however, has been taken of the passage by such commentators as Michaelis, Rosenmüller, Kuinoel, and Lücke, — and, apparently, Neander and Tholuck, — who recognize the invalidity of the Trinitarian argument which has been founded upon it. Meyer, in the first edition of his Commentary (1834), remarked, very judiciously, that expressions uttered "in such ecstatic moments" are "entirely misused when applied to the proof of doctrinal propositions." But in his second edition (1852) he does not seem quite willing to give up the passage. He speaks of Thomas as expressing "his faith in the divine nature [or essence, *Wesen*] of his Lord"; and, though he ob-

this affect our faith? We should still know the fact on which his belief was founded, the fact of the resurrection of his Master, and could draw our own inferences from it, and judge whether his were well founded. Considering into how great an er-

serves that the strong feeling under which the exclamation was uttered renders it less fitted for doctrinal use, he cites as important the remark of Erasmus, that Christ accepted the acknowledgment of Thomas, instead of rebuking him, as he would have done if he had been falsely called God. The obvious reply to this is, that Christ accepted the acknowledgment of Thomas as *he meant it*, not in the irrational sense which modern theologians have put upon the words. And as Greenwood has well remarked: —

"The answer of Jesus himself excludes the supposition that he was addressed as the Supreme God. For he said unto his disciple, 'Thomas, because thou hast seen me, thou hast believed; blessed are they that have not seen, and yet have believed.' Now this must mean, 'Because thou hast seen me here alive, after my crucifixion and burial, thou hast believed that I am raised from the dead; and it is well; but blessed are they who cannot have such evidence of the senses, and yet shall believe in the glorious truth, from your evidence, and that of your brethren.' He could not have meant, that they were blessed who, though they had not seen him, yet had believed that he was God; because there is no connection between the propositions; because the fact of the resurrection of Jesus cannot, to the mind of any one, be of itself a proof of his deity; and because no one thinks of requiring to see God, in order to believe that he exists." (Lives of the Twelve Apostles, 2d ed., p. 139.)

Nothing can be more thoroughly irreconcilable with the whole tenor of the Gospel history, than the supposition that the disciples, during their intercourse with their Master on earth, regarded him as the Supreme Being. (See before, p. 75, et seqq.) It is, accordingly, admitted by many Trinitarians, that the mystery of the hypostatic union was not revealed to them before the effusion of the Spirit on the day of Pentecost. See Wilson's "Unitarian Principles confirmed by Trinitarian Testimonies," p. 351, et seqq.

What the Apostle John understood to be implied in this confession of Thomas, may be inferred from the words with which he concludes this chapter.]

ror he had fallen in his previous obstinate incredulity, there would be little reason for relying upon his opinion as infallible in the case supposed. I make these remarks, not from any doubt about the meaning of his words, but, as I have said, for the purpose of pointing out one example of that incomplete and unsatisfactory mode of reasoning, which appears in the use of many quotations from the Old and the New Testament.

CLASS VII.

The passages to which we have had occasion to attend are of a character to excite an interest in ascertaining their true meaning, without reference to the general subject of this volume. Their explanation rests on facts and principles important to be known and attended to in the study of the New Testament. But there are others brought forward by Trinitarians of which the same cannot be said, and which require only a very brief and general notice.

I have endeavored to show, that whenever a Trinitarian meaning is given to any passage, it is given in violation of a fundamental rule of interpretation. But there are *passages adduced, in the senses assigned to which, not merely this rule is violated, but the most obvious and indisputable characteristics of language are disregarded, and the reasoning proceeds upon the assumption that they do not exist.* Thus, for example, it is said in Isaiah (xliii. 11), according to the Common Version: "I, even I, am the LORD, and beside me there is no saviour." But Christ, it is argued, is our Saviour; and, as it is proved by this passage that there can be no saviour but God, it follows that Christ is God. The reasoning proceeds upon the assumption that the same word is always used in the same sense, with the same reference, and in the whole extent of its signification; and the monstrous conclusions that would result from applying this argument to other individuals beside Christ, to whom the name "Saviour" is or may be given, are put out of sight.*

* [See 2 Kings xiii. 5; Nehemiah ix. 27; Isaiah xix. 20; Obadiah 21.

Some Trinitarians have quoted in proof of the deity of Christ a few passages in which they suppose the title "God our Saviour" to be applied to him. The following are all the passages of the New Testament in which this expression occurs: 1 Timothy i. 1; ii. 3; Titus i. 3; ii. 10; iii. 4; and Jude 25. See also Luke i. 47; 1 Timothy iv. 10.

In some of these texts, as 1 Timothy i. 1, Titus iii. 4-6, the being who is called "God our Saviour" is expressly distinguished from Christ; and one need only compare the others with these, and with their context, to perceive that it is not only without evidence, but against all evidence, that any of them are referred to Christ. A large majority of Trinitarian commentators recognize this fact.

In Jude 25 the best ancient manuscripts and versions, and other authorities for settling the text, read, "To the ONLY God our Saviour, THROUGH JESUS CHRIST OUR LORD, be glory," &c. This reading is adopted by Griesbach, Knapp, Schott, Tittmann, Vater, Scholz, Lachmann, Hahn, Tischendorf, Theile, and nearly all modern critics. There can be no reasonable doubt of its genuineness.

We may here notice also 2 Peter i. 1 and Titus ii. 13, in which it has been maintained, on the ground of the omission of the Greek article, that Christ is called "our God and Saviour," and "our great

On misinterpretations such as this it would be useless to dwell. No information can be given, no thoughts can be suggested, which are not obvious to every reader who will exercise his own understanding; and to him who will not, all assistance must be in vain.

THUS, then, with one exception, which we will immediately consider, we have taken a general view of the manner in which the passages adduced by Trinitarians are to be explained.

God and Saviour." As to the argument founded on the omission of the article, it is not necessary to add anything to what has already been said. (See p. 199, note.) But it is urged by Professor Stuart and others, in respect to Titus ii. 13, that the "appearing" of God the Father is never foretold in the New Testament, and therefore that "the great God" here spoken of must be Christ. The answer to this is, that, according to the literal and correct translation of the original, it is not "the *appearing*," but "the appearing *of the glory*, ἐπιφάνειαν τῆς δόξης, of the great God and of our Saviour Jesus Christ," of which the Apostle speaks; and that our Saviour did expressly declare that he should come "in the glory of his Father." See Matthew xvi. 27; Mark viii. 38; Luke ix. 26; and compare 1 Timothy vi. 14-16. Professor Stuart admits that "the whole argument, ... so far as the *article* is concerned, falls to the ground." (Biblical Repository for April 1834, p. 323.) The title "the great God" in this passage is referred to the Father by Erasmus, Grotius, Le Clerc, Wetstein, Doddridge, Macknight, Abp. Newcome, Rosenmüller, Heinrichs, Schott, Winer, Neander (Planting and Training, I. 509, note, Bohn's ed.), De Wette, Meyer (on Romans ix. 5), Huther, Conybeare and Howson, and others.]

CLASS VIII.

The Introduction of St. John's Gospel.

We will now attend to a passage that has been misunderstood through ignorance or disregard of the opinions and modes of conception which the writer, St. John, had in mind. This is the introduction, or proem, as it has been called, of his Gospel.

"In the beginning was the Logos, and the Logos was with God, and the Logos was God."

There is no word in English answering to the Greek word *Logos*, as here used. It was employed to denote a mode of conception concerning the Deity, familiar at the time when St. John wrote, and intimately blended with the philosophy of his age, but long since obsolete, and so foreign from our habits of thinking, that it is not easy for us to conform our minds to its apprehension. The Greek word *Logos*, in one of its primary senses, answered nearly to our word *Reason*. It denoted that faculty by which the mind disposes its ideas in their proper relations to each other; the Disposing Power, if I may so speak, of the mind. In reference to this primary sense, it was applied to the Deity, but in a wider significance. The Logos of God was regarded, not in its strictest sense, as merely the Reason of God; but, under certain aspects, as the Wisdom, the Mind, the Intellect of God. To this the creation of all things was *especially* ascribed. The conception may seem obvious in itself; but the cause why the creation was primarily referred to the Logos or Intellect of God, rather than to his goodness or omnipotence, is to be found in the Platonic philosophy, as it existed about the time of Christ, and particularly as taught by the eminent Jewish philosopher, Philo of Alexandria.

According to this philosophy, there existed an archetypal world of IDEAS, formed by God, the perfect model of the sensible universe; corresponding, so far as what is divine may be compared with what is human, to the plan of a building or city which an architect forms in his own mind before commencing its erection. The faculty by which God disposed and arranged the world of Ideas was his Logos, Reason, or Intellect. This world, according to one representation, was supposed to have its seat in the Logos or Mind of God; according to another, it was identified with the Logos. The Platonic philosophy further taught, that the Ideas of God were not merely the archetypes, but, in scholastic language, the essential forms, of all created things.* In this philosophy, matter in *its primary state*, primitive matter, if I may so speak, was regarded merely as the substratum of attributes, being in itself devoid of all. Attributes, it was conceived, were impressed upon it by the Ideas of God, which Philo often speaks

* [For an account of Plato's doctrine of Ideas, see the author's Evidences of the Genuineness of the Gospels, Vol. III. Additional Note A.]

of under the figure of *seals*. These Ideas, indeed, constituted those attributes, becoming connected with primitive matter in an incomprehensible manner, and thus giving form and being to all things sensible. But the seat of these Ideas, these formative principles, being the Logos or Intellect of God, — or, according to the other representation mentioned, these Ideas constituting the Logos, — the Logos was, in consequence, represented as the great agent in creation. This doctrine being settled, the meaning of the term gradually extended itself by a natural process, and came at last to comprehend *all the attributes of God manifested in the creation and government of the universe.* These attributes, abstractly from God himself, were made an object of thought under the name of the Logos. The Logos thus conceived of was necessarily personified or spoken of figuratively as a person. In our own language, in describing its agency, — agency in its nature personal and to be ultimately referred to God, — we might indeed avoid attaching a personal character to the Logos considered abstractly from God, by the use of the neuter pronoun *it*. Thus we might say, All things were made by *it*. But the Greek language afforded no such resource, the relative pronoun in concord with Logos being necessarily masculine. Thus the Logos or Intellect of God came to be, figuratively or literally, conceived of as an intermediate being between God and his creatures, the great agent in the creation and government of the universe.

Obsolete as this mode of conception has now become, there is a foundation for it in the nature of the being contemplated, and of the human mind. The Deity conceived of as existing within himself, removed from all distinct apprehension of created intelligences, dwelling alone in his unapproachable and unimaginable infinity of perfections, presents a different object to the mind from the Deity operating around us and within us, and manifesting himself, as it were, even to our senses. It is not strange, therefore, that these two conceptions of him have been regarded apart, and more or less separated from each other. The notion of the Logos, it is true, is obsolete; but we find something analogous to it in the use of the term *Nature* in modern times. Employed as this often is, the mind seems to rest in some indistinct notion of an agency inferior to the Supreme, or an agency, to say the least, which is not referred directly to God.

The conception and the name of the Logos were familiar at the time when St. John wrote. They occur in the Apocryphal book of the Wisdom of Solomon. The writer, speaking of the destruction of the first-born of the Egyptians, says (ch. xviii. 15): —

"Thine almighty Logos leaped down from heaven, from his royal throne, a fierce warrior, into the midst of a land of destruction."

In another passage, likewise, in the prayer ascribed to Solomon, he is represented as thus addressing God (ch. ix. 1, 2): —

"God of our fathers, and Lord of mercy,
Who hast made all things by thy Logos,
And fashioned man by thy Wisdom."

The terms, *the Logos of God*, and *the Wisdom of God*, are here used as nearly equivalent in signification. A certain distinction was sometimes made between them; but they were often considered as the same. In the book just quoted we find strong personifications of Wisdom,* considered as an attribute of God, and described in such language as was afterwards applied to the Logos. In the Proverbs there are similar personifications of Wisdom,† which the Christian Fathers commonly understood of the Logos.

The use of the word "Logos," in the sense that has been assigned to it, was derived from the Platonic philosophy. But we find among the Jews a similar mode of conceiving and speaking of the operations of God, unconnected with this philosophy, and appearing in the use of a different term, *the Spirit of God*, or *the Holy Spirit*. By either expression, in its primary theological sense, was intended those attributes, or that power of God, which operated among men to produce effects that were believed to be conformable to his will, as manifested in the laws of his moral government. Thus the miracles of a teacher from God, the direct influences of God upon the minds of men, and all causes tending to advance men in excellence, moral and intellectual, were referred to the

* Ch. vii., viii., x.

† Ch. viii. See also ch. i. 20, seqq.; ch. iii. 19.

Holy Spirit. The idea of its invisible operation was associated with it. To express what has been said in different terms, it denoted the unseen Power of God, acting upon the minds of men in the direct or indirect production of moral goodness, or intellectual ability, in the communication of truth, and in the conferring of supernatural powers. The conception is of the same class with that of the Logos; and the Holy Spirit is in some instances strongly personified, as by our Saviour in his last discourse with his Apostles. The divine Power which was manifested in Christ might be ascribed indifferently to the Spirit, or to the Logos, of God, as the reader or hearer was more conversant with the one term or the other. St. John, writing in Asia Minor, where many for whom he intended his Gospel were familiar with the conception of the Logos, has, probably for this reason, adopted the term "Logos," in the proem of his Gospel, to express that manifestation of God by Christ which is elsewhere referred to the Spirit of God.*

* It may be observed, that, amid the confusion and inconsistency of those conceptions of the earlier Fathers which afterwards settled into the doctrine of the Trinity, we often find the Holy Spirit and the Logos spoken of as the same power of God. Thus Justin Martyr, in reference to the miraculous conception of Christ, says (Apologia Prima, c. 33. p. 54): "We must not understand by the Spirit and the power from God anything different from the Logos, who is the First-born of God." Theophilus of Antioch says (Ad Autolycum, Lib. II. § 10), that "the Logos is the Spirit of God and his Wisdom"; though he elsewhere (Ibid. § 15 et § 18) makes a Trinity of God, his Logos, and his Wisdom. The Wisdom of God was commonly conceived of as the Logos of God, but Irenæus, like Theophilus, gives the former name to the Holy Spirit. (See Lib. IV. c. 20.) Ter-

But to return. The conception that has been described having been formed of the Logos, and the Logos being, as I have said, necessarily personified, or spoken of figuratively as a person, it soon followed, as a natural consequence, that the Logos was by many hypostatized or conceived of as a proper person.* When the corrective of experience and actual knowledge cannot be applied, what is strongly imagined is very likely to be regarded as having a real existence; and the philosophy of the ancients was composed in great part of such imaginations. The Logos, it is to be recollected, was that power by which God disposed in order the Ideas of the archetypal world. But in particular reference to the creation of the material universe, the Logos came in time to be conceived of by many as hypostatized, as a proper person going forth, as it were, from God in order to execute the plan prepared, to dispose and arrange all things conformably to it, and to give

tullian says (Advers. Praxeam, c. 26): "The Spirit of God [the Spirit spoken of in the account of the miraculous conception] is the same as the Logos. For as, when John says, *The Logos was made flesh*, we by the Logos understand the Spirit, so here we perceive the Logos to be intended under the name of the Spirit. For as the Spirit is the substance of the Logos, so the Logos is the operation of the Spirit; and the two are one thing. What! when John said that the Logos was made flesh, and the angel, that the Spirit was to be made flesh, did they mean anything different?" See also c. 14; Advers. Marcion. Lib. V. c. 8, et alibi sæpe; Irenæus, Cont. Hæres. Lib. V. c. 1. § 2.

* It will be convenient in what follows to use the terms *personify* and *hypostatize*, with their correlatives, as distinguished from each other according to the senses assigned them in the text.

sensible forms to *primitive matter*, by impressing it with the Ideas of the archetypal world. In many cases in which the term "Logos" occurs, if we understand by it the Disposing Power of God in a sense conformable to the notions explained, we may have a clearer idea of its meaning, than if we render it by the term "Reason," or "Wisdom," or any other which our language offers.

In the writings of Philo, who was contemporary with our Saviour, we find the Logos clearly and frequently hypostatized. According to him, considered as a person, the Logos is a god. In a passage which has been closely imitated by Origen, he says: "Let us inquire if there are really two Gods." He answers: "The true God is one, but there are many who, in a less strict use of language, are called gods." The true God, he says, is denoted by that name with the article; others have it without the article; and thus his most venerable Logos is called God without the article.* "No one," he says, "can comprehend the nature of God; it is well if we can comprehend his *name*, that is, the Logos, his interpreter; for he may be considered, perhaps, as the god of us imperfect beings, but the Most High as the God of the wise and perfect."† He represents the Logos as

* De Somniis, Lib. I. c. 39. Opp. I. 655. Comp. Origen's Comment. in Joan. Tom. II. Opp. IV. 50, 51. Clement of Alexandria, remarking on Genesis iv. 25, says, *Οὐ γὰρ Θεὸν ἁπλῶς προσεῖπεν ὁ τῇ τοῦ ἄρθρου προτάξει τὸν παντοκράτορα δηλώσας*. — Stromat. III. § 12. p. 548. [See before, p. 120, note.]

† Legg. Allegorr. Lib. III. c. 73. Opp. I. 128.

the instrument (ὄργανον) of God in the creation of the universe; as the image of God, by whom the universe was fashioned; as used by him, like a helm, in directing the course of all things; as he who himself sits at the helm and orders all things; and as his first-born son, his vicegerent in the government of the world.* "Those," says Philo, "who have true knowledge [knowledge of God] are rightly called sons of God. . . . . . Let him, then, who is not yet worthy to be called a son of God, strive to fashion himself to the resemblance of God's first-born Logos, the most ancient angel, being, as it were, an archangel with many titles." † A little after, he calls the Logos "the eternal image of God"; and elsewhere applies to him the epithet "eternal." He represents the Logos as a mediator between God and his creatures. "To the archangel, the most ancient Logos, God freely granted the high distinction of standing between and separating the creation from its Creator. With the immortal being, he intercedes for what is mortal and perishing. He announces the will of the Ruler to his subjects. Being neither unoriginated like God, nor originated like man, but standing between the two extremes, he is a hostage to both; being a pledge to the Creator that the whole race of

* De Cherubim, c. 35. I. 162. De Monarchiâ, Lib. II. c. 5. Opp. II. 225. De Migrat. Abrahami, c. 1. I. 437. De Cherubim, c. 11. I. 145. De Agriculturâ, c. 12. I. 308.

† De Confusione Linguarum, c. 28. I. 426, 427. [See before, pp. 220, 221.]

men shall never fall away and revolt, preferring disorder to order; and giving assurance to the creature that the God of Mercy will never neglect what he has made." *

Such conceptions are expressed by Philo concerning the Logos as a person. If his representations of him, so far as they have been quoted, are not perfectly consistent, they do not imply that he wavered much in the view of his character; and these representations were received by the early Fathers as the groundwork of their doctrine concerning the personal Logos. But upon further examination, the opinions of Philo will appear more unsettled and unsteady; and new conceptions will present themselves. To these we shall advert hereafter. It is only necessary here to observe, that in his opinions relating to this subject there was little fixedness or consistency. The images which floated before his mind changed their forms. Throughout his writings, he often speaks of the personal agency of the Deity in language as simple as that of the Old Testament. In a large portion of the passages in which he makes mention of the Logos, it may be doubted whether he conceived of it, *for the time*, otherwise than as an attribute or attributes of God. On the other hand, it is also to be observed, that the influence of his Platonism, when it was ascendant in his mind, did not terminate in hypostatizing the Logos alone among the powers or attributes of God.

* Quis Rerum Divinarum Hæres, c. 42. I. 501, 502.

FROM the explanations which have been given of the conceptions concerning the Logos of God, it will appear that this term properly denoted an attribute or attributes of God; and that upon the notion of an attribute or attributes the idea of personality was superinduced. Let us now consider the probable meaning of the first words of St. John's Gospel.

"In the beginning was the Logos, and the Logos was with God, and the Logos was God."

These words admit, I think, only of two explanations. Either St. John used the word "Logos" simply to denote the conception of those attributes of God which are manifested in the creation and government of the universe; and in the last clause intended to declare, that, in the contemplation of them, no other being but God is to be contemplated, and that all their operations are to be referred directly to him; — or he meant to speak of those attributes as hypostatized, and to represent the Logos of God as a proper person (such as he is described by Philo), the minister and vicegerent of God, who, always acting by the power, and conformably to the will, of God, might rhetorically be called God, according to the figure by which we transfer to an agent the name of his principal.

It is contended, indeed, that his words admit of a different meaning; that the Logos is here spoken of as a proper person; but that this person is, at the same time, declared to be, literally, God. But if we so understand St. John, his words will express a contradiction in terms. "The Logos," he says, "was WITH God," which, if the Logos be a person, necessarily implies that he is a different person from God. Whoever is WITH any being must be diverse from that being with whom he is. As far, then, as we may be assured that St. John did not affirm an absurdity in terms, so far we may be assured that he did not affirm that the Logos, being a person with God, was also, literally, God. Of the Evangelist we may here say, as Tertullian says concerning another passage quoted from him: "Secundum omnia [in suo evangelio] potius quam adversus omnia, etiam adversus suos sensus interpretandus";—"He is to be explained conformably to all, rather than in opposition to all that he has elsewhere written, and in opposition, too, to the sense of the words themselves."* Here, therefore, we dismiss the Trinitarian exposition, and proceed to consider how the passage is to be understood.

We have now only to choose between the two explanations first given. St. John has *personified*, or he has *hypostatized* the Logos. He has spoken of the Logos simply as of the attributes, or, as we may say, the Power of God, manifested in his works; or he has adopted the philosophy of some of his contemporaries, and intended to represent this Power as a person.

Whether St. John did or did not adopt this Platonic conception, is a question not important to be settled in order to determine our own judgment

* [Tertullian. advers. Praxeam, c. 26.]

concerning its truth. But that he did not, is rendered probable by his not alluding to it elsewhere in his Gospel, and by his never in any other place introducing an intermediate agent between God and his creation, or referring the Divine Power manifested in Christ to any other being but God himself. It is unlikely that he would receive a doctrine of this kind, which had not been taught by his Master; and neither he nor any other of the Evangelists has recorded that this doctrine was taught by Christ. The nature of the doctrine itself, which presents the strange conception of an hypostatized attribute or attributes, would alone forbid the supposition of its having such an origin. It is clearly traced to a different source, to a philosophy which, considering St. John's intellectual habits and his manner of life, was not likely to have a strong influence over his mind.

But, setting aside these considerations, the passage itself affords, perhaps, sufficient reason for believing that the Evangelist did not intend to speak of an hypostatized Logos. "The Logos," he says, "was God," that is, the Supreme Being. If we conceive of the Logos as a person, the agent of God, those words considered in themselves admit, as I have said, of a figurative sense. But they would express an assertion which is made by no other writer who entertained this conception of the Logos. Philo, or the earlier Christian Fathers, would, equally, have shrunk from asserting the Logos to be God, as the word "God" is used by us. The earlier Fathers understood the term "god," as here used by St. John, in an inferior sense, regarding it as denoting what we might express in English by saying, that the Logos was a "divine being." But this, unquestionably, is not its true sense. St. John, having just used the word Θεός, "God," to denote the Supreme Being, would not in the next clause thus vary its signification; and corresponding likewise to what I have before observed,* his general use of this term, like that of the other Apostles and Evangelists, was the same with our own use of the name "God." Assuming, then, that the word Θεός, "God," in the passage before us, denotes the Deity, what purpose or inducement could St. John have had to assert, in a figurative sense, that the Logos was the Deity, upon the supposition that he believed the Logos to be a distinct person, the agent of the Deity? I think none can be conjectured.

Thus far, I have been arguing merely against the supposition, that St. John adopted the Platonic conception of an hypostatized Logos. But as to the further supposition, that he believed his Master, Jesus Christ, to have been not a man, properly speaking, but that Logos clothed in flesh, it is here sufficient, after all that has been said, to remark its inconsistency with the whole character of his narrative and those of the other Evangelists, and with every other part of the New Testament. Had St. John believed his Master to be an incarnation of a great being, to whom the name Logos might be applied, superior to all other beings except God,

* See before, pp. 300, 301.

we could, with our present view of the character of the Apostle, assign no other ground for this belief than an assurance of the fact, resting upon miraculous evidence. Had he, then, held this belief, he would everywhere have spoken of his Master conformably to it. Christ would have appeared throughout his Gospel and the other Gospels, not as a man, which he was not, but as the incarnate Logos, which he was. No reason can be assigned why he should not have been usually denominated by that name, his real character kept constantly in view, and all his words, actions, and sufferings correctly represented as those of the agent intermediate between God and his universe.

Let us now examine whether the language of the Apostle can be better explained, if we understand him as using the term "Logos" merely to denote the attributes of God manifested in his works. It was his purpose, in the introduction of his Gospel, to declare that Christianity had the same divine origin as the universe itself; that it was to be considered as proceeding from the same power of God. Writing in Asia Minor, for readers by many of whom the term "Logos" was more familiarly used than any other to express the attributes of God viewed in relation to his creatures, he adopted this term to convey his meaning, because, from their associations with it, it was fitted particularly to impress and affect their minds; thus connecting the great truth which he taught with their former modes of thinking and speaking. But upon the idea primarily expressed by this term, a new conception, the conception of the proper personality of those attributes, had been superinduced. This doctrine, then, the doctrine of an hypostatized Logos, it appears to have been his purpose to set aside. He would guard himself, I think, against being understood to countenance it. The Logos, he teaches, was not the agent of God, but God himself. Using the term merely to denote the attributes of God as manifested in his works, he teaches that the operations of the Logos are the operations of God; that all conceived of under that name is to be referred immediately to God; that in speaking of the Logos we speak of God, "that the Logos is God."

The Platonic conception of a personal Logos, distinct from God, was the embryo form of the Christian Trinity. If, therefore, the view just given of the purpose of St. John be correct, it is a remarkable fact, that his language has been alleged as a main support of that very doctrine, the rudiments of which it was intended to oppose.

Considering how prevalent was the conception of the Logos as a distinct being from God, it is difficult to suppose that St. John did not have it in mind. But it is to be observed, that the preceding explanation of his words is independent of this supposition, and that they are to be understood in the same manner, whether they are supposed to refer to that conception or not.

It is, then, of the attributes of God as displayed in the creation and government of the world, that St. John speaks under the name of "the Logos."

To this name we have none equivalent in English, for we have not the conception which it was intended to express. In rendering the first eighteen verses of St. John's Gospel, I shall adopt the term "Power of God." It is, perhaps, as nearly equivalent as any that we can conveniently use. But in order to enter into the meaning of the passage, we must associate with this term, not the meaning alone which the English words might suggest according to their common use, but the whole notion of the Logos as present to the mind of the Apostle.

Adopting this term, we may say that the Power of God, personified, is the subject of the introductory verses of his Gospel. It is first said to be God, and afterwards declared to have become a man. It is first regarded in its relation to God in whom it resides, and afterwards in its relation to Jesus through whom it was manifested. Viewed in the former relation, what may be said of the Power of God is true of God; the terms become identical in their purport. Viewed in the latter relation, whatever is true of the Power of God is true of Christ, considered as the minister of God. His words were the words of God, his miracles were performed by the power of God. In the use of such figurative language, the leading term seldom preserves throughout the same determinate significance; its meaning varies, assuming a new aspect according to the relations in which it is presented. Thus, an attribute may be spoken of as personified, then simply as an attribute, and then, again, as identified with the subject in which it resides, or the agent through whom it is manifested In regard to the personification of the Logos by St John, which is a principal source of embarrassment to a modern reader, it was, as I have said, inseparable from the terms in which the conception was expressed, the actions ascribed to the Logos being of a personal character, and the use of the neuter pronoun being precluded by the syntax of the Greek language. St. John, then, says: —

"In the beginning was the Power of God, and the Power of God was with God, and the Power of God was God. He was in the beginning with God. All things were made by him, and without him nothing was made which was made. In him was the source of blessedness;* and the source of blessedness was the light for man. And the light is shining in darkness; though the darkness was not penetrated by it.

"There was a man sent from God, whose name was John. This man came as a witness, to bear testimony concerning the light, that all might believe through him. He was not the light, but he came to bear testimony concerning the light. The

* Ζωή, rendered in the Common Version *life*. It is here, however, used in the sense of *blessedness*, as often in the New Testament. But the blessedness spoken of is that which is *communicated*, not that which is *enjoyed*, by the Logos. I do not perceive, therefore, that the sense of the original can be expressed more concisely in English than by the words which I have used. This blessedness is communicated through the revelation of religious truth; the intellectual *light*; — not "of men," but "for men." In other words, the revelation made by the Power of God through Christ, which is the light of the moral world, is the source of blessedness to men.

true light,* which shines on every man, was coming into the world. He was in the world, and by him the world was made, and the world acknowledged him not. He came to his peculiar possession, and his peculiar people received him not. But to as many as received him he gave a title to be children of God, — to those who had faith in him, — they being born not of any peculiar race,† nor through the will of the flesh, nor through the will of man, but being children of God.

"And the Power of God became a man,‡ and dwelt among us, full of favor and truth; and we beheld his glory, such as an only son receives from a father. John bore testimony concerning him, and proclaimed, This is he of whom I said, He who was to come after me has gone before me, for he was my superior. — Of his inexhaustible store we all have received, even favor upon favor. For

* "The true light," that is, the Power of God, the Logos; so called because he is the source of the light, the revealer of religious truth.

† Οὐκ ἐξ αἱμάτων, literally, *not of (particular) races*, αἷμα being here used in the sense of *race*, as in Acts xvii. 26, and by profane writers. *Blood* in English is used in a similar sense; as in the expression, "They were of the same blood." The meaning of the whole thirteenth verse is, that the blessings of the Gospel were not confined to any particular race, as that of the Jews; and that none received them on the ground of natural descent, as children of Abraham and the other patriarchs.

‡ Σὰρξ ἐγένετο, rendered in the Common Version, "became flesh." The word σάρξ, in its primitive meaning *flesh*, is often used to denote *man*. When it is said that the Logos, or the Power of God, became a man, the meaning is that the Power of God was manifested in and exercised through a man. It is afterward, by a figurative use of language, identified with Christ, in whom it is conceived of as residing.

the Law was given by Moses, the Favor and the Truth* came by Jesus Christ. No man has ever seen God; the only Son, who is on the bosom of the Father, he has made him known."

In a note on this passage, I have explained the words, "the Logos became flesh," or "the Power of God became a man," as meaning that "the power of God was manifested in a man," that "it was exercised through him," "it resided in him." To one familiar with the uses of figurative language, the interpretation may appear obvious. Some Trinitarians, however, may object to it as forced. I would, therefore, ask him who believes that by the Logos is meant the second person of the Trinity, to consider the exposition which he himself puts upon the words. According to this, the second person of the Trinity, the Son, who is himself God, became a man, or, to adopt the rendering of the Common Version, was made flesh. God became a man, or was made flesh. By the word rendered *became* or *was made*, the Trinitarian understands to be meant, that he *was hypostatically united to* a man, *was so united to* a man *as to constitute with him but one person.* It is a sense of the Greek word ἐγένετο not to be found elsewhere; to say nothing of the meaning of the whole sentence, if it may be called a meaning, which results from giving ἐγένετο this unauthorized signification. The Antitrinitarian, on the other hand, understands the

* "The Favor and the Truth," ἡ χάρις καὶ ἡ ἀλήθεια. These terms are here used to denote the Christian dispensation, the religion of mercy and truth.

word as equivalent to "became," in that figurative sense in which we say that one thing is, or becomes, another, when it manifests its properties in that other thing so spoken of. He perceives as little difficulty in the language, as in that with which Thomson commences his Hymn on the Seasons:—

> "These, as they change, Almighty Father, these
> Are but the varied God."

As the Seasons are figuratively called God, because God in them displays his attributes, so the Logos is figuratively called a man, because in Christ were manifested the same Divine Power, Wisdom, and Goodness by which the universe was created.

It is by no means uncommon to find in the same passage an attribute or a quality, now viewed in the abstract and personified, and then presented to the imagination as embodied in an individual or individuals. Thus Thomson, on the same page in the volume before me from which I made the last quotation, says:—

> "Heaven-born Truth
> Wore the red marks of Superstition's scourge."

It is Truth considered in the abstract, which is described as heaven-born, or revealed from heaven; it is those who held the truth who were scourged by Superstition. Other similar examples might be adduced. I will give one expressly conformed in its general character to the passage under consideration, in which no person accustomed to the use of figurative language will suppose that its proper limits are transgressed.

Goodness is seated on the throne of God, and directs his omnipotence. It is the blessedness of all holy and happy beings to contemplate her, the Supreme Beauty, and become more and more conformed to her image. It is by her that the universe is attuned, and filled with harmony. She descended from heaven, and in the person of Christ displayed her loveliness; and called men to obey her laws, and enter her kingdom of light and joy. But she addressed those whom their vices and bigotry had made blind and deaf. She was rejected, despised, hated, persecuted, crucified.

It may appear from what has been said, that the figure by which St. John speaks of the Logos as becoming a man, or, in other words, of Christ as being the Logos, belongs to a class in common use. But it might have been sufficient at once to observe, that analogous modes of expression are used even by Philo, though he regarded the Logos as a proper person. Considering the Logos as the agent of God in the creation and government of all, the being through whom God is manifested, Philo applies that name to other beings, the agents of God's will. In this use of the term, it may seem that, the Logos being viewed as the primal, universal manifestation of God, all particular manifestations are referred to it by Philo, as parts to a whole; — or the one Logos is supposed to act in every particular Logos, using all as its ministers. However this may be, he familiarly calls the angels "Logoi"* (in the plural), and applies the term also to men. Thus he speaks of Moses as "the lawgiving Logos," as "the divine Logos," and, when he interceded for the Israelites, as "the supplicating Logos of God."† Aaron is called "the sacred Logos."‡ The same title is given to Phinehas, upon occasion of his staying the plague in the Jewish camp.§ And the high-priest is repeatedly called "Logos."|| Such language being common, the contemporaries of St. John would readily understand him, when he spoke of the Logos becoming a man, or of Christ as being the Logos. When, afterwards, the Christian Fathers, regarding the Logos as hypostatized, supposed it to have become incarnate in Christ, they, of course, put a new sense upon the words of the Apostle.

I MAY here take notice of a supposed analogy, which I believe does not exist, between the introductory verses of St. John's Gospel and those with which he commences his First Epistle. In the latter, by the expression rendered in the Common Version "word of life" (λόγος τῆς ζωῆς), he intends, I think, merely the Christian doctrine, "the life-giving doctrine"; and has no reference to the philosophical notion of the Logos of God. This

* De Posteritate Caini, c. 26. I. 242. De Confusione Linguarum, c. 8. I. 409, et alibi sæpe. [See Christian Examiner for May 1836, Vol. XX. p. 229.]

† De Migrat. Abrahami, cc. 5, 15, 21. I. 440, 449, 455.

‡ Legg. Allegorr. Lib. I. c. 24. Opp. I. 59.

§ Quis Rerum divinarum Hæres, c. 42. I. 501.

|| De Gigantibus, c. 11. I. 269. De Migrat. Abrahami, c. 18. I. 452.

expression, and others similar, are used elsewhere in the New Testament in the same sense.* The commencement of the Epistle may be thus rendered: —

"What took place from the beginning,† what we have heard, what we have seen with our eyes, what we have beheld, and our hands have handled, concerning the life-giving doctrine; — for Life has been revealed, and we saw and bear testimony, and announce to you that Eternal Life which was with the Father, and has been revealed to us; — what we have seen and heard, we announce to you, so that you may share with us, whose lot is with the Father and with his Son, Jesus Christ."

Notwithstanding the coincidence of some words, used in different senses, it is obvious that the purpose of St. John in the passage just quoted was wholly different from that which appears in the introduction of his Gospel. In the latter he intended to affirm that the Christian revelation was to be referred to the same Divine Wisdom, Goodness, and Power by which the world was created and is governed. In the first verses of his Epistle

* See Philippians ii. 16; Acts v. 20; John vi. 63, 68; Romans viii. 2, etc.

† That is, "from the beginning of the Christian dispensation." The terms, ἄπ' ἀρχῆς, or ἐξ ἀρχῆς, *from the beginning*, commonly occur in St. John's writings in reference to the beginning of a period determined only by the connection in which the words occur. Thus in the second chapter of this Epistle, verse 7, he says: "Beloved, I write you no new commandment, but an old commandment, which you have had *from the beginning* [rather, *from the first*]." See also Epistle, ii. 24; iii. 11; Gospel, vi. 64; xv. 27; xvi. 4, etc.

he merely affirms that what he had taught concerning this revelation rested upon his own personal knowledge, upon the testimony of his senses.*

We will here conclude our examination of passages adduced by Trinitarians. I have remarked upon those which will generally be considered as most important, and it would be useless to proceed further. As to any of which I have omitted to take notice, it will be easy to apply to them the principles and facts which have been stated and illustrated.

In treating of the Proem of St. John's Gospel, we have had occasion partially to consider the doctrine of the Platonic Logos, the germ of the Christian Trinity. In the next section I shall proceed to give some further account of it, and of the conceptions connected with it; my purpose being to bring into view some particulars, not generally attended to, concerning the origin, relations, and character of the doctrine of the Trinity as it existed during the first four centuries.

* There is a passage in the Epistle to the Hebrews (iv. 12, 13), and another in the Apocalypse (xix. 13), in which the conception of the Logos as an attribute or attributes of God appears to be introduced, as in the introduction of St. John's Gospel. But it would not be to our present purpose to remark upon them further.

SECTION X.

ILLUSTRATIONS OF THE DOCTRINE OF THE LOGOS.

It is in the writings of Philo that we find the doctrine of the Logos first developed; and his conceptions concerning this, as well as other subjects connected with theology, deserve to be attentively studied.

Philo, it will be recollected, was of Alexandria, a contemporary of Christ, a Jewish Platonist. No individual, since the time of the Apostles, with the exception, perhaps, of Augustine, has exercised so considerable and lasting influence upon the opinions of the whole Christian world, as this learned and eloquent Jew. His influence operated through the early Christian Fathers, particularly those of Alexandria. To the distinction which he has thus attained, he had no claim from the clearness or consistency of his speculations, or any power of argument. In his mind, imagination had seized upon the whole domain of speculative reason. As an interpreter, he melted down the literal meaning of the Old Testament, and recast it in fanciful allegories. In following him in his expositions, which constitute far the greater part of his works, the reader is bewildered by a constant succession of metamorphoses. His unsubstantial conceptions on other subjects retain no permanent form. But he sometimes pours forth noble thoughts in a stream of overflowing eloquence.* His morality is, for the most part, correct; and, considering his age and the circumstances under which he wrote, wonderfully pure and elevated. He seems to have been deeply penetrated by sentiments of true religion, and thus separated, like the early Christians, from the world around him. Though verging toward asceticism in his morality, and mysticism in his religious feelings, he stopped short of the extravagances of both. His general conceptions of the Divinity are those of an enlightened Christian; and his imaginations concerning the powers and operations of God, if untenable, are but seldom offensive even to a modern reader. His visionary speculations concerning him seem to have been rebuked by the severe genius of the Jewish religion, and to float on the confines which separate poetry and rhetoric from philosophy. For the most part, he speaks of God, not only as the first cause, but as the immediate agent in the production of beings and events, without superadding anything in this respect to the representations of the Old Testament. There are many passages in which he introduces the Logos, and other powers or attributes of God, as instrumental agents of the Deity, that might be explained as the language of

* [See, for example, a striking passage from Philo (De Opificio Mundi, c. 23. I. 15, 16), translated and illustrated by Mr. Norton in the Christian Examiner for September 1827, Vol. IV. p. 377.]

bold personification, such as is applied to Wisdom in the Proverbs and the Apocrypha. But his imaginations occasionally, or permanently, passed into opinions; and there are passages in his writings which prove that he sometimes, if not always, conceived of the Logos and of other attributes of God as proper persons. Of those relating to the Logos I have already given examples.

From Philo the Catholic Fathers borrowed their doctrine of the Logos, and the Gnostics, I may add, much of the material of their systems of Æons.* The Fathers copied his conceptions, his

* As I shall in this section occasionally refer to the Gnostics, I will here give such a brief account of them as may be necessary to illustrate those references. The term "Gnostics" is a general name applied to various sects of Christians having much in common, who early distinguished themselves from the great body of believers. They existed principally during the first three centuries. Their most distinctive opinion was the belief that the material world was created by an imperfect being, far inferior to God, — the Demiurgus or Creator; from whom also they supposed the Jewish dispensation to have proceeded. Christ was in their view the messenger of the Supreme God to deliver men from the reign of the Creator.

But those opinions to which I shall have occasion to refer concerned the development of beings from the Supreme God. Respecting this subject, different sects had different schemes. Concerning all, our information is imperfect; but that of *the Valentinians*, as reformed by Ptolemy, or the Ptolemæo-Valentinian theory, as it may be called, is the best known, was the most prevalent, and may serve as a specimen of their general character. According to this theory, God was conceived of as having dwelt from eternity with Silence, or Thought, or Benevolence, (for these different names are used,) who appears dimly shadowed forth as the hypostatized spouse of God. Silence becoming pregnant through his power, the first and greatest emanation from God, Intellect (Nous), was produced, with Truth for his spouse, and from Intellect and Truth were then emitted Reason

distinctions, his language, and his illustrations. Our interest is consequently excited to learn all that may be known of his opinions concerning this subject. The inquiry will show us how imperfect and changeable was his notion of an hypostatized Logos, and will at the same time open to us a prospect of speculations respecting the Divine Nature, the most foreign from our modes of thinking, but which have very extensively prevailed.

In the last section, I have given that view of Philo's opinions concerning an hypostatized Logos

(the Logos), with his spouse, Life; and Man, with his spouse, the Church.

The Gnostics affected the reputation of superior wisdom and discernment; and in this arrangement of emanations, we may perceive, I think, what they regarded as a more full development of ideas which, in their view, were ignorantly confounded together by other Christians. By these, generally, no distinction was made between Intellect and Reason, the Nous and the Logos; the Gnostics, on the contrary, separated them from each other, and regarded the latter as comprehended in, and emanating from, the former. We find something analogous to their conception in Origen (Comment. in Joannem. Opp. IV. 20, 21, 22, 36, 47), who represents the Logos of God as comprehended in his Wisdom, and referring to Proverbs viii. 22 (according to the Septuagint), *The Lord created me, the Beginning*, understands St. John as meaning, that the Logos was in Wisdom, when he says, *The Logos was in the Beginning.* So also, I conceive, it was another refinement of the Gnostics to separate the emanation Man from the emanation Logos. The Logos was by Philo regarded as that image of God after which man was created, the archetypal man, the primal man. But the Gnostics chose to separate these two characters, and made a distinct emanation of the Primal Man.

In order fully to explain what has been said, it is necessary to remark, that the female emanations are merely hypostatized attributes or energies of the male, and that the line of derivation from the

which is most commonly presented. But there is much more to be known. We will first consider how he speaks of the Logos in relation to the Wisdom of God.

With the Wisdom of God, the Logos is expressly identified by Philo.* He ascribes the same titles, character, and offices to both.† "God," he says, "separated Wisdom from his other powers as the head and chief."‡ He speaks of the universe as formed by Divine Wisdom.§

But though he thus identifies the Wisdom with the Logos or Reason of God, yet he elsewhere

Deity is thus to be regarded: first Intellect, then the Logos, then the Primal Man.

After those which have been mentioned, follows in the system a series of emanations, all, I conceive, hypostatized attributes or Ideas, of which it is here unnecessary to give a further account. All these emanations and the Deity himself were denominated *Æons*, that is, "Immortals." They constituted the *Pleroma* of the Gnostics, by which seems to have been meant "the Perfect Manifestation of the Deity." The word was likewise used to denote the spiritual world inhabited by them, as distinguished from the material universe.

[For further information respecting the Gnostics, see the author's Evidences of the Genuineness of the Gospels, Vols. II. and III. In relation to the principal subject of this note, see particularly Vol. III. p. 115, et seqq.]

* Legg. Allegorr. Lib. I. c. 19. Opp. I. 56. Quod Deterior Potiori insidiari soleat, c. 31. I. 213, 214.

† Legg. Allegorr. Lib. I. c. 14. Opp. I. 51, 52; comp. De Confusione Linguarum, c. 28. I. 427. — De Migrat. Abrahami, c. 8. I. 442; comp. De Somniis, Lib. I. c. 15. I. 633. — De Congressu, c. 21. I. 536; comp. De Mundi Opificio, c. 6. I. 5. — De Profugis, c. 9. I. 553.

‡ Legg. Allegorr. Lib. II. c. 21. Opp. I. 82.

§ Quis Rerum div. Hæres, c. 41. I. 501.

represents Wisdom as the mother of the Logos; "his Father being God, the Father of All, and his Mother being Wisdom, through whom all things are produced."* In another place, the figure being borrowed from a passage on which he is commenting, he says, that "to his Logos God has given his Wisdom for a country where he may dwell as native to the soil."†

He repeatedly represents Wisdom as the Spouse of God, and the Mother of all things; in the same manner (to notice his coincidence with the Gnostics) as, in the Ptolemæo-Valentinian theory, Silence, Thought, or Benevolence is assigned as a spouse to the Divine Being. "God," he says, "we may rightly call the Father, and Wisdom the Mother, of this universe"; and the language which he uses in reference to this conception is as abhorrent to our feelings of propriety, as that which Irenæus ascribes to the Valentinians.‡ Elsewhere he calls "the Virtue and Wisdom of God the mother of all"; § and in another place he describes Wisdom as the daughter of God, "always delighting, rejoicing, and exulting in God her Father alone," where, immediately after, he identifies her with the Logos.|| Again, he represents Wisdom, "the daughter of God," as properly

* De Profugis, c. 20. I. 562.

† Ibid., c. 14. I. 557.

‡ De Ebrietate, c. 8. I. 361 (conf. Irenæum cont. Hæreses, Lib. I. c. 1). Quod Det. Pot. insid. soleat, c. 16. I. 201, 202. De Cherubim, c. 14. I. 148.

§ Legg. Allegorr. Lib. II. c. 14. Opp. I. 75.

|| Ibid., Lib. I. c. 19. Opp. I. 56.

to be called both male and female, both father and mother.*

These varying accounts of the Wisdom of God seem to be, in great part, rhetorical personifications. But when we recollect that the Wisdom is identified with the Logos of God by Philo, as by the Christian Fathers, we perceive how in his mind figures of speech were mixed up with opinions, shadows with what he thought substantial beings. The process by which his fancies indurated into doctrines was left too incomplete for his scheme to possess proper consistency. This will still further appear from what follows.

The hypostatized Logos, it is to be borne in mind, is an hypostatized attribute or attributes of God. But there are other attributes, or, as Philo denominates them, Powers (δυνάμεις) of God, which appear hypostatized in his writings as distinctly and permanently as the Logos. Of this I will give some examples. From these it will be seen how imperfectly Philo's theory was adjusted in his own mind, and how far he was from having settled the relation of the other Powers of God to the Logos. His conceptions have an analogy to the Valentinian system of Æons, and his hypostatizing these other Powers of God, if it did not give occasion to, at least countenanced, their speculations.

The six cities of refuge, appointed by the Jewish Law, are, according to him, symbolical of Powers

* De Profugis, c. 9. I. 553.

of God, to whom men may fly for refuge. The most ancient, the strongest, the best, the metropolis, from which the others are, as it were, colonies, is the Divine Logos, the Mind, Intellect, or Reason of God. The other five are the Creative, by which he made the universe, which Moses, according to Philo, has called God; the Regal, by which he governs it, and which bears the name of Lord; the Merciful; the Legislative which commands and rewards; and the Legislative which forbids and punishes. "Over all these latter powers is the Divine Logos, the most ancient (or venerable) of *intelligible* things, the nearest to God, nothing intervening between him and that Being on whom he rests, Him who alone truly exists. He is the charioteer of the Powers of God, to whom God gives directions for the right guidance of the universe." *

After having given different allegorical explanations of the two Cherubim who guarded the gate of Paradise, Philo says: "I have heard a yet higher doctrine from my soul, accustomed to be divinely inspired, and to utter oracles concerning things of which itself is ignorant. This doctrine, if I am able, I will give from memory. My soul then said to me, that with the one God who possesses true being, there are two highest and principal Powers, Goodness and Authority; that by Goodness all things are made, and by Authority the creation is governed; and that a third, which connects both,

* De Profugis, cc. 18, 19. I. 560, 561. Respecting the Legislative Powers, comp. De Sacrific. Abelis et Caini, c. 39. I. 189.

being in the midst between them, is Reason (Logos), for by Reason (Logos) God both rules and is good."*

These two Powers of God under various names, sometimes called the Creative and the Regal, sometimes Goodness and Authority, sometimes the Beneficent and the Disciplinary, often appear in the writings of Philo. Sometimes they are spoken of, as in the passage last quoted, in connection with the Logos; more frequently they are denominated as the two highest Powers of God, without any mention of the Logos. To the latter, Philo, as we have seen, does not apply the name "God" in its highest sense; but of these two Powers he repeatedly says, that the proper name of the Creative, the name given it by Moses, is "God," and the name of the Regal, "Lord." †

When these Powers are spoken of by Philo as subjected to the Logos, if he regarded the Logos as a person, it is clear that he regarded them as persons also; for he would not have subjected them, considered merely as the attributes of God, to the Logos, considered as a person distinct from God.

But the idea of the conversion of an attribute or

* De Cherubim, c. 9. I. 143, 144.

† I refer to some other of the passages in which they are mentioned. De Sacrific. Abelis et Caini, c. 15. I. 173, 174. De Plantatione, c. 20. I. 342. De Confusione Linguarum, c. 27. I. 425. De Migrat. Abrahami, c. 22. I. 464. Quis Rerum div. Hæres, c. 34. I. 496. De Nominum Mutatione, cc. 3, 4. I. 581 – 583. De Somniis, Lib. I. c. 26. Opp. I. 645. De Sacrificant. c. 9. II. 258. De Legatione ad Caium, c. 1. II. 546.

power of God into a person had acquired no such fixedness and permanent form in the speculations of Philo, as in the Catholic doctrine of the Logos, or in Ptolemy's system of Æons. Accordingly the two highest Powers of God, whose names are "God" and "Lord," may seem often to be only two aspects or characters under which he regarded the Supreme Being. After having spoken of them, by the names of the Creative and Regal, as symbolized by the two Cherubim overshadowing the Mercy-seat, and entitled them, as usual, "God" and "Lord," he defends his explanation by saying: "For God, being indeed alone, is truly a Creator, since he brought into being the things which were not, and a King by nature, for none can more justly rule what is made than he who made it." * "It is customary," he says in another place, "to use two appellations of the First Cause, that of 'God' and that of 'Lord.'" † Yet there is no passage in his writings which seems more clearly to resolve them into mere attributes or characters of God, than one which is followed by such a description of their personal agency as necessarily implies the conception of their being persons distinct from God. It is in his book concerning Abraham; where he is allegorizing the appearance of the three angels to Abraham in the plain of Mamre. When the soul, he says, is circumfused by divine light, it discerns three appearances of one object, the appearance of One as properly exist-

* De Mose, Lib. III. c. 8. Opp. II. 150.

† Quis Rerum div. Hæres, c. 6. I. 476.

ing, and of two others as shadows rayed forth from Him, as we sometimes in the world of the senses see two shadows of a material object. Of these appearances, that in the midst is the Father of All, He who Is; those on each side are his two most venerable Powers, the nearest to himself, the Creative, God, and the Regal, Lord. Philo then adds, that God thus attended presents sometimes one and sometimes three images to the mental vision; *one*, when the soul, thoroughly purified, rises above all idea of plurality to that unmingled form of being which admits of no mixture, alone, and wholly independent; *three*, before it is yet initiated in the greater mysteries, and cannot contemplate Him who Is by himself alone, but needs the aid of something beside, and views him through his works as either creating or ruling.*

Philo would here seem to intend, that the language concerning the two principal Powers of God, when they are spoken of as distinct persons, is but a figurative mode of representing the operations of the Divine Being, accommodated to the weakness of those who cannot comprehend him as he is. But as he proceeds, in his earnestness to prove that the account of the three angels who appeared to Abraham is to be allegorized as relating to God and his two attendant Powers, he presents an opposite view. In the narrative of the destruction of Sodom, which immediately follows, only

* De Abrahamo, c. 24. II. 18, 19. Comp. De Sacrificiis Abelis et Caini, c. 15. I. 173, 174. [The latter passage is quoted in the Christian Examiner for May 1836, Vol. XX. pp. 231, 232.]

two angels are mentioned.* This, in his opinion, confirms his mode of interpreting the preceding account. He who had withdrawn himself was God, the two who remained were his two Powers, God judging it fit to bestow favors immediately from himself, but to commit to the ministry of his Powers the infliction of punishment. The Beneficent (another name, it will be recollected, for the Creative) and the Disciplinary (or Regal) were both present, the former to preserve the city of Zoar, which was saved, and the latter to destroy the four other cities of the plain.† To God thus using the ministry of his Powers, Philo compares human kings who bestow favors in person, but punish by the ministry of others.‡

By this and by other similar representations, Philo shows that he did often, if not uniformly, image to himself the Powers of God as agents distinct from God. But how fluctuating were his conceptions may appear, not only from the seeming discrepancy between the former and the latter part of the passage I have quoted, but from the absence of all mention of the Logos in this discussion concerning what he here and elsewhere calls the two highest Powers of God.

When, however, the light of his philosophy shone full around him, Philo discerned not merely those hypostatized Powers of God that have been mentioned, but many others, far exceeding in num-

* Genesis xix. 1, seqq. † Comp. Genesis xiv. 2, 3.

‡ De Abrahamo, c. 28. II. 21, 22.

ber the Gnostic Æons. To state a fact for which, strange as it is, what precedes may afford some preparation, Philo, as a Platonist, hypostatized, generally, the Powers of God. In commenting upon the history of the tower of Babel, he inquires whom God addressed, when he said, Come, let us go down, and there confuse their language. "He appears," he says, "to be addressing some as fellow-workers." But God is the only Maker and Father and Lord of the Universe. How, then, are the words to be explained? God, he answers, being ONE, is surrounded by innumerable Powers, all employed for the service and benefit of the creation. On these Powers the angels are attendant ministers, and the whole army of each is under the direction of God. "It is proper, then, that the King should hold converse with his Powers, and use their ministry in such acts as it is not fitting that God should effect alone." "Perceiving what was suitable for himself and his creatures, he has left some things to be wrought out by his subject Powers; not granting them, however, independent authority to complete anything by their own skill, lest some error should be introduced into the works of creation." *

After so clear an expression on the part of Philo of his conception of the Powers of God as personal agents distinct from God, it is unnecessary either to proceed with the passage which I have quoted, in which this conception is further devel-

* De Confusione Linguarum, cc. 33, 34. I. 430 – 433.

oped, or to produce at length others to the same effect.*

WE pass to other conceptions of Philo, conceptions which present new analogies to the Valentinian system of Æons. As he who is about to build a city forms a plan of it in his own mind, so God, according to Philo, before the work of creation, formed in his own Logos, or mind, a plan of the Universe. This was the Intelligible World, the world of Platonic Ideas, the archetypal world, the pattern of the visible. So far there is nothing particularly unintelligible. But Philo immediately converts the world of Ideas into the Divine Logos itself; and the confusion becomes at first view inextricable.

After comparing the archetypal world to the plan which an architect forms of a city that he is about to build, and representing its seat to be the Divine Logos (or Intellect), Philo presents the other apparently very different conception just mentioned. "To speak plainly," he says, "the *intelligible* world [the world of Ideas] is nothing else than the Logos of the Creator, as the intelligible city is only the process of thought in the architect, considering how to form a sensible city by means of an intelligible. This is not my doctrine,

* The following passages may be consulted upon this subject. De Mundi Opificio, c. 24. I. 16, 17. De Plantatione, c. 12. I. 336, 337. De Confusione Linguarum, c. 27. I. 425. De Migrat. Abrahami, c. 32. I. 464. De Profugis, c. 13. I. 556. De Legat. ad Caium, c. 1. II. 546.

but that of Moses. For in describing the production of man, he declares expressly, that he was formed after the Image of God [that is, after the Logos, whom Philo considers as the Image of God]. But if a part be an image of that Image [the Logos], it is clear that all of the same kind, the whole sensible world, which is greater than man, is a copy of the Divine Image. And it is manifest that the archetypal seal, which we say was the intelligible world, must be the archetypal exemplar, the Idea of Ideas, the Logos of God." *

"God," says Philo in another place, "gave form to the formless substance of all things [primitive matter], he stamped a character upon what bore no character, he fashioned what was without qualities, and, bringing the world to perfection, put upon it his SEAL, his Image, his Idea, his own Logos." †

Thus, according to one conception of Philo, the Logos was the hypostatized Intellect of God, the former and the seat of the archetypal world; according to another, he was himself the archetypal world. The solution of this problem is to be found in the fact, that Philo regarded the hypostatized Powers (or attributes) of God as themselves constituting the Ideas of the archetypal world, and, viewed in this aspect, as all contained in and embraced under the Logos, the most generic of Ideas.

He says, that, when Moses desired to see the

* De Mundi Opificio, c. 6. I. 5.

† De Somniis, Lib. II. c. 6. Opp. I. 665. On this subject see also Legg. Allegorr. Lib. III. c. 31. Opp. I. 106. De Profugis, c. 2. I. 547, 548.

glory of God, that is, the Powers encompassing God, "God answered him, The Powers which you desire to see are altogether invisible and *intelligible* [that is, objects of intellect alone], I myself being invisible and *intelligible*. I call them intelligible, not as if they had as yet been comprehended by intellect, but because, if it be possible they should be comprehended, it cannot be by sense, but by intellect in its highest state of purity. But though their essence is thus incomprehensible, they give forth to view impressions and images of their energy. For as the seals used by men stamp countless impressions upon wax or any similar material, without losing anything of their substance, so it is to be understood that the Powers around me give qualities to things without quality, and forms to things without form, their eternal nature remaining unchanged and without loss. Some among men not improperly call them Ideas. They confer upon each being its peculiar properties.* To the disorderly, the boundless, the undefined, the formless, [that is, to primitive matter,] they give order and bounds and limits and form, changing altogether the worse into the better." †

"It was not fit," according to Philo, "that God himself should mould the boundless and chaotic mass of matter; but by means of his incorporeal

* The original of this and the preceding sentence does not admit of a literal translation. It is as follows: Ὀνομάζουσι δ' *αὐτὰς οὐκ ἀπὸ σκοποῦ τινες τῶν παρ' ὑμῖν ἰδέας, ἐπειδὴ ἕκαστον τῶν ὄντων ἰδιοποιοῦσι.*

† De Monarchiâ, Lib. I. c. 6. Opp. II. 218, 219.

Powers, whose proper name is *Ideas*, he gave to every kind of thing the form suitable to it."*

This doctrine concerning the Powers of God, as the archetypal Ideas of all created things, was so connected in the imagination of Philo, when he wrote this passage, with his belief in God as the creator of all things, that he represents it as an impiety scarcely less than atheism to deny it.

The imaginations of Philo concerning the Powers of God, as Ideas of the archetypal world, were not peculiar to himself. They appear in the speculations of others among the later disciples of Plato, and seem to have extensively prevailed.

"Some of the Platonists and Pythagoreans," says Cudworth, "declaring the second hypostasis of their Trinity [Intellect, *Nous*, answering to the Logos of Philo] to be the archetypal world, or, as Philo calls it, *the world that is compounded and made up of Ideas*, and containeth in it all those kinds of things intelligibly that are in this lower world sensibly; and further concluding, that all these several Ideas of this archetypal world are really so many distinct substances, animals and gods, have therefore made that second hypostasis not to be one God, but a congeries and heap of Gods."† These Ideas were conceived of as existing in God, as Ideas of God. They are, in the language of Philo, the Powers of God, causing all things in the created universe to be what they are.

* De Sacrificantibus, c. 13. II. 261.

† Intellectual System, p. 553. [Ch. IV. § 36. Vol. I. p. 729, Andover ed.]

They are, as Cudworth says, "animals and gods," that is, in other terms, divine persons. For further illustration of this subject, I refer to the chapter I have quoted, the fourth of the "Intellectual System," without, however, intending to imply any general assent to the remarks and inferences of Cudworth.

HAVING long since passed the bounds of all sober speculation, we may, perhaps, be prepared for the strange chaos of opinions which has at last opened upon us, —

> "Congestaque eodem
> Non bene junctarum discordia semina rerum."

The description of the poet may be still further applied to these ancient doctrines: —

> "Lucis egens aër: nulli sua forma manebat:
> Obstabatque aliis aliud." *

The imagination of Philo with which we have at present most concern, is that by which he converted the attributes of God into proper persons. The same conception, if conception it may be called, the same formless aggregate of antagonizing ideas, is one which has made its apparition in various systems. It appears, as we have seen, in the theories of the later Platonists. It was, as I am now about to show, the basis of the doctrine of the Logos, as held by the Fathers of the first four centuries. It is the key to the Gnostic sys-

* [Ovid. Metam. I. 8, 17.]

tem of Æons, the derivative Æons being attributes and Ideas hypostatized. It is the essential principle of the speculations of the Jewish Cabalists concerning the Divinity; and through connections, which as yet have not been traced, it presents itself broadly developed in the theology of the Bramins.

Of the obscure system of the Gnostic Æons, it would be out of place here to enter into any further explanation than has been incidentally given. Between the speculations of the Cabalists and those of Philo and the later Platonists there is much coincidence, particularly as regards the topic before us. "The Cabalists," says Basnage, "regarding God as an infinite, incomprehensible essence, between which and created things there can be no immediate communication, have imagined that he has made himself known, and has operated, by his perfections which have emanated from him." "It is their style," he says, "to speak of the perfections of God as of persons different from his essence."* The first and greatest of the emanations from him they denominate "Adam Kadmon." It is in him that the Powers of God are manifested; he is the source of all subsequent existence. He corresponds to the Logos of Philo and the Christian Fathers, and to the Nous or Intellect of the later Platonists and Gnostics. He was the prototype of man, as the Logos is represented by Philo. Through him were developed ten attri-

* Histoire des Juifs, Liv. III. c. 14.

butes of the Divinity, denominated "Sephiroths" or "Splendors," each having its appropriate name. These emanations are the hypostatized Powers of God, through which he is manifested.

In the chapter from which I have quoted, Basnage is disposed to regard the whole system of the Cabalists as an allegory, and their language concerning the personal character of the Sephiroths as figurative. But he says: "They push their allegories so far that it is difficult to follow them; they so frequently speak of these perfections as of so many different persons, that the greatest attention is necessary, not to be deceived." If, however, the Cabalists had not conceived of these perfections as proper persons, they would not have represented them as emanating. Basnage, indeed, seems to have abandoned this view of their system in a subsequent volume;* in which he supposes the Cabalists to have viewed them as emanant condensations of that divine light, which, according to them, was the substance of God, "having a kind of existence separate from him, though always near him." In the chapter from which I have last quoted, he states that they believed in four modes of creation, or the production of being. The first of these was emanation from the substance of God. The Sephiroths were placed by them in the World of Emanations, corresponding to the Pleroma of the Gnostics. The Cabalists held that there was but one substance in

* Liv. IV. c. 8.

the universe, that of God; a fundamental doctrine in the theology of the Hindoos. Hence they would ascribe real personality to the Sephiroths, equally as to other beings composed of this one substance. It is the certainty that the Sephiroths were attributes of God, and the actual impossibility of an attribute being a person, that has led to the ineffectual attempts to allegorize their system. A similar cause has operated in the same way in regard to other systems of a like kind, especially that of the Gnostics. But the truth is, that in all these systems the attributes of God were regarded both as attributes and as persons, or, to express the imagination by a single term, as hypostatized attributes.

In respect to the mythology of the Hindoos, every one who has given attention to the subject is aware, that one of its most distinguishing features is the hypostatizing of the attributes and manifestations of the Deity. One Supreme Being is recognized, but no worship is paid him. He manifests himself, it is supposed, under three hypostases, as the Creator, Brahma; the Preserver, Vishnu; and the Destroyer, or Changer of Forms, Siva; with their accompanying Energies, likewise hypostatized as females. Either Siva or Vishnu, alone, or both in connection, to the exclusion of Brahma, are at the present day worshipped as Supreme. To all three, and to the goddesses who are associated with them, are ascribed personal characters and personal actions, and such too as are most abhorrent to our conceptions of the Divinity.

But these are not the only divine attributes hypostatized by the Hindoos. "The Ved having, in the first instance, personified all the attributes and powers of the Deity, and also the celestial bodies and natural elements, does, in conformity to the idea of personification, treat of them in the subsequent passages as if they were real beings, ascribing to them birth, animation, senses, and accidents, as well as liability to annihilation."*

The author from whom I have made the last extract, one of the most enlightened men whom India or the world has produced, in his labors to reclaim his countrymen from idolatry, has shown that the Vedas teach the existence and worship of him who is alone God. This, however, does not prove that the writers might not conceive of his attributes as proper persons; for Philo, and the Cabalists, and the Gnostics, all affirmed the unity of God. The Hindoo theists represent all finite spirits as portions of God's substance, as the flames of separate candles are each a portion of elemental fire; or as the numberless reflections of the sun's rays are only modifications of his light.

In endeavoring to apprehend the process of thought that has thus led to the hypostatizing of the powers and attributes of the Divinity, it may perhaps assist us if we recollect the manner in which the human mind has been decomposed, and its faculties, affections, and relations personi-

* Rammohun Roy, Second Defence of the Monotheistical System of the Veds, p. 17, note.

fied. The qualities, acts, and even sufferings, of real persons are familiarly ascribed to them. We speak of being governed by Reason, and of Reason as bewildered; Hope cheers and leads us on; Imagination pictures for us fairer scenes than reality presents; the voice of Duty is to be obeyed without hesitation; and Conscience is the vicegerent of God within us. All such expressions we recognize at once as merely figurative; because we are too well acquainted with the subject to which they relate to understand them otherwise. We may regard reason as a faculty of the mind, and, at the same time, image reason to ourselves as a person, without difficulty or absurdity. But in relation to subjects that present any considerable degree of obscurity, as, for instance, the mind of God, nothing is more common than for figurative language to harden, if I may so speak, into literal. An imagination is easily transformed into a supposed apprehension. There is a tendency in every idea that dwells long in the mind to assume a character of reality.* To the admission of metaphors as literal truths is to be ascribed a great part of the errors and follies, and consequently of the vices, of men. These errors, too, it is often difficult to expel; for when the imaginary conception that

* [See before, pp. 313, 334, 338. — "Though vivid conception is not, as it has been said to be, belief, yet we readily pass from it to the opinion, that what presents itself to our apprehension in such well-defined lineaments and permanent colors must have a real existence." (Article by Mr. Norton on the Authorship of the Epistle to the Hebrews, in the Christian Examiner for January 1828, Vol. V. p. 38.)]

has intruded itself out of place is hardly pressed, it may assume for the moment its proper character, and retreat into its own sphere, ready to return and reassume its reign whenever the conflict is over.

We come now to the purpose for which I have entered into the preceding explanations. We have seen how extensively the doctrine has prevailed of hypostatized attributes of God. This doctrine is in itself so unintelligible, and is so foreign from the philosophy of the present day, that it is not strange that the fact of its prevalence, and even of its existence, has been but imperfectly apprehended; and that modern inquirers, when they perceived that some object of thought was regarded as an attribute of God, have supposed that it could not also be regarded as a proper person. But there is no doubt that these conceptions, however incongruous, have been brought together. It was in this mode of apprehending the Divine Being that the doctrine of the Trinity had its origin. The Logos of the first four centuries was, in the view of the Fathers, both an attribute or attributes of God, and a proper person. Their philosophy was, in general, that of the later Platonists, and they transferred from it into Christianity this mode of conception.

In treating of this fact, so strange, and one which will be so new to many readers, I will first quote a passage from Origen, the coincidence of which with the conceptions of Philo and the later

Platonists is apparent. In commenting on the introduction of St. John's Gospel, he makes, as I have before said,* a distinction between the Wisdom and the Logos of God, and supposes his Logos to be comprehended in his Wisdom. The Son, or Christ, he represents as both the Logos and Wisdom of God. Of the Wisdom of God he thus speaks:† "Nor must we omit that Christ [or Jesus, for Origen uses the names indiscriminately] is properly the Wisdom of God; and is, therefore, so denominated. For the Wisdom of the God and Father of All has not its being in bare conceptions, analogous to the conceptions in human minds. But if any one be capable of forming an idea of *an incorporeal being of diverse forms of thought, which comprehend the* LOGOI [the archetypal forms] *of all things, a being indued with life, and having, as it were, a soul,* he will know that the Wisdom of God, who is above every creature, pronounced rightly concerning herself, *The Lord created me, the beginning, his way to his works.*" ‡

In this passage, the proper wisdom of God is hypostatized, and described as the Logos of Philo, or the Nous (Intellect) of the later Platonists. A little after, there is the following account of the Logos and other Powers of God as hypostatized, corresponding equally with the conceptions of Philo and the Platonists. Having declared the Logos to be comprehended in the Wisdom of God, he goes

* See before, p. 335, note. † Opp. IV. 39, 40.

‡ Prov. viii. 22, according to some copy of the Septuagint, or other Greek translation, used by Origen.

on to teach, that it has still "a proper distinct being of its own, so as to possess life in itself." In order to comprehend this, he says: "We must speak not only of the Power, but of the Powers of God. *Thus says the Lord of the Powers*,* is an expression which often occurs, in which by 'Powers' is meant certain living beings, rational and divine, the highest and best of whom is Christ, who is called not merely the Wisdom, but the Power of God. There being, then, many Powers of God, each of whom has his distinct being, and all of whom the Saviour excels, Christ is to be regarded as the Logos [the Supreme Reason over all the other rational Powers], having his personal existence in the Beginning, that is, in Wisdom; differing from that Reason which exists in us, and has no distinct being out of us." †

Obscure as these passages may be to one not familiar with the conceptions and language of the philosophy to which they belong, they are still sufficiently clear as to the main point which they have been brought to establish. It is a fact, however, which has not been, under any of its aspects, adverted to by a great majority of writers who have treated of the doctrine of the Trinity. Of the notices relating to it, there is one by Clarke, in his Scripture Doctrine of the Trinity,‡ which it may be worth while to bring forward, before adducing

* Κύριος τῶν δυνάμεων, LXX. The rendering of the Common Version is "Lord of Hosts."

† Opp. IV. 47.

‡ Part II. § 18, Notes, 3d. ed.

further quotations from the Fathers. I present it in a somewhat abridged form.

"Among the writers," he says, "before the time of the Council of Nice, Theophilus, Tatian, and Athenagoras seem to have been of that opinion, that the *Word* (the Logos) was the internal Reason or Wisdom of the Father; and yet, at the same time, they speak as if they supposed that Word to be produced or generated into a real Person; which is wholly unintelligible, and seems to be a mixture of two opinions: the one, of the generality of Christians, who believed the Word to be a real Person; the other, of the Jews and Jewish Christians, who *personated* the internal Wisdom of God, or spake of it figuratively (according to the genius of their language) as of a person.

"Irenæus and Clemens Alexandrinus speak sometimes with some ambiguity, but, upon the whole, plainly enough understand the Word or Son of God to be a real person.

"The other writers before the Council of Nice do generally speak of him clearly and distinctly as of a real person.

"About the time of the Council of Nice, they spake with more uncertainty; sometimes arguing that the Father, considered without the Son, would be without Reason and without Wisdom; which is directly supposing the Son to be nothing but an attribute of the Father; and yet at other times expressly maintaining, that he was truly and perfectly a Son. But the greater part agreed in this latter notion, that he was a real person."

In this passage there are two errors. The first is the implication that the conception of the Logos as an attribute was more prevalent about the time of the Council of Nice than it had been before. On the contrary, the fundamental idea of the Logos was as of an attribute of God. His attribute it was conceived to be, equally as reason is an attribute of man. The other error is in the supposition that the Fathers who spoke of the Logos as a person could not also have imagined him to be an attribute. The Fathers of the first four centuries, generally, believed the Logos (if we may so use the word *believe*) to be both an attribute and a person. I will quote a few examples of their language.

Justin Martyr, speaking of his "second god," whom I have formerly mentioned,* declares that "this god, produced from the Father of All, is the reason (*logos*) and wisdom and power of him who produced him," and immediately identifies him with Wisdom as personified in the Proverbs.† Justin was one of the first, perhaps the first, Christian writer who gave a form to the Catholic doctrine of the Logos. His contemporary, Athenagoras, says that "the Son is the intellect and the reason (*logos*) of the Father." "He is the first production of the Father, not with reference to any commencement of existence; for from the beginning, God, being the eternal mind, always had reason (*logos*) in himself, as being eternally rational; but

* [See before, pp. 204, 205.]

† Dial. cum Tryph. p. 267. [al. c. 61. p. 284, C.]

with reference to his going forth [his emanation from God], to be the Idea [the formative principle] and the energy of the formless nature of material things."* Theophilus of Antioch, another contemporary, calls the Logos "the spirit, the wisdom, and the power of the Most High; . . . . . the wisdom of God which was in him before the world was, and his holy reason (*logos*) which is always with him."† The Logos, he teaches, "existed always internally in the mind of God. Before anything was created, it was his counsellor, being his intellect and thought; but when God was about to form what he had determined on, he generated it externally, as the First-born of the whole creation, not making himself void of reason (*logos*), but generating reason, and always holding converse with his reason."‡

On this subject Irenæus has fallen, if it be possible, into greater confusion and contradictions than the other writers of his age. He often speaks of the Logos or Son as of a person distinct from God, and describes him as a minister of God's will. He himself says, that St. John teaches his "effectual" § generation, which, according to his use of this language elsewhere, must mean his production from the substance of God as in all respects a proper person. But in his zeal against

* Legatio pro Christianis, § 10. p. 287, edit. Paris, 1742.

† Ad Autolycum, Lib. II. § 10. p. 355, edit. Paris, 1742.

‡ Ibid., § 22. p. 365.

§ Efficabilem, i. e. efficacem. Lib. III. c. 11. § 8; comp. Lib. II. c. 17. § 2.

the Gnostic doctrine of emanation, he not only uses such language as shows that he regarded the Logos as an attribute, but such as is inconsistent with the imagination of his being anything but an attribute. Referring to the first of the Gnostic emanations, Intellect or Mind, and to the second, Logos, Reason, he says: "The Father of All is not a composite being, something else beside Mind; but Mind is the Father, and the Father is Mind." Having thus identified Mind or Intellect with the Father, he immediately proceeds to identify Intellect with Reason or the Logos.* In another passage, he describes God as being "all Mind and all Logos." "His thought," he says, "is his Logos, and his Logos his Mind, and the all-embracing Mind is the Father himself." † Speaking a little before of the Gnostic system as consisting in transferring to God conceptions of different affections and faculties of the human mind, he considers it as irreverent to regard the Divinity as thus affected and divided, "God being all mind, all reason (*ratio*, i. e. Logos), one operating spirit, all light, ever the same without change." ‡

From many passages which might be quoted it is my purpose only to produce a few, in order clearly to illustrate the conceptions of the Fathers upon this subject. Clement of Alexandria says: "The Logos of the Father of All is the wisdom and goodness of God made most clearly manifest, his almighty and truly divine power, his sovereign

* Lib. II. c. 17. § 7. † Lib. II. c. 28. § 5.

‡ Lib. II. c. 28. § 4. See further on this subject, Lib. II. c. 13.

will."* His meaning is that the Logos denotes the attributes of God as manifested in the creation and government of the universe; but there is no question that he also considered the Logos as a person. By Tertullian, Christ is described as "the power of God and the spirit of God, the discourse (*sermo*), and wisdom, and reason, and Son of God."† I have quoted passages from Origen in which he represents both the Wisdom of God, and the Logos or Reason of God, as living beings. In the following, the Logos fades away into a dim Platonic Idea. "We are reproached by Celsus," he says, "for avoiding evil deeds, and reverencing and honoring Virtue as produced by God, and being the Son of God...... If we speak of a second god, let it be understood that we mean nothing else than that Virtue which comprehends all virtues [i. e. the most generic Idea of virtue] and that Reason (Logos) which comprehends the reasons of all things properly natural, and tending to the good of the universe."‡ The Son, he expressly teaches elsewhere, is the Wisdom of God existing substantially.§

Petavius, in one of the chapters of his "Theologica Dogmata," ‖ discusses the question, "Whether the Son is the very wisdom by which the Father is wise," — *An ipsa sapientia quâ Pater sapiens est*

* Stromat. V. § 1. pp. 646, 647.

† Apologet. § 23.

‡ Contra Celsum, Lib. V. § 39. Opp. I. 608.

§ In his Commentary on John before quoted, and in his work De Principiis, Lib. I. c. 2.

‖ De Trinitate, Lib VI. c. 9.

sit Filius. After showing that this was the common doctrine of the Fathers (*plerique sic existimâsse videntur*), he produces in favor of the opposite opinion, which he himself maintains, only the vacillating authority of Augustine, who retracted on this subject the common opinion, which he had once asserted. The great argument of Athanasius and his followers for the eternity of the Logos was, that God, being always rational, always had Reason (the Logos) within him. "There is no other wisdom," according to Athanasius, "in the Father than the Lord (Christ)."* "The Son," he says, "is the very wisdom, the very reason, the very power of the Father."† He was described by others as the power, the omnipotence, and the will of the Father. It is unnecessary in this connection to quote the passages at length,‡ or to ad-

* Epistola Encyclica contra Arianos, § 14. Opp. I. 284, edit. Benedict.

† Contra Gentes, § 46. Opp. I. 46.

‡ Many passages to this effect may be found in the first volume of the work of Petavius, Lib. V. c. 8. Respecting this whole topic, the reader who wishes to pursue the inquiry may consult Petavius, as already referred to, and likewise De Trinitate, Lib. I. cc. 3, 4, 5; and Priestley's History of Early Opinions, Vol. II. pp. 44 – 144. There are considerable errors in Priestley, but none such as *essentially* affect his argument, or are likely, with one exception, much to embarrass or mislead his reader. One is, that Philo regarded the personality of the Logos as *occasional* only, a notion for which there is no foundation in his works. But the particular error to which I have referred is the implication in several passages, that the Logos conceived of as a person was not conceived of as being *at the same time* an attribute, — that he was only regarded as having been *first* an attribute, and *then* a person.

It was indeed, as has been shown by Priestley and others, the ex-duce additional proof of the general fact maintained. I will only further mention one conception, more strange than those already noticed. "Perhaps," says Origen, "if we may venture to speculate still further, we may conceive of the Only Son as the soul of God. For as the soul placed within the body moves every part, and excites all its operations, so the Only Son of God, who is his reason (Verbum, i. e. *Λόγος*), and wisdom, being placed within him, extends to and reaches every power of God."* The extravagance of this imagination becomes perhaps more striking, when we compare it with the strong language of Origen concerning the inferiority of the Son to the Father.

In all the systems before mentioned, in which attributes of God have been hypostatized, with the

press doctrine of several of the Fathers, that the Logos, existing primarily in God, was afterwards "generated," and put forth as the Son, by the voluntary act of the Father, to be his agent in the creation of the world. The doctrine is thus expressed, for instance, by Prudentius: —

"Ex ore quamlibet Patris
Sis ortus, et Verbo editus,
Tamen paterno in pectore
Sophia callebas prius."

[Cathemerin. XI. 17.]

The Fathers who held this doctrine are commonly supposed not to have ascribed personality to the Logos before his generation and emanation. But they nowhere, I think, expressly affirm that he was then not a person; and still less is it to be thought, that, after his generation, they ceased to regard him as an attribute.

* De Principiis, Lib. II. c. 10. § 5. Opp. I. 96.

exception of the later form of Trinitarian Orthodoxy, these attributes, when conceived of as persons, have been regarded as far inferior to God. The nature, indeed, and operations of the attribute belong and are to be referred immediately to God. It is indifferent whether we say that the universe was created by the disposing power of the Supreme Being, or created by the Supreme Being, if we use the former term merely to denote an attribute. But when a personal character is superadded to this attribute, then the new being becomes, as a person, inferior to the Supreme. He is not God, but a god only. Still, in regard to the Christian Logos, his substance being conceived of as derived from the substance of the Deity, as generated out of it, — a prolation or emanation from it, like a stream from a fountain, a branch from a tree, or rays of light from the sun, — he was under this aspect, as well as under the relation of an attribute, to a certain extent identified with God * by the earlier Fathers. To a certain extent only, for, in reference to the totality of

* Thus it becomes not unfrequently difficult to determine, in passages in which the name Θεός, or *Deus*, is applied by the earlier Fathers to the Logos, or Son, or Christ, whether we are to consider it as an appellative, or as to be referred through the Logos to the Supreme Being, with whom the Logos is regarded as *partially* identified. I am aware that the phrase "partially identified" is an absurdity in terms; but the imagination of which I speak was absurd, and such language alone can convey a just conception of it.

Hence the translation of the passages referred to becomes a matter of investigation and judgment, and often, from the indistinct and varying signification of the terms in question, and our different use of the name "God," it is scarcely possible to explain their sense in English by a mere translation. [See before, p. 120, note.]

each, he was regarded by them as a being far inferior to God.* The same inferiority was ascribed by the Gnostics to the derivative Æons; by the later Platonists, to the second person in their Trinity, Nous, or Intellect, considered in reference to the first; by the Cabalists, to their Sephiroths; and by the Hindoos, to all their hypostatized attributes. As respects the Logos, the imagination of a person predominating over that of an attribute, and this person being considered as far inferior to God, the way was opened for the Arian doctrine, which, dropping the idea of an attribute, and rejecting the belief that the Logos was an emanation from the substance of the Divinity, regarded him only as a person, and reduced him to the rank of created beings. But this produced a reaction on the part of their Catholic opponents, who in consequence raised the

* [Thus Tertullian says: "The Father is the whole substance; the Son, a derivation from the whole, and a portion of it; as he himself declares, *For the Father is greater than I.*" — "Pater tota substantia est; Filius vero derivatio totius et portio; sicut ipse profitetur, *Quia Pater major me est.*" (Advers. Praxeam, c. 9; comp. c. 26, and Apologet. c. 21.) Professor Stuart translates the first part of the sentence here quoted as follows: "The Father is the whole substance; the Son, *the derivation and apportionment of the whole*"! (Biblical Repository for April 1835, p. 351, note.)

So Lactantius, speaking of the Father and the Son, to whom he attributes "one mind, one spirit, one substance," goes on to remark: "But the one [the Father] is, as it were, an exuberant fountain; the other, as a stream flowing from it; the one is like the sun; the other, like a ray proceeding from the sun; and since he is faithful to the Supreme Father and dear to him, he is not separated from him, just as the stream is not separated from the fountain, nor the ray from the sun." (Institut. Lib. IV. c. 29.)

"The Son," says Origen, "is in no respect to be compared with the Father." (Comm. in Joan., Tom. xiii. c. 25. Opp. IV. 235.)]

Logos or Son to what they called an equality with God, or the Father, though they considered it as a derived and subordinate equality.

The illustrations which I have given are far from presenting a full view of the confusion and incoherence of thought that prevailed among the Catholic Fathers. But they are, perhaps, sufficient to establish the fact, that the Logos was regarded by the Fathers both as an attribute of God and a distinct person; corresponding to a mode of conception, or rather an imagination, that has spread widely through different systems of theology; — an imagination so incongruous, that those who have treated of the history of opinions seem often to have recoiled from the notice of it, or shrunk from acknowledging its existence. The words in which it is expressed, conveying in fact no meaning, are apt to pass over the mind of a modern reader without leaving the impression that what was considered as a very important meaning was once attached to them. The different aspect which it gives to the theological doctrine of the Trinity, from what that doctrine has assumed in modern times, may alone perhaps sufficiently account for the absence of all mention of it in the writings of most of those who have adverted to the opinions of the Christian Fathers respecting the Logos. That the conception of the same being as an attribute and a person was an object of what may strictly be called belief, is not to be maintained; for we cannot, properly speaking, believe a manifest contradiction. But the case was the same with this as with many other doctrines that have been zealously maintained. One part of it was believed at one time, and another at another. It was assented to successively, not simultaneously. When, of the two contrary propositions embraced in the conception, one rose upon the mind, the other set. In speaking of such doctrines as being believed, we intend, at most, what may be called an alternating belief, ever vibrating between two opposite opinions, and attaching itself, as it is repelled or attracted, first to the one and then to the other.

We will now pass to another conception concerning the Logos. In the creation of the universe, God was conceived of as having first *manifested* himself. But it was by his Disposing Power, his Logos, that the universe was created. By the same Power, as his vicegerent, God was regarded as governing all things. It was, then, in and by his Logos, that God was *manifested*. Hence the Logos, considered as a person, the agent in the creation and government of the universe, came to be regarded as an *hypostatized manifestation* of God. Thus, also, the Gnostics conceived of their Æons as *hypostatized manifestations* of God. I am aware that I use a term without meaning; but there is no other which will better convey a notion of the unformed imaginations that once prevailed upon this subject.*

* See the ingenious and agreeable work of Souverain, *Le Platonisme dévoilé,* in which, however, the view of the author is too limited.

"The Logos," says Clement of Alexandria, "is the face of God, by which he is illustrated and made known."* The Gnostics, with the same meaning, called their Æon, "Intellect," the face of God.† To the same conception of the Logos, as the manifestation of God, must be referred those numerous passages in which he is spoken of as the "name of God," the "image of God," the "irradiation" (ἀπαύγασμα) of God, the "vision" (ὅρασις) of God, the "visible god," in contradistinction to the Invisible, and as "the uttered Logos," or Discourse of God.

This last-mentioned conception of the "uttered Logos" appears particularly in the writings of the Christian Fathers, and deserves further notice. The term "Logos," it will be recollected, in one of its primary significations denotes reason, or that power by which the mind arranges its ideas in their proper relations to each other. But when thus arranged, they may be communicated in words; and to ideas thus uttered the term "Logos" was also applied, being in this sense equivalent in signification to "discourse." In the present state of our language, we have no term which answers to "Logos" in this double meaning. But in the old and now obsolete use of the word "discourse" we find the same singular union of the two principal senses of Logos; that word having

* Pædagog. Lib. I. c. 7. p. 132.

† Doctrina Orient. § 10. [In Potter's edition of Clement of Alexandria, p. 970.]

been formerly employed, not merely in its present signification, but to denote the faculty of reason. "The act of the mind," says Glanvill, "which connects propositions and deduceth conclusions from them, the schools call Discourse, and we shall not miscall it if we name it Reason."

To the Catholic Fathers, the double meaning of the word "Logos" afforded a favorite illustration of the going forth of the Divine Reason to the work of creation. Considered as previously existing with God, it was described as "the Logos within the mind of God," "the internal Logos,"* analogous to reason, or thought, in man; considered as the instrument of God in the work of creation, it was spoken of as "the uttered Logos,"† analogous to words uttered by man.

The Latin Fathers, having no word in their own language which, like Logos in the Greek, embraced the two significations of Reason and Discourse, were embarrassed in their translation of it; and hesitated between *Ratio*, Reason; *Sermo*, Discourse; and *Verbum*, Word. The first was the proper term,‡ but usage, from some cause which we cannot discover, at last settled upon the term

* Λόγος ἐνδιάθετος. † Λόγος προφορικός.

‡ "*Rationem* Græci λόγον dicunt, quo vocabulo etiam *sermonem* appellamus. Ideoque jam in usu est nostrorum [i. e. Latinorum], per simplicitatem interpretationis, *sermonem* dicere *in primordio apud Deum fuisse*, cum magis *rationem* competat antiquiorem haberi." Tertullian. advers. Praxeam, c. 5. [Compare Lactantius: "Sed melius Græci λόγον dicunt quàm nos verbum sive sermonem; λόγος enim et sermonem significat et rationem; quia ille est et vox et sapientia Dei." (Institut. Lib. IV. c. 9.)]

"Word"; and this has in consequence been adopted, in the theological dialect of modern times, as the proper rendering of "Logos," when used concerning the Deity. The term, however, is wholly inappropriate and unmeaning; and has served to confuse still further a subject in itself abundantly perplexed.

This recurrence to the double meaning of the word "Logos," this conception of the hypostatized Logos, or the Son, as the uttered *discourse* or the *word* of the Father, or God, is common throughout the writings of the Fathers. It was an imagination of their own, not derived from Philo, who, in speaking of the Logos of God, has reference only to that signification of the term in which it answers to "reason." If, in treating this subject, there be any traces in his writings of a reference to the other signification of the term, in which it answers to "discourse," they are, to say the least, few and doubtful. I think there are none.* The

* The fact has been remarked by Le Clerc: "Adi Philonem ubicunque Λόγου et Creationis Mundi meminit, videbisque de *Sermone* nusquam eum cogitâsse, sed *Rationis* potestatem animo præsentem habuisse." Nov. Test. Hammondi et Clerici. Ed. 2da. Tom. I. p. 398, col. 2.

Neander, in the Introduction to his History of the Principal Gnostic Sects (Genetische Entwickelung der vornehmsten gnostischen Systeme, p. 8), says that "Philo, in common with the Oriental theologians and the Gnostics, distinguishes between a hidden, incomprehensible God, retired within himself, not to be described or imagined, and the Manifestation of this Divinity, as the commencement of the work of creation, and of the development of life; between Jehovah (ὁ ὢν, τὸ ὄν) and his Manifestation, or, in other words, the aggregate of all the Powers hidden within the being of God." The meaning of

incongruous junction of the idea of an uttered discourse or a word, and that of the hypostatized attribute of reason, in the conception of the Logos, is to be found developed only in the writings of the Fathers.

The confusion of ideas produced by this confusion of the meanings of the word "Logos" may be easily imagined. Abundant illustrations of it may be found in most histories of the doctrine of the Trinity. I will quote only one passage, a sufficient specimen perhaps, which I find adduced as a satisfactory answer to an Arian objection, by a writer once of some note, Dr. William Sherlock.*

"As for Christ's receiving commands from the Father, though this relates to the execution of his mediatory office, and so concerns him as God Incarnate, as by the dispensation of the Gospel he is the minister of God's will and pleasure, yet I grant even as God he receives commands from his Father, but it is no otherwise than as he receives his nature from him: by nature he is the Word, the

the last clause, I presume, is *the aggregate display* of all the Powers *before* hidden within the being of God. But this seems to me not an accurate account of the opinions of Philo; and still less can I assent to what follows. "Philo has always before his eyes the opposition between εἶναι and λέγεσθαι, the former denoting the existence of God as retired within himself, and the latter, his being uttered, or manifested." — "Philo immer vor Augen hat den Gegensatz zwischen einem εἶναι, in sich selbst seyn, und λέγεσθαι, ausgesprochen, geoffenbart werden." I think it may be safely said, that Philo nowhere applies the word λέγεσθαι to God in the sense supposed, or uses concerning him the image in question.

* See his Vindication of the Doctrine of the Trinity, pp. 154, 155.

Wisdom, the Command of the Father; his reflex Image, whereby he produces all the designs of his own wisdom and counsel into act. Thus St. Austin answered the Arian objection, that Christ was but God's instrument, and made the world by God's command. 'Let them consider with what other words the Father commanded his only Word. But they frame to themselves an imagination of two [persons] near one another, but separated by their distinct places, one commanding, another obeying. Nor do they understand that the Father's command itself, that all things should be made, is no other Word of the Father, but that by which all things are made';* that is, the substantial Word, and Wisdom, and Command of the Father, his only-begotten Son."

It was from the shapeless, discordant, unintelligible speculations which have been described, *ex tantâ colluvie rerum*, that the doctrine of the Trinity drew its origin. These speculations it is now difficult to present under such an aspect as may enable a modern reader to apprehend their character. But the doctrine to which they gave birth still subsists, as the professed faith of the greater part of the Christian world. And when we look back

"* Cogitent quibus aliis verbis jusserit Pater unico verbo. Formant enim sibi in phantasmate cordis sui, quasi duos aliquos, etsi juxta invicem, in suis tamen locis constitutos, unum jubentem, alterum obtemperantem. Nec intelligunt ipsam jussionem Patris ut fierent omnia, non esse nisi verbum Patris, per quod facta sunt omnia. — Aug. contr. Serm. Arianorum, Lib. III."

through the long ages of its reign, and consider all its relations, and all its direct and indirect effects, we shall perceive that few doctrines have produced more unmixed evil. For any benefits resulting from its belief, it would be in vain to look, except benefits of that kind which the providence of God educes from the follies and errors of man.

It should be remarked, however, that little blame or discredit attaches to those earlier Fathers by whom the doctrine was introduced. They only philosophized concerning the Logos after the fashion of their age. Their only reproach is, that they were not wiser than their contemporaries. In proceeding from the same principles, they stopped far short of the extravagances of the Gnostics. Their speculations, likewise, till after the time of Origen, were obviously considered by them more as a matter of philosophy than of faith. There is sufficient evidence that, before and during his time, these speculations took little hold on the minds of common Christians. "The great body of those who are considered as believers," says Origen, "*knowing nothing but Jesus Christ and him crucified*, thinking that the Logos made flesh is the whole of the Logos, are acquainted with Christ only according to the flesh." *

* Ἕτεροι δὲ οἱ μηδὲν εἰδότες εἰ μὴ Ἰησοῦν Χριστὸν καὶ τοῦτον ἐσταυρωμένον, τὸν γενόμενον σάρκα λόγον τὸ πᾶν νομίσαντες εἶναι τοῦ λόγου, Χριστὸν κατὰ σάρκα μόνον γινώσκουσι. Τοιοῦτον δέ ἐστι τὸ πλῆθος τῶν πεπιστευκέναι νομιζομένων. Origen. Comment. in Joannem. Opp. IV. 53.

SECTION XI.

CONCLUSION.

In concluding this argument, I wish to make a few remarks concerning those general views of religion that I have directly or indirectly expressed, and which are usually connected with the opinions I have maintained. In doing so, I shall drop the singular pronoun, and blend myself with those, whoever they may be, whose sentiments correspond with my own. I speak in the name of no party; I am responsible for no opinions which I do not express, and no man is responsible for mine; but it would be false modesty, or presumption, to regard myself as standing alone.

We, then, who reject the whole system which among Protestants has been denominated "Orthodoxy," as a system of the most pernicious errors, are charged by its defenders with depriving Christianity of all its value, with contemning all its *peculiar* doctrines, with rejecting all but its name. What is it, then, that we believe? and what is it that our opponents believe?

Christianity, WE BELIEVE, has taught men to know God, and has revealed him as the Father of his creatures. It has made known his infinite perfections, his providence, and his moral government. It has directed us to look up to Him as the Being on whom we and all things are entirely dependent, and to look up to Him with perfect confidence and love. It has made known to us that we are to live for ever; it has brought life and immortality to light. Man was a creature of this earth, and it has raised him to a far nobler rank, and taught him to regard himself as an immortal being, the child of God. It calls the sinner to reformation and hope. It affords to virtue the highest possible sanctions. It gives to sorrow its best, and often its only consolation. It presents us, in the life of our great Master, with an example of that moral perfection which is to be the constant object of our exertions. It has established the truths which it teaches, upon evidence the most satisfactory. It is a most glorious display of the benevolence of the Deity, and of his care for the beings of this earth. It has lifted the veil which separated God from his creatures, and this life from eternity.

But all this, it seems, is NOTHING, unless it also teach, that there are three persons who constitute the one God; or at least that there is some threefold distinction, we know not what, in the Divinity; that one of these persons or distinctions was united in a most incomprehensible manner to the human nature of Christ, so that the sufferings of the latter were the sufferings of the former; and that it is only through these sufferings of the Son of God that we may hope for the mercy of his Father. The religion of joy and consolation will, it is contended, lose its value, unless it announce to us, that we are created under the wrath and curse of God; that it is impossible for us to perform his will, unless our moral natures be created anew; and that this is a favor denied to far the greater part of men, who are required to perform what he has made it morally impossible they should perform, with the most unrelenting rigor, and under penalty of the most terrible and everlasting torments. Such doctrines as these are represented as the *peculiar* doctrines of Christianity, those from which it derives its value; and our opponents appear to think, that if nothing better was to be effected than to make God known to men, to reveal to them his paternal character, to bring life and immortality to light, and to furnish the highest motives to virtue, it was not worth while for the Deity to interpose in a special manner to effect purposes so unimportant.

The doctrines which we believe to be established by Christianity are doctrines of inestimable value. The question of their truth is one which interests us most deeply. Our happiness and our virtue are at stake on the decision. If they are not true, we are miserable indeed. The brute, satisfied with the enjoyments of the present day, has a preferable tenure of existence to that of man, if they are both to perish together. But if these doctrines are true, there is a prospect displayed before us inconceivably glorious and delightful. They are truths which it was worthy of God to teach. Look again at the doctrines which we are opposing. Are these doctrines of any importance or value? Is it important to our virtue and happiness, that there should be a threefold distinction in the Divine Nature; or that the mercy of God which is extended toward us should have been PURCHASED with the blood of his Son? Is it desirable for us to be satisfied that our natures are so depraved, that, till they are changed by the act of God, we can do nothing to please him? Examine the creeds of what is called Orthodoxy; and read the summary of obligations which these creeds teach us that we lie under to God as our MAKER. What obligations would be due from his creatures to a being who had formed them under his "displeasure and curse," made them "bond-slaves to Satan," and "JUSTLY LIABLE" — the absurdity is as gross as the impiety — "to all punishments in this world, and in that which is to come." With what feelings might such creatures JUSTLY regard their Maker? What is the character which they would have a right to ascribe to him? It would be mockery to ask, if it be desirable that this doctrine should be true; or if Christianity would lose its value, should it appear that it taught no such doctrine.

It is because we have a strong conviction of the inestimable importance of TRUE RELIGION to human virtue and happiness, and therefore desire to promote its influence, that we wish men to know and believe that these are not the doctrines of Christianity. It is because God ought to be the object of our perfect veneration and love, that we revolt at doctrines which confound and darken our ideas of his nature, which represent one person in the Deity as exacting, and another as submitting to, the punishment of our offences; and at other doctrines far worse than these, which, if it were possible for them to have their full influence upon the mind, would make God an object of utter horror and detestation. We believe that the great truths of religion taught by Christianity are the foundation of public and private happiness, of the good order of well-regulated society, of purity of morals, of our domestic enjoyments, of all that is most generous and most disinterested in the human character, of all those qualities which endear man to man; that they make life cheerful, and reconcile us to death; and that it is on these that the character must be formed which will fit us for heaven;—and it is therefore that we wish them to be presented to men such as they really are, free from the gross errors which human folly and perversity have connected with them,—errors that have prevented their reception, and essentially counteracted their influence.

Especially at the present time, when, through the discredit and odium cast upon Christianity by the false systems that have assumed its name, its power has been annihilated through a great part of the civilized world, and it has come to be regarded by a very large portion of the educated classes of society as an obsolete superstition, the call is most imperative upon those to whom the welfare of their fellow-men is an object of concern, to use all means at their command to re-establish its true character. If they are indeed engaged in supporting the cause of TRUE RELIGION against irreligion and superstition, then the hopes of mankind are staked upon their success. All efforts to promote the influence of Christianity will be ineffectual, till its real character is understood and acknowledged; for of all the opposition to which it is exposed, that which substitutes in its place any of those false systems that have assumed its name is at the present day the most pernicious. If the doctrines against which we contend are false, then the worst enemy of Christianity is he who asserts them to have been taught by Christ.

In concluding this work, I should not speak of myself personally, were it not for the desire which every reader naturally feels to know the probable motives of one who addresses him on any important topic of practical interest. Disconnected, in a great degree, from the common pursuits of the world, and independent of any party or of any man's favor, there is, perhaps, scarcely an individual to whom it can be a matter of less private concern what opinions others may hold. No one will suppose, that, if literary fame were my object, I should have sought it by such a discussion as this in which I have engaged. Even among those who have no prejudices in favor of the errors opposed, much indifference and much disgust to the subject must be overcome, before I can expect this work to find any considerable number of readers. I commenced it not long after one of the severest deprivations of my life, the loss of a most valued, and most justly valued friend, and have continued it with sickness and death around me. I have been writing, as it were, on the tombstones of those who were most dear to me, with feelings of the character, purposes, and duties of life which my own death-bed will not strengthen. I may, then, claim at least that share of unsuspicious attention to which every one is entitled who cannot be supposed to have any other motive in maintaining his opinions, than a very serious, earnest, and enduring conviction of their truth and importance.

APPENDIX.

APPENDIX.

NOTE A.

(See p. 251.)

EXPLANATION OF JOHN vi. 61, 62.*

"Does this give you offence? What, then, if you should see the Son of Man ascending where he was before?"

In these and the following words, Jesus is remarking upon, and in part explaining, what he has before said. The purport of the words is this: Does it offend you that I speak of my death? Would your offence continue, should you see me after my death ascending to heaven?

It may be that Jesus here referred to his ascension from earth and disappearance from the view of his disciples. But if he did so, that miracle was, I conceive, present to his mind only as a proof and visible emblem of what he principally intended in his words. What he principally intended was his return to God from whom he came, after passing through his sufferings and death.

* From Mr. Norton's Notes on the Gospels.

It is to be remarked, that, here and elsewhere, the expressions "coming from" and "descending from" heaven or God, which are founded on Jewish conceptions of heaven as the local habitation of the Deity, are in their nature necessarily figurative, and do not admit of being taken in a verbal sense. God is in no one place rather than in another. There is no portion of space that may be designated as heaven on account of its being his peculiar habitation. "To be in heaven," or "to be with God," does not denote existence in any particular place. "To descend from heaven," or "to come from God," does not imply previous existence in any particular place. So to understand such expressions is to take words necessarily figurative in their literal meaning.

"Enoch *walked with* God";—"Their cry *went up* to God";—"The spirit *shall return* to God who gave it";—"Draw *near* to God";—"God *has departed* from me";—"O God, *be not far from* me";—"God will hear him *from his holy heaven*";—"Look *down from heaven*, O Lord";—"The Lord's *throne is in heaven*";—"Whom have I *in heaven* but thee?"—"God *sent* me before you";—"I (the Lord) *send* thee to the children of Israel";—"Let us *return* to the Lord, ... and he will *come* to us." In these passages, and in numberless others of a similar kind, we perceive how the imperfection of human conceptions and of human language has led to the use of expressions equally figurative with those of "descending from," and "ascending to," heaven and God.

The expressions above quoted are from the Old Testament, but they are such as are familiarly used in popular language at the present day. We do not find among them those harsher figures and ruder conceptions which elsewhere are not uncommon in the Jewish Scriptures.

In John's own writings, and particularly in his reports of the discourses of our Lord, there is much language of a similar kind. "There was a man [John] *sent from* God";—"The only Son who is *on the bosom* of the Father";—"Ye will see heaven opened, and the angels of God ascending and descending to the Son of Man";—"The Son of Man who *is in heaven*";—"The Father has not *left me alone*";—"I speak what I *have seen with* my Father";—"I speak to the world what I *have heard from* Him";—"There are many rooms in my Father's house; I am going that I may prepare a place for you";—"He who has seen me has seen the Father";—"Whoever loves me will obey my words; and my Father will love him, and we *will come to him, and make our abode with him*";—"I *came from* the Father into the world; now I am leaving the world, and *going to* the Father."

As the conceptions which we finite beings form of the Infinite Being must be inadequate and imperfect, so a great part of our language concerning him is necessarily inadequate and imperfect, and naturally assumes a figurative character. Such, of course, is particularly the case with popular language. This is full of modes of speech addressed to the imagination and feelings, but of a different character among different nations. It abounds more with figures, and becomes more remote from literal truth, in proportion as it expresses, or is conformed to, the conceptions of unphilosophical thinkers, — of such a people as the Jews. A great mistake will be committed, if from the multitude of these figures we pick out one made remarkable, perhaps, by being particularly remote from our modes of expression, and impose upon it, not the literal meaning of the words, for this may be impossible, but some imaginary, mystical meaning, which is too obscure to offend us by presenting an obvious absurdity.

Our Lord, in the passage before us, and where he speaks of descending from heaven, conforms his language to the conception of the Jews, that heaven was the peculiar abode of God. But we cannot receive this conception as true, and therefore cannot understand the words in their literal sense.*

It may be thought, however, that his declaring himself to have descended from heaven was intended as an affirmation of his pre-existence, for that by "heaven" is meant a portion of space where beings of a higher order than man reside. By "heaven" I conceive that, in the proper sense of the word, we mean that future state of blessedness on which the good will enter after death, and in which, as we have no reason to doubt, those

* [The remainder of this note is from an imperfect draught, which had not been revised by the author.]

who have been connected on earth may be near each other. But there is no rational foundation for the opinion, that those beings who are of a higher order than man exist within the limits of a certain definite portion of space which is to be called heaven.

Nor would our Lord's supposed declaration of his having been a pre-existent spirit, an angel, or an archangel, or some being of a still higher order, have anything to do with the occasion and purpose of his discourse. It could have tended only to bewilder the minds of hearers who, without this new difficulty put before them, were already confounded by his actions. The immediate occasion of the discourse was the necessity of repressing and destroying, as far as might be, the worldly passions and expectations of the Jews arising from their false notions of the temporal reign of the Messiah. Its purpose was to direct their thoughts to the true grounds of his authority, not as a warrior and earthly king, but as a teacher sent from God and speaking in God's name; — to the character necessary in his followers, who were not to be bold partisans of a temporal prince, but to do the works which God required; — to the blessings which would be conferred upon them, not such as might be looked for from a triumphant leader, but eternal life; — and to the means by which this blessedness was to be procured for his followers, not by his success as a conqueror, but by his sufferings and bloody death.

Among these thoughts there could be no propriety in his introducing the supposed doctrine that he himself was a pre-existent being. On the contrary, here, as in his other discourses, he keeps himself individually out of view. He is to be obeyed, not because he is a being in his own nature far superior to man, but because he is the minister of God. He speaks of no authority derived from what he was in himself, but of the authority conferred on him by God.

Nor does it appear that even the Jews so mistook or perverted his meaning as to put a literal sense upon his words. When he told them that he was "the true bread from heaven," "the bread of life," "the bread of God which was descending from heaven and giving life to the world," it was impossible for the Jews or any other hearers not to recognize that all these expressions were figurative, and especially, that by "descending from heaven," as used concerning the bread of God, could be meant nothing more than "coming from God." The turns of expression here employed are metaphors borrowed from the account given in the Psalms of the manna, as bread rained from heaven (the visible heavens) to preserve the lives of the Israelites. (See Psalm lxxviii. 23 – 25.) We cannot reasonably suppose that the Jews imagined our Lord to affirm that he had descended from the visible heavens in a bodily shape, or thought of his claiming to be a pre-existent spirit, coming from those abodes of the blessed which we call heaven.

* * * * *

As has already been remarked, the expressions "to come from God" and "to descend from heaven" are synonymous. (See John iii. 2, 13, 31.) They both denote the appearing among men as a minister of God miraculously authorized by him. "To go to heaven" and "to go to God" are at the present day perfectly familiar expressions, but equally figurative with those on which we are remarking. They mean, to pass from this life to a higher state of existence, in which God will confer new happiness on the good.

* * * * *

In speaking of himself as having descended from heaven, the meaning of our Lord is the same as when in this discourse he repeatedly designates himself as "him whom God has *sent*." "I *have descended from heaven*, not to do my own will, but the will of Him who *sent* me." (Verse 38; compare vv. 29, 39, 40, 44, 46, 57.)

* * * * *

Thus far, in explaining the metaphor by which Jesus represents himself as the bread descending from heaven, we find nothing which is not analogous to our own forms of expression. But in the words particularly under consideration a figure occurs, which, though it is used by writers of the Old and New Testament, and other ancient writers, Christian and Jewish, has not found a place among our modes of speech. It is connected with less philosophical conceptions of God than those which Christianity has taught us to entertain. In the use of this figure, events and persons and states of being, which it is intended to refer in the strongest manner to the appointment of God, and to represent him as having especially predestined, are spoken of as having a proper existence while yet existing only in his foreknowledge and purpose. I have elsewhere explained the design of this figure, and given many examples of it. See the notes on John xvii. 5 and viii. 58.* It is one which occurs repeatedly in the language of our Lord, as his language is reported by John; as when he says, "And now, Father! glorify me with thyself, giving me that glory *which I had with thee before the world was.*" "Thou didst *love me before the foundation of the world.*" (Ch. xvii. 5, 24.) In like manner, his being and office being predetermined by God before the world was, he here speaks of himself as having existed with God before his appearance on earth.

* [See before, pp. 235 – 246.]

NOTE B.

(See p. 284.)

ON THE EXPECTATIONS OF THE APOSTLES CONCERNING THE VISIBLE RETURN OF THEIR MASTER TO EARTH.

The language of our Saviour respecting his future coming was, I believe, more or less misunderstood by some or all of the Apostles, during a part or the whole of their ministry. They looked forward, with more or less confidence, to a personal and visible return of Christ to earth at no distant period. The first coming of the Messiah had been so wholly unlike what their countrymen had universally anticipated, that, when he spoke of a future coming while the existing generation was still living, they transferred to this some of the expectations which had been long entertained respecting his appearance and kingdom. It is necessary to attend to this fact in connection with the explanation which has been given of the language of Christ. The evidence of it may appear from what follows.

In the last chapter of John's Gospel we have the following narrative:* "Peter, turning round, cast

* John xxi. 20-23.

his eyes on the disciple whom Jesus loved, who was in the company, — the same who at the supper was lying at the breast of Jesus, and said to him, Master, who is he that will betray you? — Peter, seeing this disciple, said to Jesus, Master, and how will it be with him? Jesus answered him, If it be my will that he remain till I come, what does it concern you? Be you my follower. Hence spread that report among the brothers, that this disciple was not to die; though Jesus did not say to him that he would not die; but, If it be my will that he remain till I come, what does it concern you?"

It was a belief among the Jews, as we have good reason to suppose, that the lives of those saints who might be on earth when the Messiah should appear would be prolonged through his reign to the termination of all things.* This expectation, it would seem from the passage quoted, was now entertained by the disciples concerning the future coming of Christ.

One of the most cherished hopes of the Jews was, that the Messiah would restore the kingdom to Israel; that he would raise the nation to even far greater power and splendor than they believed it to have enjoyed during the days of David and Solomon. Similar expectations were entertained by the disciples of Christ till after his death. The two who journeyed with him to Emmaus after his resurrection said, "We were hoping that it was he

* See Pocock's Notæ Miscellaneæ in Maimon. Portam Mosis. Works, I. 177, 178.

who was to be the deliverer of Israel."* The last question which his Apostles proposed to him was, "Lord, wilt thou now restore the kingdom to Israel?" The false expectation implied in these words, it is to be observed, was not corrected by our Saviour. He only answered, "It is not for you to know the times and the seasons which are at the disposal of the Father alone." † The question of the Apostles shows that they had at the time no correct understanding of his prophecy concerning the destruction of the Jewish nation; and that their minds still dwelt on the ancient hopes of their countrymen.

The later Jews have supposed, that at the coming of the Messiah the saints who are dead will be raised from their graves to partake the glories of his kingdom.‡ It is probable that this is a traditionary belief, and that a similar supposition was entertained by the Jews in the time of Christ. If so, it may have served in part as a foundation for the following striking and eloquent passage, in which St. Paul expresses to the Thessalonians his expectation of the near return of our Saviour to earth.§

"I would have you understand, brothers, concerning those who have fallen asleep, that you may not sorrow like other men who have no hope. For

* Luke xxiv. 21. † Acts i. 6, 7.

‡ See Pocock's dissertation, "In quo variæ Judæorum de resurrectione mortuorum sententiæ expenduntur," one of his Notæ Miscellaneæ upon the Porta Mosis. Works, I. 159, seqq.

§ 1 Thess. iv. 13-18.

as we believe that Jesus died and rose again, so also will God, through Jesus, bring again with him those who have fallen asleep. For this we say to you, brothers, as teachers from God, that we who are living, we who are left till the coming of the Lord,* shall not anticipate those who have fallen asleep. For the Lord himself will descend from heaven, with a summons given by an archangel sounding the trump of God; and they who have died in Christ will arise first. Then we who are living, we who are left, shall be borne up with them into the clouds to meet the Lord in the air; and so shall we be ever with the Lord. So then comfort one another with these words."

The Thessalonians, it is evident from both of the Epistles addressed to them, were looking for the second coming of Christ as an event not distant. This expectation they would hardly have entertained so strongly as they appear to have done, had it not been countenanced by St. Paul, through whom they had just been converted to Christianity. Anticipating that our Saviour was about to come in person to establish his kingdom and reward his followers, they feared, it seems, that their friends who had died might not share in the glories and blessings to be then enjoyed by those Christians who might be living. It was the purpose of the Apostle to remove this apprehension.

* It is thus that the words, *ἡμεῖς οἱ ζῶντες, οἱ περιλειπόμενοι εἰς τὴν παρουσίαν τοῦ κυρίου*, should be rendered. St. Paul speaks of those who are alive, those who are left till the coming of the Lord, in contradistinction from those who have fallen asleep.

But if we rightly understand the passage, the conceptions of the Apostle respecting our Lord's future coming were erroneous. Undoubtedly it appears that they were so. But to what does the error amount? Does it affect any important doctrine of religion? What is the essential fact here expressed, concerning the circumstances of which St. Paul had fallen into a mistake, in consequence of the previous opinions of his countrymen? The essential doctrine — all that can properly be called *a truth of religion* — is this, that, whether the followers of Christ live a longer or a shorter time on earth, their future happiness is equally secure. The dead and the living are equally the care of God; and the time is coming when they will all meet together where their Master has gone before.

That St. Paul had in view that figurative language in which our Saviour was, as I believe, supposed to have predicted his future personal coming, appears from the words immediately following those just quoted. The Apostle adopts the thoughts and expressions which the Evangelists represent Christ as having used.

"But concerning the times and the seasons, brothers, there is no need that I should write to you. For you yourselves know well, that the day of the Lord is coming as a thief in the night.* For

* Compare Matthew xxiv. 43, 44. "But this you know, that if the master of a house is aware at what hour a thief is coming, he is awake, and suffers not his house to be broken into. So then be you always ready; for in an hour in which you do not expect him, the Son of Man will come."

when they shall say, Peace and safety, then sudden destruction will come upon them,* as the pangs of a woman with child; and they will not escape. But you, brothers, are not in darkness, that that day should come upon you as a thief. You are all children of the light, and children of the day; we are not of the night nor of darkness. Let us not sleep, then, as others, but watch and be sober." †

With their expectations of the Messiah's kingdom, the Jews had connected the belief of the overthrow and destruction of his enemies. A similar belief we find expressed by St. Paul in his Second Epistle to the Thessalonians, (written shortly after the First,) in which he encourages them with the hope that Christ was coming to deliver them from persecution by the destruction of their persecutors.

" We glory in you, telling the churches of God of your constancy and faithfulness in all your persecutions, and the afflictions that you endure; which afford a pledge of that just judgment of God, by which you will be declared worthy of the kingdom of God, for which you are suffering. Since it will be just for God to make them suffer in return who are afflicting you, and to give you who are afflicted rest with us, when the Lord Jesus shall be manifested from heaven, with the angels of his might, in flaming fire, punishing those who know not God, and those who refuse obedience to the gospel of our Lord Jesus; who will suffer the

* Compare Matthew xxiv. 37 – 39; Luke xxi. 34, 35.

† Compare Matthew xxiv. 42 – 51.

penalty of everlasting destruction, inflicted by the glorious power of the Lord himself, when he shall come in that day to be glorified in his saints, and honored in all believers." *

But the Thessalonians, it appears, had been strongly excited by the expectation of the coming of the Lord. They were regarding it as an event close at hand. St. Paul, in consequence, though he himself anticipated it as not very distant, reminds them, in order to allay the feverish state of feeling in which they seem to have been, that he had in a previous conversation with them pointed out a certain event by which it was to be preceded, and which had not yet taken place. This event I suppose to have been the rebellion of the Jews against the Romans; but it is not necessary to our present purpose to enter into a full explanation of the obscure passage to which I refer.†

We have seen that St. Paul, at the time when he wrote his First Epistle to the Thessalonians, was looking forward to a resurrection of those Christians who had died, which should take place at the coming of Christ; and that he regarded himself and those whom he addressed as individuals who might be living at the time of that event. The same anticipations appear in his First Epistle to the Corinthians. He says: —

"Through the Messiah all will be made alive. But each in his proper order; Christ the first fruits; next, they who are Christ's, at his coming.

. . . . .

* 2 Thess. i. 4–10. † 2 Thess. ch. ii.

"Brothers, I tell you a new truth. We shall not indeed all sleep, but we shall all be changed; in a moment, in the glance of an eye, at the last trump; — for the trump will sound, and the dead will be raised incorruptible, and we shall be changed."*

St. Paul elsewhere in his Epistles refers, I think, to the expected personal appearance of his Master; as, when addressing the Corinthians, some of whom were disposed to an unfriendly judgment concerning him, he says: "Judge nothing before the time, till the Lord come, who will bring to light what is hidden in darkness, and make manifest the purposes of men's hearts; and then every one's praise will be from God."†

Thus also he exhorts the Romans to obey the precepts he had given them, "understanding the time; for the hour," he says, "has come for us to awake from sleep; for now is our deliverance nearer than when we became believers. The night is far spent, the day is at hand."‡

To the Philippians (iv. 5) he says, "The Lord is at hand," apparently in the same sense in which in the Epistle of James (v. 8) it is said, "The coming of the Lord is at hand."

He tells the Corinthians: "I ever thank my God for you, on account of the favor of God bestowed upon you through Christ Jesus; for you have been enriched by him with all instruction and all knowledge, the doctrine of Christ having been firmly established among you, so that you are poor in no

* Ch. xv. 23, 24, 51, 52. † 1 Cor. iv. 5.
‡ Romans xiii. 11, 12.

blessing, whilst waiting for the manifestation of our Lord Jesus Christ; and God also will preserve you steadfast to the end, so that you may be without blame in the day of our Lord Jesus Christ."*

To the Philippians (i. 6) he expresses his confidence, that "he among them who has begun a good work will go on to perfect it till the day of Jesus Christ."

We will now take notice of a single passage in the First Epistle of St. John. It has been expected by the later Jews that the coming of the Antichrist, or of the Anti-Messiah, would precede that of the Messiah. The same notion seems to have prevailed among the Jews in the time of Christ, and to be referred to by St. John in the following passage: —

"Children, it is the last hour; and as you have heard that the Antichrist is coming, so there are now many antichrists, whence we know that it is the last hour."†

There is so little reason to suppose that the Second Epistle ascribed to St. Peter was written by him, that it is not to be quoted as evidence of his opinions. But in his First Epistle (as it is called), that is, probably, in the only writing of his which remains, he says: "The end of all things draws near. Be sober, therefore, and watch and pray."‡

"Encourage one another," says the author of the Epistle to the Hebrews, "and so much the more, because you see *the day* is approaching."§

* 1 Cor. i. 4-8.
† 1 John ii. 18.
‡ Ch. iv. 7.
§ Ch. x. 25.

I do not refer to the Apocalypse as the work of St. John, for I do not believe it to be so. But as it was written during the latter part of the first, or the early part of the second century, it affords evidence of the opinions of those who were disciples of the Apostles. I regard it as the production of some early Jewish Christian, whose imagination was highly excited by the expected coming of Christ. It does not, I think, appear that he himself intended to assume the character of the Apostle John, or that there is ground for charging him with any fraudulent design. His work, notwithstanding the imperfection of its language, is in a high strain of poetry. The mind of the writer was borne away by his subject. He intended, as I conceive, that his visions should be understood as imaginary only, like those of another work of about the same age, the Shepherd of Hermas, or, to take a more familiar example, like those of Bunyan. The conviction was strong upon him, that the second coming of Christ was near at hand; and the object of his work, which in modern times has been so ill understood, was, I believe, to describe the events by which, according to the belief of his age, or his own particular belief, it was to be preceded, accompanied, and followed. In the very commencement of his work, he professes that it relates to events soon to occur; exhorting his readers to attend to what is written, "*because* the time is near." His words are thus rendered in the Common Version: —

"The Revelation of Jesus Christ, which God gave unto him, to show unto his servants *things which must shortly come to pass;* and he sent and signified it by his angel to his servant John. . . . . . Blessed is he that readeth, and they that hear, the words of this prophecy, and keep those things which are written therein ; *for the time is at hand.*"

The words, as thus translated, show, I think, that those expositions of the book are erroneous, which suppose it to contain a prophecy of events concerning the Christian Church, extending to our own time and beyond, some of the most important not having yet taken place. Whatever the writer anticipated was, as he believed, shortly to come to pass. But I suppose that the words contain a much clearer indication of his subject, and that the first verse should be thus rendered: —

"The Manifestation of Jesus Christ, which God has granted him to show forth to his servants, — what must shortly come to pass; which he has signified, sending by his angel to his servant John."

The near coming of the Lord is several times referred to in the work in express terms. In the seventh verse of the first chapter, the language which our Saviour used when he figuratively spoke of his coming to the destruction of the Jewish nation, is quoted by the writer: "Lo! he is coming in clouds, and every eye will see him, and they who pierced him; and all the tribes of the land will lament." * There are elsewhere similar references to the words of Christ. And the book concludes, as it began, with a declaration, that the

* Compare Matthew xxiv. 30.

events anticipated in it were near at hand; and an explicit indication that the main event expected was the coming of Christ. "And the angel said to me, Seal not up the words of the prophecy of this book; for the time is near...... Lo! I am coming quickly to bring retribution with me, to give to every man according to his works...... He who testifies these things says, Surely I am coming quickly. Amen! Come, Lord Jesus!"

The principal source of illustration for this book is to be found in the language and conceptions of the later Jews, especially their conceptions of events connected with the coming of the Messiah. It is from the neglect of this means of illustration, and from the erroneous notions respecting the character of the work as, properly speaking, prophetical, that the imaginations of most modern expositors have been so bewildered in its study. The coincidence between many of the conceptions of the later Jews, and those expressed by the author of the Apocalypse, leaves little doubt that the former are traditionary, and existed in the time of Christ.

Though the Second Epistle ascribed to Peter cannot be quoted in evidence of the opinions of that Apostle, it affords proof of a state of opinion and feeling existing among Christians at some period during the first two centuries. The writer says (iii. 3–13): "Be aware of this, that in the last days scoffers will arise, following their own lusts, and saying, Where is his promised coming? For since the fathers fell asleep, all things continue as they were since the beginning of the creation.

But they wilfully forget, that of old by the word of God there were heavens, and an earth rising out of the water, and surrounded by water, which things being so, the world then existing was destroyed, being inundated by water; but the present heavens and the present earth are by his word reserved for fire, being kept for a day when the impious will be judged and destroyed. Forget not this one thing, beloved, that a day with the LORD is as a thousand years, and a thousand years as a day. The LORD is not tardy in performing his promise (as some think him tardy), but is patient toward us, not willing that any should perish, but that all should attain reformation. But the day of the LORD will come as a thief, in which the heavens will pass away with a roaring sound, and the elements will melt with fervent heat, and the earth and all its works will be burnt up. Seeing, then, that all present things are to be dissolved, what ought you to be in all holy conduct and pious dispositions, expecting and earnestly desiring the coming of the day of God, in which the heavens will be dissolved by fire, and the elements melt with fervent heat. But we, according to his promise, expect new heavens and a new earth, in which righteousness will dwell."

Though the author does not in this passage explicitly speak of the coming of Christ, — for by the title "LORD" God is here intended, — yet I suppose there is no controversy that he connected in his imagination the consummation of all present things, which he describes, with that event. It appears, then, from what he says, that there had been so much expectation among Christians of the speedy return of Christ, as to afford occasion for the ridicule of scoffers. The writer, it seems, conceived that it would be attended with the renovation of all things by fire; a conception which is not to be confounded with that of the consummation of all things by fire at the termination of the Messiah's reign. The former seems to have been peculiar, and borrowed, not from the notions of the Jews concerning the coming of the Messiah, but from Gentile philosophy, particularly the Stoic. There is nothing answering to it elsewhere in the New Testament, nor, I think, in the Jewish traditions. It is quite different from the notions entertained by the earliest Christian Fathers, which correspond to those held by the Jews, and expressed in the Apocalypse; though they comprised much which had nowhere been taught by any Apostle. The earlier Fathers believed, to quote the description of Justin Martyr, who appeals to the Apocalypse as his authority, that Jerusalem was to be rebuilt, adorned, and enlarged; that there was to be a resurrection, in which the followers of Christ who were dead, together with the patriarchs and prophets and other pious Jews, were to return to life; that these, with the body of Christians, were to inhabit that city with Christ, rejoicing, for a thousand years, at the end of which would follow the general resurrection and judgment of all. This is the doctrine of the Millennium, of the visible reign of Christ in person upon earth; a doctrine which the earlier Christians would be disposed to receive the more eagerly in consequence of the oppression, persecution, and deprivation they were suffering. It was, however, rejected and opposed by Origen. When Christianity became the religion of the state, and worldly prosperity shone on its professors, the doctrine gradually faded out of notice; but it has existed to our own age, transmitted or revived, being held at different periods by some one or other more enthusiastic sect, in connection with the belief that the expected kingdom of Christ is at hand.

We will now confine our attention to the opinions of the Apostles, which are to be carefully distinguished from all the additions made to them by others. I have quoted the writings of different Apostles. Probably there were differences of opinion among them concerning the circumstances which would attend the coming of our Lord; but they all appear to have expected his personal and visible return to earth as an event not distant; and to have believed that he would come to exercise judgment, to reward his faithful followers, to punish the disobedient, and to destroy his foes. St. Paul, likewise, expected that "the dead who were Christ's" would be raised at his coming. He further tells the Thessalonians, that the followers of Christ then living would be borne up in the air to meet the Lord and continue ever with him; — words which imply, that he believed that the end of all present things was to be connected with the coming of Christ. To the Corinthians, after speaking of the resurrection of the followers of Christ at his coming, he says: "Then will be the *end*, when he will deliver up the kingdom to God, even the Father; after destroying all dominion and all authority and power. For he must reign till He has put all his enemies under his feet. The last enemy, Death, shall be destroyed. . . . . . And when all things are put under him, then will the Son himself be subject to Him who put all things under him, that God may be all in all."* We are likewise led to the conclusion that St. Paul connected the end of the world with the coming of Christ, by the strong language that he uses concerning the general judgment of men, which was then to take place. Thus he says to Timothy: "I charge thee before God, and before Jesus Christ, who will judge the living and the dead when he shall appear in his kingdom";† and the conception, that we must "all appear before the judgment-seat of Christ to receive according to what we have done in the body, either good or evil," is one which he repeatedly expresses.‡ That he looked for the end of the world as following the coming of Christ, may be inferred also from his describing those who should then rise as passing from mortality to immortality, and as clothed with spiritual bodies. "Flesh and blood," he says, "cannot inherit the kingdom of God."§ St. Peter and St. John likewise speak of "its being the last time"; and of "the end of all things being at hand." It is to be particularly ob-

* 1 Cor. xv. 24–28. † 2 Timothy iv. 1.

‡ Romans xiv. 10; 2 Corinthians v. 10.

§ 1 Corinthians xv. 50.

served, that there is no intimation given by any Apostle of a millennial reign of Christ; a circumstance which, among many others, serves to show that the Apocalypse, in which this doctrine is clearly taught, was not the work of St. John.

Such, then, appear to have been the opinions of the Apostles respecting the second coming of their Master. I have been led to speak of this subject, so important in many of its relations, from its special bearing upon the explanations which I have given of the language of our Saviour. I have endeavored to show, that his language concerning his future coming, the establishment of his kingdom on earth, and his passing judgment upon all men, presents no difficulty when compared with subsequent events; that his expressions are figurative, and that their explanation is to be found in analogous metaphors, the meaning of which is obvious; and that, however bold some of them may appear, they do not transcend the genius of the Oriental style. But we find, on the other hand, that his Apostles, through causes which I have endeavored partly to explain, instead of a figurative coming, expected a literal return of their Master to earth, before the generation then living should pass away; that, instead of a figurative judgment, they believed that on his return he would judge all men in person; and that, in connection with these events, they anticipated the end of all things. These expectations were erroneous; and before the explanation which has been given of the words of Christ can be fully admitted, this error must be understood. We must not read over the passages in which it is expressed with a confused misapprehension of their sense, as if they related to events still future, and were at the same time coincident in meaning with the language of Christ.

Nothing more need be said to illustrate the difference which I suppose to exist between his meaning and the conceptions of the Apostles respecting his future coming. But there are questions and considerations suggested by the facts brought forward, which, though not *immediately* connected with the subject of this work, are too important to be passed over in silence. Why, it may be asked, did not our Saviour prevent his Apostles from falling into the error we have remarked? The answer to this question will open to us views of much importance to be attended to in the study of the New Testament.

On many subjects our Saviour refrained from entering into a full explanation, and correcting the errors of his hearers. They were errors not intimately connected with the essential truths of religion. The course of events, the advance of human reason, and the progress of knowledge, would afford sufficient correctives; and he was not sent to deliver men from all false opinions, and to furnish a digest of truth upon every subject. An error not important may be so interwoven with an essential truth, that it can be separated only by the hazardous experiment of unravelling the whole web.

A misapprehension of facts may be strongly associated with feelings practically true. Their roots may be so twisted round it, that there is danger of eradicating them in the attempt to remove it. Nor does the communication of truth depend upon the instructor alone. No instructor can give a child the knowledge of a man. He to whom God had opened the treasure-house of wisdom could not make all his most willing hearers as wise as himself. Putting out of view all miraculous influence upon the mind, men can be advanced in intellectual improvement only in proportion to the progress which they have already made. A truth, however clearly presented, must be in some accordance with the previous habits of thinking of him to whom it is addressed, in order to be clearly apprehended; and a truth ill apprehended, detached from the relations in which it ought to be viewed, may be more mischievous than the error which it is intended to supplant. Men must be taught, as our Saviour taught them, as "they are able to bear it." To have enabled his hearers fully to comprehend all facts and truths connected with Christianity, and to have freed their minds from all false conceptions concerning the Messiah and his kingdom, and every topic which has, or may be supposed to have, a bearing upon religion, could have been effected only by a miracle which would almost have changed their identity. Supposing that in the particular case of the Apostles such a miracle had been wrought, still their hearers would have been as dull of apprehension as were those whom Christ taught. Had the Apostles been placed in all respects on an equality with their Master; had they been guided throughout by the same perfect judgment, which implies not merely the highest intellectual, but the highest moral excellence; had they each been qualified to supply his place, and entitled to every name of honor which belongs to him, — their disciples would have held the same place which they themselves now do as disciples of Christ. They must have taught their followers as their Master had taught them; and whenever this miraculous regeneration of intellect ceased, and men's minds were left to their natural action, and the current of their opinions was suffered to pursue its ordinary course, — whenever infallibility was no longer secured by the power of God, — errors of some kind would necessarily mingle with men's religious faith. As regards the Apostles, we believe that their minds were enlightened by the Spirit of God, and by direct miraculous communications from him, in regard to the essential truths of Christianity. But we have no warrant to believe, nor is there any probable argument to show, that this divine illumination was further extended.

Our Saviour came to teach the essential truths of religion. Even these truths were but imperfectly apprehended by most of those who heard him, and, I may add, have been but imperfectly apprehended by most of those who, from his time to our own, have professed themselves to be his disciples. When we find, that on the last night of his ministry one of his Apostles said to him, "Master, show us the Father, and we shall be satisfied,"* it may be perceived that there were difficulties enough to be overcome in communicating to them a full apprehension of those elementary truths. Their attention was not to be withdrawn from them by discussions, doubts, questions, and explanations respecting subjects of comparatively little importance, concerning which they might have adopted the errors of their age. When, referring to the doctrine of the pre-existence of souls, a doctrine at that time generally connected with the belief of their immortality, they asked, "Master, who sinned, this man or his parents, that he was born blind?"† our Saviour in his answer did not explain to them the mistake implied in those words. When, under the belief common to their countrymen, that the sufferings of this life were punishments from God, certain individuals came to tell him of the "Galilæans, whose blood Pilate had mingled with their sacrifices,"‡ there was nothing in his reply to correct their false conceptions. The relative importance of different doctrines, the wide separation which divides what is essential in true religion from all the accessory notions that men have made a part of their religion, is very little understood at the present day, and was not better understood by the Jews eighteen centuries ago. In most minds, those opinions which they believe or fancy to have anything of a

* John xiv. 8. † John ix. 2. ‡ Luke xiii. 1.

religious character are disposed without regard to perspective. They all stand forward equal in magnitude. It is one of the most striking characteristics of the teaching of Christ, that the distinction between the essential truths of religion and all other doctrines, true or false, was never confounded by him. He fixed the attention of his hearers only upon what it most concerned them to know as religious beings, that is, as creatures of God and heirs of immortality. In order to effect this purpose, it was necessary for him to confine his teaching to the essential truths of religion. If he had done otherwise, if he had labored to correct the errors of his hearers upon subjects of minor importance, and to place the truth distinctly before them in all those new relations which it might present, his hearers would unavoidably have confounded the doctrines thus taught them upon divine authority with those essential principles which alone it was the purpose of God to announce. Their imaginations and feelings might perhaps have been more occupied about what it was of little consequence for them to know, than about truths which it was of the highest concern that they should understand themselves, and be qualified to teach to others.

But there is another aspect under which the subject is to be viewed. We must consider, not merely the disciples, but the enemies of Christ; we must regard the character of the ignorant, prejudiced, unstable multitudes whom he addressed, and whom his Apostles were to address; and we must recollect, that whatever he taught to his Apostles was in effect taught to all; that it was their proper office to publish his whole doctrine. Now in communicating to men the essential truths of religion, and in confining his attention to these alone, he had to encounter prejudices and passions the most obstinate and violent. Superstition, fanaticism, and hypocrisy, all that is in most direct opposition to the love of God and man, constituted the religion of a great part of the Jews. It was vital to the selfish purposes and to the authority of those who were leaders among the people, that the errors which prevailed should retain their power over men's minds. The bigotry of false religion was at the same time inflamed by national pride. This opposition Christ had to encounter, and hence he was assailed throughout his ministry with continual cavil, reproach, and persecution; and he saw from its commencement, that he should soon become their victim. The circumstances in which he was placed required the utmost circumspection, judgment, and self-command. No new prejudice was to be needlessly excited. No unnecessary occasion of cavil was to be presented. No opportunity for perverting or contradicting his words was to be given, that could be avoided consistently with the purpose of his mission. It was not for him to waste the numbered days of his ministry, in which so much was to be accomplished, to perplex his hearers, and to exasperate his foes, by entering into controversy or explanations respecting topics of minor concern. The hold which a prejudice has upon the mind is often out of all proportion to any show of proof that may be brought in its support. Questions, the discussion of which we should now regard only as an object of ridicule, have in other ages been the occasion of rancorous contention. In the fourteenth century, a dispute raged in the Greek empire concerning the question, whether the light which shone round Christ at his transfiguration was created or uncreated. Four councils were assembled, and those who affirmed it to be created, and held the consequences which were supposed to be connected with this doctrine, were anathematized as worse than all other heretics.* If a new teacher of TRUE RELIGION had been sent from God to the men of that age, we may easily comprehend, that few mistakes would have tended more to render his mission fruitless, than for him to have entered into any explanation, or to have passed any judgment, upon this controversy. In the defence of what we now consider as gross errors, a blind and deaf bigotry has been displayed, the strength of which it is hard to estimate since the delusion has passed away. It is not yet two centuries since the denial of the then common belief of witchcraft was regarded as implying the denial of the agency of any spiritual being, of the existence of the invisible world, and consequently

* See Petavii Dogmata Theologica. De Deo Deique Proprietatibus, Lib. I. c. 12. Compare Mosheim's Institutes of Ecclesiastical History, Cent. XIV. P. II. Ch. V. §§ 1, 2; Gieseler, Bd. II. Abth. III. § 129, 2te Aufl., or Vol. III. § 127, Cunningham's Translation.]

as virtual atheism.* In the time of Christ, and for a long period before, the doctrine of dæmoniacal possession prevailed among the Jews, and many diseases were ascribed to this cause. Our Saviour never taught that this was a false doctrine. He occasionally used language conformed to the conceptions of those who believed it to be true. Why was he silent on this subject? Why did he leave some, if not all, of his Apostles in error concerning it, as appears from the common belief being expressed in the first three Gospels, though not in that of St. John? Let us consider, that, if he had taught the truth, he would immediately have been denounced by his enemies as an unbeliever in the invisible world, as a Sadducee teaching that "there was neither angel nor spirit";—that the error in question was intimately connected with many others, concerning the existence of Satan, the origin of evil, the rules of God's government of the world, the mental and physical constitution of man, and the power of magic and incantations;—that it would have been idle to declare

* "For my part," says Sir Thomas Browne, "I have ever believed, and do now know, that there are witches. They that doubt of them do not only deny them, but spirits; and are obliquely and of consequence a sort, not of infidels, but atheists." (Religio Medici, Part I.) Glanvill's "SADDUCISMUS Triumphatus" is a work in defence of the common superstition, by one of the able men of his age, in which he represents, as may be supposed from the title, all disbelievers in witchcraft as destitute of religion. A great part of Dr. Henry More's "Antidote to Atheism" consists of stories of supposed supernatural events, apparitions, witchcraft, and pretended miraculous operations of God's providence.

himself against one of these errors, unless he had opposed them all; — that he was surrounded by ignorant and prejudiced hearers, wholly unaccustomed to exercise their minds upon any general truth; — and that, had it been possible to instruct them thoroughly upon any one of the subjects I have mentioned, he must, in order to effect this, have turned aside from the great purpose of his ministry, and have withdrawn their attention from it. It would have been the labor of a long life to enlighten the minds of any considerable number of Jews upon topics such as these.

Let us consider another case. The Jews had adopted what is called the *allegorical* mode of interpreting their sacred books; and had found many supposed predictions and types of their expected Messiah in factitious senses which they ascribed to particular passages. This mode of interpretation was adopted by some of the Apostles. We find examples of it as used by them in the Gospels of both Matthew and John, and in the Acts of the Apostles. One is surprised, perhaps, that this mistake was not corrected by Christ. Nothing may seem more simple, than that he should have indicated that this whole system of interpretation, and this method of proof, so far as the supposed prophecies were applied to himself, were erroneous. But would you have had him at the same time teach the whole art of interpretation? If he had not done so, errors as great might have been committed from some other cause. If he had corrected some wrong conceptions only, and left others, the latter from that very circumstance would have acquired new authority. But to have taught the art of interpretation only would not have been sufficient to enable his hearers to become skilful expositors of the Old Testament; he must have settled the yet disputed questions concerning the age, the authorship, the authority, and what has been called the inspiration, of the different writings that compose it; and whoever has studied these subjects with an unbiassed and inquiring mind may, I think, be satisfied that the truth concerning them is such as no Jew was prepared to listen to, and few indeed would have listened to without astonishment and wrath.

But let us suppose that he had attempted only to correct the single error which consisted in the false application of many passages to the Messiah; what would have been the consequence? His enemies would undoubtedly have contended, that it was idle to suppose *him* to be the Messiah. He does not even pretend, they would have triumphantly said, to be the object of the prophecies by which, according to all those learned in the Law and in our traditions, the Messiah is foretold. Perhaps he would have us believe, that no Messiah has been promised; but that he has as good a claim as any other to that title. Has he not come from Beelzebub, to teach that the prophecies are false and our hopes vain, that God has ceased to care for his people, and thus to seduce us from our faith and allegiance?

But in connection with this subject there is another fact to be attended to. In teaching or enforcing truth, the language of error may be used in order powerfully to affect the feelings; because it has associations with it which no other language will suggest. Such use of it implies no assent to the error on which it is founded. He who employs the epithets "diabolical," or "fiendish," affords from that circumstance alone no reason to suppose that he believes in the existence of devils or fiends. There is much language of the same character. We still borrow many expressions from imaginary beings of ideal beauty and grace, from fairies and sylphs, beings whose real existence was once believed. We have no reluctance to use words derived from the false opinions concerning witchcraft, possession, and magic. We use those which have been mentioned, and many terms of a similar kind, because they furnish, or seem to furnish, expressions more forcible than we could otherwise command. But this fact has been disregarded in reasoning from the language of Christ. Expressions founded upon the conceptions of the Jews, and used by him because no other modes of speech would have so powerfully affected their minds, have been misunderstood as intended to convey a doctrine taught by himself. This remark is applicable to those few passages in his discourses in which he speaks, according to the belief of the Jews, of Satan as if he were a real being, such as the following: "I saw Satan falling from heaven like lightning"; — "Your father is the Devil, and you are ready to execute his evil purposes";—"The enemy who sowed the tares is the Devil";—and particularly to the figurative and parabolic narrative in which he represented himself as having been tempted by Satan. I say in which he represented himself, for it is evident that the narrative of the Evangelists could have been derived from Christ alone. Satan was regarded by the Jews as the great adversary of God and man, the Tempter, the Accuser, the source of moral and physical evil. No words could so forcibly impress them with a conception of the odiousness and depravity of any act or character, as by resembling it to him, or referring it to him as its suggester or author. They were familiar with the imagination of such a being, and through this imagination their minds were most powerfully to be affected. The abstract idea of moral evil, if, indeed, they could have apprehended it, would have been to them a shadowy phantom, compared with it as hypostatized and vivified in its supposed malignant author. Under circumstances in which it is impossible to explain the whole truth, or in which it is certain that the whole truth cannot be understood and felt, in addressing men who are unaccustomed to exercise their understandings, and who from childhood have incorporated false conceptions with right principles of action, we may use their errors for their reformation; we may appeal to their feelings or their fears through their mistaken imaginations; we may employ one wrong opinion to counteract others more pernicious; and in reasoning, exhortation, or reproof, we may thus avail ourselves of their more innocent prejudices in opposition to their passions and vices. But in doing this, we are precluded from directly assailing those prejudices; though we may at the same time be establishing truths which will effect their gradual abolition. Such was, I believe, in some particulars, the mode of teaching adopted by Christ.

In regard to some of the errors of his disciples, it may be a question whether the plainest language would in itself alone have been sufficient to remove them. I may rather say, it evidently would not have been sufficient. The very subject of this volume shows, if the opinions maintained in it be true, that the plainest language has not been sufficient to preserve men from the grossest errors. Yet the words of Christ have not less authority as recorded in the Gospels, than when uttered by his own lips. But we are not obliged to reason thus indirectly. We may see in the accounts of his ministry, how often our Saviour was *not* understood by his disciples. As he was approaching Jerusalem for the last time, he called the Twelve together and said: "Lo! we are going up to Jerusalem," and the Son of Man "will be delivered into the hands of the Gentiles, and mocked, and insulted, and spit upon; and having scourged him, they will put him to death; and on the third day he will return to life." No language can be more simple and explicit than this. But the Evangelist goes on to relate, that the Apostles "understood this not at all; the meaning of his words was hidden from them, and they did not comprehend what he said."* How little they understood this and other declarations of Christ may appear from the fact, that the next event recorded by the Evangelists is the application on the part of James and John for the highest places, under Christ, in that temporal kingdom on which their hopes were still fixed. The prediction of his resurrection, though repeatedly made by him, was, we know, so little comprehended by them, that no hope, and apparently no thought, of that event was entertained by them after his death. It is not strange, therefore, that they expected a visible return of our Saviour from heaven, to establish his kingdom, though he himself had declared, "The kingdom of God is not coming with any show that may be watched for; nor will men say, Lo! it is here; or, Lo! it is there; for lo! the kingdom of God is within you"; and though in the clearest manner, and under circumstances the most solemn, he had affirmed, "My kingdom is not of this world."

WE are apt to fall into a great mistake, from not distinguishing between the feelings and conceptions, the whole state of character, of an enlightened Christian at the present day, and those of the Jews to whom Christ preached. It may seem to us as if a few words of his would have been sufficient to do away any error, however inveterate, because we think their effect would be

* Luke xviii. 31 - 34.

such upon our own minds. We may wonder that those words were not uttered. We may almost be tempted to ask, Why was a teacher from God so sparing of his knowledge, so limited in his instructions? Why did he not deliver his Apostles at least from all their mistaken apprehensions having any connection with the facts or truths of religion? How could he leave the world with so many false and pernicioüs opinions existing around him in full vigor, against which he had not declared himself? And why, with the same feelings, we might go on to ask, do the great truths of religion appear, as disclosed by him, in such naked, monumental, severe grandeur? Why do they stand alone, separated from all truths not essential to our faith? Why were not the many questions answered, the many doubts solved, which we might be disposed to lay before Christ, or which his disciples, if we imagine them as inquiring and as teachable as ourselves, might have proposed?

To inquiries such as these it has been my purpose to afford some answer in what has been suggested. As a teacher from God, it was the proper and sole office of Christ to make known to men, on the authority of God, the fundamental truths of religion. To inculcate these alone was a task which demanded all his efforts, his own undivided attention, and that of his most willing hearers. They were to be kept distinct from all other truths. The minds of men were not to be withdrawn from them by bringing any other subject into discussion. When we ask why Christ did not proceed further to enlighten his hearers, we forget how unprepared they were for such instruction, what prejudices must have been overcome, what wrong associations broken, how much of inquiry on their part, and of explanation on his, would have been necessary, how liable his language was to be misunderstood, and how fatal it would have been to the purpose of his mission thus to occupy their thoughts upon topics unconnected with it. We forget what opposition he had to encounter, how all his words and actions were watched with malignant eyes, how often his enemies came proposing questions to try what he would say, that they might find opportunity to injure him.* We do not remember, that no error could be touched without affording some new occasion or pretence of hatred; and that whatever he spoke would be misunderstood, perverted, misrepresented, and made a ground for false inferences. We do not keep in mind the imperfect apprehensions of his disciples, of which we find continual notices in the Gospels, and the utter indocility of the great body of the Jews, which is equally apparent. We forget, that, after a ministry of unintermitted effort, he fell a sacrifice to the truths which he did teach. In asking why his instructions did not extend to other truths, and to the correction of errors not essential, we forget how difficult was his proper office, we forget by whom he was surrounded, we forget the reproach that was forced from his lips: " O unbelieving and per-

* The Common Version says, "to tempt him."

verse race! how long shall I be with you? How long must I bear with you?" It was not to men so little ready to receive his essential doctrines that any unnecessary instruction was to be addressed. We mistake altogether the state of the case, when, in reading the Gospels, we conceive of Christ as teaching with the same freedom of explanation, and with the same use of language, with which we may perhaps reasonably suppose that he would have taught a body of enlightened men, receiving his words with the entire deference with which we now regard them.

The wisdom and the self-restraint, for so it is to be considered, of our Saviour, in confining his teaching to the essential truths of religion, and the broad distinction which he thus made between these and all other doctrines, appear to me among the most striking proofs of the divinity of his mission. I cannot believe, that a merely human teacher would have conducted himself with such perfect wisdom; that he would never have attempted to use his authority, or have displayed his superior knowledge, in maintaining other truths than those which essentially concern the virtue and happiness of mankind; that he would have refrained from exposing or contradicting the errors of his opponents on any other subjects; that he would have succeeded in communicating to his disciples those principles which are the foundation of all religion and morality, without perplexing their minds by the discussion of any topics less important; and, at last, have left his doctrine a monument for all future time, — not like the works of some enlightened men, which perish with the errors they destroy, but remaining a universal code of instruction for mankind.

But there is another very different point of view, under which the subject we have been examining affords, I think, proof of the divine origin of Christianity. If the Gospels are an authentic account of what was done and said by Christ, no question can remain whether Christ were a teacher from God. But that they are so, we have evidence in the facts which have been brought to view.

When we compare the language of Christ respecting his future coming with the expectations expressed by his Apostles, we perceive that his language was misunderstood by them. He did not predict his visible return to earth to be the judge of men. There is nothing in his words which requires or justifies such an interpretation of them. It has appeared, I trust, that the figurative language which he used is to be understood in a very different sense.

But the Apostles, from various causes, were expecting such a return of their Master. Their words admit of no probable explanation except as referring to this anticipated event. What, then, follows as a correct inference from this comparison?

It follows, that the words relating to this subject, which are ascribed to Christ in the Gospels, were truly his words. They were not falsely ascribed to him. They were not imagined for him. They were not conformed to the apprehensions of his followers. Had his followers fabricated or intentionally modified the words, they would have made their Master say what they themselves have said, in language as explicit as their own.

Here, then, we have evidence of the most unsuspicious kind, for it is clearly evidence which it was the purpose of no individual to furnish, that certain words recorded in the Gospels were uttered by Christ. The writers of these books did not in this case fabricate language expressive of their own opinions, and ascribe it to him. And if they did not in this case, concerning a subject on which they taught what he did not teach, we have no reason to suspect them of having, in any other case, intentionally ascribed to him words which he did not utter.

The words, then, ascribed to Christ in the Gospels are words of Christ. They have been reported by well-informed individuals, who had no intention of deceiving, and who did not even conform them to their own apprehension of their meaning. I will not pursue the inferences from these truths. I will only observe, that the proof of them, as we have seen, is, through the providence of God, bound up in the New Testament itself. An error of the Apostles proves the reality of their faith. In seeking to solve a difficulty, we discover unexpected evidence of the truth of Christianity. And I am persuaded, that, as the New Testament is better understood, as the false notions that have prevailed concerning it pass away, and it is made a subject of enlightened investigation and philosophical study, new and irresistible proofs will appear of that fact, of which we can hardly estimate the full magnitude and interest, that Christ was a teacher from God.

In reference, indeed, to the very subject we have been examining, there is another consideration well deserving attention. We have seen what were the anticipations of the Apostles concerning the personal return of their Master to earth, and the approaching termination of the world. But in connection with these expectations, a remarkable phenomenon presents itself. We might have supposed, that the imaginations and feelings of the Apostles would have been seized upon and inflamed by the prospect of such events; that they would have continually placed them before the eyes of those whom they addressed, and have urged them upon the thoughts of men; that their exhortations and warnings would always have borne the impress of anticipations so extraordinary and so exciting. But this is not the case. We may read far the greater part of what they have left us in writing, without discovering an intimation that they held such opinions. It is clear, that they did not insist upon the facts in question as of any considerable moment. They introduce the mention of them as accessory ideas in connection with the doctrine of immortality and retribution. Imagine any other body of individuals laboring with like earnestness and devotion for the reformation of their fellow-men, under a similar belief of the approaching end of the world; — imagine what would be the feelings and language of such individuals, and contrast them with those of the Apostles, and you may perceive what a singular phenomenon is presented in the New Testament.

In what manner is this phenomenon to be explained? How is the problem to be solved, that men, anticipating the end of the world and the final judgment of mankind as at hand, should have insisted so little upon these events for the purpose of exciting the terrors or the hopes of those whom they addressed? It can be explained, I think, but in one way. The feelings which those expected events would naturally have produced were absorbed in the deeper, the intenser feeling, produced by a thorough conviction of the essential truths of religion. To them, who knew themselves the creatures, the care, the special ministers, of the God of Love; to them, the disciples of his Son, the witnesses, nay, themselves the very agents, of that divine power by which the laws of nature were suspended; to them, before whose view the clouds resting upon eternity had been rolled away, — the consummation of this world was of little more concern than the revolution of an empire. Assured of immortality, and with everything to give strength to the feeling which this assurance is adapted to produce, it was of small moment to them or to their disciples whether with the dead they should be raised incorruptible, or whether with the living they should be changed. One all-penetrating sentiment of the truth of their religion annihilated the power of smaller excitements. Their feelings were calmed by the contemplation of one absorbing interest, which no changes could affect.

How, then, was this conviction of the truth of their religion produced, — this conviction which so wrought upon their minds that the anticipated consummation and judgment of the world had no power strongly to move them? There is one answer to this question which a Christian will give I know of no other.

NOTE C.

BY THE EDITOR.

(See pp. 183 – 191.)

VARIOUS READINGS OF CERTAIN PASSAGES SUPPOSED TO HAVE A BEARING ON THE DOCTRINE OF THE TRINITY.

Beside the three celebrated passages which have been remarked upon by Mr. Norton, — Acts xx. 28, 1 Timothy iii. 16, and 1 John v. 7, 8, — there are others, of more or less importance, whose supposed bearing on the doctrine of the Trinity is affected by various readings of the original text. It is the object of the present note to exhibit *all* the passages of this class that can be regarded as of any consequence, where a reading different from that followed in the Common Version has been adopted in any of the leading critical editions of the Greek Testament which have been published in the present century. In some instances, the reading thus adopted may be thought more favorable to the Trinitarian theory than that which before stood in the text; in others, the reverse is the case.

The examples which are about to be given of various readings of the Greek text of the New Testament, in connection with those which have already been noticed, might perhaps lead one imperfectly acquainted with the subject to suppose the differences in the original manuscripts to be more important than they really are. The number of these differences, or various readings, is very large; but an examination of them tends only to confirm our confidence in the *essential* correctness with which the text of the New Testament has been transmitted to us. At least nineteen twentieths of them, as Mr. Norton has remarked,* may be dismissed at once from consideration, as being so obviously errors of transcribers, or found in so few authorities, that no critic would regard them as having any claim to be received as genuine. Setting these aside, we shall find that about the same proportion of those which remain are of no sort of consequence as affecting the sense. A small number, however, are of a nature to excite some interest; there are a few passages of considerable length in the Received Text whose genuineness is doubtful or more than doubtful, as the doxology in the Lord's Prayer, the last twelve verses of the Gospel of Mark, and the story of the woman taken in adultery. See also, in the critical editions, Matthew xxiii. 14; xxvii. 35; Mark vi. 11; Luke ix. 55, 56; xvii. 36; John v. 3, 4; Acts viii. 37; ix. 5, 6; and xxiv. 6–8. But it may be safely said, that the various readings do not appreciably affect the evidence of any theological doctrine except the doctrine of the Trinity; and with respect to this, their importance has often been exaggerated. Still, in studying the Scriptures to ascertain what they teach, the first thing to be settled is, what *is* Scripture. If words which purport to be a part of Scripture, in the copies which are in common use, are spurious, or doubtful, the lover of truth will wish to know it; and the greater his reverence for Scripture, the more desirous will he be not to confound the mistakes of transcribers with the words of Evangelists and Apostles.

The place of true reverence for Scripture has, however,

* Evidences of the Genuineness of the Gospels, Vol. I., Additional Note A, Sect. III., "On the Character and Importance of the Various Readings of the New Testament," p. xxxviii. The substance of this Section is reprinted in Mr. Norton's Notes on the Gospels, Preliminary Note I.

too often been usurped by a blind and superstitious reverence for what has been called the "Received Text." It will be proper, therefore, before entering on the principal subject of this note, to state some facts in regard to the history of the printed Greek text of the New Testament.

THE earliest printed edition of the Greek Testament was that contained in the fifth volume of the Complutensian Polyglot. The *printing* of this volume, it appears, was completed in 1514; but it was not *published* till 1522. The manuscripts which were used for it have never been identified, though the story of their having been sold to a rocket-maker is now exploded; * and there has been much controversy respecting their value. The editors speak of them as "very ancient and correct"; but there is reason for questioning their competency to determine the fact. The art of criticism was then in its infancy; such works as Montfaucon's Palæographia Græca did not exist; and, as Bentley says, "it is not everybody knows the age of a manuscript." It is remarked by Bishop Marsh, that the text which they have given almost invariably agrees with that of the modern Greek manuscripts, — such as were written in the thirteenth century or later, — where these differ from the most ancient, and from the quotations of the early Greek Fathers. "There cannot be a doubt, therefore," he says, "that the Complutensian text was formed from modern manuscripts alone." † Wetstein had before come to the same conclusion.‡

The first *published* edition of the Greek Testament was

* See an article by Dr. James Thomson, first published in the Biblical Review for March 1847, and afterwards reprinted in Tregelles's "Account of the Printed Text of the Greek New Testament," pp. 12-18.

† Lectures, &c., p. 96.

‡ Nov. Test. Græc. (Prolegom.), Tom. I. p. 118.

printed at Basle in 1516, under the editorial care of Erasmus. The Greek text was accompanied by a revised Latin version, and a large body of annotations. Though some preparation had been made for the work, much of it was unfinished when the printing was commenced; * Erasmus was carrying through the press at the same time an edition of the works of St. Jerome, and a new edition of his Adagia; yet the whole volume, containing nearly one thousand folio pages, was printed in less than six months! *Præcipitatum fuit verius quam editum*, "it was driven headlong through the press rather than edited," as Erasmus himself says in one of his letters.† The cause of this excessive haste was the fear of the publisher, Froben, that his edition would be anticipated by the Complutensian. Only four or five manuscripts were used, all of them modern, and, with one exception, of very little value. A second and more correct edition was published by Erasmus in 1519, and a third in 1522. According to Mill, the second edition differs from the first in about four hundred places, and the third from the second in one hundred and eighteen. The text of Erasmus was worst in the Apocalypse, of which he had but a single manuscript, and that mutilated, wanting the last six verses of the book. This deficiency he supplied as well as he could by retranslating from the Latin Vulgate into Greek. In his fourth edition, which appeared in 1527, he altered the text of the Apocalypse in about ninety places on the authority of the Complutensian Polyglot, but made few other changes. His fifth edition, published in 1535, varies scarcely at all from the fourth. Compared with the first, its text would seem, according to the account of Mill, to have been altered in about six hundred places. Of these

* "Conficiebatur [*Conficiebantur* is a misprint] simul et excudebatur opus." — Erasmi Epist. CCLI. (Budæo.) Opp. III. col. 250.

† Epist. CCLXXIV. (Pirckheimero.) Opp. III. col. 268.

changes, in the judgment of the same critic, more than one hundred were not improvements.

The principal editions of the Greek Testament published in the sixteenth century subsequently to the fifth of Erasmus, were those of Robert Stephens and Beza. Among the various editions of Stephens, the third, printed at Paris in 1550, is the most celebrated, and the most important in its influence on others which succeeded it. Fifteen manuscripts and the Complutensian edition were collated for it, the various readings being noted in the margin. It was the first edition which contained a critical apparatus of this kind. The manuscripts collated, however, were used very little, if at all, for the improvement of the text. As Tregelles remarks, "the various readings seem rather to be appended as an *ornament*," the text, in reality, differing but slightly from the fifth edition of Erasmus, except in the Apocalypse, where the Complutensian was chiefly followed. The splendor of its typography, and the display of various readings, appear, however, to have given this edition a reputation to which it had no title from intrinsic merit. Its credit among Protestants was also doubtless enhanced by the fact that Stephens, who had been much harassed by the bigoted doctors of the Sorbonne, withdrew to Geneva soon after its publication, and announced himself a convert to the doctrines of the Reformation.

Beza, who published five editions of the Greek Testament, accompanied with a Latin version and notes, in 1565, 1576, 1582, 1589, and 1598, had some highly valuable manuscripts. But he made very little use of them. He mostly followed the text of Stephens's third edition, and where he differed from it often altered it for the worse, sometimes introducing readings on mere conjecture, and frequently on very slight authority. In his version and notes he has in many instances followed readings different from those which he has retained in the Greek text.

The common English version of the Bible, made by order of King James, was first published in 1611. The Greek text followed by the translators seems to accord more nearly with that of Beza's fifth edition (1598) than with any other. It agrees with Beza in opposition to the third edition of Robert Stephens in about eighty places; with Stephens in opposition to Beza, in about half that number; and in about a dozen instances it differs from both.* Most of these variations are very trivial.

We come now to the edition of the Greek Testament published by the Elzevirs at Leyden in 1624. This was based on the third edition of Stephens, a few readings, however, being derived from other sources, particularly from Beza. It differs from Stephens in only about one hundred and seventy places, the variations being, for the most part, quite insignificant, many of them, indeed, such as cannot be expressed in a translation. Meeting with favor on account of its neatness, its convenient form, and the high reputation of the Elzevir press for typographical accuracy, it was reprinted in 1633 with a preface in which the publishers assure the reader that he has "a text which is now received by all," — "*Textum ergo habes nunc ab omnibus receptum.*" This assertion, if not strictly true when it was made, soon became so, substantially; and the Elzevir text, formed by an unknown editor in the infancy of biblical criticism, was in almost universal use on the continent of Europe till near the beginning of the present century. It is this which is generally referred to as the "Textus Receptus" or "Received Text." It does not differ *materially* from the text followed in the common English version of the New Testament.

* Many of these passages are referred to in the lists given by Scrivener, in his "Supplement to the Authorised English Version of the New Testament," Vol. I. pp. 7, 8; but his enumeration is far from complete.

In Great Britain the current text has varied a little from the Elzevir, being essentially that of the third edition of Robert Stephens, — "the Vulgate of the Protestant Pope Stephens," as Bentley called it, his text having become a sort of standard among Protestants, like the Clementine edition of the Vulgate among Roman Catholics. Stephens's text was adopted in Walton's Polyglot, 1657, and was reprinted by Mill in 1707, with a few slight, unintentional variations, as the basis of his laborious collection of various readings from manuscripts, ancient versions, and Fathers, designed to serve as *materials* for a critical edition of the Greek Testament. Mill expresses his opinion of many of the various readings in his Prolegomena and Notes, and frequently condemns those adopted by Stephens; but he did not pretend to give a recension of the text. His reprint of Stephens, however, which has generally been copied in the editions of the Greek Testament published in England, has often been termed "*Mill's* text," as if it had the sanction of his critical judgment. This is the text which, now in the middle of the nineteenth century, the American Bible Union has adopted as the basis of its proposed revision of King James's version of the New Testament.

From the statements which have been made, it will be seen that the Received Text resolves itself, substantially, into that of the fifth edition of Erasmus; a scholar indeed, worthy of the highest respect and admiration, but who edited the Greek Testament, to use the language of Griesbach, "*as he could*, from a very few manuscripts and those quite modern, with no other helps except the Latin Vulgate in an interpolated state, and the writings of a few inaccurately edited Fathers." *

SINCE the time when the Received Text was formed, a

* Prolegom. in N. T., Sect. I. p. xxxvii., ed. Schulz.

vast amount of critical materials has been made available for its improvement. The great collection of various readings by Mill, published near the beginning of the last century, — the work of thirty years, — has already been referred to. This collection was much enlarged by Bengel and Wetstein. Toward the close of the last century it was again more than doubled in amount by the labors of Griesbach, Matthæi, Alter, and Birch. In the present century, Scholz, in his *Biblisch-kritische Reise*, or "Travels for the Purpose of Biblical Criticism," and in his edition of the Greek Testament, has given an account of more than three hundred manuscripts never before examined for critical purposes; but a great majority of them are comparatively recent, and his collations were very cursory and inaccurate. The indefatigable and far better directed labors of Tischendorf and Tregelles have afforded us, for the first time, an *exact* knowledge of many very ancient and important documents, which had before been but imperfectly collated. I pass over numerous minor contributions to our stock of critical materials. The result of the whole is, that the most ancient manuscripts — those written in uncial or capital letters — have now been thoroughly collated, and all the more important of them accurately transcribed and published, with the exception of the celebrated Vatican manuscript; and more than eight hundred of the later manuscripts containing the whole or parts of the New Testament have been examined in a greater or less degree, some of them thoroughly, but most of them very cursorily. The ancient versions, and numerous quotations from the New Testament in the writings of the Christian Fathers, have also been compared with the common text. There is still room for useful labor in the collation of the more important cursive manuscripts; there is need of more accurate editions and of a more careful examination of several of the ancient versions; and much remains to be done in enlarging, correcting, and sifting the critical materials which have been collected from the writings of the Fathers. But it is safe to say, that the means which we have at our command for accurately editing the Greek New Testament very far exceed those which we possess in the case of any ancient heathen writer whose works have come down to us.

Though important materials for the correction of the Received Text had been long accumulating, it was not till near the close of the last century that they were much used. The first who turned them to *proper* account was Griesbach, whose edition of the Greek Testament, published in 1775–77, marks an era in biblical criticism. His second and principal edition, in which the critical apparatus was greatly enlarged, was published at Halle and London in 1796–1806; a manual edition appeared at Leipsic in 1805. Though the second volume of his larger edition bears the date 1806, it was mostly printed several years before, so that the manual edition generally represents his later judgment.

The *leading* editions of the Greek Testament which have been published in the present century are those of Griesbach, Matthæi, Scholz, Lachmann, and Tischendorf, to which may perhaps be added that of Alford, though the last has not, like the others which have been named, added anything to our critical materials. Griesbach's has already been noticed; Matthæi's was published at Wittenberg, Hof, and Ronneburg, in 1803–7, 3 vols. 8vo; Scholz's at Leipsic, in 1830–36, 2 vols. 4to; and Lachmann's larger edition at Berlin, in 1842–50, 2 vols. 8vo. Tischendorf's second Leipsic edition appeared in 1849, 8vo, and the second edition of Alford's Greek Testament, Vols. I. and II. (ending with the Second Epistle to the Corinthians), was published at London in 1854–55. (First edition, 1849–52.) The third volume has not yet been issued.

To give a comparative estimate of the value of these editions, and to point out in detail their distinguishing characteristics, cannot here be attempted. The eminent merits of Griesbach are too well known to need particular remark. Of the other editions which have been mentioned, Lachmann's and Tischendorf's have at present the highest reputation, among those qualified to pronounce on such matters, both on the Continent and in Great Britain; while the critical judgment of Matthæi and of Scholz is little esteemed. — Matthæi's edition of 1803–7, and his earlier one published at Riga in 1782–88, 12 vols. 8vo, contain some useful materials; but his violent prejudices unfitted him for the office of a critic. — The value of Scholz's labors is greatly diminished by his want of accuracy as well as of judgment. — Lachmann's edition is founded on very ancient authorities, but too limited in number, and, in the case of some important manuscripts, not thoroughly collated. Discarding internal and collateral evidence, he adopts the reading best supported by his few select authorities, even when he does not regard it as genuine. His text is followed in the recent works of Stanley and Jowett on the Epistles of St. Paul. — The second Leipsic edition of Tischendorf, taken as a whole, is unquestionably the most important and valuable critical edition of the Greek Testament which has appeared since the time of Griesbach. Less cautious than Griesbach, he is sometimes liable to the charge of adopting readings unsupported by sufficient authority; but Alford pronounces his text "very far superior to any which have preceded it." * —

* Greek Testament, Vol. I. Prolegomena, p. 77, 2d ed. — Some account of Tischendorf and his labors may be found in the Bibliotheca Sacra for July 1852, Vol. IX. pp. 623–628. The first *fasciculus* of a new and apparently much enlarged edition of Tischendorf's Greek Testament has very lately been published at Leipsic.

Alford, in the first edition of the first volume of his Greek Testament, containing the Gospels, professedly gave only "a *provisional* text," one, he says, "which may be regarded as an experiment how far the public mind in England may be disposed to receive even the first and plainest results of the now advanced state of textual criticism." * The success of the experiment seems to have been encouraging; for in the second volume of his work, and in a new edition of the first, he has ventured to give the text according to his judgment of the evidence. He does not appear to be a critic of the highest order, but his judgment is better than might be supposed from the manner in which he commenced his editorial labors. There is no hazard in saying, that, so far as the criticism of the text is concerned, his edition is much the best which has yet been published in England. — Meyer has given a critical discussion of the various readings, in his Commentary on the New Testament, extending to the First Epistle to the Thessalonians (*not* inclusive), the notes on the remaining books, excepting the Epistle to Philemon and the Apocalypse, being prepared by his coadjutors Lünemann and Huther. Many of his remarks are acute and valuable. His "Kommentar," so far as it goes, is one of the best helps which we possess in the critical study of the text of the New Testament, to say nothing of its exegetical merits. — The long-delayed edition of Dr. S. P. Tregelles promises, when published, to be a work of great interest and value. In his "Book of Revelation in Greek, edited from Ancient Authorities; with a new English Version," &c. (London, 1844), and his "Account of the Printed Text of the Greek New Testament" (London, 1854), as well as in various articles in Kitto's Journal of Sacred Literature, Dr. Tregelles has shown himself to be a truly conscientious, independent, and intelligent critic.

* Prolegomena, p. 70, 1st ed.

His untiring zeal and industry in the *accurate* collation of the most important ancient manuscripts of the New Testament entitle him to the gratitude of all who desire to possess a pure text of the records of our religion. But this is not the place to give even a slight sketch of his arduous and disinterested labors.

Other editions of the Greek Testament of secondary importance which have been examined for the purposes of this note, it may be sufficient, with one exception, simply to mention; as Knapp's, 4th ed., Halle, 1829 (first ed. 1797); Schott's, 3d ed., Leipsic, 1825 (first ed. 1805); Tittmann's, 2d stereotype ed., Leipsic, 1828 (first ed. 1820); Vater's, Halle, 1824; Hahn's, Leipsic, 1840,—American ed. by Dr. Robinson, New York, 1842; and Theile's, stereotype ed., Leipsic, 1844 (4th ed. 1852). None of these calls for special remark, except that of Hahn, which, having been reprinted in this country under the superintendence of so distinguished a scholar as Dr. Robinson, and introduced to the American public with high commendation by Professor Stuart,* requires a notice which its intrinsic importance would not justify.

Hahn professes to give, in his notes, a view of *all* the readings approved by Griesbach, Knapp, and Scholz,† with a selection from those adopted by Lachmann in his first edition, published in 1831. Now it will hardly be pretended that a critical editor "approves" those readings which he has marked as *probably spurious*. Griesbach has so marked words of the Received Text in about four hundred and ninety instances. But Hahn takes no notice of this, leaving his readers to suppose that Griesbach, in all

* See the Bibliotheca Sacra for 1843, p. 274, et seqq.

† "Ita ut, qui nostra editione usuri essent, sine ulla difficultate *omnes* lectiones cognoscere possent, quas editores illi suo judicio probarunt."—Præfat., pp. viii., ix., ed. Amer.

these cases, received the words as genuine. — Again, there are many readings which Griesbach and Knapp have marked as *equal* in point of authority with those retained in the text. Knapp, for example, has so marked the reading κυρίου in Acts xx. 28, and ὅς in 1 Timothy iii. 16. Such readings are to be regarded as "approved" by these critics, as much as those which they have allowed to remain in the text in their stead. But Hahn affords those who use his edition no intimation of their judgment respecting them. His edition, therefore, to say the least, very imperfectly represents the opinions of Griesbach and Knapp concerning the various readings. — But, passing over the defects which have been referred to, we shall find that his work often gives *erroneously* what it professes to exhibit. I have noted more than *one hundred and thirty* instances in which the critical judgment of Knapp alone is incorrectly represented. Taking the Gospel of Matthew, for example, in twenty-two instances Knapp is said to regard a reading as *doubtful* merely,* when, by inclosing it in double brackets, he has marked it as unquestionably spurious; † in two instances the double brackets of Knapp are disregarded; ‡ and in three other places in this Gospel, the single brackets of Knapp, indicating that he considered certain words as doubtful, are passed over without remark. § In Matthew viii. 29 the word Ἰησοῦ, which stands in the Received Text, is omitted without mention of the fact in the notes. The different opinions of Griesbach, Knapp, Lachmann, and Scholz respecting it are of course not stated. In

* Matthew iv. 18; v. 27; vi. 13, 18; viii. 25, 32; ix. 13, 35; xii. 35; xiv. 22, *bis*, 25; xvi. 8; xx. 6, 22, 23; xxiii. 8; xxv. 13, 31; xxvi. 9; xxvii. 35, 64.

† "His [uncis duplicatis] ea notantur, quæ sine dubio spuria esse censebam." — Knapp, Comment. Isagog. p. xxviii.

‡ Matthew xviii. 35; xxviii. 20.

§ Matthew iv. 12; viii. 29; xxi. 12.

Matthew xxviii. 20, Hahn leaves his readers to suppose, erroneously, that 'Αμήν is retained as genuine by Griesbach and Knapp, as it is by Scholz. In further illustration of the character of Hahn's edition, I will only refer to his treatment of the passage relating to the woman taken in adultery, John vii. 53 – viii. 11. To this Griesbach prefixes a peculiar mark, indicating that its spuriousness is in the highest degree probable; Knapp has bracketed it, and in the Introduction to his Greek Testament (p. xxix.) expresses his belief that it does not belong to the Gospel of John; and Lachmann has rejected it from the text. Hahn not only retains it, but gives no hint that any of the editors who have been named had a doubt of its genuineness.

One general remark should here be made respecting the editions of Tittmann, Hahn, and Theile. These critics professedly retain the readings of the Received Text, unless the evidence against them, in their judgment, greatly preponderates. It is only when the case is very clear, that they venture to make a change.* Their authority, therefore, whatever it may be, is obviously of much less weight when they support the readings of the Received Text, than when they reject them.

We may now proceed to the examination of the passages which form the principal subject of this note. It is to be understood that the editions which have been mentioned as published within the present century retain the reading of the Received Text unless the contrary is expressly stated.

(1.) Matthew xix. 17. "Why callest thou me good?

* See, for instance, Theile's Preface, p. vii.: — "Ubi vero in utramque partem disputari posset, *si vel argumenta mutationem suadentia prævalerent*, lectionem intactam relinquere maluimus."

There is none good but one, *that is*, God." Τί με λέγεις ἀγαθόν; Οὐδεὶς ἀγαθός, εἰ μὴ εἷς, ὁ Θεός.

Here the following reading is adopted by Griesbach, Lachmann, Tischendorf, Meyer, Alford, and Tregelles, as also by De Wette, Porter, and Davidson, and is marked by Knapp and Vater as *equal* in point of authority to that of the Received Text: — Τί με ἐρωτᾷς περὶ τοῦ ἀγαθοῦ; Εἷς ἐστὶν ὁ ἀγαθός. "Why askest thou me concerning what is good? One only is good." Most of the critics who receive this reading as genuine omit the word "good" as an epithet of "teacher" in the preceding verse.

In the parallel passages (Mark x. 17, 18, Luke xviii. 18, 19) which correspond with the Received Text in Matthew, there are no various readings of any consequence; but this fact favors the supposition that transcribers altered (as *they* thought, *corrected*) the text of Matthew to make it conform to that of Mark and Luke.

(2.) Luke xxii. 43, 44. "And there appeared an angel unto him from heaven, strengthening him," &c.

These two verses are bracketed by Lachmann as doubtful, and are rejected by Granville Penn in his "Book of the New Covenant." But they are retained by all the other critical editors. Mr. Norton has given his reasons for regarding them as spurious in his Evidences of the Genuineness of the Gospels, Vol. I., Additional Note A, Section V. VI. pp. lxxxvii. – xci.

(3.) Luke xxiv. 52. "And they worshipped him, and returned to Jerusalem with great joy." Καὶ αὐτοί, προσκυνήσαντες αὐτόν, ὑπέστρεψαν, κ. τ. λ. Here the words προσκυνήσαντες αὐτόν, corresponding to "worshipped him and" in the translation, are rejected by Tischendorf. But his authorities seem altogether insufficient. The omission of the words in the Cambridge manuscript (D), the only Greek manuscript in which they are known to be wanting, and in the manuscript or manuscripts from which the Old Latin version was made, was very probably accidental, the transcriber, as Alford suggests, passing over them in consequence of the resemblance of ΑΥΤΟΝ to the preceding ΑΥΤΟΙ.

This passage has been quoted by Trinitarians as a proof that Christ was worshipped by his disciples as the Supreme Being. But, as every one acquainted with the original language knows, the word here translated "worshipped" simply denotes "to pay reverence or homage by kneeling or prostration," without defining the *kind* of reverence. It is perpetually used in the Septuagint as the translation of the Hebrew word rendered in the Common Version by "to bow down before," "to do obeisance to," and the like. See, for example, Genesis xxvii. 29; xxxvii. 7, 9, 10; xlix. 8: Exodus xviii. 7, &c. See also its use in Matthew xviii. 26; Rev. iii. 9. Dr. Robinson, in his excellent Lexicon of the New Testament, art. προσκυνέω, no. 1, explains it in this general sense, and not as denoting *divine* worship, in all the passages in which it occurs in the Gospels in reference to Christ, including the present.* Here, the words προσκυνήσαντες αὐτόν probably express the fact that the disciples, as they beheld our Lord taken up from them into heaven, knelt down, or prostrated themselves on the ground before him, in reverence.† Mr. Norton, however,

* These passages are the following: — Matthew ii. 2, 8, 11; viii. 2; ix. 18; xiv. 33; xv. 25; xx. 20; xxviii. 9, 17; Mark v. 6; xv. 19; Luke xxiv. 52; John ix. 38. The only other passage in the New Testament in which the word occurs in reference to Christ is in the Epistle to the Hebrews (i. 6), where it is used of the reverence and homage which the angels are commanded by God to pay to his Son, as their superior.

† "'Having worshipped him,' προσκυνήσαντες αὐτόν, that is, 'hav-

so far as can be judged from his translation,* seems to have understood them as denoting merely the *feeling* of reverence which filled the hearts of the disciples as they returned to Jerusalem after witnessing the ascension of their Master. But is not the use of the *aorist* participle an objection to this view?

It may be remarked that the word *worship*, both as a noun and a verb, was used in a much wider sense at the time when King James's version of the Bible was made, than it is at the present day. Examples are abundant in Shakespeare and other writers of that period. So in the marriage service of the English Episcopal Church: "With my body I thee *worship*." In Luke xiv. 10, "Then shalt thou have *worship* in the presence of them that sit at meat with thee," the noun "worship" is a translation of the Greek word δόξα, *glory*, *honor*.

(4.) John i. 18. "No man hath seen God at any time; the only-begotten Son, who is in the bosom of the Father, he hath declared *him*." Θεὸν οὐδεὶς ἑώρακε πώποτε· ὁ μονογενὴς υἱός, ὁ ὢν εἰς τὸν κόλπον τοῦ πατρός, ἐκεῖνος ἐξηγήσατο.

Here, instead of ὁ μονογενὴς υἱός, "the only-begotten *Son*," we find in some important authorities the reading ὁ μονογενὴς Θεός, "the only-begotten *God*." This strange reading (for so it will seem to most Trinitarians as well as to others) has not yet been adopted in any edition of the Greek Testament; but it deserves notice, since it is defended by a critic so worthy of respect as Dr. Tregelles. Michaelis also appears disposed to regard it as the original reading;†

ing thrown themselves prostrate before him,' as the words strictly interpreted imply." — Campbell *in loc.* See also Meyer's note.

* "And they, worshipping him, returned to Jerusalem with great joy."

† Introduction to the New Testament, Chap. X. Sect. 2. Vol. II. p. 393, 2d ed.

and Lachmann, as Dr. Tregelles assures us, would undoubtedly have received it into his text, had he known all the authorities by which it is supported.

The evidence of *manuscripts* and *versions* for and against the reading in question may first be stated. The testimony of the Fathers will require a particular discussion. It should be premised that the words υἱός (Son) and Θεός (God), in the abbreviated form in which they are written in the most ancient manuscripts (ΥC, ΘC), differ in but a single letter, so that one might easily be substituted for the other through the inadvertence of a transcriber.

The reading Θεός, then, is found in the manuscripts B C* L, 33; that is, in the Vatican manuscript, of about the middle of the fourth century, in the Ephrem manuscript (*a primâ manu*), probably written before the middle of the fifth, in another highly valuable manuscript of the eighth century, remarkable for its general agreement with the Vatican, and in a manuscript of the eleventh century, written in cursive letters, but preserving a very ancient text. As to versions, it is supported by the Peshito Syriac, as hitherto edited, the Coptic, the Æthiopic, and the *margin* of the Philoxenian or Harclean Syriac.

On the other hand, the reading υἱός is that of the Alexandrine manuscript (A), probably written not long after the middle of the fifth century, and of the manuscripts X and Δ, written in the ninth century, but often agreeing with the most ancient documents, in opposition to the later. It is also found in the other uncial manuscripts E F G H K M S U V, ranging from the middle of the eighth century to the tenth, and in several hundred manuscripts in cursive letters, mostly later than the tenth century, but some of them of much value from their usual accordance with the best authorities. The ancient versions which exhibit it are the Old Latin or Italic, the Vulgate, the Curetonian Syriac,* the Philoxenian Syriac (in the *text*), the Jerusalem Syriac, and the Armenian.

So far as the evidence has yet been stated, it will probably be admitted that the common reading is best supported. But it is on the testimony of the *Fathers* that the advocates for the reading Θεός appear chiefly to rely. The following is the account given by Dr. Tregelles of this branch of the evidence.

"As to fathers," he says, "the reading [Θεός] may almost be called *general*, for it is that of Clement of Alexandria, Irenæus, Origen, Eusebius, Epiphanius, Lucian, Basil, Gregory of Nazianzum, Gregory of Nussa, Didymus, Basil of Seleucia, Isidore of Pelusium, Cyril of Alexandria, Titus of Bostra; as also of Theodotus (in the second century), Arius, Marcellus, Eunomius, etc.; and amongst the Latins, Hilary, Fulgentius, Gaudentius, Ferrandus, Phœbadius, Vigilius, Alcuin, etc." The reading υἱός "is found twice in Origen, in Eusebius, Basil, and Irenæus (though all these writers have *also* the other reading, and in general they so speak of Θεός in the passage, that υἱός *must* have proceeded from the copyists): — the Latin writers in general agree with the Latin versions in reading *filius*. . . . . . Θεός, as the more difficult reading, is entitled to especial attention; and, confirmed as it is by MSS. of the highest character, by good versions, and by the general consent of early Greek writers (even when, like Arius, they were opposed to the dogma taught), it is necessary, on grounds

* This name has been given to a very ancient and valuable Syriac copy of part of the Gospels, — one of the Nitrian manuscripts recently added to the British Museum, — which is soon to be published (if it has not been already) by the Rev. William Cureton. It is "a version," as Tregelles remarks, "far more worthy the epithet of 'venerable' than that which is called the Peshito as it has come down to us." ("Account of the Printed Text of the Greek New Testament," p. 137; comp. pp. 160, 161.)

of combined evidence, to receive it in preference to the easier and more natural reading υἱός." *

This array of authorities is certainly imposing; and the argument would be forcible, perhaps conclusive, were it not that the *facts* in the case have been greatly misapprehended. Tregelles appears, like Griesbach, Scholz, Tischendorf, and Alford, to have relied on Wetstein, whose general accuracy might well inspire confidence. But Wetstein, in his note on this passage, has fallen into extraordinary errors, many of which have been copied, without investigation, by the critics who have just been named. One who should take the statements in Wetstein's note to be correct, would suppose that not less than *forty-four* Greek and Latin writers, in the first eight centuries, have quoted the passage in question with the reading μονογενὴς Θεός or *unigenitus Deus;* and that the number of distinct quotations of this kind in their writings, taken together, is not far from *one hundred and thirty.* I have examined, with some care, all the passages specifically referred to by Wetstein, and the whole work, or collection of works cited, when his reference is general, — as "*Epiphanius* duodecies," "*Hilarius* de Trinit. passim," "*Fulgentius* plusquam vicies," — not confining my attention, however, to these particular passages or works. The following is the result of this examination. Of the forty-four writers cited by Wetstein in support of the reading μονογενὴς Θεός, there are but *four* who quote or refer to the passage with this reading only; † *four* quote it with both readings; ‡ *nine* quote it with the reading υἱός or *filius* only, except that in one of the quo-

* "Account of the Printed Text," &c., pp. 234, 235.

† It is thus quoted in the "Excerpta Theodoti," and also by Clement of Alexandria and Epiphanius. It appears to be once referred to in the Epistle of the second Synod of Ancyra.

‡ Irenæus, Origen, Basil, and Cyril of Alexandria.

tations of Titus of Bostra υἱὸς Θεός occurs;* *two* repeatedly *allude* to it, — sometimes using the phrase "only-begotten *God*," and sometimes "only-begotten *Son*," in connection with the words "who is in the bosom of the Father," — but do not distinctly *quote* it; † and *twenty-five* do not quote or allude to it at all. ‡ Of the particular passages referred to by Wetstein, a great majority have no bearing whatever on the subject, but merely contain the *expression* μονογενὴς Θεός or *unigenitus Deus*, with no trace of an allusion to the text in question, — an expression often occurring, as will hereafter appear, in writers who abundantly and unequivocally *quote* John i. 18 with the reading υἱός or *filius*. Indeed, in some of these passages we do not find even this expression, but only the term γεννητὸς Θεός, or *genitus Deus*, applied to Christ. § Sufficient evidence that these assertions are not made at random will be given in what follows, though the mistakes of Wetstein cannot here be all pointed out in detail.

We may now examine the witnesses brought forward by Dr. Tregelles. Very few of these will stand cross-questioning. Of the *twenty-five* writers whom he has adduced in support of the reading μονογενὴς Θεός, but *four*, I believe, can be relied on with much confidence, and even their testimony is far from unexceptionable; *three* may be regarded as doubtful; *eight* really support the common

* Eusebius, Athanasius, Julian, Gregory Nazianzen, Titus of Bostra, Maximinus the Arian bishop, Hilary, Vigilius of Tapsa, Alcuin.

† Gregory of Nyssa and Fulgentius.

‡ That is, all the remaining authorities cited by Wetstein, for which see his note.

§ As in the following: — "*Origenes* in Psalm i. ap. Epiphanium," see Epiphan. Hæres. LXIV. c. 7, Opp. I. 531, B, or Origen. Opp. II. 526, E; — "*Eusebius* D. IV. 2," i. e. Dem. Evang. Lib. IV. c. 2; — "*Prudentius* in Apotheosi," viz. line 895; — "*Claudianus Mamert.* de statu animæ l. 2," where Lib. I. c. 2 must be the place intended.

reading; *two* merely allude to the passage; and *eight* have neither quoted nor alluded to it.

These statements of course require proof. This will now be presented, so far as it can be within reasonable limits. Though few passages can be quoted at length, pains will be taken to give very full and precise references to the authorities relied on. In producing the testimony of the Fathers, the time at which they flourished is indicated in marks of parenthesis after their names. In assigning these dates, either Cave or Lardner has generally been followed.

Clement of Alexandria (A. D. 194) has once quoted John i. 18 with the reading Θεός;* but this evidence is somewhat weakened by the fact that in another place, in alluding to this text, he has the words μονογενὴς υἱὸς Θεός.† Another authority for this reading is the work which bears the title "Extracts from Theodotus, and Heads of the Oriental Doctrine, so called, as it existed in the Time of Valentinus." It is sometimes quoted under the name of *Doctrina Orientalis.* This compilation is supposed by many to have been made by Clement of Alexandria, with whose works it is generally printed. "Theodotus" is several times cited in it, but more frequently "the followers of Valentinus," a famous Gnostic who flourished about A. D. 140. The passage which contains the quotation of John i. 18 with the reading ὁ μονογενὴς Θεός is introduced by the words "the Valentinians say." ‡ Didymus of Alexandria (A. D. 370) has this reading twice; § and it occurs twice in the writings

* Stromat. Lib. V. c. 12. p. 695, ed. Potter.

† Τότε ἐποπτεύσεις τὸν κόλπον τοῦ πατρός, ὃν ὁ μονογενὴς υἱὸς Θεὸς μόνος ἐξηγήσατο. — Quis dives salvetur, c. 38. p. 956.

‡ Doctrina Orient. c. 6, apud Clem. Alex. Opp. p. 968, ed. Pott.; also in Fabricii Bibl. Græc. Vol. V. p. 136, and in Bunsen's Analecta Ante-Nicæna, Vol. I. p. 211.

§ De Trinitate, Lib. I. p. 69, and Lib. II. p. 140, ed. Mingarel. Not

of Epiphanius, Bishop of Salamis in Cyprus (A. D. 368).* In another place, Epiphanius speaks of John as "calling Christ only-begotten God." † The reading Θεός also receives some support from a passage in the Epistle of the second Synod of Ancyra (A. D. 358), in which it is said that John "calls the Logos of God only-begotten God." ‡ But one who has observed the inaccuracy of such references to Scripture in the writings of the Fathers, will not attach much weight to this.

Among the numerous witnesses adduced by Wetstein and Tregelles, these are *all*, as I believe, which really support the reading Θεός; and their testimony, as has already been intimated, is far from unexceptionable. Didymus, as we

having been able to procure this volume, I take these references at second hand from the work of Guericke, "De Schola quæ Alexandrinæ floruit Catechetica," Pars II. p. 36. There is no quotation of John i. 18 in the other extant writings of Didymus, most of which exist only in a Latin translation.

* Hæres. LXV. c. 5. Opp. I. 612, C, ed. Petav. Here, in the remark which follows the quotation, Θεός and υἱός are so interchanged as to excite some suspicion of a corruption in the text. — Hæres. LXX. c. 7. Opp. I. 817, 818. Τὸ δὲ Εὐαγγέλιον ἔφη· Θεὸν οὐδεὶς πώποτε ἑώρακεν, ὁ μονογενὴς Θεὸς αὐτὸς ἐξηγήσατο.

† Μονογενῆ Θεὸν αὐτὸν φάσκων. . . . . . Περὶ πατρὸς γέγραπται, ἀληθινοῦ Θεοῦ· περὶ υἱοῦ δέ, ὅτι μονογενὴς Θεός. (Ancorat. c. 3. Opp. II. 8, C, D.) A little before, however, the passage in question is quoted thus: ὁ μονογενής, ὁ ὢν εἰς τὸν κόλπον τοῦ πατρός, αὐτὸς ἐξηγήσατο. (Cap. 2. p. 7, C.) But so far as can be judged from the confused and apparently corrupt text which precedes and follows, it seems probable that the word Θεός has here been omitted by the mistake of a transcriber.

‡ Ὁ δὲ τοῦ Θεοῦ τὸν Λόγον μονογενῆ Θεὸν . . . . φησί. (Apud Epiphan. Hæres. LXXIII. c. 8. Opp. I. 854, C.) Supposing the authors of this Epistle to have read υἱός in John i. 18, they might still have thought themselves justified in making this statement by a comparison of that verse with John i. 1, and by the fact that they regarded the term *Son*, applied to Christ, as necessarily implying his divinity. A little after the passage just cited (c. 9. p. 855, B)

are informed by his pupils Palladius and Jerome, became *blind* at four or five years of age. He has consequently quoted from memory, and often inaccurately, repeatedly assigning to one Epistle of Paul passages which belong to another. In his first quotation of the present passage, as given by Guericke, he has substituted ἐν τῷ κόλπῳ for εἰς τὸν κόλπον, and αὐτός for ἐκεῖνος; in the second, which extends only to the word πατρός, he has ἐν τοῖς κόλποις. Clement of Alexandria and Epiphanius are also notorious for the carelessness of their quotations from Scripture. Semisch, in his valuable work on the Apostolical Memoirs used by Justin Martyr, after observing that many of the Fathers have cited the New Testament from memory, says

they say: "The Son is God because he is Son of God, just as he is man because he is Son of Man," — υἱὸς Θεὸς μέν, καθὸ υἱὸς Θεοῦ, ὡς ἄνθρωπος, καθὸ υἱὸς ἀνθρώπου. So Eusebius says that Christ is "the only-begotten Son of God, and therefore God," or "a divine being," τοῦ Θεοῦ μονογενὴς υἱός, καὶ διὰ τοῦτο Θεός (Dem. Evang. Lib. V. c. 4. p. 227, B), and that "what is begotten of God must be God," or "divine," τὸ γεγεννημένον ἐκ τοῦ Θεοῦ Θεὸς ἂν εἴη (De Eccles. Theol. Lib. II. c. 14. p. 123, C, cf. p. 124, C, and Lib. I. c. 12. p. 72, D). Eusebius applies the term Θεός to Christ in an inferior sense. In quoting Eusebius here and elsewhere, I use Gaisford's edition, but refer to the pages of Viger's edition (Paris, 1628), which are noted in the margin of the former.

I will give a single illustration from Gregory Nyssen of the want of accuracy among the Fathers in such references to Scripture as that which we are considering. This writer, in mentioning the names which the Apostle Paul has given to Christ, says, among other things, "He has called him . . . . . a propitiation *for souls*, ... and first-born of the *new* creation, ... and *only-begotten Son*, crowned with glory and honor," &c. — αὐτὸν ἐκάλεσε . . . . . ἱλαστήριον ψυχῶν, ... καὶ τῆς καινῆς κτίσεως πρωτότοκον, ... καὶ υἱὸν μονογενῆ, δόξῃ καὶ τιμῇ ἐστεφανωμένον, κ. τ. λ. — De Perf. Christ. Formâ, Opp. III. 276, 277. Compare De Vitâ Mosis, Opp. I. 225, D: Ὅς [ὁ ἀπόστολος] φησιν· ὅτι ὃν προέθετο ὁ Θεὸς ἱλαστήριον τῶν ψυχῶν ἡμῶν. (See Romans iii. 25.)

that "next to Justin, Clement of Alexandria, Tertullian, Epiphanius, and Ephrem the Syrian have quoted most loosely. Verbal citations in their writings, as in those of Justin, are only to be reckoned as exceptions." * It is further to be observed in respect to Epiphanius, that his text is well known to be very corrupt,† and that he is probably the most careless, confused, and blundering writer to be found among the Fathers. Petavius, though possessing in some respects eminent qualifications for an editor, appears to have given but little attention to the criticism of the text. In many instances gross corruptions, the correction of which seems obvious, are left without any suggestion of emendation.

The three authorities adduced by Dr. Tregelles which may be regarded as doubtful, are Origen, Basil the Great, and Cyril of Alexandria. Origen (A. D. 230), according to the text of his Benedictine editors, has the reading Θεός

* Die apostol. Denkwürdigkeiten des Märtyrers Justinus, (Hamb. 1848,) p. 209; comp. p. 218, et seqq. See also Whitby's Examen Millii, Lib. I. Cap. I. Sect. 2 et 3.—I will give one or two specimens of Epiphanius's professed citations from Scripture. Just before his first quotation of John i. 18 with the reading Θεός, he adduces the following as the words of Christ:—Ζῶ ἐγώ, καὶ ζῇ ἐν ἐμοὶ ὁ ἀποστείλας με πατήρ, "I live, and the Father who sent me lives in me"; comp. John vi. 57 and Gal. ii. 20. (Hæres. LXV. c. 5. Opp. I. 612, C.)—Again, to select a passage introduced like his second quotation of John i. 18, compare the following:—Ἢ πάλιν, ὡς λέγει τὸ Εὐαγγέλιον· Καὶ ἀνῆλθεν εἰς τὸν οὐρανόν, καὶ ἐκάθισεν ἐν δεξιᾷ τοῦ πατρός, καὶ ἔρχεται κρῖναι ζῶντας καὶ νεκρούς, "Or again, as the Gospel says, 'And he ascended into heaven, and sat down at the right hand of the Father, and is coming to judge the living and the dead'"; comp. Mark xvi. 19. (Hæres. LXII. c. 5. Opp. I. 517, D.) See also Opp. I. 36, B, C; 145, C; 161, A; 486, D; 519, C, D, for a few of the numerous illustrations that might be given. Equally striking examples might be cited from Clement of Alexandria.

† See Wetstein, Nov. Test. Græc. (Prolegom.), Tom. I. p. 72.

twice; but, on the other hand, he has υἱός once, and once υἱὸς τοῦ Θεοῦ, "Son of God." In a work preserved only in the Latin translation of Rufinus, he also quotes the passage with the reading *unigenitus Dei filius.** Basil (A. D. 370) has Θεός once, and in another passage he mentions "True Son, Only-begotten God, Power of God, and Logos," as names given to Christ in Scripture, or expressions which, to use his phrase, "the Scripture knows"; but he twice quotes the text in question with the reading υἱός.† In Cyril of Alexandria (A. D. 412), as edited by Aubert, I have found Θεός four times; but he has υἱός three times.‡ I have not thoroughly examined all of his works.

* Origen reads Θεός, In Joan. Tom. ii. c. 29, and Tom. xxxii. c. 13. Opp. IV. 89, B, and 438, D. — Υἱός, Contra Cels., Lib. II. c. 71. Opp. I. 440, F. (So De la Rue, from two manuscripts; but the previous edition of Hœschel, followed by Spencer, instead of ὁ μονογενὴς υἱός, reads καὶ μονογενής γε ὢν Θεός, which has all the appearance of a marginal gloss.) — Υἱὸς τοῦ Θεοῦ, In Joan. Tom. vi. c. 2. Opp. IV. 102, D. (So De la Rue, following the Bodleian manuscript, which appears to be a very excellent one; the earlier edition of Huet, which was founded on a single manuscript, reads υἱὸς Θεός.) A little after, in two allusions to the passage, ὁ μονογενής is used alone, without υἱός or Θεός. Opp. IV. 102, E, and 114, C. — *Unigenitus Dei filius*, In Cant. Lib. IV. Opp. III. 91, E.

† Basil reads Θεός, De Spiritu Sancto, c. 6, Opp. III. 12, B, ed. Benedict., where earlier editions have υἱός, contrary to the best manuscripts. Compare c. 8, p. 14, C. — On the other hand, Basil has υἱός, De Spiritu Sancto, c. 11, Opp. III. 23, A, where the six manuscripts of Garnier appear to agree in this reading, though one of Matthæi's Moscow manuscripts has Θεός. (See Matthiæ's Nov. Test. Græc. I. 780.) Basil also reads υἱός, Epist. 234 (al. 400), c. 3. Opp. III. 358, B.

‡ In the *text* prefixed to Cyril's commentary on the passage in question, Opp. IV. 103, C, we find the reading υἱός; the commentary itself, however, as printed, has Θεός. (See p. 107, B, and comp. p. 105, B.) Cyril's remarks on this place are cited in the scholia of two Moscow manuscripts given by Matthæi (Nov. Test. Græc. et

The eight writers cited by Dr. Tregelles who *really* favor the common reading will be mentioned hereafter, when the evidence for that reading is stated.

Two others, Gregory of Nyssa (A. D. 370) and Fulgentius (A. D. 507), as has before been mentioned, have only *alluded* to the passage in question, and not in such a way as to enable us to determine with confidence how they read it.*

Lat. IV. 24). One who compares these with his text as published by Aubert, will hardly feel much confidence in the latter. — Cyril also reads Θεός in his Thesaurus, Assert. xiii. and xxv. Opp. Tom. V. P. i. p. 137, B, and 237, A; and in the Dialogue "Quod Unus sit Christus," ibid. p. 786, E. — He has the reading υἱός, Thesaur., Assert. xxxv. p. 365, C; and Advers. Nestorium, Lib. III. c. 5. Opp. VI. 90, B. This reading is also found twice in an extract which he gives from Julian in his work against that emperor. (Contra Julian., Lib. X. Opp. VI. (P. ii.) p. 333, C.) — In an *allusion* to John i. 18 we find *ὁ μονογενὴς* τοῦ Θεοῦ Λόγος, *ὁ ἐν κόλποις ὢν τοῦ πατρός.* (Apol. adv. Orient. Opp. VI. 187, C.) This is worth noting, as showing how little can be safely inferred from such allusions in regard to the reading of a passage.

* Gregory of Nyssa *alludes* to John i. 18, introducing the words "who is in the bosom of the Father" in connection with the expression "only-begotten *God*" eight times; in connection with the phrase "only-begotten *Son*," twice. I will quote one example of each kind, and refer to the others. — In the treatise De Vitâ Mosis, Opp. I. 192, B, we find, *ὁ μονογενὴς* Θεός, *ὁ ὢν ἐν κόλποις τοῦ πατρός, οὗτός ἐστιν ἡ δεξιὰ τοῦ ὑψίστου.* See also In Cantic. Homil. xiii. Opp. I. 663, A. — Contra Eunom. Orat. II. Opp. II. 432, B; 447, A; and 478, D. — Orat. III. p. 506, C. — Orat. VI. p. 595 [properly 605], A. — Orat. X. p. 681, A. —— On the other hand, Epist. ad Flavian., Opp. III. 648, A, we find, *ὁ μονογενὴς* υἱός, *ὁ ὢν ἐν τοῖς κόλποις τοῦ πατρός, ὁ ἐν ἀρχῇ ὤν, κ. τ. λ.* See also Contra Eunom., Orat. II. Opp. II. 466, C. — Once we have *ὁ ἐν* ὑψίστοις *Θεός, ὢν ἐν τοῖς κόλποις τοῦ πατρός, κ. τ. λ.* In Cantic. Homil. xv. Opp. I. 697, A.

It is to be observed that *ὁ μονογενὴς Θεός*, "the only-begotten God," is a favorite designation of Christ in the writings of this Fa-

The eight remaining witnesses produced by Dr. Tregelles — Lucian, Basil of Seleucia, Isidore of Pelusium, Arius, Marcellus, Eunomius, Gaudentius, and Ferrandus — have, as I believe, nowhere quoted or alluded to the text in question. The passages in their writings appealed to by Wetstein have merely the *expression* μονογενὴς Θεός or

ther. There are *one hundred and twenty-five* examples of its use in the treatise against Eunomius alone. It occurs fifteen times in the "Antirrheticus adversus Apollinarem," first published in Zacagni's "Collectanea," etc. (Rome, 1698); but, notwithstanding the references of Wetstein, no allusion will be found in that treatise to John i. 18.

In one place Gregory says, "The Scripture declares concerning the Logos who was in the beginning, that he is the only-begotten God, the first-born of the whole creation." (De Perf. Christ. Formâ. Opp. III. 291, A.) But the imprudence of concluding from this that he actually had the reading Θεός in the passage in question, has already been illustrated. See before, p. 445, note.

Fulgentius has alluded to John i. 18 six times. I will quote briefly all the examples, as, taken together, they clearly show how little is to be inferred from such allusions.

1. In connection with the phrase *unigenitus Deus.* — "Ut ille unigenitus Deus, qui est in sinu Patris, non solum in muliere, sed etiam ex muliere fieret homo." Epist. xvii. c. 3, in Migne's Patrologiæ Cursus Completus, Vol. LXV. col. 272, B. — "De Deo unigenito, qui est in sinu Patris, ut dixi, omnia hæc personaliter accipe." De Fide, c. 20. col. 681, B.

2. With *unigenitus filius.* — "Quis enim natus est Deus verus de Deo vero, nisi unigenitus filius, qui est in sinu Patris?" Ad Trasimund., Lib. III. c. 4. col. 272, B. — "Si vero unigenitus filius, qui est in sinu Patris, post æternam nativitatem," etc. Epist. xvii. c. 15. col. 459, C. — "Dei ergo filius unigenitus, qui est in sinu Patris, ut carnem hominis animamque mundaret," etc. De Fide, c. 17. col. 679, C.

3. With *unigenitus* alone. — "Quia unigenitus, qui est in sinu Patris, secundum quod caro est, plenus est gratiæ," etc. De Incarnatione, c. 18. col. 583, C.

The *expression* "unigenitus Deus" occurs in the writings of Fulgentius about *ninety* times.

unigenitus Deus. I have not read through the Epistles of Isidore of Pelusium; but with respect to all the other authors named, I think it may be safely said, that no trace of the reading Θεός or *Deus* occurs in their works. An examination of Wetstein's references to them will be found in the note below.* Tregelles makes no citations.

* Lucian (A. D. 290) is thus referred to by Wetstein: "*Lucianus* martyr in Confess. ap. Socrat. H. E. II. 10." The Confession of Faith here intended is the *second* Formula of the Synod of Antioch (A. D. 341), which, according to Sozomen (Hist. Eccles. Lib. III. c. 5), "*they said* was found in the handwriting of Lucian the Martyr." It may be seen in Socrates, as above referred to, and also in Athanasius de Synodis, c. 23. Opp. I. P. ii. p. 735, et seq. Learned men have not generally regarded it as the work of Lucian, who died about thirty years before it was first heard of; but the question is unimportant to our purpose. It simply says, "We believe . . . . . in one God, the Father almighty, the creator and maker of the universe; and in one Lord Jesus Christ his Son, the only-begotten God, through whom all things were made," &c.

In the case of the other authors mentioned above, it may be sufficient to refer to the places in their writings cited by Wetstein, but which will be found, on examination, to contain merely the phrase "only-begotten God."

Basil of Seleucia (A. D. 448). See Orat. I. Opp. p. 5. Paris. 1622.

Isidore of Pelusium (A. D. 412). See Epist. III. 95. Opp. p. 200, ed. Rittershus.

Arius (A. D. 316). See Athanas. de Synod. c. 15. Opp. Tom. I. P. ii. p. 728, E, ed. Benedict. In a letter of Arius given by Epiphanius, we find the words, πλήρης Θεὸς μονογενής, ἀναλλοίωτος, κ.τ.λ. (Hæres. LXIX. c. 6. Opp. I. 731, D.) But here a comma should probably be placed after the word Θεός.

Marcellus (A. D. 320). See Euseb. contra Marcel. Lib. I. c. 4. p. 19, C.

Eunomius (A. D. 360). See his Expositio Fidei, c. 3, apud Fabricii Bibl. Græc. Tom. VIII. pp. 255, 256; and his Apologeticus, cc. 15, 21, 26, *ibid.* pp. 281, 290, 298. These treatises of Eunomius may also be found in Rettberg's Marcelliana, and in Thilo's Bibliotheca Patrum Græcorum Dogmatica, Vol. II.

Such is the evidence of the Fathers in favor of the reading Θεός. I know of nothing to be added to what has been mentioned. We may now consider the testimony which supports the common reading. Only a small part of this, so far as I am aware, has ever been adduced.

The following Greek authors quote John i. 18 with the reading *υἱός*: — Irenæus, Bishop of Lyons in Gaul (A. D. 178), as preserved in a very early Latin translation;* Hippolytus (A. D. 220);† the third Synod at Antioch (A. D. 269), in their Epistle to Paul of Samosata;‡ the author of the "Acta Disputationis Archelai cum Manete" (about A. D. 300?), as preserved in the Latin version;§ Alexander, Bishop of Alexandria (A. D. 313);‖ Eusebius of Cæsarea (A. D. 315), five or six times;¶ Eustathius, Bishop

Gaudentius (A. D. 387). See Serm. XIX. in the Maxima Bibliotheca Veterum Patrum, Tom. V. p. 975, D, or in Migne's Patrol. Tom. XX. col. 990, B.

Ferrandus (A. D. 533) has the *expression* "unigenitus Deus" eight times, viz. Epist. iii. (ad Anatol.) cc. 2, 7, 9, 10, 11; v. (ad Severum Scholast.) cc. 2, 5; vii. (ad Reginum Comitem Parænet.) c. 12; in Migne's Patrol. Tom. LXVII., or in the Max. Bibl. Patr. Tom. IX.

* Contra Hæres. Lib. IV. c. 20. (c. 37, ed. Grab.) § 6. Opp. I. 627, ed. Stieren. Irenæus has also once the reading *unigenitus filius Dei* (Lib. III. c. 11. § 6. p. 466), and once *unigenitus Deus* (Lib. IV. c. 20. § 11. p. 630). The reading *filius Dei* obviously supports *filius* rather than *Deus*.

† Contra Noëtum, c. 5. Opp. II. 10, ed. Fabric.; also in Routh's Scriptorum Eccles. Opuscula, I. 58, ed. alt.

‡ Concilia, ed. Coleti, I. 869, B; also in Routh, Reliq. Sacr. II. 473 (III. 297, ed. alt.), and in Dionysii Alexandrini Opp. (Rom. 1796), p. 287.

§ Cap. 32. In Zacagnii Collectan. Monum. Vett., p. 54; also in Hippolyti Opp. ed. Fabric. II. 170, and Routh, Reliq. Sacr. IV. 213 (V. 121, ed. alt.). — On the date of this work see Lardner, "Credibility," etc. Part. II. Chap. LXV.

‖ Epist. ad Alexandrum Constantinop., apud Theodoreti Hist. Eccl. Lib. I. c. 4. (al. 3.) p. 12, ed. Reading.

¶ De Eccles. Theol. Lib. I. c. 9. p. 67, D; — c. 20. §§ 4, 5. p. 86,

of Antioch (A. D. 320);* Athanasius (A. D. 326, died A. D. 373), four times, and *Pseud*-Athanasius once;† the Emperor Julian (A. D. 362) twice;‡ Titus of Bostra

A, B; — ibid. § 7, sub fin. p. 92, D; — Lib. II. c. 23, ad fin. p. 142, C; — and Comm. in Psalm. lxxiii. 11, in Montfaucon's Collectio Nova, etc. I. 440, A.

The first passage of Eusebius which has been referred to is peculiar, reading as follows: Τοῦ τε εὐαγγελιστοῦ διαρρήδην αὐτὸν υἱὸν μονογενῆ εἶναι διδάσκοντος δι' ὧν ἔφη, Θεὸν οὐδεὶς ἑώρακε πώποτε, ὁ μονογενὴς υἱός, ἢ μονογενὴς Θεός, ὁ ὢν εἰς τὸν κόλπον τοῦ πατρός, ἐκεῖνος ἐξηγήσατο; that is, "The Evangelist expressly teaches that he is the only-begotten Son, when he says, '*No man hath seen God at any time; the only-begotten Son*, or only-begotten God, *who is in the bosom of the Father, he hath declared him*.'" But here it is evident, as Montagu remarks in his note on the place, that the words ἢ μονογενὴς Θεός, "or only-begotten God," form no part of the quotation. They appear to be a marginal gloss which has crept into the text. — The only passage which I have found in Eusebius that seems to countenance the reading Θεός is the following. After using the strongest language respecting the supremacy of the Father over all other beings, and quoting Ephesians iv. 5, 6, he proceeds: "And He alone may be called (χρηματίζοι ἂν) the one God, and Father of our Lord Jesus Christ; but the Son [may be called] only-begotten God, who is in the bosom of the Father (ὁ δὲ υἱὸς μονογενὴς Θεός, ὁ ὢν εἰς τὸν κόλπον τοῦ πατρός); and the Paraclete, Spirit, but neither God nor Son." (De Eccles. Theol. Lib. III. c. 7. pp. 174, 175.) Here it will be observed that Eusebius does not assert that the Son *is* called "only-begotten God" in Scripture, but only that it is proper to give him that name. This passage, therefore, does not weaken the force of his express quotations of John i. 18 with the reading υἱός.

* De Engastrimytho, as printed (from the edition of Leo Allatius) in Tom. II. p. 1150, med. of the *Critici Sacri*, ed. Amst. 1698; in Tom. VIII. col. 443, l. 34, of the London edition.

† Athanasius de Decret. Nic. Synod. c. 13. Opp. I. 219, E, ed. Benedict. — *Ibid.* c. 21. p. 227, D. — Orat. II. contra Arian. c. 62. p. 530, D. — Orat. IV. contra Arian. c. 26. p. 638, A. — *Pseud*-Athanasius contra Sabellian. c. 2. Opp. II. 38, D.

‡ Apud Cyril. Alex. Lib. X. contra Julian. Opp. VI. (ii.) 333, also in "Défense du Paganisme par l'Empereur Julien en Grec et en

A. D. 362);* Gregory Nazianzen (A. D. 370);† the author of a Homily published with the works of Basil;‡ Rufinus Syrus or Palæstinensis (about A. D. 390), as preserved in a very early Latin translation;§ Chrysostom (A. D. 398), at least eight times;‖ Theodoret (A. D. 423), at least four times;¶ and Proclus, Patriarch of Constantinople (A. D. 434).** To these may be added several Greek writers of less weight, being later, and some of them of quite uncertain date; as *Pseudo*-Cyril,†† *Pseudo*-Cæsa-

Français, avec des Notes par Mr. le Marquis d'Argens," 3e éd., II. 120, 122.

* Contra Manichæos, Lib. III., apud Basnage, Thesaur. Monum. Eccles. et Hist. sive Canisii Lectiones Antiq., I. 144, 145. —But *ibid.* p. 153, we have the reading *ὁ μονογενὴς υἱὸς Θεός*; compare the interpolation on the same page in the quotation of Matthew iii. 17 or xvii. 5, as follows: *Καὶ μαρτυρεῖ μὲν ἡ τοῦ κυρίου φωνή· Οὗτός ἐστιν ὁ υἱός μου ὁ μονογενὴς καὶ ἀγαπητός, ἐν ᾧ ἐγὼ εὐδόκησα.*

† Orat. XXXV. c. 17. Opp. I. 573, C, ed. Bill.

‡ *Pseudo*-Basil. Homil. in Psalm. xxviii. c. 3. Opp. I. 359, F.

§ De Fide, Lib. I. c. 16, in Sirmondi Opera Varia, Tom. I. (Venet. 1728) col. 166, A. — Garnier supposes the Latin translation to have been made by Julian of Eclanum (A. D. 420), the famous Pelagian bishop.

‖ De Incomprehensibili Dei Naturâ, Hom. IV. c. 3, *bis.* Opp. I. 475, A, E, ed. Montf. — *Ibid.* c. 4. p. 476, B. — *Ibid.* Hom. V. c. 1. p. 481, A. — Ad eos qui scandalizati sunt, c. 3. Opp. III. 470, B. — In Isaiam, cap. vi. § 1. Opp. VI. 64, A. — In illud, *Filius ex se nihil,* etc. c. 6. Opp. VI. 264, D. — In Joan. Hom. XV. (al. XIV.) Opp. VIII. 84, B (*text*). — *Ibid.* c. 2. p. 86, C, compared with p. 87, B.

¶ Interp. in Psalm. cix. 1. Opp. I. 850, A, ed. Sirmond. — Eranist. Dial. I. Opp. IV. 14, B. — Hæret. Fab. Lib. V. c. 1. Opp. IV. 251, B. — *Ibid.* c. 2. p. 253, D.

** Orat. XV. Analect. p. 440, ed. Riccard.

†† I refer to the "Capitula de Trinitate," published as a work of Cyril of Alexandria by Angelo Mai in his "Script. Vet. Nova Collectio," Tom. VII. P. II. In this work, cap. 6. p. 31, John i. 18 is quoted with the reading *υἱός*; but Dr. Tregelles ("Account of the

rius,* Andreas Cretensis (A. D. 635 Cave, 680 Saxe, 850 Oudin), † Joannes Damascenus (A. D. 730), three times, ‡ Theophylact (A. D. 1070), § and Euthymius Zigabenus (A. D. 1110). ||

The testimony of the Latin Fathers may now be produced. The most important part of this was long ago exhibited by Sabatier with his usual diligence and accuracy. A careful examination of his citations might have saved Dr. Tregelles from some errors.

The following Latin writers quote John i. 18 with the reading *filius*: — Tertullian (A. D. 200); ¶ Hilary (A. D. 354), at least seven times; ** Phæbadius (A. D.

Printed Text of the Greek N. T.," p. 232, note †) is probably correct in regarding it as the production of a later writer than Cyril.

* John i. 18 is quoted with the reading υἱός in a work entitled "Quæstiones et Responsiones," or "Dialogi IV.," which appears to be as late as the seventh century, but which has been attributed to Cæsarius, the brother of Gregory Nazianzen. It passed current under his name in the time of Photius (A. D. 858), who has described it. The quotation of John i. 18 may be found in Dial. I. of the work, as published, in a Latin version, in the Max. Bibl. Vet. Patr., V. 753, G. The Greek, which is contained in Vol. VI. of Galland's Bibliotheca Veterum Patrum, I have not been able to consult.

† Orat. in Transfigurat. Opp. p. 44, ed. Combefis.

‡ De Fide Orthodoxâ, Lib. I. c. 1. Opp. I. 123, C, ed. Le Quien. — Advers. Nestorianos, c. 32, *bis*. Opp. I. 562, E.

§ Comment. in loc.

|| Comment. in loc.

¶ Advers. Praxeam, c. 15.

** Tract. in Psalm. cxxxviii. c. 35. Opp. col. 520, ed. Benedict. — De Trinitate, Lib. II. c. 23. col. 799, E. — Lib. IV. c. 8. col. 831, C. — *Ibid.* c. 42. col. 852, C. — Lib. V. c. 33. col. 873, D. — *Ibid.* c. 34. col. 874, A. — Lib. VI. c. 39. col. 905, E. Hilary's comment on this passage shows *conclusively* that he read *filius*.

Wetstein quotes in favor of the reading Θεός "*Hilarius* de Trinit. passim," and Hilary is also one of Dr. Tregelles's witnesses. The *expression* "unigenitus Deus" occurs in the treatise "De Trinitate" about one hundred and four times; but the only *quotations* of John i. 18

359);* Victorinus Afer (A. D. 360), six times;† Ambrose (A. D. 374), at least seven times;‡ Faustinus (A. D. 384);§ Augustine (A. D. 396), three times;‖ Adimantus the Manichæan (A. D. 396);¶ Maximinus, the Arian bishop (A. D. 428), twice;** the author of,

to be found in it have been referred to above, and they all (six in number) have the reading *filius*. The only passage in this work, and, so far as I know, in Hilary's writings, which can be imagined to support the reading *Deus* is in Lib. XII. c. 24, Opp. col. 1125, A, where we find the words "cum unigenitus Deus in sinu Patris est." It will be seen, on examining the context, that *est* is the emphatic word in this sentence, and that there is no more reason for regarding the expression "unigenitus Deus" as a citation from the Apostle John, than there is for supposing it to be quoted from the Apostle Paul in c. 26 of the same book, where Hilary says, "cum secundum Apostolum ante tempora æterna sit unigenitus Deus"; compare 2 Tim. i. 9.

* Contra Arianos, c. 12, in Migne's Patrol. Tom. XX. col. 21, D, or in Max. Bibl. Patr. IV. 302, F. — Phæbadius (or Phœbadius) is another of Dr. Tregelles's witnesses; but even the *expression* "unigenitus Deus" does not occur in his writings.

† De Generat. Verbi Divini, ad Candidum, c. 16 (unigenitus Dei filius) — *Ibid.* c. 20. — Advers. Arium, Lib. I. cc. 2, 4. — *Ibid.* c. 15 ("unigenitus" alone). — Lib. IV. c. 8. — *Ibid.* c. 33 (unigenitus solus filius). In Migne's Patrol. Tom. VIII. col. 1029, 1030, 1041, 1042, 1050, 1119, 1137, or Max. Bibl. Patr. IV. 167, 169, 254, 255, 257, 282, 289.

‡ De Joseph. c. 14, al. 84. Opp. I. 510, D, ed. Benedict. — De Bened. Patriarch. c. 11, al. 51. col. 527, F. — In Luc. Lib. I. c. 25, col. 1274, D. — *Ibid.* Lib. II. c. 12. col. 1286, B. — De Fide, Lib. III. c. 3, al. 24. Opp. II. 501, C. — De Spir. Sanct. c. 1, al. 26. col. 605, F. — Epist. xxii. c. 5. col. 875, E.

§ De Trinitate, Lib. I. c. 2. § 5, in Migne's Patrol. Tom. XIII. col. 54, A, B, or Max. Bibl. Patr. V. 642, F, G.

‖ In Joan. Tract. xxxi. c. 3. — Tract. xxxv. c. 5. — Tract. xlvii. c. 3. — Opp. Tom. III. P. II. col. 1638, 1660, 1734, ed. Migne.

¶ Apud Augustinum contra Adimant. c. 9. § 1. Opp. Tom. VIII. col. 139, ed. Migne.

** Apud Augustini Collat. cum Maximin. cc. 13, 18. Opp. Tom. VIII. col. 719 et 728, ed. Migne.

the work against Virimadus ascribed to Idacius Clarus (A. D. 385), three times; * Vigilius of Tapsa (A. D. 484), or the author, whoever he was, of Libri XII. de Trinitate; † Junilius (A. D. 550); ‡ and Alcuin (A. D. 780). §

SUCH is the *external* evidence respecting the reading of the passage in question. It does not seem worth while to give a formal summary of it. The preceding examination of the testimony of the Fathers does not profess to be exhaustive. But it has been pursued so far that there is no probability that subsequent investigation will add many important facts, or affect the general conclusion to which we are led by those which have been produced.

It will be observed that a great majority of the witnesses for the reading Θεός, whose locality can be determined, are *Alexandrian*, or belong to places under Alexandrian influence; though the Alexandrian authorities are far from being unanimous in support of it.‖ The witnesses on the other side are not only much more numerous, but are *far more widely diffused*, representing almost every important part of the whole Christian world. In respect to *antiquity*, we have in favor of the reading υἱός, *before the middle of the*

* Advers. Virimadum, in Max. Bibl. Patr. V. 731, E, and 740, B, E. Montfaucon ascribes this work, and also the first eight books of the one next mentioned, to Idatius the Chronicler (A. D. 445). See his edition of Athanasius, Tom. II. pp. 602, 603.

† De Trinitate, Lib. IV. in Max. Bibl. Patr. VIII. 783, A, or in Athanasii Opp. II. 615, A, ed. Montf.

‡ De Part. Div. Legis, Lib. I. c. 16, in Max. Bibl. Patr. X. 342, H, or Migne's Patrol. Tom. LXVIII. col. 22, C.

§ Comm. super Joan. in loc. Opp. I. 472, 473, ed. Froben. — The passage referred to by Wetstein, De Fide S. Trin. Lib. I. c. 12 (al. 13, al. 14), has only the *expression* "unigenitus Deus." Opp. I. 712.

‖ Thus the Philoxenian or Harclean Syriac, revised and collated with two Greek manuscripts at Alexandria, A. D. 616, has the reading "God" in the *margin*, but not in the text.

fourth century, — the date assigned by Tischendorf to our oldest Greek manuscript of the New Testament, — the evidence of the Old Latin and Curetonian Syriac versions, both belonging probably to the second century, and that of Hippolytus, the third Synod of Antioch, Alexander of Alexandria, Eusebius of Cæsarea, and Eustathius of Antioch, besides Irenæus, Tertullian, and the author of the "Discussion between Archelaus and Manes," to whose testimony exception may perhaps be taken. During the same period we have on the other side only Clement of Alexandria, the *Doctrina Orientalis*, and the Coptic version, with the Peshito Syriac as commonly edited, if that form of the Syriac text is of so early a date. In the period that follows, though the four manuscripts which support the reading Θεός are of the highest character, yet the weight of the *whole* evidence of manuscripts, versions, and Fathers must certainly be regarded as greatly preponderating against it.

LET us now see what view is to be taken of the *internal* evidence. In respect to this Dr. Tregelles says: "In forming a judgment between these two readings, it must be remembered that μονογενής would *naturally* suggest υἱός as the word which should follow it, whereas Θεός strikes the ear as something peculiar, and not elsewhere occurring in Scripture; the change, being but of *one letter* (ΥC for ΘC), might be most inadvertently made; and though the evidence of the Latin versions and the Curetonian Syriac is not of small weight, yet the same chance of a change would, in a case of this kind, affect the copyists of a version (or indeed the translators) [?] just as much as the transcribers of Greek MSS. Θεός, as the more difficult reading, is entitled to special attention," &c.*

* Account of the Printed Text of the Greek N. T., p. 235.

There is some force in these remarks; but not so much as may at first be thought. Though μονογενὴς Θεός is a harsh expression and an unusual combination to us, it was not so to copyists of the fourth century and later. "The only-begotten God" was, as we have seen, an exceedingly common appellation of Christ in the writings of that period, the Father being distinguished from him as ἀγέννητος, ἄναρχος, ἀναίτιος, "unbegotten, unoriginated, uncaused." It is strange that Dr. Tregelles should regard it as an expression to which the Arians of those days would object. The Arians did not hesitate to apply the term Θεός or *Deus* to Christ, using it, as the Ante-Nicene Fathers had done before them, in an inferior sense; * and though no example of a *quotation* of John i. 18 with the reading Θεός has been produced from any Arian writer, we find the *expression* μονογενὴς Θεός in the so-called Apostolical Constitutions (seven times), in the larger Epistle of the Pseudo-Ignatius to the Philadelphians, and in the fragments which remain to us of the writings of Arius and his followers, Asterius, Eunomius, and others, referred to by Wetstein. Being a phrase, then, so frequently used both by the Catholic Fathers and their opponents, transcribers must have been very familiar with it. In the passage in question Θεόν had just preceded, bringing Θεός before the mind of the copyist. The word Θεός occurs in the New Testament three times as often as υἱός. Is it strange, then, that one or more transcribers, under such circumstances, should inadvertently substitute the more common for the less frequent word, the one differing from the other, in the abbreviated form, only in a single letter? And might not this mistake have been easily propagated, so as to extend to the comparatively few authorities which exhibit the reading Θεός?

* See before, p. 120, note.

But there is another aspect of the internal evidence, as important as that to which we have just attended. "No man hath seen *God* at any time; *the only-begotten God*, who is in the bosom of the Father, he hath declared him." Does not every one perceive that the introduction of the phrase "only-begotten God," after the use of the word "God," alone and absolutely, immediately before it, is a harshness which we can hardly suppose in any writer? Does not the word "Father," in a sentence like this, almost necessarily imply that the correlative "Son" has just preceded? And is there anything analogous to this expression, "the only-begotten God," in the writings of John, or in any other part of the New Testament?

One can hardly believe that so fair-minded and impartial a critic as Dr. Tregelles, after a careful re-examination of the whole evidence, will regard himself as justified in introducing the reading μονογενὴς Θεός into the text. But supposing this to be the true reading, it is obvious that the being so designated is here distinguished in the clearest manner from Him to whom the name "God" is emphatically and absolutely applied; and that the word Θεός, in this expression, must therefore be used in an inferior sense, unless John taught the existence of two Supreme Beings. It will also strike every one, that the title "*only-begotten* God" is not suitable to a being who possesses the attribute of self-existence.

In respect to the meaning of the appellation "only-begotten Son," or "only Son," repeatedly given to Christ in the writings of St. John, it may be sufficient to refer to the remarks of Mr. Norton in the former part of this volume.* The corresponding Hebrew word is repeatedly rendered in the Septuagint by ἀγαπητός or ἀγαπώμενος, "beloved."

* See before, p. 220.

(5.) John iii. 34. "For he whom God hath sent speaketh the words of God; for God giveth not the Spirit by measure *unto him*," οὐ γὰρ ἐκ μέτρου δίδωσιν ὁ Θεὸς τὸ πνεῦμα.

Here ὁ Θεός, answering to the word "God" in the last clause, is bracketed by Lachmann, and omitted by Tischendorf, Meyer, and Alford, as also by Mr. Norton; Griesbach marks it as probably spurious. De Wette, Meyer, and Alford suppose that ὁ Θεός (understood) is the subject of δίδωσι, so that the omission would make no difference in the sense. Mr. Norton, however, regards "He whom God has sent," the Messiah, as the subject, and translates, "He gives not the spirit by measure." See his note.

(6.) Acts xvi. 7. "After they were come to Mysia, they essayed to go into Bithynia; but the Spirit suffered them not."

Here, instead of τὸ πνεῦμα, "the Spirit," the best manuscripts and versions, with other authorities, read τὸ πνεῦμα Ἰησοῦ, "the spirit of Jesus." This reading is adopted by Griesbach, Knapp, Schott, Tittmann, Vater, Scholz, Lachmann, Hahn, Theile, Tischendorf, and Alford; also by De Wette, Meyer, Mr. Norton, and many others. See before, p. 225, et seqq.

(7.) Romans ix. 5. "Whose *are* the fathers, and of whom as concerning the flesh Christ *came*, who is over all, God blessed for ever. Amen." The Greek is as follows: ὧν οἱ πατέρες, καὶ ἐξ ὧν ὁ Χριστὸς τὸ κατὰ σάρκα· ὁ ὢν ἐπὶ πάντων Θεός, εὐλογητὸς εἰς τοὺς αἰῶνας. Ἀμήν.

If the remarks which have been before made (pp. 207–212, note) on this much controverted text are correct, the original is grammatically ambiguous, admitting of at least three different constructions; — 1. that of the Common Version, according to which the last clause, ὁ ὢν ἐπὶ πάντων, etc., refers to *Christ*; — 2. that of Mr. Norton, according to which it relates to *God*, the Apostle, in enumerating the privileges of the Jews, mentioning as their last great distinction the fact that God himself had presided over all their concerns in a particular manner; (the literal rendering of the words being, "He who was over all [was] God, blessed for ever";) — and 3. that of many eminent German critics, who regard the clause as a doxology, translating, "God, who is over all, be blessed for ever."

This passage cannot, with strict propriety, be introduced here, as there are no *various readings* of any consequence; but as involving a question of *punctuation*, it is not wholly unconnected with the subject of this note. It has already been mentioned, that the punctuation adopted by Mr. Norton and many other interpreters, as well as by Lachmann and Tischendorf among the critical editors, is found not only in some manuscripts in cursive letters, but also in the celebrated Ephrem manuscript. I have since observed that a stop is also placed after σάρκα in the Alexandrine manuscript, as edited by Woide. The Alexandrine and Ephrem manuscripts are the two oldest Greek manuscripts of the New Testament in which there is any kind of punctuation, the Vatican having no stops *a primâ manu*. The single point, or very short line, used in the earliest manuscripts where any marks of this kind appear, denotes a pause sometimes answering in length only to our comma, but usually equivalent to a colon or a period. Manuscript authority in a case of this kind is really of no importance; but some writers have laid stress on the supposed want of it as an objection to the punctuation adopted by Mr. Norton.

The orthodox Fathers who have quoted the passage, and the authors of the ancient versions, refer the clause to Christ; but it is not strange that they should give to ambiguous language the interpretation most favorable to their theological opinions.

It may be worth while to mention, that Mr. Jowett, now Regius Professor of Greek in the University of Oxford, in his recent work on the Epistles of Paul to the Thessalonians, Galatians, and Romans, adopts the punctuation of Lachmann and Tischendorf, and translates, "God, who is over all, is blessed for ever. Amen."

But supposing it to have been shown that the last part of this verse may grammatically refer to God as well as to Christ, is there any *philological* reason, it may be asked, for preferring the former construction to the latter? In respect to this point, one who has any doubt on the subject may examine the use of the word Θεός, "God," first in this Epistle, and then in the other Epistles of St. Paul; noting the examples, if he can discover any, in which it is applied to Christ, and also those in which it is applied to a being clearly distinguished from Christ, as in 1 Corinthians iii. 23; viii. 6; xi. 3; xv. 24, 28; 1 Timothy ii. 5, &c. He will find in the Epistles of Paul, not including the Epistle to the Hebrews, more than *five hundred* instances of the use of the word in question; and he will also find, I believe, that there is not among them all a *single* clear and unequivocal example of its application to Christ. But if this be the case, the presumption is very strong that it is not so applied here. The argument rests, it will be perceived, not on the inconsistency of the Trinitarian construction with the *theology* of St. Paul as gathered from his other writings, — that is another weighty consideration, — but on its inconsistency with his habitual or uniform *use of language.*

(8.) Romans xiv. 10. "For we shall all stand before the judgment-seat of Christ."

Here, instead of Χριστοῦ, "Christ," the reading Θεοῦ,

"God," is adopted by Lachmann, Tischendorf, Alford, and Tregelles, as also by Meyer and others. It is to be observed, that the Vatican and Ephrem manuscripts agree with the other leading uncial manuscripts in the latter reading, though this fact was not known to Griesbach and Scholz.

Supposing the common reading to be correct, some Trinitarians have inferred the deity of Christ from a comparison of this verse with the two following. In respect to this point, it may be sufficient to refer to Acts xvii. 31; Romans ii. 16. See also before, p. 68, note, and p. 285.

(9.) Romans xv. 29. "And I am sure that, when I come unto you, I shall come in the fulness of the blessing of the gospel of Christ."

The words τοῦ εὐαγγελίου τοῦ, corresponding to "of the gospel," are bracketed by Vater as doubtful, and are omitted by Griesbach, Schott, Scholz, Lachmann, Theile, Tischendorf, Alford, Tregelles, and Meyer. De Wette regards them as probably spurious.

(10.) Romans xv. 32. "That I may come to you with joy by the will of God," διὰ θελήματος Θεοῦ.

Lachmann reads διὰ θελήματος κυρίου Ἰησοῦ, "by the will of the *Lord Jesus*." This reading is supported by only one manuscript, the Vatican; though a few authorities have the words Χριστοῦ Ἰησοῦ, "Christ Jesus," instead of Θεοῦ, "God."

(11.) 1 Corinthians x. 9. "Neither let us tempt Christ, as some of them also tempted," &c.

Here, for τὸν Χριστόν, "Christ," or "the Anointed One," the reading τὸν κύριον, "the Lord," is adopted by Lachmann, Meyer, and Alford, as also by Wetstein, Archbishop

Newcome, Rückert, Norton, and others. Griesbach (in his manual edition) and Knapp mark it as of equal authority with Χριστόν. Compare Griesbach's Symbolæ Criticæ, II. 114.

"As some of them also tempted," καθὼς καί τινες αὐτῶν ἐπείρασαν. Καί, "also," is omitted by Lachmann, Tischendorf, Meyer, and Alford, is marked by Griesbach as probably spurious, and bracketed by Vater.

Archbishop Newcome observes, "If we read Χριστόν, the sense is, 'Nor let us tempt, try, prove, provoke Christ now, as some of them did God at that time.'" The passage is thus understood by many Trinitarian commentators; but others, supplying the word "him" instead of "God" after "tempted," suppose that Paul represents Christ as the being described in Numbers xxi. 5, 6, as tempted by the Israelites in the wilderness.

(12.) 1 Corinthians xv. 47. "The second man *is* the Lord from heaven."

Ὁ κύριος, "the Lord," is here marked by Griesbach as probably spurious, bracketed by Vater, and omitted by Lachmann, Tischendorf, Meyer, and Alford, as also by Rückert, De Wette, Mr. Norton, and others.

(13.) 2 Corinthians iv. 14. "Knowing that he which raised up the Lord Jesus shall raise up us also by Jesus."

Instead of διὰ Ἰησοῦ, "by Jesus," the reading σὺν Ἰησοῦ, "with Jesus," is adopted by Lachmann, Theile, Tischendorf, Meyer, Alford, Rückert, and De Wette.

(14.) Ephesians iii. 9. "God, who created all things by Jesus Christ."

The words διὰ Ἰησοῦ Χριστοῦ, "by Jesus Christ," are marked by Knapp and Vater as doubtful, and are rejected by Griesbach, Schott, Tittmann, Scholz, Lachmann, Hahn, Theile, Tischendorf, Olshausen, De Wette, Meyer, Mr. Norton, and others.

(15.) Ephesians v. 21. "Submitting yourselves one to another in the fear of God," ἐν φόβῳ Θεοῦ.

The reading ἐν φόβῳ Χριστοῦ, "in the fear of *Christ*," is adopted by Griesbach, Knapp, Schott, Tittmann, Vater, Scholz, Lachmann, Hahn, Theile, Tischendorf, Meyer, and De Wette.

(16.) Philippians iii. 3. "For we are the circumcision, which worship God in the spirit," οἱ πνεύματι Θεῷ λατρεύοντες.

Matthæi, Scholz, Lachmann, Tischendorf, Meyer, and Wiesinger read Θεοῦ for Θεῷ. So also Wetstein. Supposing this reading to be genuine, the literal translation will be, "who worship (*or* pay religious service) in (*or* through) the Spirit of God." The words also grammatically admit of the rendering, "who worship the Spirit of God"; and so Granville Sharp translates.* But this interpretation introduces an idea so foreign from the context, to mention no other objection, that Mr. Sharp has had few, if any, followers.

(17.) Philippians iv. 13. "I can do all things through Christ which strengtheneth me."

The word Χριστῷ, "Christ," is bracketed as doubtful by Knapp and Vater, and omitted by Griesbach, Schott, Scholz, Lachmann, Theile, Tischendorf, Meyer, Conybeare and Howson, and others. If it is omitted, the translation will be, "I can do (*or* bear) all things through Him who strengthens me."

* Remarks on the Uses of the Definitive Article, &c., pp. 33, 34, 3d ed.

(18.) Colossians ii. 2, 3. "To the acknowledgment of the mystery of God, and of the Father, and of Christ; in whom are hid all the treasures of wisdom and knowledge," εἰς ἐπίγνωσιν τοῦ μυστηρίου τοῦ Θεοῦ καὶ πατρὸς καὶ τοῦ Χριστοῦ, ἐν ᾧ εἰσὶ πάντες οἱ θησαυροὶ τῆς σοφίας καὶ τῆς γνώσεως ἀπόκρυφοι.

The words καὶ πατρὸς καὶ τοῦ Χριστοῦ, "and of the Father, and of Christ," are marked as doubtful by Knapp, and omitted by Griesbach, Schott, Scholz, Lachmann, Tischendorf, Olshausen, De Wette, Conybeare and Howson, Professor Eadie, Mr. Norton (see p. 297), and others.

Lachmann, Meyer, Steiger, Huther, and Granville Penn adopt the reading τοῦ μυστηρίου τοῦ Θεοῦ Χριστοῦ, which admits, grammatically, of different interpretations. It may mean, 1. "of the mystery of the God of Christ" (comp. Ephes. i. 17); so Huther and Meyer; or, 2. "of the mystery of God, namely, Christ," the word "Christ" being in apposition with "mystery" (comp. Col. i. 27). Steiger understands Χριστοῦ to be in apposition with Θεοῦ, but, to justify his interpretation, the Greek, as De Wette and Olshausen remark, should be τοῦ Χριστοῦ Θεοῦ, and not τοῦ Θεοῦ Χριστοῦ.

Theile reads, τοῦ μυστηρίου τοῦ Θεοῦ πατρὸς τοῦ Χριστοῦ, "of the mystery of God, the Father of Christ."

Whichever of these readings is genuine, ἐν ᾧ, "in whom," or "in which," in the last clause, should probably be understood as referring to μυστηρίου. So Grotius, Hammond, Bengel, Schleusner, De Wette, Meyer, and others explain the words, and Professor Eadie translates, — "to the full knowledge of the mystery of God, in which all the treasures of wisdom and knowledge are laid up."

The meaning of the word translated "mystery" in the Common Version would be better conveyed to most readers by the term "new doctrine," or "new religion."

(19.) Colossians iii. 13. "Even as Christ forgave you, so also do ye."

Here, instead of ὁ Χριστός, "Christ," the reading ὁ κύριος, "the Lord," is adopted by Lachmann, Tischendorf, Olshausen, and Meyer.

(20.) Colossians iii. 15. "And let the peace of God rule in your hearts."

"The peace of *Christ*" is the reading adopted by Griesbach, Knapp, Schott, Tittmann, Vater, Scholz, Lachmann, Hahn, Theile, Tischendorf, Meyer, and De Wette.

(21.) 2 Thessalonians ii. 8. "Whom the Lord shall consume with the breath of his mouth."

For ὁ κύριος, "the Lord," Griesbach, Knapp, Tittmann, Schott (in his 3d ed., 1825), Scholz, Lachmann, Hahn, Theile, and Lünemann read ὁ κύριος Ἰησοῦς, "the Lord Jesus." But Matthæi, Pelt, Schott (in his Commentary, 1834), Tischendorf, De Wette, and others, retain the common reading, regarding Ἰησοῦς as a gloss.

(22.) 1 Peter iii. 15. "But sanctify the Lord God in your hearts."

Here, instead of Θεόν, "God," the reading Χριστόν, "Christ," is adopted by Lachmann, Theile, Tischendorf, Tregelles, and Huther. Tregelles argues from this reading as compared with Isaiah viii. 12, 13, that "the expression 'Jehovah of Hosts himself' in the prophet finds its New Testament exposition as an equivalent in κύριον τὸν Χριστόν, 'the Lord Christ,' thus marking the divine glory of our Lord in the most emphatic manner." * But nothing is more common than for the writers of the New Testament to borrow the language of the Old to express their own

* Account of the Printed Text of the Greek New Testament, p. 235.

thoughts, and thus to apply it to very different subjects from those to which it relates in its original connection. See, for example, 1 Peter ii. 9, comp. Exodus xix. 6; — Romans x. 6 – 8, comp. Deut. xxx. 12 – 14; — Romans x. 18, comp. Psalm xix. 4.

(23.) 1 John iii. 16. "Hereby perceive we the love of God, because he laid down his life for us."

Here the words τοῦ Θεοῦ, "of God," are rejected as spurious by all modern editors. They are found, so far as is known, only in one Greek manuscript, and in the Latin Vulgate version. In most editions of the Common Version they are now printed in Italics; but they are not so distinguished in the original edition of 1611. Our translators followed Beza and the Complutensian Polyglot in reading τοῦ Θεοῦ.

(24.) Jude 4. "Denying the only Lord God, and our Lord Jesus Christ," τὸν μόνον δεσπότην Θεὸν καὶ κύριον ἡμῶν Ἰησοῦν Χριστὸν ἀρνούμενοι.

Supposing the common text to be correct, Granville Sharp would render, "Denying our only Master, God, and Lord, Jesus Christ." (See before, p. 199, note.) But the word Θεόν, "God," is omitted by Griesbach, Knapp, Schott, Tittmann, Vater, Scholz, Lachmann, Hahn, Theile, Tischendorf, Huther, De Wette, and others. We may then translate, "Denying the only Sovereign Lord, and our Lord Jesus Christ." Compare Norton's Evidences of the Genuineness of the Gospels, Vol. II. p. 166.

(25.) Jude 5. "The Lord, having saved the people out of the land of Egypt, afterward destroyed them that believed not."

For ὁ κύριος, "the Lord," the reading ὁ Ἰησοῦς, "Jesus," is adopted by Lachmann, and favored by Huther.

(26.) Jude 25. "To the only wise God our Saviour, be glory and majesty, dominion and power," &c.

Here the word σοφῷ, "wise," is omitted, and the words διὰ Ἰησοῦ Χριστοῦ τοῦ κυρίου ἡμῶν are inserted after μόνῳ Θεῷ σωτῆρι ἡμῶν, by Griesbach, Knapp, Schott, Tittmann, Vater, Scholz, Lachmann, Hahn, Theile, Tischendorf, Huther, De Wette, and others. The passage may then be translated, "To the *only* God our Saviour, *through Jesus Christ our Lord*, be glory and majesty, dominion and power," &c. See before, p. 305, note.

(27.) Revelation i. 8. "I am Alpha and Omega, the beginning and the ending, saith the Lord," &c.

Instead of ὁ κύριος, "the Lord," κύριος ὁ Θεός, "the Lord God," is adopted by all the modern critical editors who have been mentioned in this note, and even by Bloomfield, who also remarks, "By most recent commentators these words are understood of God *the Father*." He himself, however, explains them as referring to Christ. Professor Stuart observes, in his note on the passage, that "the weight of external testimony is greatly in favor of κύριος ὁ Θεός," and that, admitting this reading, "it is more facile to regard God as the speaker."

The words, "I am Alpha and Omega," are explained in ch. xxi. 6 and xxii. 13 by "the beginning and the end," "the First and the Last." (The words translated "the beginning and the ending" in the present passage are an interpolation.) Compare Isaiah xli. 4; xliv. 6; xlviii. 12. These expressions have been variously interpreted; by some, as denoting eternity, or unchangeableness; — but "the beginning and the end" can hardly mean "without beginning and without end"; — by others, as signifying completeness, or perfection. Here, and in ch. xxi. 6, where they are also applied to God, they seem rather used to denote the certain accomplishment of his purposes; that what he has begun he will carry on to its consummation. Thus Hengstenberg remarks: "The emphasis is to be laid upon the Omega. It is as much as: I am as the Alpha, therefore also the Omega. The beginning is surety for the end." *

The words in question may be understood in a similar manner when applied to Christ, as in ch. xxii. 13; comp. i. 17, ii. 8. Thus Erasmus remarks in his note on John viii. 25, as cited by Wilson in his Concessions of Trinitarians: "Christ is called *the beginning and the end*, because he is the beginning and the consummation of the Church, which was founded by his first, and will be completed by his second appearance." † So one of the Latin Fathers, Fulgentius, says, though he gives other meanings to the words: "*Principium* Christus, quia ipse inchoavit perficienda; *finis* Christus, quia ipse perficit inchoata"; that is, "Christ is *the beginning*, because he himself commenced the work to be accomplished; Christ is *the end*, because he accomplishes the work begun." ‡ It is, perhaps, in a somewhat similar sense that he is called by the author of the Epistle to the Hebrews "the Author and Finisher of the faith," ὁ τῆς πίστεως ἀρχηγὸς καὶ τελειωτής. §

(28.) Revelation i. 11. "I am Alpha and Omega, the First and the Last; and, What thou seest, write in a book," &c.

Here, the words which precede "What thou seest" are rejected as spurious by all the modern critical editors.

* "The Revelation of St. John, expounded," &c., Vol. I. p. 107, Amer. ed. of the Engl. translation.

† Opp. Tom. VI. col. 376, E.

‡ Ad Trasimundum, Lib. II. c. 5; in Migne's Patrol. Tom. LXV. col. 250, C.

§ Hebrews xii. 2.

Dr. Doddridge observes, in his note on this verse: "That these titles ["Alpha and Omega," &c.] should be repeated so soon, in a connection which demonstrates that they are given to Christ, will appear very remarkable, whatever sense be given to the *eighth verse.* The argument drawn in the preceding note upon it would have been strong, wherever such a passage as this had been found; but its immediate connection with this greatly strengthens it. And I cannot forbear recording it, that *this text* has done more than any other in the Bible toward preventing me from giving in to *that scheme,* which would make our *Lord Jesus Christ* no more than a *deified creature.*"

It is a pity that this excellent man did not take a little more pains to distinguish the genuine text of Scripture from the corruptions introduced by transcribers.

(29.) Revelation ii. 7. "To him that overcometh will I give to eat of the tree of life, which is in the midst of the paradise of God."

Instead of τοῦ Θεοῦ, "of God," the reading τοῦ Θεοῦ μου, "of *my* God," is marked by Vater as probable, and is adopted by Matthæi, Griesbach, Knapp, Schott, Tittmann, Scholz, and Tischendorf.

(30.) Revelation iii. 2. "I have not found thy works perfect before God," ἐνώπιον τοῦ Θεοῦ.

Here the reading ἐνώπιον τοῦ Θεοῦ μου, "before *my* God," is marked by Vater (in his note on ch. ii. 7) as probable, and is received into the text as genuine by all the other critical editors of the present century who have been mentioned in this note.

THIS completes the view proposed of passages whose supposed bearing on the doctrine of the Trinity is affected by various readings of the original text. I refer, it will be understood, to readings which have been adopted in any of the leading critical editions published within the present century. In a large majority of these passages, the variation of reading seems to me to be of little or no consequence, so far as the doctrine in question is concerned; but I wished to include all where it had been, or might be, thought of any importance. I have certainly endeavored to omit nothing which a Trinitarian might regard as favoring his belief.

INDEX

TO

PASSAGES OF SCRIPTURE QUOTED OR REFERRED TO.

2 COR. (*continued*). Page

GENERAL INDEX.

46 *

GREEK WORDS AND PHRASES.

THE END.

www.ingramcontent.com/pod-product-compliance
Lightning Source LLC
LaVergne TN
LVHW021241110826
845150LV00002B/380

9781425561321